HANDBOOK OF BIBLICAL HEBREW

VOLUME ONE — LESSONS

HANDBOOK
of
BIBLICAL HEBREW

An Inductive Approach Based on the Hebrew Text of Esther

by

WILLIAM SANFORD LaSOR

VOLUME ONE

Reading Lessons Keyed to the Grammar

WILLIAM B. EERDMANS PUBLISHING COMPANY
Grand Rapids, Michigan

TO
MY STUDENTS
AND ESPECIALLY TO
THOSE WHO SERVED AS
MY TEACHING ASSISTANTS
WHO HAVE TAUGHT ME MORE THAN I TAUGHT THEM
THIS WORK IS
GRATEFULLY AND LOVINGLY
DEDICATED

HANDBOOK OF BIBLICAL HEBREW

Printed in the United States of America
ISBN 0-8028-2381-5

PREFACE

This *Handbook* is designed to be a complete tool for the student who wishes to learn Biblical Hebrew. It combines lessons, grammar, basic vocabulary, and learning methodology. The student who follows the method faithfully will not only learn the elements of Hebrew, but in addition, and more important, he or she will learn *how to observe and how to learn by observation.* In addition, the *Handbook* is keyed to the classical 28th edition of the Kautzsch-Cowley *Gesenius' Hebrew Grammar* for fuller study of many points. It has been set up in 80 lessons, each lesson on two facing pages so as to be completely visible at a glance, planned for a course of 90 class-hours. Thus it can be covered in a 3-hour course in 30 weeks (whether semesters or quarters) or (as I have done many times) in a 15-hour course in six weeks.

The *method* is largely *inductive,* i.e. working from the text to the grammar. The learned William Rainey Harper did much to develop this method of language study, and for decades his work on Hebrew has been well recognized, going through many editions. However, this method has fallen somewhat into disrepute. In my opinion, this was due more to improper use of the inductive method than to the method itself. See my article, "The Inductive Method of Teaching Hebrew — Its Advantages and Its Pitfalls," *Hebrew Abstracts,* 15 (1974) 108-119, for fuller discussion. I have tried to remedy this defect in using the inductive method by requiring *more synthesis* of what is learned inductively.

The inductive method has advantages and disadvantages. First of all, *it holds student interest,* because the student is at once into reading the language. The learning of paradigms, rules of grammar and syntax, vocabulary, and other features of conventional language study for a year (more or less) before ever reading connected text can kill the interest of all but the most persistent student. Moreover, much that is taught is *useless.* Who has not learned pluperfect or other forms he has not seen in years of reading? Who has not learned to write, "My aunt's male elephant loves my uncle's female elephant," only to find that he never has had the chance to use that literary gem? The inductive method is free from these faults. The student learns only what he or she encounters.

On the other hand, many students *observe without integrating their observations.* After a year of inductive study they cannot tell what they have seen. (This, contrary to the false idea among many language teachers, does not necessarily mean ignorance of the language. Many persons can read, speak, and even write a language well, who have no grammatical integration of the language.) As a result, teachers and students conclude that the inductive method does not work. I strongly disagree, and I have the experience and evidence to back up my opinion.

This work started out as "Notes on Biblical Hebrew" in 1950, and developed into *Hebrew Handbook,* which went through two or three revisions. It has been used to teach more than 2,000 students at Fuller Theological Seminary, and an unknown number at other institutions. I used the same method to develop my *Handbook of New Testament Greek,* which went through several revisions (1963-1969) and was brought out by Eerdmans in 1973. I have used the same method, with various amounts of helps available to the students, to teach Old Babylonian, Biblical Aramaic, New Testament Syriac, several other Aramaic dialects, Ugaritic, Phoenician, Ethiopic, Old South Arabic, and, most recently, Sumerian. I may have omitted one or two others. Without hesitation I state categorically, *the system works.* I make no claim that this is the *best* method; I simply say that, *if it is used properly, it produces excellent results.*

Perhaps the greatest obstacle to the inductive method is *what it demands* of both teacher and student. The teacher must be ready to *face* (not necessarily to *answer*; he or she can say frankly, "I don't know; I'll try to work it out and give you the answer tomorrow") *any question at any time*. Preparing tomorrow's lesson is easily done when the lesson is on the *Pe Guttural* verb. But when the teacher is faced with students who will ask anything from the utterly stupid to the most discerning question, the teacher must know the language and the *Handbook* thoroughly. At the same time, the student must think for him/herself. He/she must learn to observe and to question. The student is faced with a vast amount of heterogeneous material *from the very start*.

This is an advantage, however. When learning a language by the conventional method, the student finds the work increasingly more difficult as he/she learns more material. He/she tends to forget what he/she learned a few weeks ago. But when learning by the inductive method he/she will never find it more difficult than it is between the tenth and twentieth lessons. From that point on, learning is almost entirely by repetition of things already observed, and there is little chance to forget, for the student is constantly using what has already been seen.

The learning of a language involves at least three things – more, if you plan to speak and write in that language. First is the *meaning of words*, those units of thought that compose the message being expressed. Some teachers seem to think that all a student needs for this is a dictionary of word-for-word equivalents – but this obviously is extremely limited. To read with understanding, the student needs to know how the meaning of a word is affected by its context.

Next, for an inflected language the student needs to be able to identify correctly the *changes in form* that indicate the relationship of a word to its context. The student can achieve a degree of success by memorizing paradigms, or he or she can learn the same thing by encountering the word in many contexts. We all learned our mother-tongue by this inductive method, therefore it is *not* necessary to learn paradigms. Learning paradigms is faster – but is it better in the long run? Teachers will argue this point at length without convincing one another. I would simply point out that in any case it is still necessary to learn to read in context.

Third, and most important, the student needs to understand the meaning that is conveyed by the *putting together of these inflected words into a meaningful group*, or what the Greeks called "syntax." According to the "classical" method of teaching a language, syntax always comes last (if at all), and since it is of little meaning to the student without contexts, it is rarely mastered. Again, it is only when the student begins to read connected passages that syntax begins to make sense.

I have been asked many times, "Why did you use Esther?" For one thing, it is a story, with literary character, a plot, denouement, etc. This makes it interesting. Masculine and feminine forms, as well as singular and plural, are used throughout the work. (Much of the narrative material in the rest of the Hebrew Bible is seriously lacking in feminine forms.) Esther presents little difficulty in theological or textual matters. When we begin with the first chapter of Genesis, we immediately encounter all sorts of discussions concerning theology, historicity, cosmology, etc., when we ought to be learning the elements of Hebrew. Esther is long enough to present most of what the first-year student needs to know, with enough repetition to impress certain points on the student's mind. Some might object that Esther is late Hebrew, but the difference between Esther and, let us say, Genesis is not all that great. The vocabulary of Esther is excellent, containing about 500 words, most of which are of high frequency and relatively few of low frequency. That is to say, the student is constantly encountering words that will be needed wherever he or she turns in the Hebrew Bible. And, since I have included readings from other portions of the Bible, including several chapters from Genesis, the student will have opportunity to read Hebrew other than that of Esther.

I have a deep debt of gratitude that should be expressed. First and foremost I am indebted to my mentor at Dropsie University, Dr. Cyrus Gordon, for introducing me to the reduction of observations to simple rules. Some of the "Rules" herein are in the form in which he gave them to us; others have been reworked by me or by one of my assistants, particularly by my now-colleague, Dr Frederick Wm. Bush; still others have been formulated from my own observations. Most of these I have not learned from Grammars, and some are not to be found in any Grammar; they are proof that an observant student can learn many things *directly from the text.*

Starting in 1950, I applied the principle that "the best way to learn a subject well is to teach it," by giving my best students the responsibility of teaching sections of Hebrew. These *Teaching Assistants* or *Teaching Fellows* were continually feeding back to me the reactions to the method, pointing out places where clarification was needed, helping to make the length of lessons more reasonable, and in many other ways helping make this *Handbook* what it is today. To review their names is to give a veritable Who's Who, for quite a number of them have gone on to be teachers and administrators of excellence that would make any teacher proud. Some of them got their first experience in teaching in this manner. At least two of them have gone on to their eternal reward. My former assistants are: David Allan Hubbard (my first, and now the president of our Seminary), †Robert H. Emery, †Robert B. Laurin, Robert P. Dugan Jr, Marvin Webster, Haskell I. Stone, Gerald Swaim, Frederick W. Bush, Roy Hayden, Dwight Paine, John D. Koeker, Kurt G. Jung, Duncan W. McIntosh, Richard J. Saley, George VanAlstine, J. William Whedbee, Willard A. Parker, D. Dale Gerard, Ronald F. K. Ching, Timothy P. Owen, Glenda Fisk, Roger Fung, William Jeffrey Sweeney, W. Allan Gravely, Thomas F. Johnson, Michael F. Kopesec, David Lee Foxgrover, Kent A. Meads, Walter C. Wright Jr, Stephen J. Kobernik, Howard J. Loewen, Gary A. Tuttle, Gerald Sheppard, Edward E. Breeden, Robin A. Moore, Timothy E. Udd, Gerald H. Wilson, Richard C. Meyer, David M. Watson, B. Michael Blaine, Kenneth Brewster, Karen L. Hammeras, John H. Hull, Garth Moller, John C. Puckett, Mark A. Sereduck, Eugene Carpenter, Robert S. Goffigon, and Dawn Waring. If I have lost any names from this list, it is entirely unintentional and regrettable, but trying to reconstruct the details of three decades is a difficult task.

To some of these associates I have a particular indebtedness. Gary Tuttle, Gerald Wilson, and David Watson worked long and hard over numerous details in the revision. David Watson checked over the Basic Vocabulary, adding numbers and word-counts wherever they were lacking. Thomas McAlpine struggled, as I have done, to try to put the Synoptic Paradigms into some form that would be both useful and pleasing to the eye. Dawn Waring and Leon Mashchak opaqued the negatives from which the page-plates were made. Michael Blaine carried countless pages and galleys back and forth between the Seminary and Church Press. All of the recent teaching assistants have worked with and taught from these pages and have furnished me with numerous corrections that need to be made. And again, if I have forgotten anyone, I truly am sorry. Hearty thanks to each one who helped.

Finally, I want to thank Allan Farson of Church Press, Glendale, for creative ideas and much time and patience in making possible the typography in this *Handbook.* He designed the photographic disk used on the Photon by which the type was photographically set. Working with me, he created the beautifully clear Hebrew font, which he has graciously named "LaSor Hebrew." He patiently taught me how to set the type (by typewriter and punched tape), and he helped me work out countless mistakes. That many others remain I have no doubt. If anyone thinks he or she is infallible, try setting type for a book like this! I must add, also, my warm appreciation to William B. Eerdmans Jr for his willingness to venture the publication of my Handbooks.

To God be the greater glory!

William Sanford LaSor

Altadena, California
19 April 1978

ABBREVIATIONS

abs. absolute
acc. accented, accusative
adj. adjective, adjectival
adv. adverb, adverbial
Akk. Akkadian
Arab. Arabic
Aram. Aramaic
art. article
attrib. attributive

BDB Brown-Driver-Briggs *Lexicon*
Bib. Biblical

c conversive, see p.59
c. construct
c common (m. and f.)
C consonant, see §29.02
cf. compare
cl. clause, closed
cohort. cohortative
coll. collective
comp. complementary
cond. condition(al)
conj. conjunction, conjunctive
conv. conversive, converted
cstr. construct

d. dual
D *Piʿel*, cf. §28.12
dat. dative
d.d.o. definite direct object
d.o. distant open
def. definite
demon. demonstrative
denom. denominal
dir. direct
disc. discourse
du. dual

e.g. for example
Eng. English
esp. especially
Est. Esther

f., ff. following
f. feminine
f.b. from bottom
fda, fdc, fds fem. dual abs., cstr., suf.
fem. feminine
fpa, fpc, fps fem. plur. abs., cstr., suf.
fsa, fsc, fss fem. sing. abs., cstr., suf.
ft. foot, feet
fut. future

G *Qal*, cf. §28.12
GCC cf. §29.02
gen. genitive
Gen. Genesis
Ges. Gesenius' Hebrew Grammar 28th ed.
Gk. Greek
GNB Good News Bible
GNP gender, number, person
GNS gender, number, state
Gp *Qal* passive, cf. p.59

H *Hiphʿil*, cf. §28.12
Heb. Hebrew
Hp *Hophʿal*, cf. §28.12
HtD *Hithpaʿel*, cf. §28.12

i.e. that is
imperf. imperfect
impers. impersonal
impf. imperfect
impv. imperative
ind. indirect
indef. indefinite
indir. indirect
inf. infinitive
interrog. interrogative
intr. intransitive
intrans. intransitive

juss. jussive

kg. kilogram(s)
KJV King James' Version
Kt *k*^{e}*tîḇ*, written

l., ll. line(s)
L *Poʿel*, cf. §28.121
lb., lbs. pound(s)
lit. literally
loc. local, locative
LXX Septuagint

m. masculine
m. meter(s)
mda, mdc, mds masc. du. abs., cstr., suf.
mid. middle
mpa, mpc, mps masc. pl. abs., cstr., suf.
msa, msc, mss masc. sg. abs., cstr., suf.

N *Niphʿal*, cf. §28.12
n. neuter
neg. negative

neut. neuter
n.o. near open
num. number, numeral
obj. object, objective
OPers Old Persian
p passive, plural
part. particle
pass. passive
perf. perfect
Pers. Persian
PGN person, gender, number
phr. phrase
pl. plural
plur. plural
pred. predicate
preform. preformative
prep. preposition
pr.n. proper noun
pres. present
pron. pronoun
PS Proto-Semitic
ptcp. participle, participial
Q *qᵉrî*, read
R *Pilpel*, cf. §28.121
R. Rule (number)
rad. radical
rel. relative
RSV Revised Standard Version
s suffixed, suffixial, cf. p.59
s singular
Sem. Semitic
sg. singular
sing. singular
suf. suffix, suffixial
Swed. Swedish
syll. syllable(s)
t infixed *t*, cf.§28.12
T. Table (number)
tr. transitive
trans. transitive
u.c. unaccented closed
un.cl. unaccented closed
v vowel, cf. §16.3
vb. verb
VDC Verb Diagnosis Chart
voc. vocative
WCC *Pe Waw*, cf. §29.02
x times
YCC *Pe Yod*, cf. §29.02
2, 3, etc. see p.59
* hypothetical form
+ added to
< develops from
> develops into, becomes
/ or
= is equivalent to
=? is equivalent to what?

ADDITIONS AND CORRECTIONS

p.6, ¶ 6, l.1 read §11.15
p.10, ¶ 3, l.1 read לְ|מָלְ|כוֹ
p.16, ¶ 5, l.3 read m.p.c.
p.16, ¶ 7, l.1 read m.p.c.
p.19, ¶ 4, l.3 read *wā-îš*
p.21, ¶ 9, l.4 read לַמֶּלֶךְ
p.21, 4 ll. f.b. read תּוֹכַחַת
p.24, ¶ 4, l.4 read suf.
p.29, 1 line f.b. read שֶׁבֶת
p.34, ¶ 2, l.5 read Root is *ʿśy*
p.39, ¶ 5, l.4 read עָשָׂה
p.41, 5 ll. f.b. read יְכָבֵּב
p.41, 4ll. f.b. read תְּכָבֵּב
p.51, ¶ 4, l.7 read *yišlōᵃḥ*
p.54, ¶ 1, l.6 read *ʾmn*
p.60 ¶ 6, l.1 read –הַ
p.63 1 line f.b. read כָּמוֹךָ
p.66 ¶ 5, l.1 read (a) 2:10²
p.70 ¶ 5, l.2 read ‘And
p.75 ¶ 6, l.1 read *yešnô*
p.83 2 lines f.b. read הַגּוֹרָל
p.109 4 lines f.b. read אֵלַי
p.113 add Learn the words in BVG 1-11, 34-45.
p.113 delete repetion f. b. of p.112.
p.135 ¶ 5, l.1 read *šṓmaᶜ*
p.156 last ¶ read *ʿal*
p.158 ¶ 5, l.1 read וְאָבִיו
p.166 ¶ 5, l.3 read *Ges.* §101*l*

TABLE OF CONTENTS

Part 1
LESSONS

TO THE TEACHER

You may pick up a copy of this *Handbook*, look at the Table of Contents, examine the detailed presentation of Phonology, the unusual Synoptic Paradigms, and the quantity of Hebrew to be read (about 15 chapters), and be tempted to put it aside with the comment, "It won't work!" Or you may have had some experience with "the inductive method," and found that, while it is certainly a more enjoyable method of learning, nothing is really learned. At the end of the course the student still does not know the language. Well, before you make a decision, please let me have this chance of explaining what this method entails and how it is expected to work.

The method used in this *Handbook*, simply described, is *to begin with the context*. Orthography, phonology, morphology, syntax, and vocabulary are all learned by encountering the various elements in a connected passage. This method, of course, plunges the student into everything all at once. It is like teaching a person to swim by throwing him or her into a deep lake. Obviously, some planned approach is necessary. In this *Handbook* certain features indicate the approach I use.

Transliteration is used, along with Hebrew orthography. You and I, after years of experience, can look at a Hebrew word and pronounce it almost as easily as we can pronounce a word in Roman characters – but the student has not yet reached that stage. Some years ago, my friend Dr. G. Douglas Young attempted to reduce all Hebrew to transliteration for his grammar. His argument was basically sound: the student could read, recall, and reproduce transliteration much more readily than he could do the same with Hebrew characters. The basic flaw in that system is obvious: only Dr. Young's work was transliterated. To read the Bible, the student must read Hebrew orthography. I have attempted to use both, sometimes Hebrew without transliteration, sometimes only transliteration, and often both side by side. The goals are to learn the approximate and recognizable sound of a word from the start, and to learn to read Hebrew as soon as possible. Teachers who look upon Hebrew orthography as an esoteric mystery will resent transliteration. I consider my task to teach, rather than to impress my students with a self-awarded Master of Mysteries.

Learning is through *repetition*, rather than through attempted mastery at the first encounter. At this point, I would caution the teacher *not* to expect mastery of each new item as it is introduced. Repetition is built into the system. Not every encounter is meaningful, and nothing is learned through meaningless encouters. I have attempted to build in many meaningful encounters of the more significant elements of the language. Please don't ignore them. Remember that some students learn more slowly than others.

The *more frequent elements* of the language receive *more emphasis*. For example, about 10% of the vocabulary makes up about 90% of the text on any given page. Therefore, the student who knows 850 high-frequency words will read much better than one who knows 850 words drawn at random. I stress frequency vocabulary. The same fact is true, *mutatis mutandis*, of other elements of the language. Why spend as much time on the Hithpalpel as on the Qal imperfect? Why not emphasize the things that the student will see most often? In Volume 2 of this *Handbook*, I have attempted to include everything significant, so the student has access to it. In addition, I have given copious references to *Gesenius' Hebrew Grammar* (ed. E. Kautzsch, trans. A. E. Cowley, 2d ed. 1910). But in the lessons, I have concentrated on the more common phenomena. The *Handbook* is designed to be used by working from the lessons to the grammar, not the reverse.

Each lesson has a primary purpose, but this is not the total purpose of that lesson. The teacher should use the lesson to make encounters with the indicated subject as meaningful as possible. Do not attempt, however, to use that as an occasion to present material other than that which is in the lesson.

Along about Lesson 12, the student begins to be overwhelmed by the amount of material being presented. For the next fifteen or twenty lessons, he or she will need a great deal of understanding and encouragement. Those of us who have been through the system several times know that this takes place, and that it always comes out satisfactorily – but students do not know that, and some drop the course at this point. What is happening is simply this: the quantities of new material must be assimilated at the student's own pace. Nothing is gained by *reducing* the pace; it is *repetition* that counts. But the student needs your help to assure him or her that a learning plateau has been reached, and that there will be a period of no apparent progress until assimilation at that level is nearly complete. Then once again there will be noticeable progress.

All learning is *in context*. The context, however, is not artificial, composed perchance by one who does not use the language naturally, but rather it is the actual language of those who used it as their mother-tongue. For this reason, I refuse to ask the students to compose sentences in Hebrew. To do so is to impress errors on the student's mind. And, frankly, most of us who teach Biblical Hebrew do not have sufficient fluency in the language to speak or write in it. I differentiate here between Biblical and Modern Hebrew.

Most of all, I attempt to make the learning process *enjoyable*. Not *easy*, but *enjoyable*. The student should have a constant feeling that he or she is learning a very useful tool, that there is a sound reason for learning elements of phonology (no pun intended!) as well as morphology and syntax, and that the teacher's role is to teach, to help to learn, and to encourage, not to test, to criticize, and to ridicule. The worst epitaph I can imagine is one that would read, "He loved to teach, but he taught his students to hate the subject."

I have used proverbs, pithy sayings, and scriptural portions as space-fillers. Some of these may profitably be used to illustrate points in the lessons; others may be memorized. But, above all, teach *what is in the lesson*.

Encourage the student to keep some systematic record of his or her observations. The major weakness of the inductive method is the lack of a synthesizing process. I have endeavored to compensate for this by synthetic illustrations, but the student should carry this out by entering observed phenomena systematically in a notebook, both in Hebrew characters and in transliteration. Teach the student to observe, and he or she will be learning the rest of his or her life.

The ear to hear and the eye to see,	אֹ֣זֶן שֹׁ֭מַעַת וְעַ֣יִן רֹאָ֑ה
The Lord made both of them.	יְ֝הוָ֗ה עָשָׂ֥ה גַם־שְׁנֵיהֶֽם׃

Proverbs 20:12

1

Purpose: To get acquainted with the *Handbook* and the method.
Materials: Handbook, Parts 1, 2, 3, and 4

Since this course is designed for *inductive* study, let's get acquainted with the *Handbook* inductively. Note that it is divided into four parts. For your convenience, Part 1 has been bound separately. Parts 2, 3, and 4 have been bound as Volume 2. You will normally work with Vol. 1 open to the lesson you are studying (as you are doing right now), and you will be referring continually to Vol. 2 for information that is designed to help you learn certain points in the lesson. *Note the order:* Always work from the lesson to the grammar, not the reverse.

Now turn to Vol. 2. The front portion (Part 2) is the *Grammar.* It is divided into three divisions: Phonology, Morphology, and Syntax. Note that these 3 divisions are subdivided into many sections (indicated by the sign § 'section,' followed by numbers). Look at §01: it defines Phonology. Don't bother to learn it now, since this is simply a familiarization run on the *Handbook.* Now look at §20, where Morphology is defined. Next look at §30. What is defined there? Turn now to §06ff and read about the numbering system. Look over the examples at the bottom of that page. What have you learned?

Turn to Part 3, Tables and Paradigms. Leaf through it and get an idea of what is contained there. Note that the Paradigms are "synoptic." If you don't know the meaning of "paradigm" and "synoptic," where would you look? Do it. In most grammars, paradigms give all significant examples of a particular type of a verb or a noun. In this *Handbook,* we get a synoptic view of a certain feature of several different types, e.g. the "G-stem" of "regular" and "irregular" verbs. You are *not* expected to memorize entire paradigms; rather, you are expected to *observe* (and, of course, learn) the significant characteristics of forms so you can recognize them quickly and accurately.

Now look at Part 4, Basic Vocabulary. In this *Handbook,* we stress the learning of a *basic* vocabulary (i.e. the words that occur most frequently in a language). About 10% of the words occur about 90% of the time. Of the more than 8,600 words in the OT vocabulary, only about 1,100 (about 12.5%) occur 25 times or more. Obviously, these are the words to learn first. The basic vocabulary is arranged alphabetically, and each word is numbered (following the numbering of *Strong's Concordance*). In addition a letter-and-number symbol indicates the word's frequency. All words that occur 15x or more (except proper names) are listed. Beginning with Lesson 4, you will be learning groups of words. These groups, fitted to the lessons, will be found in the back of Vol. 1.

Now, how do we go about studying? We go through each *Lesson,* point by point. We look up the references to the Grammar and the Tables and Paradigms. We observe, record observations, compare our records, learn a few points, and move on. Concentrate on a *few* points in each lesson. *Do not try to learn everything* in a lesson, but work to the limit of your own ability. Repetition has been built into the *Handbook,* so if you do not learn a point in one lesson, you will have many more opportunities to learn it.

Learning is *repetition.* We have deliberately–even mechanically–built repetition into the *Handbook.* Not only are there periodic reviews, but each point that is introduced will be repeated in subsequent lessons, then ignored for several lessons, and then reintroduced for relearning. If it takes 5 meaningful encounters to learn a point, we have built in 10 or even 15 encounters that are designed to be meaningful. If you get bored by such repetition, remember that another student needs that extra encounter to learn the matter. If after several lessons, you find that you no longer need to look up §13.111, skip it. If you can look at a Hebrew word and tell at a glance its form, its root, and other details that are significant for the understanding of that word in its context, pass on to the next. Just remember, some learn more slowly, some more rapidly. You should work at your own pace.

We shall make use of *synthetic* materials (grammars, lexicons, commentaries, etc.), in order to draw upon knowledge already gained—for no one in his right mind would seek to cover the entire field of human knowledge inductively. At the same time, we must not let the conclusions arrived at by other students blunt our own observations of the data.

Keep a *notebook*, and record carefully your observations. Periodically review and rearrange them, until you have a small grammar of your own. Inductive learning breaks down if the student fails to synthesize what he observes inductively.

Plan to spend *two hours* on each lesson. Make the time count. Don't spin your wheels, but keep learning new points. Jot down points that are not clear. Learn to ask questions of the text, and soon it will be answering you. If you are weak in English grammar, spend time on §30ff. The first 25-30 lessons will be the hardest, especially from about Lesson 12 on. The reason: you are continually encountering new items, far more rapidly than you can assimilate them. From about Lesson 30 on, you will encounter few *new* items, but you will be constantly reviewing what you have previously seen (and probably not learned, or not fully understood). *Stay with it!* There is no *easy* way to learn a language. The inductive method can be *more enjoyable* and, properly used, can be more *effective.*

Read over §§01.-05, §§10., 10.1, 10.2, 10.3, 10.4.

2

Purpose: To start learning the alphabet and the pointing
Materials: Esther 1:1

וַיְהִי בִּימֵי אֲחַשְׁוֵרוֹשׁ הוּא אֲחַשְׁוֵרוֹשׁ הַמֹּלֵךְ מֵהֹדּוּ וְעַד־ א
כּוּשׁ שֶׁבַע וְעֶשְׂרִים וּמֵאָה מְדִינָה׃

וַיְהִי[1]—Hebrew is read *from right to left* (←), see §11., §11.1. Consonants: ו *wāw,* י *yôd,* ה *hê,* י *yôd*. Compare (cf.) ו and י. See TABLE B. Vowels: ַ *pattāḥ,* ְ *šᵉwâ,* ִ *ḥîrîq*. For vowels see TABLE C. Accent under ה, *ṭip̄ḥâ*, §11.53. Read §§11.5-.52. Final *yôd* is a vowel lengthener, §11.2. Transliteration, *wa-yᵉ-hîʸ*. 'And it was.'

בִּימֵי[2]—ב *bêṯ,* מ *mêm*; you should recognize *yôd* (1:1[1]). Vowels: *ḥîrîq,* ֵ *ṣērê*. Note בּ with *dāḡēšᵉ*, §§11.44, .441. Accent, *mûnāḥ*, §11.54. י without vowel is a vowel letter, §11.21. *bîʸ-mêʸ* 'in the days of.'

אֲחַשְׁוֵרוֹשׁ[3]—א *'ālep̄* (§12.51, §12.35), ח *ḥêṯ* (§§12.331, .341), שׁ *šîn* (pronounce *sheen;* §11.41). ו *wāw,* ר *rêš,* וֹ *ḥôlā-wāw* (§11.3231). ֲ *ḥăṭap̄-pattāḥ* (§11.32); you have had the others. ֑ is *'aṯnāḥ* (§11.533, §11.55). וֵ: *wāw* with vowel must be consonantal. וֹ could be *wō* or *ôʷ*– but note the ר. Since it has no vowel written under it, וֹ must be its vowel. ַ is a short vowel (§14.2); וֹ is a long vowel (§14.1). *'ă-ḥaš-wē-rôʷš* 'Ahasuerus.'

הוּא[4]—*hê*, spirant, §12.42. §11.54. No vowel under ה, but וּ *šûrûq* follows, §11.324. א is quiescent, §13.55. *hû'* 'he, that.'

אֲחַשְׁוֵרוֹשׁ[5]—See 1:1[3]. Nore *rᵉḇîᵃ'* over ר, §11.534. א is a stop, §12.411. ח, שׁ, consonantal ו, and ר are spirants, §12.421. ו *w,* originally a bilabial, §12.31. ר *r* probably uvular, §12.341, originally alveolar flap, §12.321. שׁ *š*, sibilant, §12.322.

הַמֹּלֵךְ[6]—ל *lāmeḏ,* '11.15. ךְ *kap̄ sôp̄ît* 'final kaph,' §11.131; if it has no vowel, it is always written with shewa. מּ, with strong dagesh, §11.431, read §11.43. Note ֹ *ḥôlām*, §11.323. Read §§12.-12.22, and start using §12.5. Accent is postpositive, §11.571. *ham-mô-lēḵ* 'the (one) ruling.'

מֵהֹדּוּ[7]—First letter? vowel? §12.5. §11.32. Second letter? vowel? accent? §11.54. ד *dāleḏ* with *dāḡēš*: read §11.44. Dagesh both doubles and hardens, §11.43, §11.442. וּ *šûrûq. mēhōd-dû* 'from India.'

וְעַד־כּוּשׁ[8]—ע *'áyin* (not Y!), strong glottal stop, §12.351. ־ *maqqēp̄*, §11.45. כּ *kap̄* with dagesh, cf. 1:1[6], §11.131, and read §11.44 carefully. This is the light dagesh, §11.441. Note וְ and וּ—which is consonant, which is vowel letter? (1:1[4]). Note that ד and שׁ at word-end have no vowels. Accent, *zāqēp̄-qāṭôn*, §11.535. *wᵉ-aḏ—kûš* 'and unto Cush.'

שֶׁ֫בַע[9]—ב is *rāpê'*, read §11.44, §11.443. ע is pronounced how? Squeeze your glottis! Accent conjunctive; read §11.57. *šé-ḇa'* 'seven.'

וְעֶשְׂרִ֑ים[10]—שׂ *śîn*, §11.41. Note שׁ and שׂ. ם *mêm sôp̄ît*, §11.131. ֶ *s*^{e}*gôl*, §11.32. ִי *ḥîrîq-yôḏ*, §14.13, §11.322. First *š*^{e}*wâ* is vocalic, second is silent (read §15.251). *w*^{e}*-'eś-rîm* 'and 20.'

וּמֵאָה[11]—ָ *qāmāṣ gāḏôl*, §11.321. וּ *šûrûq* is the only vowel that stands at beginning of word, §16.3f. Review §11.21, §11.53. *û-mē-'ā*^{h} 'and 100.'

מְדִינָֽה׃[12]—נ *nûn*. ׃ֽ *sillûq* and *sôp̄ pāsûq*, read §11.531, §11.46. *m*^{e}*-ḏî*^{y}*-nā*^{h} 'province(s).'

The following consonants have appeared: שׁשׂרענםמלךכּיחוהדדּבבּא. Be sure you know them, names, transliteration, pronunciation, and how to write them (TABLE D).

The following vowels have appeared: ַ ֵ ֶ ְ ִ ָ ָה ֵי ִי וֹ וּ. Know their names and values (TABLE C).

Note carefully: שׁשׂ ךד חה נו יו רד כב.

Read over §§01.—04. Read over §§10.—10.442.

Learn the terms: consonant, vowel, diphthong, transliteration, quiescent, vowel lengthener, conjunctive, disjunctive (accent); dagesh, begadkepat, athnaḥ, sillûq, sôph pasûq.

Learn to write Hebrew clearly and accurately. *Write* the letters; don't *draw* them. Omit serifs and shading, just as you do when writing English.

```
with serifs and shading:   A B C D E F G H I J
with serifs, no shading:   A B C D E F G H I J
no serifs, no shading:     A B C D E F G H I J
```

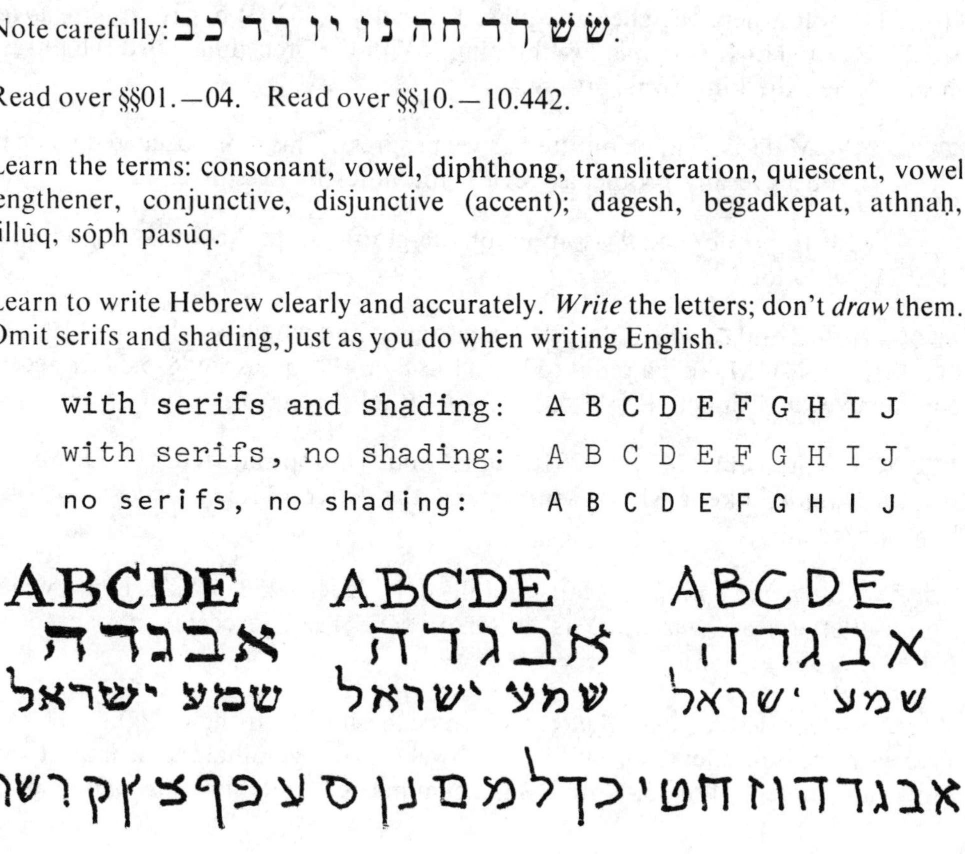

3

Purpose: To learn the orthography
Materials: Esther 1:2

2 בַּיָּמִ֖ים הָהֵ֑ם כְּשֶׁ֣בֶת ׀
הַמֶּ֣לֶךְ אֲחַשְׁוֵר֗וֹשׁ עַ֚ל כִּסֵּ֣א מַלְכוּת֔וֹ אֲשֶׁ֖ר בְּשׁוּשַׁ֥ן הַבִּירָֽה׃

בַּיָּמִ֖ים[1]—בַּ, read carefully §11.441, §12.4, .41. What vowel follows? §11.32. Read carefully §11.431. Compare מּ and מ and read §11.13f. Read §11.2. *bay-yā-mî^y m* 'in the days.'

הָהֵ֑ם[2]—For *qāmāṣ gāḏôl* read §11.32, Table C. For *ṣērê* §11.32, and for *'aṯnāḥ* §11.533. Read §11.5. *hā-hēm* 'the those' 'in those days.'

כְּשֶׁ֣בֶת ׀[3]—Fpr כּ §11.441. For ְ §11.44, §15.25, .2521. שֶׁ §11.41, §11.54, §17.11. Read §17. ב read §12.422, §11.443. ת is also spirantized, §12.422. For ׀ §11.72. Note that it cannot be a major pause here. *k^e-š-ḇeṯ* 'when the sitting of.'

הַמֶּ֣לֶךְ[4]—Cf. 1:1[6]. מּ §11.431, §13.31. Read §11.43 and §13.3. For ֶ read §11.54, §11.57. Read also §17.11, and start to notice where stress-accent is placed. For ךְ §11.1311; note where the shewa is placed. Read §16.363. What is an *allophone*? §10.23. Read §11.44. *ham-mé-leḵ* 'the king.' With the preceding word the phrase means 'when the king [was] sitting.'

אֲחַשְׁוֵר֗וֹשׁ[5]—Material will be omitted as we progress. This word occurred twice in 1:1[3 5]. If you have any problems, review the notes in Lesson 2.

עַ֚ל[6]—Learn to pronounce ע as an emphatic glottal stop. Accent is conjunctive §11.521. *'al* 'upon.'

כִּסֵּ֣א[7]—Note כּ and סּ: which dagesh is a hardener and which is a doubler? Review §11.431, §11.441. Make it a point to learn this *now*. א is quiescent §15.54. Is accent conjunctive or disjunctive? §11.521. *kis-sē'* '[the] throne of.'

מַלְכוּת֔וֹ[8]—Note וֹ §11.324, §11.3231. Both כ and ת are spirantized, §11.44. Accent is *zāqēp̄ qāṭôn*, like a shewa on top of the letter §11.535. *mal-ḵû-ṯô^w*, his kingship/royalty.'

אֲשֶׁ֖ר[9]—Note *ḥaṭap̄ pattāḥ* ֲ. Read carefully §11.325, §15.253, §15.42. Learn which sounds (letters) are *gutturals*. Is שׁ *šîn* or *śîn*? §11.41. Accent conj. or disj.? §11.521. *ă-šer* 'which.'

בְּשׁוּשַׁ֥ן[10]—New letter ן *nûn sôp̄îṯ* §11.131. Is dagesh in בּ strong or light? §11.43ff. Is shewa vocal or silent? §16.35. Is וּ a vowel (*û*) or a geminate consonant (*ww*)? How can you tell? §11.433. Note: if וּ is a geminate consonant, *it must have a vowel with it*–is there one? In an accented syllable, *qāmāṣ* must be *ā*, §15.11, cf. §11.321. What kind of accent? *b*^{e}*-šû*^{w}*-šan* 'in Susa.'

הַבִּירָֽה׃''—After vowel, dagesh in בּ must be strong (doubling) §16.3612, therefore syllable must be *closed* §16.11, and the vowel a *normal short* vowel §14.232. Start to master Table E. For ִי cf. §§11.2, .21, .211. ָ is *ā*, §15.11, cf. §14.2. ָה is a vowel, §11.2. Note ֽ silluq, §11.531 it looks like metheg (§11.58), but where is silluq found?. Soph pasuq ׃, §11.46. *hab-bî*^{y}*-rā*^{h}, 'the palace/citadel.'

New consonants: ת ם ן.

Note carefully the differences: דרך תחה סם ןוי.

Long vowels thus far: ָה, ֵי, וֹ, וּ/. Read §14., §14.1, §14.13.

Short vowels thus far: ַ ָ ֶ ִ ֻ ֳ ָ. Read §14.2, §14.232.

Know the meanings: closed syllable, open syllable, geminate consonant; begadkepat, athnaḥ, silluq, soph pasûq; light dagesh, strong dagesh; stop, spirant, spirantization. Put them in your notebook.

Transliterate from Heb. characters to Roman Zephaniah 3:8, using the system of transliteration found in Tables B and C. You will have difficulty with the shewa and the dagesh, but these will be cleared away in the next few lessons. Concentrate on getting a useful phonetic equivalent for the Heb. orthography.

לָכֵ֣ן 8
חַכּוּ־לִ֣י נְאֻם־יְהוָ֗ה לְי֛וֹם קוּמִ֖י לְעַ֑ד כִּ֣י מִשְׁפָּטִי֩ לֶאֱסֹ֨ף
גּוֹיִ֜ם לְקָבְצִ֣י מַמְלָכ֗וֹת לִשְׁפֹּ֨ךְ עֲלֵיהֶ֤ם זַעְמִי֙ כֹּ֚ל חֲר֣וֹן אַפִּ֔י
כִּ֚י בְּאֵ֣שׁ קִנְאָתִ֔י תֵּאָכֵ֖ל כָּל־הָאָֽרֶץ׃

RULES

1a. A *dagesh* in a *begadkepat* at the beginning of a word or following a shewa is a light dagesh, indicating stopped pronunciation (§11.44). A dagesh in any other letter, or in a begadkepat in any other position, is a strong dagesh, indicating a geminate (doubled) consonant (§11.43). A strong dagesh in a begadkepat both doubles and hardens it (§11.442).

1b. Consonants with shewa, except begadkepat and ט, frequently lose the strong dagesh (§13.41). This particularly applies to י.

4

Purpose: To study syllabification and vowel quantity
Materials: Esther 1:3

בִּשְׁנַת שָׁלוֹשׁ לְמָלְכוֹ עָשָׂה מִשְׁתֶּה לְכָל־שָׂרָיו וַעֲבָדָיו 3
חֵיל ׀ פָּרַס וּמָדַי הַפַּרְתְּמִים וְשָׂרֵי הַמְּדִינוֹת לְפָנָיו׃

1:3 בִּשְׁנַת [1]—Always start from the *end* of a word to syllabify. Every syllable must begin with a consonant (read §16.3). Read §16. בִּשְׁ|נַת, 2 syllables, both closed, §§16.11, .32. The word is *in construct,* hence has no primary stress-accent (Rule 3), §25.4. Both syllables are *unaccented closed,* §16.33. The word is composed of the prep. *b*^{e}- + *š*^{e}*nat̲,* hence a zero shewa, §15.2522, §16.3624. The *ḥîrîq* ִ develops from 2 shewas, §15.651. Read §15.243. *biš-nat̲* 'in the year of.'

שָׁלוֹשׁ [2]—שָׁ|לוֹשׁ, primary accent on ultima, §16.1. Pure long vowel, §14.1, .11, written full (§11.322. The *penult* (§16.1) is open, §16.32; since it is immediately before the stress-accent, it is *near-open,* §16.321, .3211. Be sure you know this thoroughly. A short vowel normally lengthens in a near-open syllable, hence *šā-lô*^{w}*š* 'three.'

לְמָלְכוֹ [3]—לְ|מָלְ|כוֹ, 3 syllables, read §16.2. Ultima open, accented, pure-long vowel; penult closed, unaccented; antepenult open, hence distant-open, §16.3212. Look at the short vowels: in the penult מָלְ, therefore ָ must be *qāmāṣ-ḥăṭûp̄,* short *o,* §11.321. Shewa in distant open (d.o.) is a reduced vowel, §15.252. כ is spirantized after silent shewa, §15.2522. *l*^{e}*-mol-k̲ô*^{w} 'to (= of) his ruling.'

עָשָׂה [4]—עָ|שָׂה, ultima accented (open), penult near-open, hence lengthened, ה is a vowel-letter, §11.2. *ʿā-śā*^{h} 'he made.'

מִשְׁתֶּה [5]—Note dagesh in תּ: since this is a begadkepat, the dagesh could be light or strong, §11.43ff. But since it follows shewa, it must be light, Rule la. Study §16.3622. Review §11.441. The shewa must be a syllable divider, §15.251, and שׁ must close a syllable. For ֶ in accented syllable, read §15.732, .7322. Review §11.535. *miš-tê*^{h} 'a banquet.'

לְכָל־שָׂרָיו [6]—Syllabify, working from end. What does maqqeph (§11.45) tell you about accent on לְכָל? §15.321. Then what is ָ? §11.321, §14.23, .231. Is the shewa silent or vocal? §15.25, .252. Whis syllable is near-open (n.o.)? §15.12. The combination רָיו is pronounced [rɑw] or [rɑv], read §13.52, .525. *l*^{e}*-k̲ol-śā-rā*^{y}*w* 'for all his princes.'

וַעֲבָדָיו [7]—Syllabify, identify each syllable (acc., n.o., d.o., cl). There are 2 d.o. syll., neither with simple shewa. Read §15.253, then §15.653 (Rule 21). Review §11.58f, §15.23, §15.12, §14.31, and 1:3[6]. What does ֲ tell you? §11.533. *wa-ʿă-b̲ā-d̲ā*^{y}*w* 'and his servants.'

חֵיל[8]—One syll., §16.2, a monophthong §15.7, in cstr., hence no primary accent (Rule 3), cf. §15.7324. Review §11.54, §11.72. *ḥê^{y}l* 'the might of.'

פָּרַ֫ס[9]—Syllabify, identify each syll. Note pattaḥ in acc. cl. The mark * above ר is a Masoretic note (§11.7), telling us that *qāmāṣ* is found in some texts. Which would you expect? Rule 13. *pā-ras,* 'Persia.'

וּמָדַי[10]—Syllabify, identify syllables. How many vowels and diphthongs? Therefore, how many syllables? Learn §16.2 *now.* Read §16.31, review §15.12, §14.33, §15.72. Loan-words often do not follow the rules. *û-mā-ḏay* 'and Media.'

הַפַּרְתְּמִים[11]—Syllabify. There are 2 begadkepats with dagesh: read §§11.441, .442 carefully, and identify the strong dagesh (Rule 1a). Read §15.2511 carefully. You should have cvc-cvc-cv-cvc. For n.o. with shewa, possibly §15.241, but this is a loan word. Review §14.13. *hap-par-t^{e}-mîm* 'the nobles.'

וְשָׂרֵי[12]—Without further instruction, *you are expected to syllabify every word in the next several lessons,* until you can do it easily and accurately. Review §17.12. Word in cstr., hence שָׂ may be compensation vowel §15.14. Note §15.73. *w^{e}-śā-rê^{y}* 'and [the] princes of.'

הַמְּדִינוֹת[13]—Identify the long vowels. §11.322, §11.3231, §14.1. Which dagesh? §16.3612. Does §16.3622 apply? *ham-m^{e}-ḏî-nôṯ* 'the provinces.'

לְפָנָיו׃[14]—How many vowels? How many syllables? Is the shewa a syllable? §16.21. Does the begadkepat that follows have dagesh?. Cf. 1:2[13]. *l^{e}-p̄ā-nā^{y}w* '[were] before him.'

New consonants: כ פּ פ ת; new vowel: ָ (*o*); diphthongs: ֶה ֵי ָיו.

Know the meanings of: closed, open, accented, unaccented, near-open, distant-open, lengthened, reduced, pure-long vowel, lengthened short vowel, zero shewa.

Learn Rules 1a, 3, 13.

Syllabify Est. 1:1.

Memorize the words in Vocabulary Group 1.

3. Words joined by maqqeph and words in construct have only one major accent (§17.12).

יִרְאַת יְהוָה רֵאשִׁית דָּעַת

The fear of the Lord is the beginning of wisdom.

(Prov. 1:7)

5

Purpose: To introduce morphology
Materials: Esther 1:4

4 בְּהַרְאֹתוֹ אֶת־עֹשֶׁר כְּבוֹד מַלְכוּתוֹ וְאֶת־יְקָר תִּפְאֶרֶת
גְּדוּלָּתוֹ יָמִים רַבִּים שְׁמוֹנִים וּמְאַת יוֹם׃

Read carefully §§20.-20.31.

בְּהַרְאֹתוֹ [1]—Syllabify all words. בְּ|הַרְ|אֹ|תוֹ. Be sure you understand why it is divided in this manner. Read §§20.1,.12, 20.2,.212. –בּ is a preposition (§30.35). וֹ– is a pronominal suffix, §23.121, §30.312. The balance is a verb, to be discussed in later lessons. א is defective, §11.324f, תוֹ is *plene* $\hat{o}^h$, §11.322. Read §11.3241. Review §11.534, §17. 'In his causing to see' = 'when he showed.'

אֶת־עֹשֶׁר [2]—For עשׁ see §11.411. Note maqqeph, §11.45. We have here the beginning of a chain of constructs (§36.31f). Read §17.12f carefully. Accent on ר is postpositive (§11.571), and since the stress-accent (secondary) is on the penult, the accent is repeated over ע. Review §11.52f, §11.45. אֶת is the sign of the definite direct object (d.d.o.), §34.113. 'The wealth of.'

כְּבוֹד [3]—Cstr., hence כְּ is d.o. §17.121. בוֹד is unacc. cl., hence long *ô,* §15.22. 'The glory of.'

מַלְכוּתוֹ [4]—וֹ– is pron. suf., 1:4[1], §2321. \וּת\ indicates an abstract idea, '-ship, -ness,' §24.56. The root is מלך *m-l-k,* §20.3. *It will be easier to learn a basic vocabulary if you learn to group words from the same root.* A pron. suf. makes a word definite, §30.3222, §36.523. If the last word in cstr. is definite, all words in the chain are def., §36.3161. 'His kingship' = 'the wealth of the glory of his kingship.'

וְאֶת־יְקָר [5]—w^e is d.o., *'et* unacc.cl., y^e is d.o. in cstr. §17.121. The word $y^eq\hat{a}r$ has the same form in abs. and cstr., hence *â* must be long (Rule 2a). 'And the costliness of.'

תִּפְאֶרֶת [6]—תִּפְ|אֶ|רֶת with accent on penult, a segolate (§17.11). ֶ ֶת is a fem. morpheme, §25.131; for development, see §15.61. Originally the word was something like **tip'artu.* 'The beauty/adornment of.'

גְּדוּלָּתוֹ [7]—וֹ is what morpheme? §23.121. ַת is an original fem. sg. morpheme, preserved in cstr. and suf. forms (as well as fem. of segolates), §25.13. Is the word definite? §36.523. What does this do to the chain of cstrs.? §36.3131. Review §11.53. 'His greatness.' [Note that the word 'greatness' is fem. (abstract), but the pron. suf. is masc.]

יָמִים רַבִּים [8]—We shall begin to study words in phrases. Note the ending ־ים– and read §25.12. This is a masc. pl. absolute (m.p.a.) morpheme. Note position of adjective: in Heb. it regularly follows the noun it modifies, §30.32, §36.12, and is in concord (i.e. it agrees in gender, number, and state), §36.11.

שְׁמוֹנִים [9]—ִ־ים– is what morpheme? §25.12. Syllabify and identify each syllable. The pl. of '8' is '80'–don't ask why! §26.26.

וּמְאַת יוֹם׃ [10]—*û-m^{e}-at*, §16.3. ַ־ת– is what morpheme? §25.13. *yô^{w}m* < **yawm*, §15.7211. Review §11.531. 'Eighty and one hundred of day' = '180 days.'

This is just an *introduction* to morphology. We must study it from now on, until every morpheme is quickly apparent. If you have not yet started a notebook, do so now. Record your observations until you no longer need to do so (which should be for at least the next 40 lessons!)

New consonants: ג ק. Review others. Note differences: ג נ כ.

Note these words: הַמֹּלֵךְ 1:1[6], הַמֶּלֶךְ 1:2[4], לְמָלְכוֹ 1:3[3], and מַלְכוּתוֹ 1:4[4]; what do you see? Read §20.2. What is the common *root* of these words? What does it mean? *Don't look it up until you have tried to figure it out!* Learn to use your power of reasoning.

Now go back over Lessons 2–4 and analyze –ל and –ו similarly. See if you can figure out the morphemes ִ־ים– and –וֹת. Look for other morphemes. You may see some that are not there, but at least you're looking.

Learn Rules 2, 4, and 5. Learn the basic vocabulary in Group 2.

13a. Short vowels normally *lengthen* in accented or near-open syllables, and *reduce* in distant-open syllables (§15.11, §15.12, §15.23)

13b. Compensatory vowels do not reduce (§15.233).

13c. The original vowel of a segolate does not reduce in sg. cstr. (§15.232). It does, however, reduce in pl. abs. forms.

13d. In many forms, *ṣêrê* does not reduce (§15.223).

פּוֹרֵעַ מוּסָר מוֹאֵס נַפְשׁוֹ.

He who ignores instruction despises himself.

(Prov. 15:32)

6

Purpose: To study the behavior of short-vowels
Materials: Esther 1:5

ה וּבִמְלוֹאת ׀ הַיָּמִים
הָאֵלֶּה עָשָׂה הַמֶּלֶךְ לְכָל־הָעָם הַנִּמְצְאִים בְּשׁוּשַׁן הַבִּירָה
לְמִגָּדוֹל וְעַד־קָטָן מִשְׁתֶּה שִׁבְעַת יָמִים בַּחֲצַר גִּנַּת בִּיתַן
הַמֶּלֶךְ׃

1:5 וּבִמְלוֹאת [1]—Masoretic note (§11.61) calls attention to unusual form. Correct form is given in the *q*^{e}*rê* in bottom margin (§16.31). Form here is built by analogy, §20.6. –ו is conjunction, §30.36. –בּ is prep., §30.35. §20.2, §20.211, §22.41. Balance is a verb, in cstr., hence no major accent (Rule 3). Now note the vowels: וּ is pure-long (Rule 2a). *w*^{e}*b̲*^{e}*m*^{e}- developed to *û-b̲im-* under Rule 8 (§16.31) and Rule 19 (§15.651). §11.5, .521, .54. 'and in the filling of.'

הַיָּמִים הָאֵלֶּה — ־ים §25.321. הַ· is def. art. §22.2. So is –הָ. Start to master Table G. For אֵלֶּה note accent; *'ēl-* is acc. cl., hence vowel is lengthened (R. 13). *-lê*^{h} is a monophthong §15.7, §15.73; this word is an exception to §15.7322. In a similar way work out the vowels in *hay-yā-mî*^{y}*m.* For the demonstrative pronoun, see §30.3123, and for concord §§36.11, .12. Review §11.534. 'the days the these.' With the previous word, read 'when these days were filled.'

עָשָׂה הַמֶּלֶךְ [3]—Cf. 1:3^4, 1:2^4. Read §30.33, §30.31. In future lessons we shall omit words which you are supposed to know without explanation, but be sure you can explain them. הַמֶּלֶךְ is a segolate, §24.21. Such words do not lengthen ֶ under accent, §15.232. Read §15.35, §17.11. Is שׂ *šîn* or *śîn*? Explain the vowels in עָשָׂה. 'He made, the king' = 'the king made.'

לְכָל־הָעָם [4]—Identify the def. art., note vowel, see Table G. 1:5^2. –ל is a prep., §20.25, §20.2. For כָּל see 1:3^6. Which *qāmāṣ*? What kind of syllable? For עָם, §15.133. 'for all the people.

הַנִּמְצְאִים [5]—See §15.2511, and then syllabify. הַ· 1:5^2, §22.2. ־ים is what morpheme? §25.231. נ is a stem-indicator (to be discussed when we get to verbs) often passive, and the word is a participle (ptcp.), §30.382, a verbal adjective, hence in concord with הָעָם. As in Eng., 'people' can be sg. or pl.; here pl., 'the [ones who are] being found.' The form should be **nimṣā'îm,* cf. §15.241f and read §20.6.

בְּשׁוּשַׁן הַבִּירָה [6]—(a) 1:2^{10}. This word is always vocalized with *pattāḥ*. For בּ §22.4. (b) 1:2^{11}. §22.2 ־ָה is fem. sg. absolute morpheme, §25.121.

לְמִגָּדוֹל וְעַד־קָטָן [7]—(a) *l*[e]- 1:5[4]. *migg-* for *ming-,* read §13.1, .111, Rule 11. §22.42. *gāḏôl* is an adj. used substantivally, §30.31, §24.42. Explain each vowel. (b) *w*[e] is a conjunction, §30.36, §22.1. *ʿaḏ* is a prep., §30.35f. *qāṭān* is adj. used substantivally (§30.31). Explain the quantity of each vowel (§15). *l*[e]*min . . . we*ʿ*aḏ* is an idiom, 'from . . . to;' 'from great to small' is a merism, meaning 'everybody.'

מִשְׁתֶּה [8]—Cf. 1:3[5]. There is no indefinite article in Heb., §36.25. For *-tê*[h] §15.7322 and Table F.

שִׁבְעַת יָמִים [9]—(a) ־ַת *-aṯ* is what morpheme? §25.122. Does this tell us how to relate the two words? R.3. 1:1[9]. (b) *-îm* is what morpheme? 1:2[1], 1:4[8]. Note 1:4[10] '100 of day'; here '7 of days.' With numbers 2-9 use pl. nouns, from 10 up, use sg. Don't ask why!

בַּחֲצַר גִּנַּת בִּיתַן הַמֶּלֶךְ׃ [10]—Note the vowels: all short vowels are reduced except in closed syllables or in the last word. This is your clue to a chain of constructs, §36.316. (a) Read §15.653. *ba-* is what morpheme? 1:5[1]. (b) What morpheme is *-aṯ*? §25.122, 1:5[9]. (c) Long vowels do not reduce, §15.22. (d) 1:2[4]. 'in the court of the garden of the house of the king.'

New consonants: צ ט. Note differences: א ע צ מ ט.

Study the accents in this verse and note how they break up the sentence into phrases and clauses. Read over §§11.5–11.59.

Learn Rules 2a, 10b, 11, 19.

Learn the basic words in Group 3.

Analyze the following words: יום 1:4[11], בַּיָּמִים 1:2[1], הַיָּמִים 1:5[2], בִּימֵי 1:1[2]. Make notes in your notebook. Do the same with וּמֵאָה 1:1[11] and וּמְאַת 1:[10], and with שֶׁבַע 1:1[9] and שִׁבְעַת 1:5[9]. How many observations can you list? How many morphemes have you identified?

11. Nun נ assimilates to a following consonant when no vowel separates (§13.111).

19. When two successive simple (vocal) shewas would occur, the first becomes *ḥîrîq* and the second becomes zero-shewa (§15.651).

לֵךְ־אֶל־נְמָלָה עָצֵל רְאֵה דְרָכֶיהָ וַחֲכָם׃

Go to the ant, O sluggard; consider her ways, and be wise.

(Prov. 6:6)

7

Purpose: To introduce the segolates
Materials: Esther 1:6

חוּר ׀ כַּרְפַּס וּתְכֵלֶת אָחוּז בְּחַבְלֵי־בוּץ וְאַרְגָּמָן 6
עַל־גְּלִילֵי כֶסֶף וְעַמּוּדֵי שֵׁשׁ מִטּוֹת ׀ זָהָב וָכֶסֶף עַל רִצְפַת
בַּהַט־וָשֵׁשׁ וְדַר וְסֹחָרֶת׃

1:6 ׀ חוּר[1]—Masoretic note calls attention to the large *ḥêṯ*. The reason for the large letter is no longer known. וּ is a long vowel, §14.1. For *pāsêq,* 1:1[3]. Closed syllable, §16.33. 'white cotton/linen.'

כַּרְפַּס[2]—Review R.1 (why?). Two closed syllables; we would expect *qāmāṣ* in the ultima. Why? §16.3. 'fine linen.'

וּתְכֵלֶת[3]—Syllabify *û-ṯ*^{e}*-ḵē̆-leṯ*. Read and apply §16.31, §15.23, §16.3212, §17.1, §17.11, §16.33. Now study carefully §15.161. Be sure you understand anaptyxis, §15.61, and doubly-closed syllable, §16.34. Rules 4, 5, 6b. The word originally was probably **tukiltu* or *tikiltu. 'and violet/blue.'

אָחוּז[4]—Syllabify, read §16.3211, §16.33. Identify the long vowel. This is a passive participle (pass. ptcp.), §30.382. 'seized/held.'

בְּחַבְלֵי־בוּץ[5]—Maqqeph, §11.45. R. 3. §17.121. (a) *b*^{e}*-ḥaḇ-lê*^{y}. Identify each syllable and each vowel. Read §14.3, §15.7, §15.72ff, .73ff, §16.33, §15.23. Cf. 1:5[1, 10]. ־ֵי is masc. pl. cstr. (m.s.c.) morpheme. Take it away, and you have *ḥabl*–a doubly-closed syllable. Rule 6b would suggest a development to *ḥéḇel,* a segolate, §16.3432. (b) What kind of vowel? 'With bands/cords of *βυσσος* (fine linen).'

וְאַרְגָּמָן[6]—וְ|אַר|גָּ|מָן, identify each syllable (acc. cl., n.o., d.o., u.c.), and explain each vowel, whether it is lengthened (§15.1) or reduced (§15.2). Start to work on the Short-Vowel Chart (SVC), Table E. Read §16.3622, §16.361. 'and purple.'

עַל־גְּלִילֵי כֶסֶף[7]—Note m.s.c. morpheme (־ֵי) and maqqeph, recall R. 3. What is true of all syllables except the next-to-last? (a) Prep., §30.35, u.c. §16.33. (b) Which dagesh? §11.44f. Both *yôḏ*s are vowel letters, §11.21. Which is a long vowel (§14.13) and which is a monophthong (§15.73)? §11.322. What is the m.p.c. morpheme? §25.421. Cf. 1:6[5]. (c) כ is spirantized because the word is closely joined to the preceding which ends in a vowel-sound. Originally **kaspu* (cf. Akk. *kaspum*), the word has become a segolate, §15.611. Study carefully §15.61. 'on rings of silver.'

וְעַמּוּדֵי שֵׁשׁ[8]—(a) ־ֵי tells us what? 1:6[7]. §25.421. What does this tell us about the stress-accent? §17.121. Which dagesh in מּ? R.1. What does this do to preceding syllable? §16.3611. What kind of vowel is וּ ? §14.13. Since it is a d.o. syll., וּ

cannot be a short vowel, §15.23. (b) What accent is under שֵׁ? §11.53. What does this tell us? §15.533. Syllabify. 'and pillars of marble.'

זָהָב וָכֶסֶף | מִטּוֹת[9]—(a) Two syllables–why? §16.361, .3613. Neither can reduce–why? §15.243, §15.22. Hence the *form* does not tell us whether the word is in cstr., but the *context* does. Note *pāsêq*, 1:2[3]. (b) Syllabify *zā-hā<u>b</u>*, §16.3211, .33. R. 13. (c) וָ, note vowel, §16.3211. כֶּסֶף, note where the accent is–a fairly reliable clue to a segolate, §15.611. Here we find one ruling noun (§36.311) with two governed nouns (§36.312). Read §36.313. We therefore probably should read 'beds of gold-and-silver' rather than 'beds of gold and (other beds) of silver.'

עַל רִצְפַת[10]—(a) Prep. in cstr. followed by noun. (b) Note vowels: both short, §15.243. Which dagesh in פּ? Master Rule 1a *now*. Identify the morpheme ת–ַ. 'upon a pavement of.'

בַּהַט־וָשֵׁשׁ[11]—(a) Note vowels and accent, §15.161. The guttural accounts for the *a*-vowels, §15.43. This type of noun is often classified as a segolate, §15.611; more accurately, it develops by anaptyxis, §15.61. (b) 1:6[8]. Note vowel under ו. Perhaps 'porphyry and marble.'

וְדַר וְסֹחָרֶת[12]—(a) The vowels suggest a cstr., but the following ו makes this impossible. *dar* is doubly-closed, cf. Arab. *durru,* hence §15.112, R.6a. The conj. *wa* does not always lengthen in n.o. (b) Note silluq and soph pasuq, §11.531. The word is *in pause,* hence the original *a*-vowel has lengthened (§15.131), possibly **suḥartu* > *sōḥére<u>t</u>,* pausal *sōḥāre<u>t</u>*. Here four nouns are governed by one ruling noun (*regens*), hence we are to understand that the floor was composed of (inlays? of) porphyry and marble, and mother-of-pearl and tortoise-shell (?), possibly a mosaic. The meanings of the words are uncertain.

New letters: ץ ף ז. All letters have now appeared. Compare: ק ף ע ץ ו ז.

Go back over Lessons 2–6 and list all the segolates you can recognize. This type of noun is very common, so you should learn to recognize it as soon as possible.

Learn Rules 6a, 10d, 14, 16.

Learn the basic vocabulary in Group 4.

14. Short *a* does not lengthen in *erstwhile doubly-closed syllables* except in pause (§15.111, cf. §15.132).

16. In *near-open* syllables, *i*- or *u*-class short vowels *reduce* to shewa when preceded by a long *syllable* or by no syllable at all (§15.241).

8

Purpose: To Learn the Short-Vowel Chart
Materials: Esther 1:7-8

7 וְהַשְׁקוֹת בִּכְלֵי זָהָב וְכֵלִים
8 מִכֵּלִים שׁוֹנִים וְיֵין מַלְכוּת רָב כְּיַד הַמֶּלֶךְ׃ וְהַשְּׁתִיָּה
כַדָּת אֵין אֹנֵס כִּי־כֵן ׀ יִסַּד הַמֶּלֶךְ עַל כָּל־רַב בֵּיתוֹ
לַעֲשׂוֹת כִּרְצוֹן אִישׁ־וָאִישׁ׃

1:7 והשקות[1]—Read §§ 14., 14.1, 14.2, .21, .22, .23, 15., 15.1. וְ|הַשְׁ|קוֹת w^{e}-*haš-qô*^{w}*ṯ*. Always syllabify from the *end* of the word. Ultima is acc. cl., pure-long vowel. Penult is unaccented closed (u.c.), short-vowel is normal, §14.232. Antepenult is distant-open (d.o.), short-vowel reduces, §15.2, §15.23, R.13. Turn to Table E, and be sure you can find the syllable and the vowels. 'and drinking/causing to drink.'

בִּכְלֵי זָהָב[2]—בִּ|כְ|לֵי זָ|הָב. Note ֵי: what morpheme? §25.433. Cstr. (§25., §§36.31, .325). Only one major accent. *hāḇ* is acc. cl., §15.11. *zā* is n.o., §15.12. Cf. 1:6[9]. *lê*^{y} is monophthongized, hence short-vowel rules do not apply (but diphthong rules do!). *biḵ* develops from (<) b^{e}*ḵ*^{e}, §15.53, §15.651. 'in/with vessels of gold.'

וכלים מכלים שונים[3]—There is no sign of a cstr. chain, so we treat each word separately. (a) w^{e}-*ḵē-lî*^{y}*m* d.o. §15.2, §16.3212, n.o. §15.12, §16.3211, acc. §15.11. 'and vessels.' (b) *mik-kē-lî*^{y}*m,* u.c. §14.232, n.o. §15.12, d.o. §15.11, §16.3212. *mikk* < *min* + *k,* §13.111, R.11. Figure out the meaning. (c) *šô*^{w}*-nî*^{y}*m,* penult has pure-long vowel (§15.21), read §15.22. Ultima has pure-long vowel. 'differing.'

וְיֵין מַלְכוּת רָב[4]—The monophthong ֵי tells us that this is cstr. (Table F), hence w^{e}-*yê*^{y}*n mal-ḵûṯ,* d.o. §16.3212, Monophthong §15.7, .71, .73, .7324. u.c. §14.232, acc. cl. §15.11. Be sure you understand how to find these syllables and vowels on Table E. *-ûṯ* is fem. §24.56. *rāḇ* is masc., hence it cannot modify *malḵûṯ*; it must therefore modify *yên,* §36.11. 'much wine of royalty' = 'much royal wine.'

כְּיַד הַמֶּלֶךְ׃[5]—Vowels in k^{e}-*yaḏ* are unaccented or reduced, suggesting cstr. Find them on Table E. (a) כ– is a prep., יָד 'hand,' = 'according to the generosity of.' (b) 1:2[6]. Note accent, note segols, rev. §15.611, §15.61.

1:8 וְהַשְּׁתִיָּה כַדָּת[1]—w^{e}-*haš-š*^{e}*-ṯî*^{y}*-yā*^{h}. Identify each syllable, d.o., u.c., long, acc., and explain each vowel. Table E, §14.232, §15.11, §§15.2, .21, .22. Note form of def. art. (Table G). ָה– is fem., §25.412. 'and the drinking.' (b) *kad-dāṯ*. Identify syllables, explain vowels. *kadd-* < k^{e} + def. art., §13.521. '[was] according to the decree.'

אֵין אֹנֵס[2]—(a) Accent (§11.54), monophthong (§14.32), Table F, = cstr. 'nonexistence of' = 'there is/was not.' (b) *'ōnēs,* defective writing, §11.3241. This is a participle (ptcp.), §24.23, §27.6111, *ô* < *â,* §14.11, §15.31, §27.611.

'compelling'; the king's decree concerning the drinking was 'there is no compelling.'

כִּי־כֵן ׀ יִסַּד הַמֶּלֶךְ[3]—(a) *kî* conj. (§30.362), pure-long vowel, §15.22. 'for, because.' (b) *k̲ēn,* adv. (§30.34), acc.cl., spirantized כ because closely joined to previous word which ends in a vowel. 'thus.' (c) Verb, see §15.113. Rule 15. 'he ordained, commanded.' (d) Segolate, CvCC, §24.21, §15.61, .611.

עַל כָּל־רַב בֵּיתוֹ [4]—(a) Prep., §14.232, §30.35f. (b) This is in a chain of cstrs., hence u.c., hence *qāmāṣ-ḥăṭûp̄* (§11.321). 'every.' (c) u.c., §14.232. 'great (one).' (d) **bayt* (CaYC) > *báyit̲,* §24.213, §15.72. However, the added suffix *-ô* causes an accent shift with resulting change of the diphthong: **baytô* > *bêt̲ô,* §15.73, .7324. 'his house.'

לַעֲשׂוֹת[5]—*la-ʿă-śô^{w}t̲* < **l^{e}-ʿ^{e}-śôt̲;* read §15.4, .42, R. 10b, and §15.653, R. 21. The form is an infinitive construct (inf. cstr.), §27.65. 'to do.'

כִּרְצוֹן אִישׁ־וָאִישׁ׃ [6]—*k^{e}-r^{e}-ṣô^{w}n* > *kir-ṣô^{w}n,* §15.651. 'according to the will/pleasure of.' (b) *ʾî^{y}š* contains a long vowel; the metheg is used with a long vowel in a closed syllable before maqqeph (*Ges.* §16*f*). 'a man.' (c) *wā-ʾîš,* vowel of conj. ו often lengthens (but not always) in near-open. אִישׁ־וָאִישׁ is distributive, 'each individual man.'

Your primary task in this lesson is *to master the Short-Vowel Chart* (Table E). *Do it.* Many of the problems of recognizing verb and noun forms will not be understood until you understand the rules governing vocalic alteration. Look over the major points in §15 (i.e., the sections with one and two decimals, §15.1, §15.11, etc.).

Learn the words in Vocabulary Group 5.

The Short-Vowel Chart

	a-type vowel	*i*-type vowel	*u*-type vowel
Unacented closed	◌ַ	◌ִ/◌ֶ	◌ָ/◌ֻ
Accented or Near-open	◌ָ	◌ֵ	◌ֹ
Distant-open	◌ְ	◌ְ	◌ְ
" with gutturals	◌ֲ/◌ֱ	◌ֱ/◌ֲ	◌ֳ

9

Purpose: To study the definite article
Materials: Esther 1:9-10

גַּם וַשְׁתִּי הַמַּלְכָּה עָשְׂתָה 9
י מִשְׁתֵּה נָשִׁים בֵּית הַמַּלְכוּת אֲשֶׁר לַמֶּלֶךְ אֲחַשְׁוֵרוֹשׁ׃ בַּיּוֹם
הַשְּׁבִיעִי כְּטוֹב לֵב־הַמֶּלֶךְ בַּיָּיִן אָמַר לִמְהוּמָן בִּזְּתָא
חַרְבוֹנָא בִּגְתָא וַאֲבַגְתָא זֵתַר וְכַרְכַּס שִׁבְעַת הַסָּרִיסִים
הַמְשָׁרְתִים אֶת־פְּנֵי הַמֶּלֶךְ אֲחַשְׁוֵרוֹשׁ׃

1:9 גַּם וַשְׁתִּי הַמַּלְכָּה [1]—(a) Conj., v.1571, BDB 168 gives root as *gmm.* §30.36f. (b) Pr. n. 'Vashti,' not bound by the *w* > *y* shift, §12.66. (c) *ham-mal-kā*^{h}, v. (vocab., see Part 4) 4436. Def. art. is –ּ‑הַ, §22.2, .231. Start to study Table G. ‑ָה is fem. sg. abs. (fsa) morpheme, §25.1, .13. If מֶלֶךְ is 'king,' what is מַלְכָּה?

עָשְׂתָה [2]—*ʿā-ś*^{e}*-ṯā*^{h}, a verb, study Rules 15 and 17 and §11.581. 'she made.'

מִשְׁתֵּה נָשִׁים [3]—Note ‑ֵה, §15.7323, Table F, cstr., 1:3[5], voc. 4961. (b) ‑ִים is mpa morpheme, but the word means 'women.' The morphological gender does not always indicate the sex gender, §15.1. Gen. of reference, §36.3291. Voc. 802.

בֵּית הַמַּלְכוּת [4]—(a) *bê*^{y}*ṯ* for *b*^{e}*ḇê*^{y}*ṯ* 'in the house of,' cf. BDB 108, 1a. (b) *ham-mal-ḵûṯ,* 1:2[8], note def. art., §22.2. If the last word in a cstr. relation is definite, the preceding word is definite, §36.3161. 'In the house of the royalty' = 'in the royal house.'

אֲשֶׁר לַמֶּלֶךְ [5]—(a) Relative pronoun (rel. pron.), 1:2[9], note syllables and vowel quantities. §30.3128, §38.411. *ʾăšer* modifies 'the royal house,' §30.2, which is its antecedent, §30.313. (b) *lammélek̲* < *l*^{e} + *hammélek̲,* §22.24, learn §13.521 now. *ʾăšer l*^{e}- 'which [was] to ...' = 'which belonged to ...'; an adj. clause, §30.323.

1:10 בַּיּוֹם הַשְּׁבִיעִי [1]—(a) *bayy-* suggests what? §13.521, §22.24. **yawm* > *yô*^{w}*m,* §24.212. 'in the day.' (b) Do you see a def. art.? We had שֶׁבַע in 1:1[9]; the form with *î-î* is an ordinal numeral, §24.55; for numeral adj., §30.32; voc. 7637. Note that def. art. is repeated on an adj. in concord, §36.11.

כְּטוֹב לֵב־הַמֶּלֶךְ —(a) *k*^{e}- 1:2[3], 'as, when.' *ṭô*^{w}*ḇ* adj. 'good' voc. 2896, Cv̂C §24.12. This word is used as a predicate adjective, §30.321. (b) *lēḇ* 'heart,' voc. 3820, < *libb-,* §13.42. Note maqqeph, §11.45. The *ṣērê* does not reduce in this word, §15.223. Since המלך is def., this word is also def., 'the heart of the king.' With pred. adj., translate 'when the heart of the king (was) good.'

בַּיָּיִן [3]—*bayy-* suggests what? §22.24. *yáyin* 'wine' (3196) is CaYC, §24.212, but here in pause, §11.533. 'with (the) wine.'

אָמַר [4]—Verb, ‘he said’ (559), R. 15.

לִמְהוּמָן ... וְכַרְכַּס [5]—l^e- introduces indirect object, §30.22, §35.1. Use the 7 names to review alphabet, vowels, and short-vowel rules.

שִׁבְעַת הַסָּרִיסִים [6]—(a) 1:5[9]. (b) Def. art.? *sârîs* ‘eunuch, official’ (v.5631). Metheg is often replaced by other weak accents, *Ges.* §16*f*. Cf. 1:5[9]: does this mean ‘7 of the eunuchs’ or ‘the 7 eunuchs’? §36.325.

הַמְשָׁרְתִים [7]—Article? *m*^{e}*šārēṯ* ‘ministering’ (v.8334) is D participle (ptcp.), §24.33f. Review §13.38, §15.15f, §15.233, Rule 13b. Note *mûnāḥ* for *méṯeḡ*, cf. 1:10[6].

אֶת־פְּנֵי[8]—(a) Prep. ‘with, close by’ (v.854, BDB 816, II 2). (b) *pānî*^{y}*m* (pl.) ‘face,’ in cstr. often = ‘before,’ §36.42.

Review the def. art. in previous notes: 1:2[1,2], 1:5[2], 1:8[2]? These were selected because they illustrate different points. What do you see? How many other def. arts. can you find in 1:2, 1:5, 1:8?

Study Table G carefully. You should now recognize: הַ·—, בַּ·—, כַּ·—, הָ—.

Learn the words in vocabulary group 6.

---

hammōlēḵ	הַמֹּלֵךְ	*hāhēm*	הָהֵם
bayyāmîm	בַּיָּמִים	*hā'ēllê*^{h}	הָאֵלֶּה
kaddāṯ	כַּדָּת	*hā'ām*	הָעָם
lammélek	לַמֶּלֶךְ	*beḥāṣēr*	בֶּחָצֵר

21. When *simple (vocal) shewa* would occur before *compound shewa,* the simple shewa is changed to the normal short vowel of the same vowel-class as the compound shewa (§15.653).

22. When *compound shewa* would occur before simple (vocal) shewa, the compound shewa develops to its corresponding normal short vowel, and the simple shewa becomes zero shewa (§15.2532).

אֹהֵב מוּסָר אֹהֵב דָּעַת וְשׂוֹנֵא תוֹכַחַת בָּעַר׃
Whoever loves discipline loves knowledge,
but he who hates reproof is stupid.
Proverbs 12:1

10

Purpose: To Introduce Noun Morphology
Materials: Esther 1:11

לְהָבִיא אֶת־ **11**
וַשְׁתִּי הַמַּלְכָּה לִפְנֵי הַמֶּלֶךְ בְּכֶתֶר מַלְכוּת לְהַרְאוֹת הָעַמִּים
וְהַשָּׂרִים אֶת־יָפְיָהּ כִּי־טוֹבַת מַרְאֶה הִיא׃

Read §20.–20.6 before working on the text.

1:11 לְהָבִיא אֶת־וַשְׁתִּי הַמַּלְכָּה [1]—(a) l^e + inf. cstr. 'to cause to enter, to bring,' in indirect discourse, §38.82. (b) 1:4[2]. 1:9[1]. 'Vashti' is definite (pr. n.) and dir. obj. of verb, §34.1, .113. (c) 1:9[1]. Basic pattern of this type of noun is CaCC (an *a*-vowel after the first consonant, no vowel between 2d and 3d consonants). In msa and msc, anaptyxis occurs, §24.21.

לִפְנֵי הַמֶּלֶךְ [2]—(a) l^e- + $p^e n\hat{e}^y$ 'to the face of' > *prep.* 'before.' Cf. 1:3[14]. It is followed by its object, §30.351. (b) Basic pattern is CaCC *malk*, but this develops to *mélek̲* (Rule 6b), §24.21. This is a *segolate* (Lesson 7).

בְּכֶתֶר מַלְכוּת [3]—(a) You should recognize b^e- –בְּ. *kéṯer* 'crown' (v.3804 3x in OT, 3x in Est. [3/3]) is CvCC. It could be *katr* or *kitr*—possibly the latter (Arab. has both *katr* and *kitr,* Aram. has *kitrâ*). It is a segolate, §24.21. (b) 1:2[8]. Basic pattern is CaCC + ût, §24.56.

לְהַרְאוֹת הָעַמִּים וְהַשָּׂרִים [4]—(a) –לְ + inf. cstr., 'to cause to see, to show.' (b) Note form of def. art. *'ammî* has mpa *-îm* ים–ִ morpheme, §25.231. Basic form of the noun *'amm* is CvC^2, with geminate 2d rad., §24.214. §13.42 applies (Rule 6a): *'amm* > *'am,* then Rule 14 applies, §15.111, עַם, pausal or with def. art. *'ām* עָם, 1:5[4]. This is the first object of the verb (§34.3). (c) Note conj. and def. art., note mpa morpheme. What remains is שָׂר. The basic form is **śarr* (cf. Σαρρα), CaC^2, §24.214, but ר resists gemination (§13.38) and there is compensation (§15.14). The first obj. of the verb is compound (§34.17).

אֶת־יָפְיָהּ [5] —(a) §34.113. The verb takes two objects, §§34.3, .35, *whom* he caused to see and *what* he caused them to see. (b) Basic form CuCY *yopy,* §24.213, but §15.67 (R.9) applies > $y^e p\hat{\imath}$ יְפִי (§15.241, R. 16) 'beauty' (v.3808, 19/1). הּ–ָ *-āh* is 3fs suffix 'her'; note *mappîq* (§11.42). 'to cause *the peoples and the princes* to see *her beauty.*'

כִּי־טוֹבַת מַרְאֶה הִיא׃ [6]—(a) *kî* conj. 'because,' introduces causal clause, §30.3623. (b) *ṭôḇaṯ* ends with fsc morpheme *-aṯ* ת–ַ, 1:10[2]. Pattern is CvCat, §24.121. (c) *mar'ē^h* 'appearance, sight' (4758); pattern maCCaY *mar'ay,* §24.33. Nouns can be formed with preformative *mêm.* (d) Pers. pron. 3fs 'she' §21.1. The copula is omitted, and a verbless clause results, §31., the subj. is הִיא §31.21, and the pred. is a pred. adj. phrase, §31.23. ‘for she [was] good of appearance.’

Read carefully: §25.11, §25.231, §25.41, §§25.421, .424, §§25.4211, .4212.

Know these morphemes: *-îm* ־ִים, *ê^y* ־ֵי, *-ê^h* ־ֶה, *-ē^h* ־ֵה.

Learn the words in Group 7.

Study the following noun types and their morphology. Enter them in your notebook, and add others as you see them. *Begin* (do not attempt to master at this time) the study of noun formation and gender-number-state (GNS) morphology.

CaC	yad	*yad̲*	יַד	1:7	m.s.c.
CaCat	ŝanat	*š^{e}nat̲*	שְׁנַת	1:2	f.s.c.
CiCat	mi’at	*mē’ā^h*	מֵאָה	1:1	f.s.a.
		m^e’at̲	מְאַת	1:4	f.s.c.
CaC^2	‘amm	*‘ām*	עָם	1:3	m.s.a. + הָ
		‘ammîm	עַמִּים	1:11	m.p.a.
CaC^{2}at	gannat	*ginnat̲*	גִּנַּת	1:5	f.s.c.
CiC^2	libb	*lēb̲*	לֵב	1:10	m.s.c.
CaCC	malk	*mélek̲*	מֶלֶךְ	1:2	m.s.a.
	kasp	*késep̄*	כֶּסֶף	1:6	m.s.a.
CaCCat	malkat	*malkā^h*	מַלְכָּה	1:11	f.s.a.
CaWC	yawm	*yôm*	יוֹם	1:10	m.s.a.
CaYC	yayn	*yā́yin*	יָיִן	1:10	m.s.a. (paus.)
		yên	יֵין	1:7	m.s.c.
CiCG	ŝib‘	*šéb̲a‘*	שֶׁבַע	1:1	f.s.a. (num.)
CiCGat	ŝib‘at	*šib̲‘at*	שִׁבְעַת	1:5	m.s.c. (num.)
CiCC	kitr	*két̲er*	כֶּתֶר	1:11	m.s.c.
CuCC	‘uθr	*‘ṓšer*	עֹשֶׁר	1:4	m.s.c.
CaCaC	ðahab	*zāhāb̲*	זָהָב	1:6	m.s.a.
	dabar	*d^{e}b̲ar*	דְּבַר	1:12	m.s.c.
CaCiG	ḫaṣir	*ḥăṣar*	חֲצַר	1:5	f.s.c. (!)
CâCiC	mâlik	*môlēk̲*	מֹלֵךְ	1:1	m.s.a.
	’ânis	*’ônēs*	אֹנֵס	1:8	m.s.a.
CaCâC	gadâl	*gād̲ôl*	גָּדוֹל	1:5	m.s.a.
	kabâd	*k^{e}b̲ôd̲*	כְּבוֹד	1:4	m.s.c.
CaCîCat	madînat	*m^{e}d̲înā^h*	מְדִינָה	1:1	f.s.a.
miCCaY	miŝtay	*mištê^h*	מִשְׁתֶּה	1:3	m.s.a.
CaCCût	malkût	*malk̲ût̲*	מַלְכוּת	1:11	f.s.a.

4. Original short vowels in final open syllables have generally vanished (§§15.51, .52).

11

Purpose: To study feminine noun morphology
Materials: Esther 1:12

12 וַתְּמָאֵן הַמַּלְכָּה
וַשְׁתִּי לָבוֹא בִּדְבַר הַמֶּלֶךְ אֲשֶׁר בְּיַד הַסָּרִיסִים וַיִּקְצֹף
הַמֶּלֶךְ מְאֹד וַחֲמָתוֹ בָּעֲרָה בוֹ׃

1:12 וַתְּמָאֵן הַמַּלְכָּה [1]—(a) Verb, 'and she refused,' subject follows, §30.111. (b) 1:11[1], fsa morpheme *-ā*^{h} ־ָה. Read §25.12 carefully. §33.1. וַשְׁתִּי is in apposition, §30.251.

לָבוֹא [2]—Inf. cstr., 'to enter'; complementary inf. after 'refused,' §34.6.

בִּדְבַר הַמֶּלֶךְ [3]—(a) *d*^{e}*b̲ar* has reduced or normal short vowels, hence no major accent. Why? R.13a. Normal pattern CaCaC *dāb̲ār,* §24.22; 'word, affair' (v.1697). 'And the queen, Vashti, refused to enter into (participate in?) the king's matter' or 'to enter at the king's command.'

אֲשֶׁר בְּיַד הַסָּרִיסִים [4]—(a) 1:2[9], §21.3. (b) *yad̲* (is it cstr.?), pattern CvC §24.12, lengthens under accent to *yād̲* יָד. 'by the hand of' = 'by.' (c) 1:10[6]. Probably a loan-word, pattern either CvC^{2}v̂C or Cv̂Cv̂C; in either case there is no possible reduction of vowels in cstr., suff., or pl. forms.

וַיִּקְצֹף הַמֶּלֶךְ מְאֹד [5]—(a) Verb 'and he was angry,' subj. follows. (b) What kind of noun formation? §24.21. §33.1f. (c) Adv. 'exceedingly' (v.3966); §35.2, §30.34. Possibly developed from a noun, **mi'âd.*

וַחֲמָתוֹ [6]—Conj., §30.36f. Suf. (s0) *–ô* §36.52. The rest is *ḥămāt̲,* with fsc *-at* morpheme §25.12. The abs. would be **ḥămā*^{h} or *ḥēmā*^{h}, since the guttural would obscure the reduced vowel. We find it as *hēmā*^{h} (v.2534), according to BDB 404, from *y*^{e}*ḥēmā*^{h} with apheresis §13.51. For our purposes, we can analyze the word that we have, not the hypothetical form. It is fem. of CvCat type §24.122. Note what happens when adding the suffix: accent shifts, n.o. lengthens, d.o. reduces, influence of guttural (§15.42, R. 10b). Be sure you understand this; it is almost impossible to locate the lexicon form if you cannot reconstruct it from the textual form.

בָּעֲרָה בוֹ׃ [7]—(a) Verb, 'she/it burned,' subj. precedes, 'his wrath burned.' For concord, §33.11. Note influence of guttural on penult. (b) Prep. + s0 וֹ– 'in him.' The prep. phrase is adverbial, §30.341, §30.354, §30.412. It tells *where* his anger burned.

Read carefully: §§25.12, .121, .232, .422, .425, .52, .54.

Go back over 1:1-11 and look for fem. nouns. Note the following: מֵאָה 1:1^{11}, מְאַת 1:4^{10}, מְדִינָה 1:1^{12}, הַמְּדִינוֹת 1:3^{13}, תִּפְאֶרֶת 1:4^{6}; גְּדוּלָּתוֹ 1:4^{7}; תְּכֵלֶת 1:6^{3}; מִטּוֹת 1:6^{9}; בִּשְׁנַת 1:3^{2}. Why have I selected these words? Can you identify every one? Make notes of your observations.

Learn the words in Group 8.

Study the following noun types and their morphology. Enter them in your notebook, and add others as you see them.

m.s.a.	m.s.c.	m.p.a.	m.p.c.
dāḇār 1:21	*d^{e}ḇar* 1:12	*d^{e}ḇarîm* 2:1	*diḇrê^{y}* 2:23
דָּבָר	דְּבַר	דְּבָרִים	דִּבְרֵי
yāḏ 2:21	*yaḏ* 1:7	*yāḏîm*	*y^{e}ḏê^{y}* 3:9
יָד	יַד	יָדִים	יְדֵי
yôm 1:4	*yôm* 9:18	*yāmîm* 1:4	*y^{e}mê^{y}* 2:12
יוֹם	יוֹם	יָמִים	יְמֵי
ʿam 1:22	*ʿam* 3:6	*ʿammîm* 1:11	*ʿammê^{y}*
עַם	עַם	עַמִּים	עַמֵּי
raḇ	*raḇ* 1:8	*rabbîm* 1:4	*rabbê^{y}*
רַב	רַב	רַבִּים	רַבֵּי
		kēlîm 1:7	*k^{e}lê^{y}* 1:7
		כֵּלִים	כְּלֵי
		śārîm 1:11	*śārê^{y}* 1:3
		שָׂרִים	שָׂרֵי

f.s.a.	f.s.c.	f.p.a.	f.p.c.
ṭôḇā^{h} 1:19	*ṭôḇaṯ* 1:11	*ṭôḇôṯ*	*ṭôḇôṯ* 2:2
טוֹבָה	טוֹבַת	טוֹבוֹת	טוֹבוֹת
mēʾā^{h} 1:1	*m^{e}ʾaṯ* 1:4	*mēʾôṯ* 9:6	
מֵאָה	מְאַת	מֵאוֹת	
šānā^{h} 9:21	*š^{e}naṯ* 1:3		
שָׁנָה	שְׁנַת		
rabbā^{h} 1:20		*rabbôṯ* 2:8	
רַבָּה		רַבּוֹת	
m^{e}ḏînā^{h} 1:1		*m^{e}ḏînôṯ* 1:3	*m^{e}ḏînôṯ* 1:16
מְדִינָה		מְדִינוֹת	מְדִינוֹת

	Masculine		Feminine			
sg.abs.	–	–	*–ā^{h}*	or *–t*	־ָה	־ֶ־ֶת
sg.cstr	–	–	*–aṯ*	or *–t*	־ַת	־ֶ־ֶת
pl.abs.	*–îm*	־ִים	*–ôṯ*		־וֹת	
pl.cstr.	*–ê*	־ֵי	*–ôṯ*		־וֹת	

12

Purpose: To review your progress to this point
Materials: Esther 1:1-12, Tables, Rules

At this time there is value in reading (rather rapidly) the entire Phonology part of the *Handbook,* §§10.–17.41. Some of the §§ that meant little when you first encountered them, will now be meaningful. Skip over the others. Mark for further study any that need it.

Be sure you know the meanings of all terms used so far, both Eng. and Heb. terminology. When starting any new field of study, one of your great problems is "vocabulary control," which means the vocabulary of that particular field. Our present field is language, specifically Hebrew.

Be sure you know the alphabet. Go over Zephaniah 3:8, which contains all letters of the alphabet, all vowel signs except ֳ, all final letters, and all of the important accents (except *'ôlê w^e^yôrē̱d*). If you can do it completely, you know the orthography.

Study Tables B and C. Students who fail to get the details of orthography at this stage do a lot of wheel-spinning through most of the rest of the course.

Study Tables E and F. Be sure you know Rule 13.

Be able to identify pure-long vowels written full; start to work on distinguishing pure-long written defectively from lengthened short, and lengthened short written with false *plene* from pure-long. This will take many more meaningful encounters.

Be able to recognize the mpa and mpc morphemes, and also the fsa, fsc, and fpa morphemes.

Be able to recognize all bound prepositions (–בּ, –כּ, –ל, –מֵ) and the conjunction (–ו).

Be able to spot possible construct forms from reduction of vowels.

Know the meanings of the words in Basic Vocabulary Groups 1-8.

Pronounce the following Hebrew characters:

ע	[y] as in *yet*	[ts] as in *hats*	[ʔ] as in *unh-unh*
שׁ	[ʃ] as in *shish*	[s] as in *sis*	[ts] as in *hats*
ף	[p] as in *pep*	[f] as in *fife*	[q] as in *kook*
ט	[m] as in *mom*	[t] as in *taught*	[ts] as in *hats*
ם	[m] as in *mom*	[s] as in *sis*	[k] as in *kick*
פּ	[p] as in *pep*	[f] as in *fife*	[b] as in *bob*
ס	[m] as in *mom*	[s] as in *sis*	[k] as in *kick*
ח	[h] as in *hah*	[x] as in *ach!*	[t] as in *tat*
א	[ks] as in *kicks*	[ʔ] as in *naïve*	[w] as in *wow*
נ	[g] as in *gig*	[z] as in *zoo*	[n] as in *none*

Transliterate from Roman to Hebrew characters:

'ēṯ	*qēṣ*	*bêʸṯ*
'ēṯ	*'ēṣ*	*'aḏ*
'ēṯ	*gan*	*yaḏ*
kāp̄	*dôr*	*sārîs*
qôp̄	*ṣûm*	*śārîm*

Transliterate from Hebrew to Roman characters:

קֶצֶף	יִכְתֹּב	הַזֶּה
עָמַד	יִכָּתֵב	הַכְּתָב
וַתִּשָּׂא	יְכַתֵּב	גִּנְזֵי
וַתְּצַוֵּהוּ	פַּתְשֶׁגֶן	יַצִּעַ
הֶחֱרַשְׁתִּי	טַבַּעְתּוֹ	הָאֲחַשְׁדַּרְפְּנִים

Check the words that *have* the definite article:

הַיּוֹם	לַעֲשׂוֹת	הָעָם
בַּיַּיִן	הֶגְלָה	בָּעֶרֶב
לַמֶּלֶךְ	בֶּחָצֵר	הָמָן
לְהָבִיא	וְהַנַּעֲרָה	לְבַדּוֹ
כָּרֶת	מִתְהַלֵּךְ	בַּחֹדֶשׁ

5. A doubly-closed syllable never occurs within a word and rarely occurs at word-end (§16.34).

6. When a doubly-closed syllable would result from the loss of a short vowel (Rule 4), one of the following occurs:
   a. If a geminate consonant would result, it loses gemination (§13.42);
   b. If a consonantal cluster would result, an anaptyctic vowel is inserted (§15.61);
   c. In a few cases, the doubly-closed syllable remains (§16.3423).

13

Purpose: To examine the student's progress
Materials: Esther 1:1-12, student's notebook

The first hour examination will be given at this point. It will be thorough but (we hope!) not unfair.

1. You will be asked to transliterate from Hebrew to Roman characters, and from Roman to Hebrew, both consonants and vowels. This is to test your knowledge of the orthography and your ability to read Hebrew text. You may get Zeph. 3:8.

2. You will be tested on your knowledge of the Short-Vowel Chart and short-vowel rules, by being given forms to point. You will also be tested on pure-long vowels and diphthongs.

3. You will be asked to identify the definite article, with or without prepositions, in the normal form and in the forms before gutturals. You may be given words to point to show that you know these details.

4. You will be asked to identify morphemes, both bound- and free-form, both prefixed and suffixed.

5. You will be questioned about the significance of the most important conjunctive and disjunctive accents.

6. You will be asked to translate simple clauses either from Est. 1:1-12 or closely similar clauses. This is to test your ability to put together the words in context and get meaning therefrom.

7. You will be tested on the basic vocabulary to date.

Do your own best–that is all that is expected of you.

2a. *Pure-long vowels* do not reduce except in originally-closed syllables (§15.22), where they become the corresponding short vowel, subject to the short-vowel rules (§15.222)

2b. Long *â* became long *ô* in the Canaanite dialects (§14.11).

8. The conjunction —ו, when it occurs before labials (ב, מ, פ, called *bumep̄*), or before consonants with shewa, develops to vocalic וּ *û*; before yod with shewa, however, long *î* is formed (§15.652).

Given	Point	Given	Point
דָּבָר	דבר הַמֶּלֶךְ׃	מַ֫יִם	המים
כֹּל	כלָּם	אִמּוֹ	אם
נַפְשִׁי	נפש	עוֹלָם	העולם
קוֹל	קל יְהוָה	כֹּל	כל־יום
ʿammî	עמי	*báyiṯ*	בית
lᵉ + ʿăḇōḏ	לעבד	*kᵉ + kᵉṯōḇ*	ככתב

Be able to recognize all bound prepositions (–בְּ, –כְּ, –לְ, –מֵ) and the conjunction (–וְ).

Identify the following morphemes:

——ֵי	כְּ——	——ֶ֫ת
הַ·——	——וֹ	הָ——
וְ——	——ַת	לְ——
——ָה	——ָיו	בְּ——
——ִים	——וֹת	——ָהּ

What is the *significance* of each of the following?

silluq	revia'	metheg
maqqeph	zaqeph-qaṭon	athnaḥ

Translate the following:

דְּבַר הַמֶּ֫לֶךְ	בִּשְׁנַת שֶׁ֫בַע	מִכָּל־עֲבָדָיו
עַמִּים רַבִּים	שָׂרִים טוֹבִים	לַמַּלְכָּה הַטּוֹבָה

Behold, how good and how pleasant
for brothers to dwell in unity!

הִנֵּה מַה טּוֹב וּמַה נָּעִים
שֶׁ֫בֶת אַחִים גַּם יָֽחַד.

(Psa. 133:1)

14

Purpose: To introduce the Hebrew verb
Materials: Esther 1:1–12

We now begin to study the Hebrew verbal system. Read §27., §27.1, and §27.11. Read §§30.33, .332. If you are weak in Eng. grammar, read §§30.–30.339.

אָמַר, 1:10[4], means 'he said.' It is third person, masculine singular, perfect, of the simple stem (G or Qal). All of these data are indicated by the vowel pattern and the presence or absence of preformatives. In this *Handbook* we call such a form 'G10'–which is much easier to write. G = G-stem, 1- = perfect, -0 = 3 masc. sing. The full system is given in §27.151, but we shall not attempt to learn it just yet. The G10 pattern is CaCaC > *CāCaC.* Note operation of Rule 15.

עָשָׂה, 1:5[3], 'he made,' is also G10. Rule 15 is not operative, since the ultima is open, *CāCā*^{h}. The perfect is *not a tense,* but rather it indicates *completed action.* The tense of the action must be determined from the context, §27.1111. The perfect is most frequently translated by an Eng. past tense.

בָּעֲרָה, 1:12[7], is 3 fem. sg. (G11). The subject is fem., hence the verb form is fem. The 3fs perf. (11) is indicated by the morpheme *-ā*^{h} ָה. See §27.221, but don't try to learn it now.

עָשְׂתָה, 1:9[2], is also G11. In verbs that have *-ā*^{h} ָה for G10 (called CCY or *Lamed Hê* verbs), the G11 morpheme is *-tā*^{h} ָתה. All other verbs have the regular G11 ending, so you must learn the regular ending first, then the CCY ending. CCY verbs are very common.

יִסַּד, 1:8[3], 'he commanded,' is also perf. 3ms, but it is built on the D stem (*Pi'el*), hence is D10. Read §28 carefully, and look over §28.1–but don't try to learn it yet.

הַנִּמְצְאִים, 1:1[5], is a ptcp. built on the N stem (*Niph'al*). The N stem often has a passive meaning. Here the word means 'the being-found ones' or 'those that (were) found.' The ptcp. has no tense; you must get the tense from context.

לְהָבִיא, 1:11[1], and לְהַרְאוֹת, 1:11[4], are infinitives construct (inf. cstr.), built on the H stem (*Hiph'il*). The H stem usually has a causative meaning, 'to cause to enter' (= 'to bring in') and 'to cause to see' (= 'to show').

So far we have seen the G, D, H, and N stems. There is also the HtD (*Hithpa'el*) as well as some less-common stems. The *root* of the word gives us the basic meaning; the *stem* gives some special significance. Now read §§27.115–.1153.

The names of the stems give us a clue to their morphology. The G (ground) stem, or Qal (קַל 'light') is the basic form and generally has the basic root-meaning.

The D (doubled) stem doubles the middle radical. *yissad* from the root *ysd,* shows this gemination. Hebrew grammarians used the verb פִּעֵל for their basic paradigm, and unfortunately it cannot show the doubling in *pi'ēl* because of the guttural. The D stem often gives an idea of repetition, intensity, or the like. יִסַּד 'he commanded,' and וַתְּמָאֵן, 1:12[1], 'and she refused' both convey some intensity or repetition.

The H stem is basically formed by the addition of a preformative –ה, hence הִפְעִיל *hip̄'îyl.* Besides indicating causation, this stem can turn an intransitive verb into a transitive (§§30.3391f).

The N stem is basically formed by the addition of a preformative –נ, hence נִפְעַל or *nip̄'al.* Besides indicating the passive voice (§30.334, .3342), it sometimes indicates a reflexive sense (§30.3343).

Most of the finite (§30.3321) verbs that we have seen so far are perfs. (10s or 11s), but we have also seen two impfs., וַיְהִי 1:1[1], and וַתְּמָאֵן 1:12[1]. The *imperfect* (§27.3) indicates *incomplete action/state.* We indicate it by 2- in the tens place, hence G20 would be G imperf. 3ms, and G21 G imperf. 3fs. In Bib. Heb., however, it is possible to *convert* the impf. to have the force of a perf. by adding –·וַ to the verb. Both of these verbs are thus converted, and we indicate this fact by adding 'c' before the indicator: Gc20, Dc21.

We have also seen several infs. cstr. (G65, H65), and a number of ptcps. (G50, N55, and Gp50, 'p' after the stem symbol indicates 'passive').

It is therefore obvious that we have a bit of a job ahead of us to learn how to distinguish the elements that are indicated by verb morphology. There are certain vowel patterns, and there are person–gender–number (PGN) morphemes (preformative and sufformative), and there are also stem indicators. How do we go about learning to recognize these morphemes? When a Hebrew heard *wattᵉmā'ēn lāḇô'* how did he immediately recognize the tense, voice, mood, person, and number of the verb, plus the fact that it was followed by a complementary infinitive? This will be our task for the next 12 or more lessons.

Read §27.15. Know precisely what is required when parsing a verb. Start to become familiar with Paradigm V-1.

Learn the basic words in Group 9.

תֵּן לְחָכָם וְיֶחְכַּם עוֹד

Give instruction to a wise man and he will be still wiser.

(Prov. 9:9)

15

Purpose: To study the G stem of the verb
Materials: Esther 1:13-14

13 וַיֹּאמֶר הַמֶּלֶךְ
לַחֲכָמִים יֹדְעֵי הָעִתִּים כִּי־כֵן דְּבַר הַמֶּלֶךְ לִפְנֵי כָּל־יֹדְעֵי
14 דָּת וָדִין׃ וְהַקָּרֹב אֵלָיו כַּרְשְׁנָא שֵׁתָר אַדְמָתָא תַרְשִׁישׁ
מֶרֶס מַרְסְנָא מְמוּכָן שִׁבְעַת שָׂרֵי ׀ פָּרַס וּמָדַי רֹאֵי פְּנֵי
הַמֶּלֶךְ הַיֹּשְׁבִים רִאשֹׁנָה בַּמַּלְכוּת׃

1:13 וַיֹּאמֶר הַמֶּלֶךְ לַחֲכָמִים[1]— (a) Start to learn the process of "stripping" a verb form. Here we see וַ-יּ-אמֶר. וַיּ– is the conj., but with pattaḥ and the strong dagesh, it is a "conversive" or "converting" waw. Read §32.53. In this form (with dagesh) it occurs only on the imperfect. Read §32.52. The impf. is formed by adding preformatives to the root, and for some PGNs, a sufformative. Read §20.212, §20.3. The preformative here is –י *y*–, §§27.3, .31, .311. v.559, 'and he said.' (b) This is the defined subj. of the verb, §§33., 33.1. (c) Note –לַ, prep. and def.art., Table G. Note –ִים. חָכָם v.2450, 'wise (man).'

יֹדְעֵי הָעִתִּים [2]—(a) G ptcp. mpc (G57) of יָדַע, v.3045. Read §27.61. The vowel pattern of G50 is CâCiCu > *CôCēC yôḏē*^{a}*ʿ*. The clue to look for is long *ô* (often written defectively) after the first radical. Read §§27.6111, .6112. Read §30.382. 'knowers of.' (b) Note –הָ and see Table G. Note –ִים, §25.423. עֵת v.6256 'time,' obj. of the ptcp. The clause, 'knowers of the times,' modifies 'wise men,' §36.7.

כִּי־כֵן דְּבַר הַמֶּלֶךְ [3]—(a-b) Cf. 1:8[3]. (c-d) Cf. 1:12[3].

לִפְנֵי כָּל־יֹדְעֵי|דָּת וָדִין׃ [4]—(a) 1:11[2]. (b-c) 1:13[2], review notes on ptcp. (d) 1:8[1]. (e) v.1779 'law.' 'For thus [was] the word of the king before all who know custom and law.'

1:14 וְהַקָּרֹב—(a) Identify the bound-form morphemes. קָרֹב v.7138, here written defectively, 'near,' used substantivally, §30.31.

אֵלָיו[2]—Prep. אֵל v.413, always in the form אֵלַי* with suff. –ָיו, Table H. 'unto him.'

כַּרְשְׁנָא ... מְמוּכָן[3]—7 pr.n., use them to review consonants, vowels, and accents. Be sure you can read proper nouns! You cannot recognize them if you can't read them. They are not included in the basic vocabulary.

שִׁבְעַת שָׂרֵי ׀ פָּרַס וּמָדַי[4]—(a) 1:5[9]. What morpheme is –ַת? §25.422. (b) 1:3[6]. –ֵי is what morpheme? §25.424. (c-d) 1:3[9,10]. Since a pr.n. is definite (§30.3144), the cstr. chain is def. Is this 'seven of' or 'the seven'?

רֹאֵי פְּנֵי הַמֶּלֶךְ ^{1}—(a) *rô'ê^{y}*: note clues, long *ô* after 1st rad. = G ptcp., ־ֵי mpc, hence G57, v.7200. 'The ones seeing' = 'those who saw.' Read §38.43. (b) פָּנִים (pl.) 'face,' v.6440. In this form (mpc), this word is often used as a prep., but not here. 'the face of the king,' §36.322.

הַיֹּשְׁבִים ^{6}—Strip the form הַ—ִים, identify the morphemes. The remainder is יֹשְׁב < יָשַׁב, v.3427, cf. $1:2^{3}$. What clue do you see after 1st rad.? Does transliteration *yôšēb̲* help you?. §27.6111, 'the ones sitting/dwelling.'

רִאשֹׁנָה בַּמַּלְכוּת׃ ^{7}—(a) *rî'šônā^{h}*, quiescent א, §13.523, *-ôn* §24.431, adv. *-ā^{h}* (identified as fem. in BDB 912), 'foremost.' (b) Note ־ַּבּ: what morpheme is hidden? §13.521. Cf. $1:2^{8}$, v.4438.

Analyze the following forms: הַמֶּלֶךְ $1:1^{6}$, שׁוֹנִים $1:7^{3}$, אֹנֵס $1:8^{2}$.

Analyze the following: וַיִּקְצֹף $1:12^{5}$, cf. $1:13^{1}$.

Start to memorize the G10 and G20 morphemes, §§27.21, .31. Learn them as *recognition elements:* י ככב 'he will ...,' ככב 'he did ...,' etc.

Learn the basic words in Group 10.

CaCaC	> *CāCaC*	*qāṭal*	קָטַל
CaCiC	> *CāCēC*	*kāb̲ēd̲*	כָּבֵד
CaCuC	> *CāCōC*	*qāṭōn*	קָטֹן
yaCCuC	> *yiCCōC*	*yiqṭōl*	יִקְטֹל
yiCCaC	> *yiCCaC*	*yik̲bad̲*	יִכְבַּד
yaCCiC	> *yiCCēC*	*yittēn*	יִתֵּן

עַל שְׁלֹשָׁה דְבָרִים הָעוֹלָם קַיָּם׃
עַל הָאֱמֶת, עַל הַדִּין , וְעַל הַשָּׁלוֹם.
On three things the world is established:
on truth, on justice, and on peace.
(פרקי אבות א)

16

Purpose: To learn more of the G stem
Materials: Esther 1:15-16

טו כְּדָת֙ מַה־לַּעֲשׂ֔וֹת
בַּמַּלְכָּ֖ה וַשְׁתִּ֑י עַ֣ל ׀ אֲשֶׁ֣ר לֹֽא־עָשְׂתָ֗ה אֶֽת־מַאֲמַר֙ הַמֶּ֣לֶךְ
16 אֲחַשְׁוֵר֔וֹשׁ בְּיַ֖ד הַסָּרִיסִֽים׃ וַיֹּ֣אמֶר מוֹמְכָ֗ן לִפְנֵ֤י הַמֶּ֙לֶךְ֙
וְהַשָּׂרִ֔ים לֹ֤א עַל־הַמֶּ֙לֶךְ֙ לְבַדּ֔וֹ עָוְתָ֖ה וַשְׁתִּ֣י הַמַּלְכָּ֑ה כִּ֤י
עַל־כָּל־הַשָּׂרִים֙ וְעַל־כָּל־הָ֣עַמִּ֔ים אֲשֶׁ֕ר בְּכָל־מְדִינ֖וֹת
הַמֶּ֥לֶךְ אֲחַשְׁוֵרֽוֹשׁ׃

1:15 כְּדָת֙[1]—Cf. 1:8[1]—what difference do you see between the form here and in 1:8?

מַה־לַּעֲשׂוֹת[2]-(a) Interrog. pron., §21.42f. (b) לַ–עֲשׂ–וֹת. Note dagesh, §13.3, §13.36. Only two radicals are seen, ע–שׂ, hence one is missing, but is it the 1st, 2d, or 3d? Clue: ל—וֹת is almost certainly an inf. cstr. (G65) of a verb with 3d rad. weak (CCY). Read §29., §29.7. Note §29.71, to which you will return often. Read §32.38. Root is *'ss*, v.6213. 'What to do?' = 'what shall we do?' At this point, review עָשָׂה 1:3[4], which is G10, and עָשְׂתָה, 1:9[2], which is G11. Look at §29.71 again, and locate the CCY endings.

בַּמַּלְכָּה[3]—Cf. 1:12[1].'With the queen.'

עַל ׀ אֲשֶׁר [4]—(a) v.5921. (b) v.834. Together, they form an idiom, 'because that,' cf. BDB 758 IIIa.

לֹא־עָשְׂתָה [5]—(a) Neg. part., v.3939, §35.221. (b) Can you work it out without going back to 1:9[2]? Learn *now* that ־תָה with 2 rads. is G/D/H/N/HtD 11 morpheme of CCY verbs. 'She did not do.'

אֶת־מַאֲמַר֙ ... בְּיַד הַסָּרִיסִים׃ [6]—(a) Sign of d.d.o., §34.113. Why is the word that follows definite? §30.3144. (b) *ma'ămar* msc of מַאֲמָר (3982 3/3) 'commandment,' a noun built on the pattern maCCaC, §24.33. (e-f) 1:12[4]. 'Because she did not do the commandment of king A. (delivered) by the eunuchs.'

1:16 וַיֹּאמֶר מוֹמְכָן לִפְנֵי הַמֶּלֶךְ וְהַשָּׂרִים [1]—(a) Review 1:13[1]. This is an 'CC verb, §29.21, note especially §29.212. Conv. waw has caused accent shift, §17.341. **ya'mir* > **yâ'mēr* > *yô'mēr*, with conv. waw *wayyố'mer.* This word is so very common, that you should learn וַיֹּאמֶר 'and he said.' (b) Masoretic note calls attention to misspelling מומכן for *מְמוּכָן. (e) 1:11[4].

לֹא עַל־הַמֶּלֶךְ לְבַדּוֹ[2]—(a) 1:15[5]. (b) *'al* prep. 'against,' v.5921, BDB 757 II 7d. (c) *l^e-b̲add- -ô,* analyze the elements. בַּד v.905, 'alone': 'not against the king alone.'

עָוְתָה[3]—Cf. 1:15[5]. Here the verb is *ʿ-w-y* עָוָה (v.5753) 'to do wrong, be perverse. The form is G11 of CCY, as the ending תָה– tells us. Because of the very high frequency of CCY verbs, start to master them *today*. 'she has done wrong.'

כִּי עַל־כָּל־הַשָּׂרִים [4]—(a) After a neg. 'but,' v.3588, BDB 474 3e. (b) 1:16[2]. You should be able to work this out.

וְעַל־כָּל־הָעַמִּים[5]—(a) Note that the prep. is repeated. This is more common, but we sometimes find one prep. governing two objects. Cf. 1:16[2]. (c) 1:5[4], v.5971.

אֲשֶׁר בְּכָל־מְדִינוֹת [6]—(a) Relative clause, §38.4, modifying 'all the princes' and 'all the peoples.' (b) *kol* before pl. = 'all': 'in all the provinces of the king.'

Analyze the following forms:

כְּשֶׁבֶת *k^{e}šéḇeṯ* G65 of *yšb* with *k^e*-, §§29.3, .322:

לְמָלְכוֹ *l^{e}molḵô*, 1:3[3], G65 of *mlk* with *l^e*-, §§27.65f.

וּבִמְלוֹאת *ûḇimlô^w'ṯ*, §1:5[1], G65 (irreg.) of *ml'*, read §29.22, §29.2213.

לָבוֹא *lāḇô'*, 1:12[2], G65 (irreg.) of *bw'*, §29.54, §29.6, §29.631.

Learn the basic vocabulary in Group 11.

Study the following verb developments:

CCC	מלך	**yamluk*	> *yimlōḵ*	יִמְלֹךְ
CCC	כבד	**yikbad*	> *yiḵbaḏ*	יִכְבַּד
'CC	אלף	**ti'lap*	> *te'lap̄*	תֶּאְלַף
'CC	אמץ	**yi'maṣ*	> *ye'ĕmaṣ*	יֶאֱמַץ
'CC	אסר	**ya'sur*	> *ye'sōr*	יֶאְסֹר
			or *ye'ĕsōr*	יֶאֱסֹר
GCC	הפך	**yahpuk*	> *yahăpōḵ*	יַהֲפֹךְ
GCC	חמס	**yaḥmus*	> *yaḥmōs*	יַחְמֹס
GCC	חלם	**yaḥlum*	> *yaḥălōm*	יַחֲלֹם
GCC	חנן	**yiḥnan*	> *yeḥĕnan*	יֶחֱנַן
GCC	עבד	**yaʿbud*	> *yaʿăḇōḏ*	יַעֲבֹד
GCC	ערב	**yiʿrab*	> *yeʿĕraḇ*	יֶעֱרַב
NCC	נדר	**yandur*	> *yiddōr*	יִדֹּר
NCC	נגש	**yingaš*	> *yiggaš*	יִגַּשׁ
NCC	נתן	**yintin*	> *yittēn*	יִתֵּן
WCC	יעף	**yiyʿap*	> *yî^{y}ʿap̄*	יִיעַף
WCC	ילד	**taylid*	> *têlēḏ*	תֵּלֵד
YCC	ישר	**yiyšar*	> *yî^{y}šar*	יִישַׁר

17

Purpose: To introduce derived stems of verb forms
Materials: Esther 1:17-18

17 כִּֽי־יֵצֵא דְבַר־הַמַּלְכָּה עַל־כָּל־הַנָּשִׁים
לְהַבְזוֹת בַּעְלֵיהֶן בְּעֵינֵיהֶן בְּאָמְרָם הַמֶּלֶךְ אֲחַשְׁוֵרוֹשׁ אָמַר
לְהָבִיא אֶת־וַשְׁתִּי הַמַּלְכָּה לְפָנָיו וְלֹא־בָאָה׃ וְהַיּוֹם הַזֶּה 18
תֹּאמַרְנָה ׀ שָׂרוֹת פָּרַס־וּמָדַי אֲשֶׁר שָׁמְעוּ אֶת־דְּבַר הַמַּלְכָּה
לְכֹל שָׂרֵי הַמֶּלֶךְ וּכְדַי בִּזָּיוֹן וָקָצֶף׃

1:17 כִּי־יֵצֵא[1]—(a) Conj., v.3588, 'for, because,' introduces causal clause, §30.3623. (b) *yêṣē'* < **yayṣi'u,* yaCCiC or *yaqtil* impf. of *yṣ',* v.3318, 'to go out.' The verb is YCC < *WCC. Read §29.3, §29.321. Now read §27.33. Since most grammars fail to distinguish the *yaqtil*-type of impf., this formation is often misunderstood. The impf. here is not converted, hence may be translated as a future, §32.522, 'it shall go out.'

עַל־כָּל־הַנָּשִׁים[2]—(a) The preps. אֶל and עַל often interchange, particularly in the later books; but cf. BDB 757. Here it seems to mean 'unto.' (c) 1:9[3]. The morpheme ־ִים *-îm* is mpa, but this word means 'women' (listed under אִשָּׁה in BDB 61). The word is fem., and takes fem. adjs..

לְהַבְזוֹת[3] בַּעְלֵיהֶן בְּעֵינֵיהֶן—(a) *l^e-habz-ôt,* לְ—וֹת could be 65 (inf. cstr.) of CCY, §29.71. That leaves הבז of which only 2 can be radicals (in CCY the 3d rad is weak), hence ה must be a stem indicator of H stem, §28.3, cf. §32.82. בָּזָה 'to despise,' v.959, cf. 1:18[7] below, H 'to cause to despise.' (b) *ba'al-ê^y-hen,* from בַּעַל 'lord, master, husband,' v.1167. ־ֵי tells us that it is mps (§25.5) and the ־ֶהֶן is 3fp (s6), 'their husbands.' Note that in Heb. the pron. suf. is in concord with its antecedent; in French it is in concord with the word it modifies, *son mari* 'her husband,' *sa femme* 'his wife.' (c) *b^e-'ên-ê^y-hen,* from עַיִן 'eye,' v.5989, mps6 (masc. pl. with 3fp suffix.), 'their (f) eyes,' 'to make their husbands despicable in their eyes.'

בְּאָמְרָם[4]—*b^e-'omr-ām,* prep., G65, s5. For *'omr* < ***'umur,* cf. §27.65, §27.652. Study this carefully. 'In their saying' = 'when they say,' §35.421. What follows is direct discourse, §38.31.

אָמַר[5]—Rule 15. No preformative or sufformative = G stem, and vowel pattern CaCaC indicates G10, 'he said'; subj. precedes. What follows is indirect discourse, §38.82.

לְהָבִיא[6] אֶת־וַשְׁתִּי ... לְפָנָיו—(a) *l^e- hābî'* gives 3 clues: the prep. ־לְ, which often signals an inf. cstr., the ־ה, which may signal an H stem, and the ־ִי־, which often indicates an H stem. There are other possibilities, but we should start with the most likely. Since there is no indication of loss of first radical and no indication of loss of 3d rad. (points that you will learn by analyzing many verbs), we may assume that it comes from *bw'* בּוֹא 'to enter,' v.935. Cf. 1:11[1]. H65 of בּוֹא. (b) v.853, ddo., §34.113. (e) 1:3[14].

וְלֹא־בָ֫אָה׃[7]—(a) Conj. and neg. part. (b) ָה could be one of several morphemes: replacement for weak 3d rad. (CCY, G10), fsa of noun, or 11 of verb. Note accent, which indicates that it is not a noun or a G10. It is G11 (perf. 3fs) of בּוֹא, Cv̂C, see §29.6, §§29.63f. In verbs of this category (Cv̂C), G11 is accented in the penult, and G51 on the ultima. 'and she did not come.'

1:18 וְהַיּ֫וֹם הַזֶּה [1]—(a) 1:4[10]. (b) זֶה demon. pron. 'this,' v.2088, §21.2, cf. 1:2[12]. Note position of pron. and concord (agrees in gender, number, definiteness).

תֹּאמַ֫רְנָה[2]—ת—נָה are afformatives that indicate 3fp (26) or 2fp (28) of impf., §27.31. The balance is אמַר, which has no indication of D, H, N, or HtD stem, hence must be G. Context requires G26 of אמר 'they (f) will say,' referring to the women, 1:17[2].

שָׂר֫וֹת[3]—If שָׂרִים is 'princes,' what is this? What morpheme is וֹת-? §25.232. Since the vowels cannot reduce (ָ is a compensation vowel), there is nothing but the accent ֫ to indicate cstr., 'the princesses of Persia and Media.'

אֲשֶׁר שָׁמְעוּ [4]—(a) Introduces rel. cl., §38.4. (b) Note וּ— and no preformative. This can be 15, 16 (§27.21) or 37 (§27.422), and only the vowel under the 1st rad. tells the difference. Here is it ָ, hence it must be G15/16, and context requires the 3fp or G16. שָׁמַע 'he heard,' v.8085. In context, this must be translated as future perfect, 'and all the princesses who shall have heard ... shall say.'

לְכֹל שָׂרֵי הַמֶּלֶךְ[5]—Indirect object after verb of saying, §35.11. You should be able to work it out. What the ladies will say is left unsaid—any married man will know!

וּכְדַי[6]—For *û*, Rule 8. *kᵉ*-, 'like, as.' The expression is cryptic, and many explanations have been given, possibly 'according to the abundance of' (BDB, reading וּכְדֵי). For דַּי 'enough,' see v.1767.

בִּזָּיוֹן וָקָצֶף׃ [7]—(a) *bizzay* + *ôn*, 'contempt' (963 1/1), cf. 1:17[3](a). (b) *qéṣep̄*, pausal *qā́ṣep̄*, 'wrath,' v.7110, cf. 1:12[5](a). 'and (there will be) like plenty of contempt and wrath.'

Start to work in earnest on Paradigm V-1.

Analyze the following verbs:
בָּעֲרָה, *bāʿărāʰ*, 1:12[7], ה— with ָ under 1st rad., G11 of *bʿr*, §27.21.
עָשְׂתָה, 1:9[2], תָה— with ָ under 1st rad. = ? §29.7131.
עָוְתָה, 1:16[3].

Learn the vocabulary in Group 12.

18

Purpose: To continue study of the Hebrew verb
Materials: Esther 1:19-20

19 אִם־עַל־הַמֶּלֶךְ טוֹב
יֵצֵא דְבַר־מַלְכוּת מִלְּפָנָיו וְיִכָּתֵב בְּדָתֵי פָרַס־וּמָדַי וְלֹא
יַעֲבוֹר אֲשֶׁר לֹא־תָבוֹא וַשְׁתִּי לִפְנֵי הַמֶּלֶךְ אֲחַשְׁוֵרוֹשׁ
וּמַלְכוּתָהּ יִתֵּן הַמֶּלֶךְ לִרְעוּתָהּ הַטּוֹבָה מִמֶּנָּה׃ וְנִשְׁמַע כ
פִּתְגָם הַמֶּלֶךְ אֲשֶׁר־יַעֲשֶׂה בְּכָל־מַלְכוּתוֹ כִּי רַבָּה הִיא
וְכָל־הַנָּשִׁים יִתְּנוּ יְקָר לְבַעְלֵיהֶן לְמִגָּדוֹל וְעַד־קָטָן׃

1:19 אִם־עַל־הַמֶּלֶךְ טוֹב [1]—(a) Conj., 'if,' v.518; introduces a condition §38.6. (d) 1:11[6]. This is a common cliché to a superior. The clause is verbless (§31), 'if (it is) good.'

יֵצֵא דְבַר־מַלְכוּת [2]—(a) 1:17[1]. There it is impf. (G20), but here context suggests jussive (G40, §30.3355); there is no formal difference in this word. 'let there go forth.' (b-c) Cf. 1:7[4]; here 'a royal word.'

מִלְּפָנָיו [3]—*min* + *l*^{e}- + *p*^{e}*nê* + s0, lit. 'from (reference) to face of him' = 'from before him,' an idiom found 73x in OT (BDB 817 II 5).

וְיִכָּתֵב [4]—*w*^{e}*yikkāṯēḇ* < **w*^{e}*yinkāṯēḇ,* possibly < **w*^{e}*y*^{e}*hinkāṯēḇ,* read §28.4 on N stem. Clues to the N perf.: preformative n —נ, with *i* < *a* under the preformative. Clues to the N imperf., strong dagesh in 1st rad. and vowel pattern yiC^{2}āCēC. What clues do you see here?. This could be N20 (—·י) or N40 (juss.); context suggests juss., 'and let it be written.' The *wāw* cannot be conversive, for on impf. it would be —·וַ, and it cannot stand on juss. כתב 'to write,' v.3789.

בְּדָתֵי פָרַס־וּמָדַי [5]—(a) Note ֵי-. You should know the word (1:8[1]). (b-c) You should know this expression (1:3[9,10]).

וְלֹא יַעֲבוֹר [6]—(a) You should know (v.3939). (b) Written with a false plene (§11.3241), it may confuse you. —י indicates a 3ms impf. (20) form, §27.21. Vowel pattern yaCCuC, §27.32, usually > *yiCCōC yiqtōl* (Rule 18), but with GCC verbs (§29.1f.), Rule 10c applies > *yaGăCōC. Study this carefully.* עבר 'to cross over, pass away,' v.5674. 'and it shall not pass away.'

אֲשֶׁר לֹא־תָבוֹא [7]—(a) Introduces indir. disc. BDB 833.8, or possibly final clause (§30.3624). (b) —תָ: morpheme is either impf. 3fs (21) or 2ms (22), §27.31. There is no indication that this is CCY (21/22 of CCY ends in -ê^h). It could be CC^2 or CvC, but the final א rules out the former, so we try בוא, v.935, 'to enter.' Subj. follows, 'Vashti,' hence verb is G21, and clause is translated 'Vashti shall not enter.' The form could be G41 (juss.), 'Let Vashti not enter,' but לֹא is usually used with indicative and אַל with juss. (you haven't learned this yet), hence this is indic.—לֹא + indic. is a strong prohibition.

וּמַלְכוּתָהּ יִתֵּן [8]—(a) הּ‍ָ -*āh* (with mappiq, §11.42) is 3fs suffix (s1), hence 'her royalty.' (b) *yittēn* < **yintēn* (R.11), yaCCiC, §27.334. Preformative —י must be 20, and *i*-vowel under preformative is a fairly sure sign of G20. Strong dagesh (R.1a) suggests that a consonant has been assimilated. It could be an N stem, but the vowel-pattern does not confirm this. It could be D10 of **ytn*, or G20 of *ntn*. In a case like this, we try both for fit. G20 of נתן 'to give,' v.5414, fits context. It could be G40 (juss.). Object precedes, subj. follows: 'her kingdom let the king give.'

לִרְעוּתָהּ [9]—*l*^{e}*-r*^{e}*ʿûṯ-āh*, with R.19. רְעוּת (7466 6/1) 'friend, neighbor.'

הַטּוֹבָה מִמֶּנָּה׃ [10]—(a) Def. art. used like rel. pron. What does -*ā*^{h} suggest? Cf. טוֹב, 1:10[2]. It is in concord with 1:19[10], §36.1f. (b) Possibly < *min* + *min* + *hā*^{h}, with reduplication of the prep. (v.4480), 'from her.' This is מִן of comparison, §38.71. 'The good from her' = 'who is better than she.'

1:20 וְנִשְׁמַע פִּתְגָם הַמֶּלֶךְ [1]—(a) *w*^{e}*-nišmaʿ*: *ni— —a—* = niCCaC. The preformative can be impf. 1cp (29) or N perf 3ms (N10); context favors the latter. See §28.42. שמע 'to hear' (v.8085), N10 'it shall be heard.' The subj. is more closely defined by the next word. (b) *piṯgām* (Pers. *patigâma*) 'edict' (6599 2/1), in cstr. with following word.

אֲשֶׁר־יַעֲשֶׂה [2]—(a) Rel.pron., modifying *piṯgām*. (b) ה—יַ. We see only 2 rads. and the form ends in הֶ‍, hence it must be 20 of CCY. The vowel pattern could be H20 of CCY or G/H20 of GCY, §29.11. Since this verb has a guttural in 1st rad., our first try will be G20 of עָשָׂה, 'he shall make.'

כִּי רַבָּה הִיא [3]—(a) Causal, 'for,' §[8].53. (b) masc. *raḇ*, fem. *rabbā*^{h}, hence CvC[2] type noun/adj. (v.7227). Here it is pred. adj., §30.321, §31.23. (c) Independent pron. 3ms, §21.1 (v.1931b), 'she, it (f).' Subj. of the verbless clause, §31.122. A copula is not used in Heb. but must be added in translation: 'for it (is) great.'

וְכָל־הַנָּשִׁים יִתְּנוּ יְקָר לְבַעְלֵיהֶן [4]—(a-b) 1:9[3], 1:17[2]. (c) וּ—יִ must be impf. 3mp (25), §27.31. Strong dagesh in 1st rad. suggests assimilated *nûn* < **yint*^{e}*nû*, G25 of נתן, cf. 1:19[9]. Subj. precedes and is fem.; possibly the *-îm* ending attracted a masc. form of the verb. Context suggests that juss. (G45) is possible, 'let all the women give.' (d) 1:4[5]. (e) 1:17[3]. לְמִגָּדוֹל וְעַד־קָטָן׃ [5]—Cf. 1:5[7].

Analyze the following verbs:

יִסַּד *yissaḏ*, 1:8[3]. Careful! There are some YCC verbs, and the –יִ can be the 1st rad. Can this be a D10 form?

וַתְּמָאֵן, 1:12[1]. –וַ tells us what? —תְּ‍ָ tells us (1) form is 21/22 and (2) it is D (shewa under preformative, vowel pattern), §28.21.

לְהַרְאוֹת, 1:11[4]: וֹת—לְ suggests 65 of CCY, §29.71, but that leaves הרא. The ה must therefore be stem indicator, hence H65 of *r'y* רָאָה.

Learn the vocabulary in Group 13.

19

Purpose: To continue analysis of the Hebrew verb
Materials: Esther 1:21-22

21 וַיִּיטַב
הַדָּבָר בְּעֵינֵי הַמֶּלֶךְ וְהַשָּׂרִים וַיַּעַשׂ הַמֶּלֶךְ כִּדְבַר מְמוּכָן׃
22 וַיִּשְׁלַח סְפָרִים אֶל־כָּל־מְדִינוֹת הַמֶּלֶךְ אֶל־מְדִינָה וּמְדִינָה
כִּכְתָבָהּ וְאֶל־עַם וָעָם כִּלְשׁוֹנוֹ לִהְיוֹת כָּל־אִישׁ שֹׂרֵר
בְּבֵיתוֹ וּמְדַבֵּר כִּלְשׁוֹן עַמּוֹ׃

1:21 וַיִּיטַב הַדָּבָר [1]—(a) *way - yî*^{y}*ṭab: yi—a–* is yiCCaC type of YCC verb. Read §29.3 carefully. Look at יֵצֵא, 1:17[1], and compare with יִיטַב. Read §29.33 and then read carefully §29.331. In this *Handbook* we distinguish WCC from true YCC. WCC verbs often lose 1st rad. י in G impf., and YCC verbs usually keep 1st rad י in the same forms. יטב (v.3190) 'to be good'; subj. follows. (b) 'The word, thing' (v.1697). What does *wāw* conv. do to tense of verb?

בְּעֵינֵי הַמֶּלֶךְ וְהַשָּׂרִים [2]—(a)1:17[3], CaYC-type noun, §24.212. In cstr. with *two* nouns, contrary to normal grammar, *Ges.* §128*a*.

וַיַּעַשׂ [3]—Note carefully *way - yáʿaś,* note accent. This is *apocopated;* read §13.533 and Rules 5,6. Read §17.341. Apocopation is a common feature of CCY verbs with wāw conv. and impf. Decide now to learn this. 'and he did.' *yiGCay* > *yaGăCê*^{h} יַעֲשֶׂה + *way* > *wayyáʿaśe̸h̸* וַיַּעַשׂ

כִּדְבַר מְמוּכָן׃[4]—(a) Note vowels, *kiḏbar* < *k*^{e}*ḏ*^{e}*ḇar,* R.19. -כְּ prep., 'according to.' It is necessary to study the wide range of meanings the preps. have. (b) Note spelling and cf. 1:16[1] and Masoretic note there.

1:22 וַיִּשְׁלַח סְפָרִים [1]—(a) –וַ tells us what?. *yi--a-* suggests yiCCaC, here yiCCaG, a CCG-type verb, §29.13. שלח v.7971, 'to send.' What form here? §27.31. How should you translate it? (b) *s*^{e}*pārîm* is pl. of *sēper,* v.5612, 'document,' a CiCC-type noun. Why is אֵת omitted? §34.113.

אֶל־כָּל־מְדִינוֹת הַמֶּלֶךְ [2]—How does the accent here and that of the following word help us? (a) אֶל v.413, 'unto.' Which is correct? 'The king sent documents unto all the cities,' or '... unto every city,' or 'and he sent documents to all the cities of the king.'

אֶל־מְדִינָה וּמְדִינָה כִּכְתָבָהּ [3]—(a-c) Cf. 1:8[6]; this is distributive, = 'to each province.' (d) *k*^{e}*- k*^{e}*ṯāḇ -āh* , prep. + כְּתָב v.3792 'writing,' cf. 1:19[4]. 'according to its writing.'

וְאֶל־עַם וָעָם כִּלְשׁוֹנוֹ[4]—(a-c) Distributive. (b,c) Note vowels: עָם is pausal form. Translate. (d) *k*^{e}*-l*^{e}*šôn-ô.* לָשׁוֹן v.3956, 'tongue,' CvCv̂C-type noun. Why is it *kilšônô* but *kik<u>t</u>*^{e}*<u>b</u>āh?* Why are the suffixes different? What are their antecedents?

לִהְיוֹת כָּל־אִישׁ[5]—(a) *l*^{e}*- h*^{e}*yô<u>t</u>:* ל—וֹת could be an inf. cstr. (65) of a CCY, §29.71. Work from there; what consonants remain? What would the root be? Is היה the right answer? Does it make sense in context (v.1961)? (b-c) כֹּל before sing. means 'every.' This phrase is subj. of the inf., 'every man to be....'

שֹׂרֵר בְּבֵיתוֹ[6]—(a) *-ô-ē-* CôCēC is G50 pattern, §27.611. שׂרר is prob. a denominal verb from שַׂר. meaning 'to be prince, ruler' (8323 5/1). ר was heard as geminate by LXX translators (**Σαρρα = שָׂרָה**). An *r* can be prolonged when it is trilled, but not when it is guttural (contrast Span. and Ital. *r* with Ger. and Fr.). Tiberian Heb. (i.e. Masoretic) was guttural, cf. Matt. 26:73.

וּמְדַבֵּר[7]—*û- m*^{e}*<u>d</u>abbēr: m*^{e}*CaC*^{2}*iC* is the pattern of D50, §28.21. Your clues are: (1) shewa under preformative, (2) *-a-i-* vowel pattern, and (3) dagesh in middle radical—*in this order!* דִּבֵּר 'he spoke,' v.1696; 'and speaking.'

כִּלְשׁוֹן עַמּוֹ׃[8]—(a) 1:22[4]. (b) 1:16[5]. Does the dagesh in עַמּוֹ explain why the sing. is עַם? Rules 6a and 14. 'and speaking according to the tongue of his [not his wife's] people.'

Be sure you have recorded in your notebook all the verb forms that we have encountered. Now it is time to categorize them and to work seriously on methodical verb analysis. You will make very slow progress if you do not master the verbal system outline at this point!

In the following forms, כ stands for any strong consonant. Can you recognize the forms?

כְּכַב	יִכְבֹּכ	תִּכְבַּכ	יִכְבְּכוּ
כּוֹכֵב	יִכֵּב	יַעֲסֹם	יִכְּכוּ
כָּכָה	יִכְכֶּה	מְכַכְּבִים	יְסַסֵּם
תְּסַבֵּב	לִכְכוֹת	לְהָכִיב	לְהַכְכוֹת

Learn the words in Group 14.

---

20. In originally closed accented syllables, in certain forms original short *i* becomes short *a* (§15.33).

20

Purpose: To learn to use the Verb Diagnosis Chart
Materials: Verb Diagnosis Chart, student's notebook

Note: Some students and instructors find the VDC of little value. In my experience, it has been very useful, and a few former students report that they still use it for difficult forms. I have no zeal for the VDC, but I am certain that there is no substitute for developing a *methodical approach* to verb analysis. The following steps, with or without the VDC, are of primary importance.

Preliminary steps

1. Remove all prepositions and suffixes. If there is a prep., form must be a verbal noun. If there is a suf., vowel pattern may have to be restored, using SVC.

2. Identify all preformatives and sufformatives. *You cannot parse a verb form if you do not know these morphemes.* If there is a preformative –י, –ת, –א, or –נ, the form is impf. (20) or juss. (40). If there is a sufformative but no preformative, the form is perf. (10) or impv. (32).

3. Identify any stem-indicator (strong dagesh, stem preformative or the effect of one). Stem preformatives are –ה, –נ, –הִת, and –הִנ, or resultant forms with PGN preformatives added to stem preformatives (e.g. –יִת, –אֶת, etc.), assimilation of *nûn,* ellision (syncopation) of –הָ–, and other phonetic alterations.

4. What remains is the *root* or one or two radicals of the root. Step 2 has given us PGN and possibly other data, such as stem, aspect (tense), voice, and mood, and Step 3 has given us the stem if the form is a derived stem. But the parsing of a verb is not complete until the root is given, for it is impossible to know the meaning of the word without knowing its root (unless, of course, you grow up with the language).

5. Are there apparent causes for irregularity? Is there a guttural, a *rêš*, signs of a hollow verb (*CûC, CîC*), signs of first radical weak (*WCC, YCC*) or third radical weak (*CCY*), a dagesh indicating an assimilated *nûn* or a compensation vowel giving the same clue? Carefully check each step.

Parsing procedure

6. Easiest to recognize are HtD and D forms of the "strong" verb (CCC, plus GCC and CCG and some forms of CC^2 and NCC). See Table 1 of VDC.

a. Is there a preformative –הִת, –תִת, –אֶת, –נִת, of –מִת? The form is HtD, §28.5. Is there any sign of metathesis and/or assimilation, §28.53? The middle radical should be doubled (that's the D in HtD), but if it is a guttural or *rêš* or if it has a shewa, doubling may be absent.

b. Is there a strong dagesh in the second radical? If everything else seems to be in order, the form is either D or Dp (Pi'el or Pu'al), §28.2. However, be sure you have the second *radical* and not just the second consonant in the word. The N perf. of NCC or CC² verbs, the N32 of strong verbs, certain forms of CC² verbs, etc., may have a dagesh in the second consonant. It is for this reason that you *must* be able to identify the preformatives (steps 2 and 3).

c. Is there a shewa under the preformative? This is often a better indicator of the D than the gemination of the middle radical, see §§28.21, .22. However, beware of pronominal suffixes which may pull the accent to the end of the word, leaving a shewa under the first radical. You may mistake the radical for a sufformative, particularly if it is י, ת, א, נ, or מ.

d. Is there there the correct vowel pattern? Short *a* after the first radical is HtD or D active, *u* (usually *o*, ָ, *qāmāṣ ḥăṭûp̄*) after the 1st rad. is Dp (HtDp is very rare, §28.52).

7. Is the *first radical* doubled? See Table 2 of VDC. This is a fairly sure sign of the N stem, §28.4.

a. The N perf. and ptcp. will have preformative stem indicator, hence no doubling of 1st rad.

b. When the *nûn* is assimilated, doubling the 1st rad., the vowel pattern confirms the clue: —*i*—*ā*—*ē*—, ־ִ־ָ־ֵ־.

c. Be sure three radicals are present; NCC and CC² forms may have the first apparent radical doubled (see Table 7 of VDC).

d. In GCC verbs, gemination is impossible, but compensatory lengthening may give the clue; check the vowel pattern.

8. Is there a *silent shewa* under the 1st radical? In other words, does the preformative and the first radical form a closed syllable? See Table 3 of VDC. The form may be G20/40, H or Hp, N10/60; look for further clues.

a. Start with H or Hp. H/Hp10/60 will have the preformative ־ה. The other H forms will have *pattāḥ* under the preformative, and Hp forms will have *qāmāṣ-ḥăṭûp̄*.

b. The N forms will have preformative *nûn*. Study the vowel pattern. niCCaC is N10, niCCāC is N50, niCCôC is N60.

c. G20/40 forms will have *i* under the preformative. GCC verbs, of course, do not fall into this category (see Table 4 of VDC).

continued on next page

9. Is there *both* a preformative *and* a vowel under the first radical? Make further analysis.

a. If there is a shewa under the preformative, it is probably a D; see step 6c above or Table 1 of VDC.

b. If the first radical is a guttural, the form may be N or G. Check the vowel pattern (step 7b, Table 2 VDC) for N.

c. If 7a and 7b are negative and there is a guttural in 1st rad., the form is G impf. or juss.

d. If the form is *not* GCC, have you overlooked a pron. suf. that has shifted accent?

10. Are there three radical consonants, no sufformative, all consonants separated by vowels? The form can only be G, D/Dp of CGC or CC^2, or you have not identified a pre-/suf-formative.

a. If the form is CGC, it could be D or Dp perf. Check the vowel pattern. The D has an *i*-vowel under the first radical; the Dp10 has a *u*-vowel.

b. The G10 has an *a*-vowel under the 1st rad.

c. The G50 has a long *ô* after the 1st rad. It is possible to confuse this with a Pô'ēl (§28.6), but such forms are comparatively rare.

d. The Gp50 has long *û* after 2d rad., and the G60 has long *ô* after 2d rad.

e. The G12/13/14/19 of CCY have long *î* after 2d rad.—don't let this mislead you to identify the form as H. See Table 3 VDC and step 8a above.

f. Is there a shewa under the first radical? The form may be G17/18, G32/65. Look for further clues.

g. Is there an *i* vowel under 1st rad.? The form may be D10 of CGC or G33/37. Look for further clues.

11. If *only two radicals* are present, see Tables 6-10 of Verb Diagnosis Chart and follow these steps.

12. Does the form end in ָה-, ֵה-, וֹת-, or a pron. suf.? It can only be CCY (see Table 6 VDC).

a. Read carefully §§29.7-.723.

b. Take all of the form up to and including the 2d rad. and apply the steps above (or Tables 1-5 VDC).

13. Is the *first radical* doubled? Careful! Do not confuse this with step 7, which is

for *three* radicals; this is only for forms with *two* radicals. The form can be NCC, CC², or N stem of Cv̂C. See Table 7 VDC.

a. If first vowel is *u* (ֻ), form is Hp of NCC, §29.43.

b. If first vowel is *o* (ָ), form is Hp60 of CC², with "Aramaic" doubling, §29.5115.

c. If first vowel is *a* (ַ), form is H (but not Hp) of NCC, §29.4.

d. If first vowel is *i* (ִ), note the second vowel, use Table 7 VDC.

14. Is the *second radical* doubled? Remember, we are dealing here *only* with forms that have only *two* radicals showing. The form is either CC² or D of CCY. See Table 8 VDC.

a. For CC², read through §§29.5ff.

b. For CCY, review §§29.7ff.

c. Beware of נָתַתִּי, the only verb that assimilates its *third radical nûn*, §29.44.

15. Is there a preformative? There are a number of possibilities. Study Table 9 VDC carefully. It will take some time to master this category.

a. If there is *ô* (וֹ or ֹ) in preformative, it is H or N of WCC, §29.32.

b. If there is *ê* (ֵ for ֵי) in preformative, it is WCC (§29.321) or possibly YCC (*Ges.* §70*c*, Rem. 1).

c. If there is *û* (וּ) in preformative, it is Hp of WCC, Cv̂C, or CC².

d. In other cases, follow Table 9 of VDC carefully. Note that G and H forms are often remarkably similar.

16. Are there *just two radicals* with no preformative? See Table 10 VDC.

a. If the consonants are separated by ִי, form is CîC, §29.64.

b. If the consonants are separated by וּ, form is CûC, §29.63ff.

c. In other cases, use Table 10 VDC

17. Is *only one radical* present? Form is NCY or G65 of נתן. See Table 11 VDC.

a. If the separating vowel is *a* (ַ), form is H.

b. If the separating vowel is *i* (ִ), form is G20 or H10.

c. If the vowel is *ē* (ֵ), form is G40.

d. If the vowel is *u* (ֻ), form is Hp10.

Using the verbs in your notebook, start analyzing them by using these steps.

Learn the words in Vocabulary Group 15.

VERB DIAGNOSIS CHART

If *three* radicals are present, use Tables 1-5.

1 Middle radical doubled; ± *hiṯ*- stem-indicator

cac^{2}ēc	*dabbēr*	דִּבֵּר	D32[3]	CCC
cac^{2}ôc	*yassôr*	יַסֹּר	D60	
cic^{2}ac	*limmaḏ*	לִמַּד	D10	
	yissaḇ	יִסַּב		T.7
cic^{2}ác-	*biššáltā*	בִּשַּׁלְתָּ	D12	CCC
cic^{2}ēc	*'iwwēr*	יִעוֵּר	D10	
cic^{2e}cv	*kibb^{e}ḏû*	כִּבְּדוּ	D15	
	tiss^{e}ḇû	תִּסַּבּוּ		T.7
cuc^{2}ac	*puqqaḏ*	פֻּקַּד	Dp10	
	huggaš	הֻגַּשׁ		T.7
cuc^{2}ôc	*quṭṭôl*	קֻטּוֹל	Dp60	CCC
y^{e}cac^{2}ac	*y^{e}ḡallaḥ*	יְגַלַּח	D20	CCG
y^{e}cac^{2}ēc	*y^{e}ḏabbēr*	יְדַבֵּר	D20	CCC
	n^{e}ḇaššēl	נְבַשֵּׁל	D29	
	m^{e}ḏabbēr	מְדַבֵּר	D50	
'ăcac^{2}ēc	*'ăḵappēr*	אֲכַפֵּר	D24	
y^{e}cac^{2e}c-	*t^{e}ḏabb^{e}rûn*	תְּדַבְּרוּן	D27	
	m^{e}ḇašš^{e}lîm	מְבַשְּׁלִים	D55	
y^{e}cic^{2}ēc-	*y^{e}sibbḗnî*	יְסִבֵּנִי		T.8
y^{e}cuc^{2}ac	*y^{e}ḇuqqaš*	יְבֻקַּשׁ	Dp20	CCC
	t^{e}ḇuššal	תְּבֻשַּׁל	Dp21[7]	
m^{e}cuc^{2}āc	*m^{e}p̄uzzār*	מְפֻזָּר	Dp50	
m^{e}cuc^{2e}c-	*m^{e}lumm^{e}ḏê^y*	מְלֻמְּדֵי	Dp57	

*h*itcac^{2}ac	*hiṯ'annap̄*	הִתְאַנַּף	HtD10	CCC
	tiṯhaddar	תִּתְהַדַּר	HtD42	
	yiṯgabbār	יִתְגַּבָּר	HtD20	CCG
	yiṯhall^{e}ḵû	יִתְהַלְּכוּ	HtD25	
*h*iṯcac^{2}ēc	*'eṯhallēḵ*	אֶתְהַלֵּךְ	HtD24	
	hiṯhallēḵ	הִתְהַלֵּךְ	HtD32[3]	
	hiṯḥannēn	הִתְחַנֵּן	HtD10[3]	GCC
	miṯhallēḵ	מִתְהַלֵּךְ	HtD50	
*h*ictac^{2}ēc	*mistattēr*	מִסְתַּתֵּר	HtD50	R.12
	hištabbē^{a}ḥ	הִשְׁתַּבֵּחַ	HtD65	R.12
	niṣṭaddēq	נִצְטַדֵּק	HtD29	R.12
hotcac^{2}ac	*huṭṭammā'ā^h*	הֻטַּמְּאָה	HtDp11	R.12
*h*itc^{2}ac^{2}ēc	*middabbēr*	מִדַּבֵּר	HtD50	R.12
	'eddammê^h	אֶדַּמֶּה	HtD24	CCY

2 First radical doubled; with preformative or stem-indicator

*y*ic^{2}ācac	*yiwwada'*	יִוָּדַע	N20	CCG
	hiššāma'	הִשָּׁמַע	N32[2]	CCG
*y*ic^{2}ācac-	*tiqqāṭálnā*	תִּקָּטַלְןָ	N26[8]	CCC
*y*ic^{2}ācēc	*yikkāṯēḇ*	יִכָּתֵב	N20	CCC
	tillāḥēm	תִּלָּחֵם	N21[7]	
	hiqqāḇēṣ	הִקָּבֵץ	N32[2]	
hic^{2}ācôc	*hinnāṯôn*	הִנָּתוֹן	N60	
*y*ic^{2}āc^{e}cv	*yillāḥămû*	יִלָּחֲמוּ	N25	CGC
hic^{2}îc	*higgîḏ*	הִגִּיד		T.7
tic^{2}ōccā	*tissōḇnā*	תִּסֹּבְנָה		T.7
*y*ic^{2e}cv	*yipp^{e}lû*	יִפְּלוּ		T.7
	yigg^{e}lû	יִגְּלוּ		T.6
huc^{2}ac	*huggaḏ*	הֻגַּד		T.7

[1]32 = 60
[2]32 = 65
[3]32 = 60 = 65
[4]10 = 32 = 60 = 65
[5]60 = 65
[6]15 = 16
[7]21 = 22
[8]26 = 28
[9]40 = c20
[10]20 = 40
[11]10 = 50
[12]CWC = CYC
y-/h- = any preformative

Verb Diagnosis Chart

If *less than three* radicals are present, use Tables 6-11

3 — 1st and 2d radicals *not* separated by vowel

yaccac	*yaṣmaḥ*	יַצְמַח	H40[9]	CCG
yaccēc	*yalbēš*	יַלְבֵּשׁ	H21[7]	CCC
	nā*taqṭēlnā*	תַּקְטֵלְנָה	H26[8]	
yaccîc	*talbîš*	תַּלְבִּישׁ	H21[7]	
'eccac	*'elbaš*	אֶלְבַּשׁ	G24	
'eccōc	*'eḏrōš*	אֶדְרֹשׁ	G24	
yiccac	*yiškaḇ*	יִשְׁכַּב	G20*a*	CCC
yiccāc	*yimṣā'*	יִמְצָא	G20*u*	CC'
yiccōc	*yisgōr*	יִסְגֹּר	G20*u*	CCC
yicc^{e}c-	*yiśr^{e}ṣû*	יִשְׁרְצוּ	G25	
yō'cac	*yō'mar*	יֹאמַר	G20	'CC
yuccac	*yušlaḵ*	יֻשְׁלַךְ	Hp20	CCC
haccēc	*haḇdēl*	הַבְדֵּל	H32[3]	
haccîc	*halbîš*	הַלְבִּישׁ	H65	
-v̂	*haḇdîlû*	הַבְדִּילוּ	H37	
heccác-	*heḵlámnû*	הֶכְלַמְנוּ	H19	
hiccác-	*hilbáštā*	הִלְבַּשְׁתָּ	H12	
hiccēc	*himṣē'ṯ*	הִמְצֵאת	H13	CC'
hiccîc	*hiḏrîḵ*	הִדְרִיךְ	H10	CCC
hoccac	*hohpaḵ*	הָהְפַּךְ	Hp10	
hoccēc	*hoḥtēl*	הָחְתֵּל	Hp60	
huccac	*huškaḇ*	הֻשְׁכַּב	Hp10	
hucc^{e}c-	*hušl^{e}ḵû*	הֻשְׁלְכוּ	Hp15	
maccîc	*maḏrîḵ*	מַדְרִיךְ	H50	
moccac	*mošlaḥ*	מָשְׁלָח	Hp50	
muccāc	*mušlāḵ*	מֻשְׁלָךְ	Hp50	
neccac	*nehpaḵ*	נֶהְפַּךְ	N10	GCC
niccac	*nikbaḏ*	נִכְבַּד	G29	CCC
	nišmar	נִשְׁמַר	N10	
niccāc	*nistār*	נִסְתָּר	N10 paus.	
	nip̄rāṣ	נִפְרָץ	N50	
	nimṣā'	נִמְצָא	G29/N10	
niccac-	*nišmartem*	נִשְׁמַרְתֶּם	N17	
niccēc-	*niqrē'ṯî*	נִקְרֵאתִי	N14	CC'
nicc^{e}c-	*nip̄q^{e}ḥû*	נִפְקְחוּ	N15	CCC
niccōc	*niḵtōḇ*	נִכְתֹּב	G29	CCC
niccôc	*nilḥôm*	נִלְחוֹם	N60	

6 — Only 2 radicals: Note ending; Up to and including 2d rad., Tables 1-5

	—ā^{h}	־ָה	10	CCY
Up to and	—e^{h}	־ֶה	20/50	CCY
including	—ē^{h}	־ֵה	32	CCY
2d radical,	—îṯ	־ִית	12	CCY
in Tables	—ô^{h}	־ֹה	60	CCY
1 to 5.	—ôṯ	־וֹת	65	CCY
Read	—ûy	־וּי	p50	CCY
§§29.7ff.	—ṯā	־ְתָה	11	CCY

4 — 1st and 2d radicals separated and *with* preformative or stem-indicator

cacăcēc	*haḥărēš*	הַחֲרֵשׁ	H32[3]	GCC
cacăcîc	*haḥăṭî'*	הַחֲטִיא	H60	GCC
	yaḥălîp̄	יַחֲלִיף	H20	GCC
	maḥărîš	מַחֲרִישׁ	H50	GCC
cacăcōc	*ya'ăḇōr*	יַעֲבֹר	G20*u*	GCC
cacac^{e}cv	*yahar^{e}ḡû*	יַהַרְגוּ	G25	GCC
cecĕcac	*ye'ĕhaḇ*	יֶאֱהַב	G20*a*	GCC
	neḥĕlāṣ	נֶחֱלָץ	N10	GCC
cecĕcîc	*he'ĕmîḏ*	הֶעֱמִיד	H10	GCC
cecĕcōc	*'eḥĕḇōš*	אֶחֱבֹשׁ	G24*u*	GCC
cecec^{e}cv	*teḥeṭ^{e}'û*	תֶּחֶטְאוּ	G27	GCC
cēcācēc	*yē'āḵēl*	יֵאָכֵל	N20	'CC
c^{e}cacēc	*y^{e}ḇahēl*	יְבַהֵל	D20[10]	CGC
c^{e}cācēc	*t^{e}mā'ēn*	תְּמָאֵן	D21[7]	CGC
	m^{e}ḇārēḵ	מְבָרֵךְ	D50	CGC
c^{e}cācaccv	*t^{e}hārāḡnā*	תְּהָרַגְנָה	G26	GCC

5 — All radicals separated; *no* preformative or stem-indicator

cácac	*dá'aṯ*	דַּעַת		T.10
cācac	*'āmar*	אָמַר	G10*a*	CCC
	nāsaḇ	נָסַב		T.9
cācáccv	*'āḇádtî*	אָבַדְתִּי	G14	CCC
cācāc	*qārā'*	קָרָא	G10	CC'
	'āśā^{h}	עָשָׂה		T.6
	nāsāḇ	נָסָב		T.9
cācēc	*kāḇēḏ*	כָּבֵד	G10*i*[11]	CCC
	bārēḵ	בָּרֵךְ	D32[3]	CGC
cācîcv	*'āśîṯā*	עָשִׂיתָ		T.6
cācōc	*qāṭōn*	קָטֹן	G10*u*[11]	CCC
cācôc	*nāṯôn*	נָתוֹן	G60	CCC
cācûc	*'āḥûz*	אָחוּז	Gp50	CCC
cécec	*šéḇeṯ*	שֶׁבֶת		T.10
cēcac	*bēraḵ*	בֵּרַךְ	G10	CGC
cic^{e}cv	*šim^{e}'û*	שִׁמְעוּ	G37	CCC
coc^{e}cv	*mol^{e}ḵô*	מָלְכוֹ	G65s0	CCC
cōcac	*bōraḵ*	בֹּרַךְ	Dp10	CGC
côcac	*sôḇaḇ*	סוֹבַב	Lp10	CC[2]
côcēc	*môlēḵ*	מֹלֵךְ	G50	CCC
	sôḇēḇ	סוֹבֵב	L10	CC[2]
c^{e}cac	*š^{e}ma'*	שְׁמַע	G32*a*	CCG
c^{e}caccv	*q^{e}ṭaltem*	קְטַלְתֶּם	G17	CCC
	ḥăzáqnā^{h}	חֲזַקְנָה	G38	GCC
c^{e}cōc	*š^{e}lō^{a}ḥ*	שְׁלֹחַ	G65[2]	CCG

If *less than three* radicals are present, use Tables 6-11

7 Only 2 radicals, 1st radical doubled

*y*ac^{2}ē**c**	*yassēḇ*	יַסֵּב	H20	CC^2
	tappēl	תַּפֵּל	H40	NCC
*y*ac^{2}î**c**	*yassîṯ*	יַסִּית	H20	CWC
	taggîḏ	תַּגִּיד	H22[7]	NCC
*y*i**c**^{2}a**c**	*yimmal*	יִמַּל	G20[10]	CC^2
	yiggal	יִגַּל	N40	CC^2
	yissag	יִסַּג	N20	CWC
	tiggaʿ	תִּגַּע	G21[7]	NCC
	nittan	נִתַּן	N10	NCC
	yiqqaḥ	יִקַּח	G20	לקח
*y*i**c**^{2}á**c**^{2}û	*yiqqállû*	יִקַּלּוּ	N25	CC^2
*y*i**c**^{2}ā**c**	*tiśśā'*	תִּשָּׂא	G21[7]	NC'
	tiggāl	תִּגָּל	N40	T.6,2
*y*i**c**^{2}ā**c**û	*yiqqāwû*	יִקָּווּ	N15	T.6,2
*y*i**c**^{2}ō**c**	*yimmōl*	יִמֹּל	N20	CWC
	yiddōḏ	יִדֹּד	G20	NC^2
	nissōḇ	נִסֹּב	N29	CC^2
'e**c**^{2}ō**c**	*'eddōm*	אֶדֹּם	G24	CC^2
*y*u**c**^{2}a**c**	*yuṣṣaʿ*	יֻצַּע	Hp20	YṢC
ha**c**^{2}a**c**	*hannaḥ*	הַנַּח	H32	CWC
ha**c**^{2}ē**c**	*haṣṣēl*	הַצֵּל	N32	NCC
ha**c**^{2}ô**c**	*hakkôṯ*	הַכּוֹת	N65	NCY
hi**c**^{2}ē**c**	*hissēḇ*	הִסֵּב	N60[5]	CC^2
hi**c**^{2}î**c**	*higgîḏ*	הִגִּיד	H10	NCC
	hinnîᵃḥ	הִנִּיחַ	H10	CWC
hu**c**^{2}ô**c**	*himmôl*	הִמּוֹל	N60	CWC
.	*hiqqôm*	הִקּוֹם	N60	CC^2
hic^{2}ocv	*himmṓlû*	הִמּוֹלוּ	N37	CWC
hi**c**^{2}û	*hiṣṣû*	הִצּוּ	H15	NCY
ho**c**^{2}a**c**^{2}v	*hoššammā^h*	הָשַּׁמָּה	Hp60	CC^2
hu**c**^{2}a**c**tv	*huggáštî*	הֻגַּשְׁתִּי	N14	NCC
ma**c**^{2}é**c**et	*maggéḏeṯ*	מַגֶּדֶת	H51	NCC
ma**c**^{2}î**c**	*maggîᵃʿ*	מַגִּיעַ	H50	NCC
ni**c**^{2}a**c**	*nittan*	נִתַּן	N10	NCC
	nissaḇ	נִסַּב	N29	CC^2
ni**c**^{2}a**c**tv	*niggáštā*	נִגַּשְׁתָּ	N12	NCC
ni**c**^{2}ō**c**	*nissōḇ*	נִסֹּב	G29	CC^2
	nimmōl	נִמּוֹל	N10	CWC
ni**c**^{2}ō**c**îm	*nimmōlîm*	נִמֹּלִים	N55	CWC
ni**c**^{2}ô**c**	*nimmôl*	נִמֹּל	N10	CWC

[1] 32=60
[2] 32=65
[3] 32=60=65
[4] 10=32=60=65
[5] 60=65
[6] 15=16
[7] 21=22
[8] 26=28
[9] 40=c20
[10] 20=40
[11] 10=50
[12] CWC = CYC
y-/h- = any preformative

8 Only 2 radicals, 2d radical doubled

ca**c**^{2}v	*ḥáttā^h*	חַתָּה	G11	CC^2
	qállû	קַלּוּ	G15	CC^2
	máttā	מַתָּ	G12	CWC
	máttî	מַתִּי	G14	CWC
ca**c**^{2}v-	*sabbū́nî*	סַבֻּנִי	G15s4	CC^2
	sabbṓṯî	סַבֹּתִי	G14	CC^2
	ḥannôṯ	חַנּוֹת	G65	CC^2
cā**c**^{2}v	*rā́bbā^h*	רָבָּה	G11	CC^2
	dā́mmû	דָּמּוּ	G15	CC^2
ci**c**^{2}v	*tillû*	תִּלּוּ	D15	CCY
cō**c**^{2}v	*sṓbbî*	סֹבִּי	G33	CC^2
	ḥṓttû	חֹתּוּ	G37	CC^2
*y*ā**c**ḗ**c**^{2}v	*yāhḗllû*	יָהֵלּוּ	H15	CC^2
*y*ā**c**ṓ**c**^{2}v	*tāmṓddû*	תָּמֹדּוּ	G27	CC^2
	nāḇṓzzû	נָבֹזּוּ	G49	CC^2
*y*ē**c**ṓ**c**^{2}v	*yērṓmmû*	יֵרֹמּוּ	N15	CC^2
*y*ᵉ**c**a**c**^{2}v	*yᵉḇallû*	יְבַלּוּ	D25	CCY
*y*ᵉ**c**i**c**^{2}ê-	*yᵉsibbḗnî*	יְסִבֵּנִי	H25s4	CC^2
	tᵉḥilléʸnā^h	תְּחִלֶּינָה	H26	CC^2
*y*ᵉ**c**u**c**^{2}v	*tᵉhummēm*	תְּהֻמֵּם	G22s5	CC^2
	lᵉhummām	לְהֻמָּם	G65s5	CC^2
	tᵉsubbéʸnā^h	תְּסֻבֶּינָה	G26[8]	CC
ha**c**i**c**^{2}ôt-	*haḥillṓṯā*	הַחִלּוֹתָ	H12	CC^2
hē**c**á**c**^{2}v	*hēsábbû*	הֵסַבּוּ	H15	CC^2
hē**c**ḗ**c**^{2}v	*hēḥḗllû*	הֵחֵלּוּ	H15	CC^2
hē**c**ṓ**c**^{2}v	*hērṓmmû*	הֵרֹמּוּ	N37	CC^2
na**c**á**c**^{2}v	*nāsábbû*	נָסַבּוּ	N15	CC^2
	nātáttā	נָתַתָּ	G12	NCC
nā**c**ḗ**c**^{2}v	*nāsḗbbā^h*	נָסֵבָּה	N11	CC^2
nā**c**ṓ**c**^{2}v	*nāqṓṭṭû*	נָקֹטּוּ	N15	CWC
	nābṓzzā^h	נָבֹזָּה	G49	CC^2

11 only *one* radical, with preformative or stem-indicator

ca**c**	*haḵ*	הַךְ	H32	NCY
	taṭ	תַּט	H40	NCY
	yaḵ	וַיַּךְ	Hc20	NCY
ca**c**^{2}v	*hakkû*	הַכּוּ	H37	NCY
	yaššê^h	יַשֶּׁה	H20	NCY
	makkîm	מַכִּים	H55	NCY
cā**c**	*'āṭ*	אָט	G24	NCY
cē**c**	*yēṭ*	יֵט	G40[9]	NCY
	tēṭ	וַתֵּט	Gc21	NCY
ci**c**^{2}v	*yiṭṭû*	וַיִּטּוּ	Gc25	NCY
cu**c**^{2}v	*tukkû*	תֻּכּוּ	Hp27	NCY
	hukkā^h	הֻכָּה	Hp10	NCY
	mukkā^h	מֻכָּה	Hp51	NCY

Verb Diagnosis Chart

If *three* radicals are present, use Tables 1-5

9 — 2 radicals separated by vowel, *with* preformative or stem-indicator

yācac	*nāsab̲*	נָסַב	N10	CC[2]
	yāšab̲	יָשַׁב		T.5
yācēc	*yāqēl*	יָקֵל	H20	CC[2]
	yāqēm	יָקֵם	H40	CWC
	yāḡēl	יָגֵל	G40	CYC
yācîc	*ʼāqîm*	אָקִים	H20	CWC[12]
	yāḡîl	יָגִיל	G20	CYC
yācōc	*yāsōb̲*	יָסֹב	G20	CC[2]
	yāmōt̲	יָמֹת	G40	CWC
yācôc	*tāb̲ôʼ*	תָּבוֹא	G21[7]	CWC
yācûc	*ʼāṣûm*	אָצוּם	G24	CWC
	yādû^{a}ʿ	יָדוּעַ		T.5
yácac	*-yáʿan*	וַיַּעַן		T.6,4
cécec	*lédet̲*	לֶדֶת	G65	WCC
yêcac	*yêdaʿ*	יֵדַע	G20	WCC
yécec	*yéšeb̲*	יֵשֶׁב	G20	WCC
yêcēc	*yêṭēb̲*	יֵיטֵב	H40	YCC
	yêṣēʼ	יֵצֵא	G20	WCC
yêcîc	*têṭîb̲*	תֵּיטִיב	H21[7]	YCC
yícec	*yígel*	יִגֶל	G40	CCY
yî́cec	*yî́qeṣ*	וַיִּיקֶץ	Hc20	YCC
yîcac	*yîṭab̲*	יִיטַב	G20	YCC
yôcēc	*tôsēp̄*	תּוֹסֵף	H40	WCC
	yôšēb̲	יוֹשֵׁב	G50	YCC
yôcîc	*yôšîb̲*	יוֹשִׁיב	H20	WCC
yûcac	*yûsab̲*	יוּסַב	Hp20	CC[2]
	yûšab̲	יוּשַׁב	Hp20	WCC
	yûqam	יוּקַם	Hp20	CWC

y^{e}cac	*y*^{e}*ṣaw*	יְצַו	D40	CCY
yit̲cac	*yit̲gal*	יִתְגַּל		T.6,1
mēcēc	*mēsēb̲*	מֵסֵב	H50	CC[2]
mēcîc	*mēqîm*	מֵיקִים	H50	CWC[12]
mêcîc	*mêṭîb̲*	מֵיטִיב	H50	YCC
mûcāc	*mûšāb̲*	מוּשָׁב	Hp50	WCC
nācac	*nāsab̲*	נָסַב	N10	CC[2]
	nāṯan	נָתַן		T.5
nācāc	*nāsāb̲*	נָסָב	N50	CC[2]
nācēc	*nāsēb̲*	נָסֵב	N10	CC[2]
nācôc	*nāqôm*	נָקוֹם	N10[11]	CWC[12]
	nāṯôn	נָתוֹן		T.5
nôcāc	*nôšāb̲*	נוֹשָׁב	H20[10]	WCC
	nôdaʿ	נוֹדַע	N10[11]	WCC
nôcîc	*nôšîb̲*	נוֹשִׁיב	H20	WCC
hācēc	*hāšēb̲*	הָשֵׁב	H32[1]	CWC
	hāsēb̲	הָסֵב	H32[3]	CC[2]
hācîc	*hābîʼ*	הָבִיא	H65	CWC
hēcac	*hēsab*	הֵסַב	H10	CC[2]
hēcēc	*hēḥēl*	הֵחֵל	H10	CC[2]
hecĕcv	*heḥĕlî*	הֶחֱלִי	H11	CCY
hēcîc	*hēbîʼ*	הֵבִיא	H10	CWC
hêcîc	*hêṭîb̲*	הֵיטִיב	H60[4]	YCC
hôcîc	*hôdî*^{a}ʿ	הוֹדִיעַ	H65[4]	WCC
	hôšîb̲	הוֹשִׁיב	H10	WCC
hûcac	*hûḥal*	הוּחַל	Hp10	CC[2]
	hûšab̲	הוּשַׁב	Hp10[4]	WCC
	hûqam	הוּקַם	Hp10[4]	CWC

10 — 2 radicals, *no* preformative

cac	*tam*	תַּם	G10	CC[2]
	gaš	גַּשׁ	G32	NCC
	daʿ	דַּע	G32	WCC
	gal	גַּל	D32	CCY
	qaḥ	קַח	G32	לקח
cacc-	*gašnā*^{h}	גַּשְׁנָה	G38	NCC
	tammû	תַּמּוּ		T.8
cácac	*daʿat̲*	דַּעַת	G65	WCC
cāc	*qām*	קָם	G10	CWC
	bān	בָּן	G10	CYC
câc	*qâm*	קָם	G50	CWC
	qâmê^{y}	קָמֵי	G57	CWC
	bân	בָּן	G50	CYC
cēc	*mēt̲*	מֵת	G10[11]	CWC
	šēb̲	שֵׁב	G32	WCC
	tēt̲	תֵּת	G65	נתן

	lēk̲	לֵךְ	G32	הלך
	tēn	תֵּן	G32	נתן
cēcv	*mĕṯā*^{h}	מֵתָה	G11	CWC
cēcc	*ṣēʼt̲*	צֵאת	G65	WCʼ
cécet	*šéb̲et̲*	שֶׁבֶת	G65	WCC
	géšet̲	גֶּשֶׁת	G65	NCC
cîc	*bîn*	בִּין	G65[2]	CYC
	śîm	שִׂים	Gp50	CYC
cōc	*šōk̲*	שֹׁךְ	G32[2]	CC[2]
côc	*bôn*	בֹּן	G60	CYC
	qôm	קוֹם	G60	CWC
cûc	*qûm*	קוּם	G32[2]	CWC
	qûm	קוּם	Gp50	CWC
c^{e}cv	*g*^{e}*šî*	גְּשִׁי	G33	NCC
	š^{e}*bû*	שְׁבוּ	G37	WCC
	l^{e}*k̲û*	לְכוּ	G37	הלך
yvcc^{e}	*wayyašq*^{e}	וַיַּשְׁקְ	Hc20	CCY
	wattēb̲k^{e}	וַתֵּבְךְּ	Gc20	§29.721
	wayyišb^{e}	וַיִּשְׁבְּ	Gc20	”

21

Purpose: To study the D stem
Materials: Esther 2:1-3a

ב CAP. II. ב

א אַחַר הַדְּבָרִים הָאֵלֶּה כְּשֹׂךְ חֲמַת הַמֶּלֶךְ אֲחַשְׁוֵרוֹשׁ זָכַר
אֶת־וַשְׁתִּי וְאֵת אֲשֶׁר־עָשָׂתָה וְאֵת אֲשֶׁר־נִגְזַר עָלֶיהָ׃
2 וַיֹּאמְרוּ נַעֲרֵי־הַמֶּלֶךְ מְשָׁרְתָיו יְבַקְשׁוּ לַמֶּלֶךְ נְעָרוֹת בְּתוּלוֹת
3 טוֹבוֹת מַרְאֶה׃ וְיַפְקֵד הַמֶּלֶךְ פְּקִידִים בְּכָל־מְדִינוֹת
מַלְכוּתוֹ

2:1 אַחַר הַדְּבָרִים הָאֵלֶּה [1]—(a) Prep. 'after' (v.310), **'aḥḥar* with implied doubling, §15.1411. (b) ־הַ· §22.2. ־ִים §25.231. (c) 1:5[2], §21.2. Cf. §36.11. This is a prep. phrase used adverbially.

כְּשֹׂךְ חֲמַת[2]—(b) In the Letteris text, this is pointed as though from *śkk,* but BDB 1013 lists it under *škk* 'to be assuaged' (7918 5/2). k^e + *šōḵ,* cōc, Table 10 VDC, CC^2 G65. On CC^2, §29.51. k^e- + inf. cstr., 'when, while.' (b) 1:12[6], note vowels and ־ַת; what do they tell us?. §25.12. You know the next words. 'When the anger of the king decreased.'

זָכַר אֶת־וַשְׁתִּי[3]—(a) Three consonants, no pre- or sufformative, cācac in Table 5 VDC. The vowel pattern indicates G10 of CCC, §27.221, from *zkr* 'to remember' (v.2142). The subj. is in the verb form, §§32., .1, .113, mentioned in previous clause. (b) Why אֶת? Is Vashti definite? Why?

וְאֵת אֲשֶׁר־עָשָׂתָה [4]—(a) Note pointing. This indicates a second dir. obj. in a compound obj., §34.17. (b-c) Noun cl. used as obj., §34.12, §21.3. 'He remembered *what she had done.*' (c) ־תָה— indicates 11 of CCY, §29.7131. The pausal form is found here with *zāqēp-qāṭôn*, §17.2231.

וְאֵת אֲשֶׁר־נִגְזַר עָלֶיהָ׃ [5]—(a) 3d obj. of compound object, §34.17. (b-d) Noun cl., obj. of verb, §34.12. (c) *ni*— is G29 or N10, §27.31, §28.42. *gzr* 'to cut, divide, decide' (1504 13/1). (d) עַל always takes the form עלי when adding a suf. Cf. 1:14[2]

2:2 וַיֹּאמְרוּ נַעֲרֵי [1](a) *way-* tells us what? §22.13, §27.117. י——וּ tells us what? §27.31. *yô'm^{e}rû* < **ya'mirû* ya'CiC, §29.2, §29.212. Cf. 1:13[1]. Subj. follows. (b) ־ֵי = ? §25.424. נַעַר (v.5288) here 'servants.' CaGC type noun, §24.21, .211.

מְשָׁרְתָיו[2]—Cf. 1:10[7]. ־ָיו = ? §23.1121. ——מְ = ? §28.22, Table 1 VDC. *m^e–ā—*, note §15.141. Don't expect to find a dagesh in every D form.

יְבַקְשׁוּ לַמֶּלֶךְ [3]—(a) וּ——יְ, this could be 25 or 45 (jussive, §27.5f.); context tells. Note shewa under preform.: a strong clue of D. §28.21. ק usually omits dagesh when with reduced vowel (shewa); you must learn the vowel patterns, here *y^e-a-^{e}-û.* D25/45 of *bqš*, D 'to seek' (v.1245). (b) *l^e-*, §35.42. 'Let them seek for (on behalf of) the king.'

נְעָרוֹת בְּתוּלוֹת [4]—(a) *naʿărā^h* (v.5291), f. of נַעַר, §24.211, note the pl., §24.215. (b) Adj. in concord, note GNS (gender, number, state), §36.11. *b^{e}ṯûlā^h* 'unmarried woman, virgin' (v.1330). Noun type, §24.241. Attrib. adj., §36.1. Note position of adj. 'virgin maidens.'

טוֹבוֹת מַרְאֶה׃ [5]—(a-b) 1:11[6]; what difference do you see? ת‐ = ? וֹת‐ = ? §25.12, §25.232. (b) מַ—ֶה tells two things: *-ê^h* is 20/50 of CCY, §29.71, Table 6 VDC; *ma-* is H ptcp., §28.31. Hence form is H50 of *r'y* ראה. However, it is usually taken as a noun, here in apposition with *n^{e}ʿărôṯ*, §36.6.

2:3 וְיַפְקֵד הַמֶּלֶךְ פְּקִידִים [1]—(a) וְ, is this *wāw* conv.? §22.1, .13. ‐יַ suggests H20/40,-n§28.31, .313. The vowel pattern *-a--ē-* could be Hc20 (conv. impf.) or H40 (juss.). Which is it? *pqd* H 'to appoint' (v.6485). (c) CvCv̂C-type noun, §24.24, cf. §15.21. *p^{e}qîḏ* 'officer, one appointed' (6496 13/1). Why is there no אֵת?. 'and let the king appoint appointees.'

בכל־מדינות מלכותו [2]—(a) 'all' or 'every' ?. (b) 1:1[12]. (c) 1:3[4].

Go over the D stem (§28.22ff) and spot the identifying morphemes.

CiC²ēC	*qiṭṭēl*	קִטֵּל
CēGēC	*bē'ēr*	בֵּאֵר
m^{e}CaC²ēC	*m^{e}qaṭṭēl*	מְקַטֵּל
m^{e}CāGēC	*m^{e}šārēṯ*	מְשָׁרֵת

Start to familiarize yourself with Paradigm V-4.
Go back over previous lessons and look for D-stem forms. Analyze them.

Learn the basic vocabulary in Group 16.

---

9. At word-end, original *-cw > *-cû* and *-cy > *-cî* (§15.67).

10a. *Gutturals* reject dagesh (§11.432); before א, ע, and ר there is compensatory lengthening (§15.141).
 b. Gutturals do not take simple vocal shewa (§15.42).
 c. Gutturals often vocalize a silent shewa (§15.421).
 d. Gutturals prefer *a*-class vowels, especially before them (§15.43).
 e. At word-end, ע, ח, or הּ (*he^h with mappiq*) attract pattaḥ furtive after *i-* or *u*-class vowels (§15.4321).
 f. *i > e* (*ḥîrîq > s^{e}gôl*) before nonfinal gutturals (§15.434).
 g. Initial א prefers *i*-class vowels when near the accent (§15.433).
 h. א at word-end and frequently at syllable-end is quiescent (§15.54).

22

Purpose: To study the G stem
Materials: Esther 2:3b-4

וְיִקְבְּצוּ אֶת־כָּל־נַעֲרָֽה־בְתוּלָה טוֹבַת מַרְאֶה אֶל־
שׁוּשַׁן הַבִּירָה אֶל־בֵּית הַנָּשִׁים אֶל־יַד הֵגֶא סְרִיס הַמֶּלֶךְ
שֹׁמֵר הַנָּשִׁים וְנָתוֹן תַּמְרוּקֵיהֶן׃ וְהַֽנַּעֲרָה אֲשֶׁר תִּיטַב 4
בְּעֵינֵי הַמֶּלֶךְ תִּמְלֹךְ תַּחַת וַשְׁתִּי וַיִּיטַב הַדָּבָר בְּעֵינֵי
הַמֶּלֶךְ וַיַּעַשׂ כֵּן׃

2:3b וְיִקְבְּצוּ[3]—*way-*, §221.3, tells us what aspect (tense)?. §32.5, .52. Will it be translated past or future? §32.53. *yi——û* is what PGN (person, gender, number)? §27.31. Will you translate it 'they,' 'we, or 'you'? *yiCC*^{e}*Cû,* Table 3 VDC, no vowel between 1st and 2d radicals, *i*-vowel under preformative, G25/45, §32.35. *qbṣ* 'gather, collect' (v.6908). 'Let them gather.'

אֶת־כָּל־נַעֲרָה־בְתוּלָה [4]—(a) This tells us what?. כל is used to determine a noun, *Ges.* §117*c.* (c-d) What is the difference between this and 2:2[4]?

טוֹבַת מַרְאֶה [5]—(a-b) 1:11[6].

אֶל־ שׁוּשַׁן הַבִּירָה[6]—1:2[10.11].

אֶל־בֵּית הַנָּשִׁים [7]—(b) 1:8[4]. Table F. (c) 1:17[1].

אֶל־יַד הֵגֶא סְרִיס [8]—(b) 1:7[5] (c) Pr.n. Hegai. (d) Note that -ָ has reduced, cf. 1:10[6]. Note how the directions get increasingly precise.

שֹׁמֵר הַנָּשִׁים[9]—(a) For שׁ, §11.411. Vowel pattern -ֹ-ֵ- strongly suggests G50, §27.61, cf. §27.6, .6111. *šmr* 'to watch, keep, protect' (v.8104). Read §27.6112. This is cstr., G52.

וְנָתוֹן תַּמְרֻקֵיהֶן׃[10]—(a) *nātôn, -ā-ô-* is vowel pattern of G60, §27.64. Read §§30.381, .3812, §32.39f; 'to give.' (b) *tamrûq* is taCCûC, §24.36, *mrq* 'to scour, polish,' *tamrûq* 'detergent' (8562 4/3). For הֶן-, §23.1211. The heavy ending takes the accent.

2:4 וְהַנַּעֲרָה[1]—(a) Compare the forms in 2:2[4] and 2:3[4]. Identify them.

אֲשֶׁר תִּיטַב בְּעֵינֵי[2]—(a) Rel. cl. (b) *t*—— can be 3fs or 2ms impf (20/40). The pattern *ti-a-* is G20/40 of yiCCaC type, Table 3 VDC. *tiYCaC* is YCC. If you can't work it out, see 1:21[1]. (c) 1:21[2]

תִּמְלֹךְ[3]— —ת is 21/22 or 41/42. *ti--ō-* is G of yaCCuC type, §27.321. The vowel following the 2d rad. is called the *thematic* (or *theme*) vowel, §27.231. At this point you should begin to get familiar with "Barth's Law," §27.331f. What does the root מלך mean? 1:1[6], 1:3[3]. Is the form 3fs or 2ms? How can you tell?

תַּ֫חַת וַשְׁתִּ֑י[4]—(a) Denominal prep. 'under,' v.8478, here 'in the place of, as the successor to.'

וַיִּיטַ֧ב הַדָּבָ֛ר בְּעֵינֵ֥י[5]—(a) Work it out. Then cf. 1:21[1]. (a-d) 1:21[12].

וַיַּ֥עַשׂ כֵּֽן׃[6]—(a) Note –ַ וַ. *yáʻaś*: *yá–*, only 2 radicals. The accent is like CvCC nouns (*náʻar*), hence no true vowel separates the consonants, hence it is not the 2d rad. that is lost. There is no lengthening of preformative vowel, hence it is unlikely that the 1st rad. is lost. That suggests CCY, §29.7), and we should think at once of the possibility of apocopation, §29.72. Review 1:21[3] carefully. (b) 1:8[3].

This is a good place to try to nail down the G stem, particularly the G impf.

yaCCuC	*yiqṭōl*	יִקְטֹל
yiCCaC	*yik̲bad̲*	יִכְבַּד
yaCCiC	*yittēn*	יִתֵּן
yaGCuC	*yaḥălōm*	יַחֲלֹם
yaCCuG	*yišlaḥ*	יִשְׁלַח
	yišlôᵃḥ	יִשְׁלֹ֫חַ
yaYCi'	*yêṣē'*	יֵצֵא
yiYCaC	*yîʸṭab̲*	יִיטַב

Go back over previous lessons and analyze the G-stem verbs you have encountered. Make plenty of notes in your notebook. You will always have trouble until you conquer the G stem of the verb.

Learn the basic vocabulary in Group 17.

---

23. The connecting vowel of a pronominal suffix, if any, takes the accent (§17.32). If a shewa precedes the suffix, it is zero shewa and the כְ of the suffix is spirantized.

24. In verbal forms, thematic *a* in G-perf. generally yields thematic *u* in G-impf., andnthematic *i* or *u* in G-perf. yields thematic *a* in G-impf. (§27.331).

25. In G-impf., the vowel of the preformative is determined usually by the thematic vowel, as follows: thematic *a* preformative *i*, thematic *i* or *u* preformative *a* (§27.332).

23

Purpose: To study the H stem
Materials: Esther 2:5-6

אִישׁ יְהוּדִי הָיָה בְּשׁוּשַׁן הַבִּירָה ה
וּשְׁמוֹ מָרְדֳּכַי בֶּן יָאִיר בֶּן־שִׁמְעִי בֶּן־קִישׁ אִישׁ יְמִינִי׃ אֲשֶׁר 6
הָגְלָה מִירוּשָׁלַיִם עִם־הַגֹּלָה אֲשֶׁר הָגְלְתָה עִם יְכָנְיָה
מֶלֶךְ־יְהוּדָה אֲשֶׁר הֶגְלָה נְבוּכַדְנֶאצַּר מֶלֶךְ בָּבֶל׃

2:5 אִישׁ יְהוּדִי הָיָה [1]—(a) 1:8[6]. Indef., 'a man,' §30.3223. (b) י— is a gentilic (a people of a place), §22.45. y^{e}hûḏ 'Judah, Judea,' hence, 'Jew.' The word in in apposition with (a). (c) *–ā–ā^{h}* tells us two things: -ā^{h} ָה– is 10 of CCY, §29.71. and the vowel after the 1st rad. tells us that it is G. *hy^{h}* 'to be' (v.1961).

בְּשׁוּשַׁן הַבִּירָה [2]—1:2[10,11].

וּשְׁמוֹ מָרְדֳּכַי [3]—(a) *û,* §16.31. *š^{e}m + ô,* from *šēm,* §15.121, R. 16, 'name' (v.8034). (b) Pr.n. 'Mordecai,' מָרְ is unaccented closed, Table E.

בֶּן יָאִיר בֶּן־שִׁמְעִי בֶּן־קִישׁ [4]—A genealogy, not necessarily complete. Jair may have been his father, and Shimei and Kish more remote ancestors. Note בֵּן but בֶּן in cstr.

אִישׁ יְמִינִי׃ [5]—(a) Cstr.–why not reduced vowel? (b) For *ben-y^{e}mînî,* Benjamite.

אשר הגלה[1]—(a) Rel. cl., modifying 2:5[1]. (b) *ho--ā^{h}:* note *-ā^{h},* Table 6 of VDC, §29.71. Note *hoḡ-* (un. cl, therefore *qāmāṣ ḥāṭûp̄,* sign of Hp[ass.], §28.32. *gl^{y}* גלה (v.1540), here 'to go into exile'; Hp 'was caused to go ..., was taken exile.'

2:6 אֲשֶׁר הָגְלָה [1]—(a) Rel. cl., modifying 2:5[1].

מִירוּשָׁלַיִם [2]—*mî-* from *min* + *y^{e}-*. *y^{e}rûšāláyim,* pr. n.— can you figure it out? This is a prep. phrase used adverbially ('he was taken *from where?*').

עִם־הַגֹּלָה [3]—(a) עִם prep. 'with' (v.5973); do not confuse it with עַם. (b) *hag* + *gôlā^{h}:* CôCē^{h} is masc., CôCā^{h} fem., G51 of *gl^{y}*, 2:6[1]. The fem. is often an abstract noun, here 'the exile' (v.1473). Another prep. phr. used adverbially.

הָגְלְתָה[4]—Note ָתה–, sign of 11 of CCY, §29.71. Learn the CCY indicators now. Note –הָג: if ָ is *o* and not *ā,* this is Hp, §28.32. Now cf. 2:6 . Why is this form fem.? The subj. is אֲשֶׁר, but its antecedent is הַגֹּלָה.

עִם יְכָנְיָה מֶלֶךְ־יְהוּדָה [5]—(a) 2:6[3]. (b) Pr.n., *y^{e}ḵonyā^{h}*–can you figure it out? (d) *y^{e}hûḏā^{h}* syncopated later > *yûḏā^{h};* can you figure it out?

הֶגְלָה[6]—הּ—ָ is what of CCY? §29.71. —הֶ (or —הִ) is sign of H (act.), §28.31. Now compare *heḡlāʰ* הֶגְלָה with *hoḡlāʰ* הָגְלָה. The subj. follows.

נְבוּכַדְנֶאצַּר מֶלֶךְ בָּבֶל׃[7]—(a) *nᵉḇûḵaḏneṣṣar*–can you figure it out? (c) *bāḇel* from Akk. *bab ilim* 'gate of god' = Babylon.

This is a good time to work on the H stem. Get familiar with Paradigm V-5.

Study these forms:

hiCCîca	*hiqṭîl*	הִקְטִיל
yᵉhaCCîCu	*yaqṭîl*	יַקְטִיל
yᵉhaCCîC	*yaqṭēl*	יַקְטֵל
mᵉhaCCîC	*maqṭēl*	מַקְטֵל
hiCCaY (?)	*heḡlāʰ*	הֶגְלָה
huCCaC	*hoqṭal*	הָקְטַל

Analyze the following:

הֶגְלָה	2:6[6]	וַיַּמְלִיכֶהָ	2:17[6]
הָגְלָה	2:6[1]	וּבְהַגִּיעַ	2:12[1]
הִגִּידָה	2:10[1]	בְּהַרְאֹתוֹ	1:4[1]
הָגְלְתָה	2:6[4]	לְהָבִיא	1:11[1]
תַּגִּיד	2:10[4]	בְּהִשָּׁמַע	2:8[2]
וְיַפְקֵד	2:3[1]	לְהַרְאוֹת	1:11[4]
וַיַּגֵּד	2:22[2]	וְהַשְׁקוֹת	1:7[1]
וַיָּשֶׂם	2:17[5]	לִהְיוֹת	1:22[1]
וַיַּעַשׂ	2:18[1]	לְהַבְזוֹת	1:17[3]

Memorize the basic vocabulary in Group 18.

---

17. In finite verbal forms *without sufformatives*, the accent is on the *ultima* (§17.21). In such forms *with sufformatives*, the following rules prevail:

a. If the *ultima* is *closed*, the accent is on the ultima, and the form follows the short-vowel chart (§17.221).

b. If the *ultima* is *open* and the *penult* is *long*, the accent is on the *penult*, and the form follows the short-vowel chart (§17.222).

c. If the *ultima* is open and the *penult* is *short*, in *nonpausal* forms the accent is on the *ultima*, the vowel of the *penult* reduces to shewa, and the vowel of the antepenult has its pausal form (lengthened) and is marked by metheg (§17.223).

d. Under the same conditions (17c) but in *pausal form*, the accent is on the *penult*, and the form follows the short-vowel chart (§17.2231).

18. Short *a* frequently attenuates to short *i* in unaccented closed syllables (§15.32).

Purpose: To study the N stem
Materials: Esther 2:7-8

7 וַיְהִי אֹמֵן
אֶת־הֲדַסָּה הִיא אֶסְתֵּר בַּת־דֹּדוֹ כִּי אֵין לָהּ אָב וָאֵם
וְהַנַּעֲרָה יְפַת־תֹּאַר וְטוֹבַת מַרְאֶה וּבְמוֹת אָבִיהָ וְאִמָּהּ
8 לְקָחָהּ מָרְדֳּכַי לוֹ לְבַת׃ וַיְהִי בְּהִשָּׁמַע דְּבַר־הַמֶּלֶךְ וְדָתוֹ
וּבְהִקָּבֵץ נְעָרוֹת רַבּוֹת אֶל־שׁוּשַׁן הַבִּירָה אֶל־יַד הֵגָי
וַתִּלָּקַח אֶסְתֵּר אֶל־בֵּית הַמֶּלֶךְ אֶל־יַד הֵגַי שֹׁמֵר הַנָּשִׁים׃

2:7 וַיְהִי אֹמֵן אֶת־הֲדַסָּה [1]—(a) 1:1[1]. This form is somewhat difficult to analyze, and since it is very common, you would do better to memorize it *now*. Gc20 of היה. Analysis: *yôḏ* with shewa drops dagesh (R.1b), hence this is way- (conv. *wāw*). CCY apocopates in conv. impf. (c20) and juss. (40), *way* + *yihyê*^{h} > **wayyihy*, §29.72. *-cy* > *-cî*, **wayyihî* (R.9); application of R.16 > **wayy*^{e}*hî*^{y}, and application of R.1b > *way*^{e}*hî*^{y}. (b) Vowel pattern *-ô-ē-*, G50, §27.6122, of *ʾamn* 'to be firm, support, rear, foster' (v.539). G10 + G50 denotes continuous or habitual action in past time (§32.551), 'he was (had been) supporting.' (c-d) Pr.n. 'Hadassah.'

הִיא אֶסְתֵּר [2]—(1:20[3], §21.1f.). Verbless cl., 'she/that (was) Esther.' (b) Pr.n.

בַּת־דֹּדוֹ [3]—(a) **bin* 'son' + *-t* > **bint* (cf. Arab. *bint*) 'daughter' > **bitt* > **bit* > *baṯ* (v.1323). Explain each step. (b) *dôḏ* 'uncle' (v.1730). Whose uncle? What was Esther's relationship to Mordecai?

כִּי אֵין לָהּ אָב וָאֵם [4]—(a) Causal (v.3588), §38.53. (b) 1:8[2]. *ʾên l*^{e}*-* = 'he/she does/did not have.' (c) Prep. + s1, §23.121. (d) *ʾāḇ* 'father' (v.1); CvC-type noun, §24.12. (e) *ʾēm* 'mother' (v.517); CiC^{2}-type noun, §24.214.

וְהַנַּעֲרָה יְפַת־תֹּאַר [5]—(a) 2:2[4]. (b) Cf. 1:11[5]; here יָפֶה adj. 'fair, beautiful' (v.3303), fem. יָפָה, f. cstr. יְפַת. (c) *tṓʾar* 'outline, form' (v.8389); CuCC-type noun. Note postpositive accent, repeated on stressed syllable, §11.571.

וְטוֹבַת מַרְאֶה [6]—Cf. 1:11[6]. Verbless cl., §31. Compound pred., §30.123. 'The maiden (was) (1) beautiful of form and (2) good of appearance' (= 'shapely and comely').

וּבְמוֹת אָבִיהָ וְאִמָּהּ [7]—(a) *û* + *b*^{e}- + *môṯ*. Table 10 VDC shows that G65 of CûC would be מוּת; the form here therefore must be a noun < *mā́weṯ* 'death' (v.4194). 'And on the death of' followed by two governed nouns. (b) 2:7[4](d); note that אָב adds י- when adding suf., *ʾāḇî-*, §23.1211. (c) 2:7[4](e); אֵם with suf. restores gemination: *ʾimm-*. Why *ʾāḇî-hā* but *ʾimm-āh*? §23.121.

לְקָחָהּ מָרְדֳּכַי לוֹ לְבַת׃ [8]—(a) *Watch out!* ָהּ is s1, §23.122, not sufformative. The accent shift has altered the vowel quantities, §27.72. G10 *lāqáḥ* + *āh* > *l^eqāḥāh*. *lqḥ* 'to take' (v.3947). (b) 2:5[3]. Subj. of preceding verb, 'Mordecai took.' (c) Indir. obj. (like dat. of reference) 'for himself.' (d) 'for a daughter' 2:7[3].

2:8 וַיְהִי [1]—Note the *r^eḇî^aʿ*. Cf. 1:1[1]. 'And it was,' και εγενετο.

בְּהִשָּׁמַע דְּבַר־הַמֶּלֶךְ וְדָתוֹ [2]—(a) *û* + *ḇ^e* + *hiššāmaʿ*. 1st rad. geminate, Table 2 VDC; it must be N stem. **hin-* is found only in N32/65, and *b^e-* is found only on 65, hence N65. The vowel pattern hiC²āCēC is affected by guttural > hiC²āCaG. 'In the being heard of' = 'when was heard.' *šmʿ* 1:18[4]. (b-c) 1st obj. of N65. (d) 2d obj. (compound) of N65. Note that the obj. of the inf. cstr. becomes the subj. in Eng. trans.: 'in the being heard of the word' = 'when the word was heard.'

וּבְהִקָּבֵץ נְעָרוֹת רַבּוֹת [3]—(a) *û* + *ḇ^e* + *hiqqāḇēṣ,* see notes on 2:8[2](a). Can you see a similarity? Here hiC²āCēC. qbṣ, 2:3[3]. (c) 1:20[3]. Why is form different here? On translation, see previous note.

אֶל־שׁוּשַׁן הַבִּירָה אֶל־יַד הֵגָא [4]—(a-c) 1:2[10 11]. (d-f) 2:3[8]. Note different spellings, הֵגֶא, הֵגַי, and pausal הֵגָי.

וַתִּלָּקַח אֶסְתֵּר אֶל־בֵּית הַמֶּלֶךְ [5]—(a) *wat* + *tillāqaḥ* tiC²āCaG, cf. 2:8[2]. —וַ tells us what? Doubled 1st rad. tells us what? (Table 2 VDC). Preformative tells us what? —ת is 21/22, and the subj. that follows tells us that it is 21, hence N21 of *lqḥ* (2:7[8]). (b) 2:7[2]. (c-e) Cf. 2:3[7]. Translate the clause.

אֶל־יַד הֵגַי שֹׁמֵר הַנָּשִׁים׃ [6]—(a-c) 2:3[8] and 2:8[4]; note spelling. (d-e) 2:3[9].

Analyze the following forms: הַנִּמְצְאִים 1:5[5]. וַיִּכָּתֵב 1:19[4]. נִשְׁמַע 1:20[1]. נִגְזַר 2:1[5].

niCCaC	*niqṭal*	נִקְטַל
y^ehanCaCiCu > yiC²āCēC	*yiqqāṭēl*	יִקָּטֵל
naCCaCu	*niqṭāl*	נִקְטָל
hanCaCiCu	*hiqqāṭēl*	הִקָּטֵל

Read §28.4. Work on the peculiarities of the N stem.

Learn the words in Basic Vocabulary Group 19.

7. Syllables do not begin with consonantal clusters, except in forms of the word for 'two' (§16.35).

25

Purpose: To review for the examination
Materials: Esther 2:9-10

9 וַתִּיטַב הַנַּעֲרָה בְעֵינָיו וַתִּשָּׂא חֶסֶד לְפָנָיו וַיְבַהֵל אֶת־
תַּמְרוּקֶיהָ וְאֶת־מָנוֹתֶיהָ לָתֶת לָהּ וְאֵת שֶׁבַע הַנְּעָרוֹת
הָרְאֻיוֹת לָתֶת־לָהּ מִבֵּית הַמֶּלֶךְ וַיְשַׁנֶּהָ וְאֶת־נַעֲרוֹתֶיהָ
י לְטוֹב בֵּית הַנָּשִׁים׃ לֹא־הִגִּידָה אֶסְתֵּר אֶת־עַמָּהּ וְאֶת־
מוֹלַדְתָּהּ כִּי מָרְדֳּכַי צִוָּה עָלֶיהָ אֲשֶׁר לֹא־תַגִּיד׃

2:9 וַתִּיטַב הַנַּעֲרָה בְעֵינָיו [1]—(a) See 1:21[1]: what is the difference? Work out the parsing (§27.15). Then cf. 2:4[2]. (b) How is this related to the verb? §32.113. Cf. 2:4[5]. (c) What is the difference betwen בְּעֵינָיו here and בְּעֵינֵי in 1:21[2]?

וַתִּשָּׂא חֶסֶד לְפָנָיו [2]—(a) Note the dageshes, R. 1a. *wat-* tells what? (§22.13). Then *tiśśā'* must be what aspect (tense)? Therefore only 2 radicals are present, for the second *t* must be a preformative. If you do not understand the logic here, you need much more study of the points covered. ת must be geminate, *tt*. Conv. *wāw* of this form only stands before impf., therefore *t*— indicates 21/22 form. First *radical* (שׂ) is doubled; Table 7 VDC indicates that yiC^2aC is G20 of NCC. Verb is therefore *nś'* 'to lift up, carry' (v.5375). (b) *ḥéseḏ* is a very rich word (v.2618), but here it simply means 'favor'; idiom 'to take up favor, to be liked.' (c) 1:17[6]

וַיְבַהֵל [3]—Cf. R.1b. *way(y)-* tells us what? §22.13. Preformative with shewa tells us what? §28.21. Vowel pattern *yᵉ-a-ē-* tells us what? §28.21. Why no dagesh in 2d rad.? R.10a. Look at Table 4 VDC. Identify as Dc20 of CGC. Why no compensatory lengthening? §15.1411. בלה D 'to hasten' (v.926).

אֶת־תַּמְרוּקֶיהָ וְאֶת־מָנוֹתֶיהָ [4]—(a-b) 2:3[10]. What suffix here? §23.1211. (d) *mānāʰ* 'part, portion' (4490 13/3). Note fps *-ôṯê* –וֹתֵי– §25.54.

לָתֶת לָהּ [5]—(a) לָ|תֶת prep. + G65 of נתן. This is difficult, so it is best to memorize לָתֶת 'to give.' *nᵉṯin (G65) > *tin + t (§13.513) > *tint > *titt (R.11) > *tiṯ (R.6a) > tēṯ (R.13a). For shift of accent, §17.35. (b) Pron. + s1, indir. obj.

וְאֵת שֶׁבַע הַנְּעָרוֹת [6]—(a) 2d compound obj. after וַיְבַהֵל, 'to hasten (1) her detergents and her portions, and (2) the seven maidens....' (b) Cf. 1:10[6]. Here the noun is f. so the num. adj. has the "masc." form, §36.141.

הָרְאֻיוֹת לָתֶת־לָהּ [7]—(a) *hā* + *rᵉʾûyy* + *ôṯ*. *rāʾûy* is Gp50 of CCY, §27.63, §29.71. The pl. may double the *yôḏ* (also *rᵉʾûyôṯ*, BDB 906). The pass. of 'to see' is 'to be seen, to seem, to appear'; here 'seemly,' modifying נְעָרוֹת. (b-c) 2:9[5].

וַיְשַׁנֶּהָ וְאֶת־נַעֲרוֹתֶיהָ [8]—(a) Can this be conv. *wāw*? R.1b. *y*[e]*šannê* + *hā,* §23.122. Preformative with shewa, 2d rad. doubled, it must be D20/40. The 3d rad. lost, it must be CCY. If you don't know why, go back over your notes on verbs in your notebook. Dc20s1 of *šny* G 'to double,' D 'to remove' (v.8138). (b) 2d compound obj.: 'he removed (l) her and (2) her maidens. Note form of suffix; on verb it is accusative, on noun genitive.

לְטוֹב בֵּית הַנָּשִׁים׃ [9]—(a) 'to the good of' = 'to the best (part) of.' On superlative, §36.3252.

2:10 לֹא־הִגִּידָה אֶסְתֵּר [1]—(a) Neg. adv., negating either a following word or a clause. (b) *higgîḏā*[h]: *-ā*[h] could be an 11 ending of CCY, §29.71. hiC– could be H perf., §28.31. For hic²îc, Table 7 VDC, which identifies form as H10 of NCC. The ָה then must be 3fs (11), and correct parse is H11 of *ngd* H 'to declare, tell, proclaim' (v.5046). (c) Subj. of verb.

אֶת־עַמָּהּ וְאֶת־מוֹלַדְתָּהּ [2]—Note the compound obj. (a-b) and (c-d). (b) *ʿamm* + s1, 'her people.' (d) *môladt* + s1; *môladt* > *môle̱det* < **mawladt,* WCC. The form can be parsed as H51 of *yld,* but it is listed as a noun 'kindred' (v.4137) from **wld* > *yld* 'to bear, give birth'

כִּי מָרְדֳּכַי צִוָּה עָלֶיהָ [3]—(a) Causal, 1:17[1]. (b) 2:5[3]. (c) Note וָּ: the ָ tells us that וּ is *wāw* with strong dagesh, hence *ṣiwwā*[h], cf. §11.433. Then *-ā*[h] cannot be an 11 morpheme, hence it must be 10 of CCY, Table 6 VDC, §29.71. cic²ā[h] must be D10 of CCY (note that ָה is for *all* 10 morphemes in CCY, G10, D10, H10, N10). *ṣwy* צוה 'to give charge/command' (v.6680). (d) The verb does not take direct object of the person: 'Mordecai gave charge to her.'

אֲשֶׁר לֹא־תַגִּיד׃ [4]—(a) Introduces indirect discourse. (b) לֹא + impf. is a strong prohibition. (c) *taggîḏ,* cf. 2:10[1]. Here *pattāḥ* under preformative may be a sign of H20/40. —ת is 21/22/41/42. tac²îc, Table 7 VDC, must be H21/22; tac²ēc would be H41/42, cf. *yap̄qēḏ,* 2:3[1]. 'that she should not declare.'

In view of the upcoming exam, you should use this occasion to review verbs. If you are weak in any particular area(s), now is the time to work specifically. Can you identify the following?

כָּבַב	יְכֹבֵב	תְּכֻבַּב	תְּכֻבֶּבְנָה
יַעֲכֹב	יֹאכֵב	כֹּבֵב	כְּבֹב
לְכַבֵּב	מַכְבִּיב	נִכְבַּב	נִכְבָּב
לְכַבּוֹת	בְּכָבְכֶם	כָּבַבְתָּ	כְּבַבְתֶּם
וַיֵּכֶב	וַיִּיכַב	כָּבוֹב	

Learn the basic words in Group 20.

26

Purpose: To review the student's progress to this point
Materials: Esther 1:1–2:10

The second hour examination should be given at this point, and it should deal mainly with the verb. Elements of phonology that are significant for verb morphology, noun morphemes that are used on participles, and similar material, will be included.

Read: §§30.12ff, 30.33–.3394, 30.38–.382.
Read: §§32., .11, .12, .31, .35, .38, .4, .5, .51, .52.
Read *carefully* §32.53.

Now, let's get the morphology in hand.
Read: §§27., .11, .1111, .1112, .1121, .1131, .1134.
Read §§27.114, .211; *memorize* §27.21 and §27.31.
Read: §§27.115, .1153, §§28., 28.1, and work carefully on Paradigm V-1.

Read: §§28.2, .21; §§28.3, .31; §§28.4, .42, .421
Read: §§29., .01, .02.

This review should be fairly meaningful to you, since you have encountered the forms and meanings in the last 12 lessons. You will have to review many more times to gain an ability to handle the verb with facility. There is no substitute for careful analysis and observation. You should havenseparate pages for various types of verbs, and you should have all verbs recorded and arranged to show **similarities and differences. You should also be studying the synoptic paradigms in the *Handbook*.**

You should be able to answer questions like the following:

1. Identify the following preformatives and sufformatives: —י, —א, וּ—, וּ—י, הָ—, הָ— (only 2 other consonants present), —תּ, תֶּם—, תָה— (only 2 other consonants present), נָה—תּ, תָּ—.

2. Know the operation of Rules 1a, 1b, 2a, 9, 10a-f, 11, 13b, 15, 18, 20.

3. Know the meanings of technical terms used in connection with the study of the Heb. verb.

4. Know the thematic vowels and their general significance in the perf. (CaCaC, CaCiC, CaCuC), and in the imperf. (yaCCuC, yiCCaC, yaCCiC).

5. Parse the following, using the indicators (§27.151, reprinted below).

אָכַל	דִּבֵּר	הַבְדִּיל	נִקְדַּשׁ
אָכַלְתָּ	צִוָּה	הִמְשַׁלְנוּ	תִּגְנֹב
יִרְגַּז	יִצְדַּק	תְּקַבֵּץ	גָּלְתָה
תִּיטַב	יַעֲבֹר	תִּתֵּן	תֵּצֵא
מַשְׁלִימִים	אָחוּז	מְדַבְּרִים	מְבַקְשׁוֹת
הָשְׁלַךְ	סֵפֶר	גֹּלֶה	שָׁמוֹעַ

Know all the basic vocabulary in Groups 1-20.

TABLE OF INDICATORS

Stem	Conjugation	PGN	Perf.	Impf.	Impv.	Juss./ Cohort.	Ptcp.	Inf.	Pron. Suf.	PGN
G	qtl	3 ms	10	20	--	40	50 m.s.a.	60 inf.abs.	s0	3 ms
Gp	qtl pass.	3 fs	11	21	--	41	51 f.s.a.		s1	3 fs
N	nqtl	2 ms	12	22	32	42	52 m.s.c.		s2	2 ms
D	qttl	2 fs	13	23	33	43	53 f.s.c.		s3	2 fs
Dp	qttl pass.	1 cs	14	24		44			s4	1 cs
HtD	htqttl									
HtDp	" pass.	3 mp	15	25	--	45	55 m.p.a.	65 inf.cstr.	s5	3 mp
H	hqtl	3 fp	16	26	--	46	56 f.p.a.		s6	3 fp
Hp	hqtl pass.	2 mp	17	27	37	47	57 m.p.c.		s7	2 mp
HtŠ		2 fp	18	28	38	48	58 f.p.c.		s8	2 fp
		1 cp	19	29	--	49			s9	1 cp

c *after stem indicator and before the number,* indicates *wāw* conversive; *wāw* conj. not indicated.
s *after the number* plus suffix indicator indicates pron. suf.
e.g. וַיִּתְּנָהּ is identified as Gc20s1 of נתן, which is much simpler than writing 'third masculine singular, imperfect, of נתן, with 3 fem. sing. suf. and *wāw* conversive.'

Those who wait on YHWH shall renew strength,
they shall ascend on wings like the eagles,
they shall run and not grow weary,
they shall walk and not grow faint.

וְקֹוֵי יהוה יַחֲלִיפוּ כֹחַ
יַעֲלוּ אֵבֶר כַּנְּשָׁרִים
יָרוּצוּ וְלֹא יִיגָעוּ
יֵלְכוּ וְלֹא יִיעָפוּ׃

(Isaiah 40:31)

27

Purpose: To study the numerals
Materials: Esther 2:11-13

11 וּבְכָל־
יוֹם וָיוֹם מָרְדֳּכַי מִתְהַלֵּךְ לִפְנֵי חֲצַר בֵּית־הַנָּשִׁים לָדַעַת
12 אֶת־שְׁלוֹם אֶסְתֵּר וּמַה־יֵּעָשֶׂה בָּהּ׃ וּבְהַגִּיעַ תֹּר נַעֲרָה
וְנַעֲרָה לָבוֹא ׀ אֶל־הַמֶּלֶךְ אֲחַשְׁוֵרוֹשׁ מִקֵּץ הֱיוֹת לָהּ כְּדָת
הַנָּשִׁים שְׁנֵים עָשָׂר חֹדֶשׁ כִּי כֵּן יִמְלְאוּ יְמֵי מְרוּקֵיהֶן שִׁשָּׁה
חֳדָשִׁים בְּשֶׁמֶן הַמֹּר וְשִׁשָּׁה חֳדָשִׁים בַּבְּשָׂמִים וּבְתַמְרוּקֵי
13 הַנָּשִׁים׃ וּבָזֶה הַנַּעֲרָה בָּאָה אֶל־הַמֶּלֶךְ אֵת כָּל־אֲשֶׁר
תֹּאמַר יִנָּתֵן לָהּ לָבוֹא עִמָּהּ מִבֵּית הַנָּשִׁים עַד־בֵּית הַמֶּלֶךְ׃

2:11 וּבְכָל־יוֹם וָיוֹם[1]—(a-c) This is distributive, 'each day.' 1:8[6], 1:22[34]. Note the vowel: וָיוֹם. It does not always lengthen in near-open with the conj.

מָרְדֳּכַי מִתְהַלֵּךְ[2]—(a) 2:5[3]. (b) *mit̠hallēk̠,* note מת– and –ל–, Table 1 VDC. For HtD, read §§28.5, .51, .511. Preformative –מ is often the sign of a ptcp. (not G). הלך 'to walk' (v.1980), in HtD 'to walk back and forth.'

לִפְנֵי חֲצַר בֵּית־הַנָּשִׁים[3]—(a) 1:11[2]. (b) Note vowels; what should the quality tell us? 1:5[10]. (c-d) You should know this.

לָדַעַת אֶת־שְׁלוֹם אֶסְתֵּר[4]—(a) l^e + *dáʿat̠*. Cf. 1:2[3]. ת– could be "ballast," §13.513. If so, there are only 2 rads., cf. Table 10 VDC. The form is WCC or YCC with apheresis, §13.511, and anaptyxis, §15.61. Your clues are the prep. l^e- and the *-t,* §29.322. ידע 'to know' (v. 3045). With –ל the inf. cstr. often expresses purpose, §38.54. (c) *šālôm* 'peace, welfare' (v. 7965). What does the reduced vowel tell us? §25.42f. (b-d) Noun clause, obj. of inf. cstr.. 'in order to know Esther's welfare.'

וּמַה־יֵּעָשֶׂה בָּהּ׃[5]—(a) Indef. pron., §21.5, 'whatever' (v. 4100), subj. of following verb. (b) יֵעָשֶׂה *yēʿāśê*^{h}, note dagesh, §13.36. ה–ֶ could be 20 of CCY, §29.71. Learn this *now.* Guttural in 1st rad. resists gemination, with compensatory lengthening (R.10a), hence vowels indicate N stem, §28.42; Table 4 VDC also identifies as N20 of GCC. (a-c) Noun cl., 2d compound obj. of *dáʿat̠* 'to know ... whatever would be done with her.' Note that in Heb., since the subjunctive has disappeared, you must get the mood from the context (§27.1132).

2:12 וּבְהַגִּיעַ תֹּר נַעֲרָה וְנַעֲרָה[1]—(a) *û* + b^e + *haggî*^{aʿ}. –הַ could be H stem indicator; if so, only 2 rads. are present, 1st geminate, suggesting NCC, §28.31. A prep. occurs on a verb form only in the inf. cstr., hence H65. Table 7 VDC. Read §15.4321. נגע H 'to arrive, reach' (v.5060). (b) *tôr* 'turn' (8447 4/2). (c-d) Distributive, §36.15. 'In the reaching of the turn of maiden and maiden' = 'when each girl's turn arrives.'

לָבוֹא[2]—(a) 1:12[2].

מִקֵּץ הֱיוֹת לָהּ[3]—(a) *min* + *qēṣ* 'end' (v.7093), cstr., note *ṣērê*, §15.223. (b) וֹ– could be fpa/c or 65 of CCY, Table 6 VDC. *hĕyôṯ* is G65 of *hyʰ* היה 'to be.' 'From the end of being to her ... 12 months' = 'at the end of her 12-month period.'

כְּדָת הַנָּשִׁים שְׁנֵים עָשָׂר חֹדֶשׁ [4]—(a) 1:8[1]; *dâṯ* should not reduce in cstr. (R. 2a), cf. 9:13[4]. (b-c) Numeral, §26.2, '12,' composed of (b) *šnêm,* the form of '2' used in '12'; note the initial cluster, §16.351, (v.8147); and *'āśār* the form of '10' used in the teens (v.6235b). Read §26.25. (d) *ḥōḏeš* 'month' (v.2320); CuCC-type noun, §24.21. Note that the sg. form is used with numbers from 10 up (1:1[12]), §36.142.

כִּי כֵּן יִמְלְאוּ [5]—(a-b) 1:8[3]. (c) וּ—יִ = ? –ְ = ? מלא, cf. 1:5[1] (v.4390). 'For thus they fulfilled'; subj. follows.

יְמֵי מְרוּקֵיהֶן [6]—(a)1:1[2], §24.212; pl. of *yôm* is irregular, as if from **yᵉwāmîm* > *yāmîm* (v.3117). (b) Cf. 2:3[10], note difference; *mārûq* 'scouring, rubbing' (4795 1/1).

שִׁשָּׁה חֳדָשִׁים בְּשֶׁמֶן הַמֹּר [7]—(a) *šiššāʰ* '6' (v.8337), §26.234. The 'fem.' form with -*āʰ* is used with masc. noun, §36.141. (b) 2:12[4](d), *ḥōḏeš,* pl. *ḥŏḏāšîm,* Paradigm N-3. R. 10b. (c) *bᵉ-* + *šémen* 'oil (vegetable)' (v. 8081), cstr., but segolates do not reduce in cstr., §15.232. (d) *ham* + *mōr* 'myrrh' (4753 12/1), Akk. *murru,* Gk. *μύῤῥα*.

וְשִׁשָּׁה חֳדָשִׁים בַּבְּשָׂמִים וּבְתַמְרוּקֵי הַנָּשִׁים׃ [8]—(a,b) 2:17[7]. (c) *bᵉ-* + *hab* + *bᵉśāmîm,* pl. of בֶּשֶׂם 'balsam' (v. 1314). (d) 2:3[10].

2:13 וּבָזֶה הַנַּעֲרָה בָּאָה[1]—(a) *û* + *ḇā* + *zêʰ*, §21.2. 'and in this (manner).' (c) Note carefully: *bā'āʰ* is G11, and *bā'āʰ* is G51, cf. 1:17[7]. Learn this *now.* 'The maiden (is) entering.'

אֵת כָּל־אֲשֶׁר תֹּאמַר[2]—(a) The grammar is distorted, for the noun cl. which begins as object becomes the subject of the main verb, possibly by attraction to the nearer verb: '*all* that she shall say *shall be given.*' (d) *tô'mar* < **ta'mir,* ya'CiC (R. 10d). —ת = ? Parse it.

יִנָּתֵן לָהּ [3]—(a) Note accent, §17.35. Normalize it *yinnāṯēn,* 1st rad. doubled, sign of N stem, Table 2 VDC. N20 of *ntn,* 2:3[10].

לָבוֹא עִמָּהּ [4]—(a) 1:12[2]. (b) *'imm-,* 2:6[3].

מִבֵּית הַנָּשִׁים עַד־בֵּית הַמֶּלֶךְ׃ [5]—(b) Note dagesh in בּ. What does this suggest? R. 11. (c) Cf. 1:5[7].

Learn the basic words in Group 21.

28

Purpose: To study the participle
Materials: Esther 2:14-15

14 בָּעֶרֶב ׀ הִיא בָאָה וּבַבֹּקֶר הִיא שָׁבָה אֶל־בֵּית הַנָּשִׁים
שֵׁנִי אֶל־יַד שַׁעַשְׁגַז סְרִיס הַמֶּלֶךְ שֹׁמֵר הַפִּילַגְשִׁים לֹא־
תָבוֹא עוֹד אֶל־הַמֶּלֶךְ כִּי אִם־חָפֵץ בָּהּ הַמֶּלֶךְ וְנִקְרְאָה
טו בְשֵׁם׃ וּבְהַגִּיעַ תֹּר־אֶסְתֵּר בַּת־אֲבִיחַיִל ׀ דֹּד מָרְדֳּכַי אֲשֶׁר
לָקַח־לוֹ לְבַת לָבוֹא אֶל־הַמֶּלֶךְ לֹא בִקְשָׁה דָּבָר כִּי אִם
אֶת־אֲשֶׁר יֹאמַר הֵגַי סְרִיס־הַמֶּלֶךְ שֹׁמֵר הַנָּשִׁים וַתְּהִי
אֶסְתֵּר נֹשֵׂאת חֵן בְּעֵינֵי כָּל־רֹאֶיהָ׃

2:14 בָּעֶרֶב ׀ הִיא בָּאָה [1]—(a) For b^e- + *hā* + *'éreḇ* 'evening' (v.6153), with syncopation §13.521, and compensatory lengthening §15.14. For | §11.72. Anaptyxis, §15.6. Noun is GvCC type, §24.211. (b) Pers. pron., §22.2. (c) 1:13[1]; is this G51 or G11? בוֹא, v.935. ָה cannot be a radical, for הִיא is fem., hence there are only 2 rads. The root cannot be CCY, for then we would have תָה– in 11 or ֶֶה in 51. There is no way it can be 1st rad. weak in this form. Therefore it must be CvC. Be sure you can follow the logical steps in indentifying such a form.

וּבַבֹּקֶר הִיא שָׁבָה [2]—(a) Identify the morphemes. Is there a def. art.? The accent is prepositive, §11.571. *bṓqer* 'morning' (v. 1242), is CuCC-type noun, §24.21. (c) *šûḇ* 'to return' (v.7725), CvC verb: G51 and G11 are distinguished by accent, §29.6318. 'In the evening she is entering and in the morning she is returning.'

אֶל־בֵּית הַנָּשִׁים שֵׁנִי [3]—(a-c) You can now do this without help. (d) *šēnî* 'second' (v.8145), an ordinal numeral, §26.32. We would expect a def. art., since בֵּית is def. because of the noun it governs. 'To the second harem.'

אֶל־יַד שַׁעַשְׁגַז סְרִיס הַמֶּלֶךְ [4]—(a-c) Cf. 2:8[6]; note the differences and explain them. (c) Pr. n. 'Shashgaz.' (d-e) You can do.

שֹׁמֵר הַפִּילַגְשִׁים [5]—(a-b) Cf. 2:8[6]. *šômēr,* pattern *-ô-ē-* is G50, §24.24, §27.611. (b) *pîléḡeš* 'concubine' (v.6370), a 4-consonant form, §03.12, §24.28, which has developed similar to a segolate < **pîlagš,* note the pl. When the girl entered the king's house she was בְּתוּלָה; when she returned she was פִּילֶגֶשׁ. She left the (first) house of the women; she returned to the second. She was first under Hegai; later she was under Shaashgaz. With exquisite reserve the story is fully told—yet devoid of sensual details.

לֹא־תָבוֹא עוֹד [6]—(a) 1:17[7]. (b) *tāḇô',* —ת can be 21/22 or 41/42. Table 9 VDC suggests G20 of CWC, but context requires 21. (c) *'ôḏ* 'again' (v.5750), modifying the verb, §35.2. 'She shall not enter again.'

כִּי אִם־חָפֵץ בָּהּ הַמֶּלֶךְ [7]—(a-b) After a neg. *kî 'im* usually means 'except' (v.3588). (b) *ḥāpēṣ,* pattern is G10/50 of CaCiC, a stative verb. Read §27.23f, and note well §27.232. חפץ 'to delight, take pleasure' (v.2654), followed by prep. –בְּ, see (d). (e) Subject. 'Except the king was delighted with her.'

וְנִקְרְאָה בְשֵׁם׃ [8]—(a) נ—ָה, *n—ā*^{h}, with 3 rads. between, therefore most likely N stem perf. 3ms, or N11 of *qr'* 'to call' (v. 7121). *w*^{e}- could be simple or conversive, §27.117. If we read, 'unless the king was delighted with her and she was called by name,' it is simple *wāw.* The Masoretic note calls attention to ָ, but no good reason is given. (b) 2:5[3]. Note application of R.16 in *š*^{e}*mô,* 2:5[3]. *b*^{e}- 'with, in,' here is better translated 'by.'

2:15 וּבְהַגִּיעַ תֹּר־אֶסְתֵּר בַּת־אֲבִיחַיִל | דֹּד מָרְדֳּכַי [1]—(a) 2:12[1]; go over the analysis again. (b-c) Cf. 2:12[1]. Now it's Esther's turn. (d-e) Name formula, like Swed. *Svensdotter.* (f-g) Cf. 2:7[3].

אֲשֶׁר לָקַח־לוֹ לְבַת [2]—(a-c) Cf. 2:7[8]. (b) *lā́qaḥ;* CāCaC is G10 pattern; accent has shifted because of proximity of next accent, §17.35. (a) is obj. of verb, 'whom he took to him for a daughter.'

לָבוֹא אֶל־הַמֶּלֶךְ [3]—Cf. 2:12[2].

לֹא בִקְשָׁה דָּבָר [4]—(b) *biq*^{e}*šā*^{h}. We see 4 consonants; *b*^{e}- could be prep., but only on 65 and the pattern is wrong. *–ā*^{h} could be 11 sufformative. The *i*-vowel with 1st rad. suggests D stem, but there is no gemination of 2d rad. Is there a reason? R.1b. *biqq*^{e}*šā*^{h} is D11 of *bqš,* 'he sought' (v.1245), cf. 2:2[3]. 'She did not seek a thing.'

כִּי אִם אֶת־אֲשֶׁר יֹאמַר [5]—(a-b) 2:14[7](a-b). (c-d) Noun clause, obj. of verb which is understood from previous clause. (e) *yô'mar* < **ya'mir,* 'CC. Cf. 2:13[2](d). What is the difference between the two forms? For the following words, cf. 2:8[6] or 2:3[8].

וַתְּהִי אֶסְתֵּר נֹשֵׂאת חֵן [6]—(a) Cf. וַיְהִי in 1:1[1]; what is וַתְּהִי? Cf. Rule 1b. (c) G51 of CC' verb. Normally CôCēCt > CôCéCe̱t, but the א quiesces > CôCē't *nôśē't̠.* For *nś',* 2:9[2]. (d) *ḥēn* 'favor, grace, acceptance' (v.2580).

בְּעֵינֵי כָּל־רֹאֶיהָ׃ [7]—(a) 1:21[2]. (c) *rô'ē*^{y} + *hā. CôCē*^{h} is G50 pattern of CCY. Learn it *now.* ֶיהָ is masc. pl. of the noun, and 3fs suf. of the pronoun, 'the (ones) seeing her.' A ptcp., particularly when definite, often serves as a relative clause, 'in the eyes of all *who saw her.*'

Learn the words in Group 22.

Love your neighbor as yourself. וְאָהַבְתָּ לְרֵעֲךָ כָּמוֹךָ.
Lev. 19:18

29

Purpose: To study the *wāw*-conversive
Materials: Esther 2:16-18

16 וַתִּלָּקַח אֶסְתֵּר אֶל־
הַמֶּלֶךְ אֲחַשְׁוֵרוֹשׁ אֶל־בֵּית מַלְכוּתוֹ בַּחֹדֶשׁ הָעֲשִׂירִי הוּא־
17 חֹדֶשׁ טֵבֵת בִּשְׁנַת־שֶׁבַע לְמַלְכוּתוֹ׃ וַיֶּאֱהַב הַמֶּלֶךְ אֶת־
אֶסְתֵּר מִכָּל־הַנָּשִׁים וַתִּשָּׂא־חֵן וָחֶסֶד לְפָנָיו מִכָּל־הַבְּתוּלוֹת
18 וַיָּשֶׂם כֶּתֶר־מַלְכוּת בְּרֹאשָׁהּ וַיַּמְלִיכֶהָ תַּחַת וַשְׁתִּי׃ וַיַּעַשׂ
הַמֶּלֶךְ מִשְׁתֶּה גָדוֹל לְכָל־שָׂרָיו וַעֲבָדָיו אֵת מִשְׁתֵּה
אֶסְתֵּר וַהֲנָחָה לַמְּדִינוֹת עָשָׂה וַיִּתֵּן מַשְׂאֵת כְּיַד הַמֶּלֶךְ׃

2:16 וַתִּלָּקַח אֶסְתֵּר [1]—(a) Work out the analysis and then look at 2:8[5]. Note the use of *wāw* to invert the tense significance. Read §27.117f. When parsing a form with conversive *wāw,* you identify the *form* (here impf.) and not the meaning (here past time). Use a 'c' before the symbol: Nc21. You should be able to do the rest to the next note.

בַּחֹדֶשׁ הָעֲשִׂירִי [2]—(a) Is there a def. art.? R.10a. §15.1411. 2:12[7]. (b) *hā* + *'ăśîrî:* the pattern —*î*–*î* suggests an ordinal number, §26.32. עשׂר gives us the idea of 'ten,' hence ordinal '10th' (v.6224). Note concord, §36.11. Note word order, §26.87. 'In the month the tenth' = 'in the 10th month.'

הוּא־חֹדֶשׁ טֵבֵת [3]—(a) Demon. pron., §21.2. Noun clause, 'that (is) the month Tebet,' §31.122. (b) Cstr., but a segolate, §15.232. (c) Pr.n. 'Tebet,' 10th month counting from Nisan (Mar.), hence about January. Since the pr. n. is definite, the noun in cstr. is def., §36.3121.

בִּשְׁנַת־שֶׁבַע לְמַלְכוּתוֹ׃ [4]—(a) b^e + $š^e na\underline{t}$, R.19. $šānā^h$ 'year' (v.8141). Note carefully §26.871. (b) 1:1[9]. 'In the year of 7' = ? (c) If Ahasuerus = Xerxes I, this would be 479 BC, but scholars are divided on this identification.

2:17 וַיֶּאֱהַב [1]—Note *wāw* and strong dagesh, §22.13. This can only be on the impf., and always converts the meaning of impf. to that of the corresponding perf. —י 3ms, vowel pattern is yiCCaC of 'CC. אהב 'to love' (v. 157). This verb is often pointed אָהֵב, which is stative vocalization, and G20 form agrees with this (cf. Barth's law, §27.331). The theory is good, but formal statives (i.e. having the form of a stative) often, as here, take direct objects.

מִכָּל־הַנָּשִׁים [2]—מִן of comparison, cf. 1:7[3], 1:19[11]. 'More than all the women.'

וַתִּשָּׂא־חֵן וָחֶסֶד [3]—(a) 2:9[2]. What kind of *wāw*? §27.117. (b) 2:15[6](d). (c) 2:9[2].

מִכָּל־הַבְּתוּלוֹת [4]—(a) מִן of comparison, 2:17[2]. (b) 2:3[4](d). What difference(s) do you see in the two forms?

וַיָּ֣שֶׂם כֶּֽתֶר־מַלְכוּת֙ בְּרֹאשָׁ֔הּ[5]—(a) Note *wāw*. Note shift of accent, Rule 27. The impf. without conv. *wāw* would be *yāśîm* יָשִׂים, CîC verb. G20 and H20 fall together in this type verb, §§29.6, .64, .6413. Note especially §29.641. שִׂים 'to place' (v. 7760). (b-c) 1:11[3]. (d) בְּ|רֹאשׁ|ָהּ, *rôš* 'head' (v. 7218). 'And he put the royal crown on her head.'

וַיַּמְלִיכֶ֖הָ תַּ֥חַת וַשְׁתִּֽי׃[6]—(a) Note *wāw*. Preformative with *a* (—ַי) tells us what? Long *î* after 2d rad. (–ִי—) is a clue to what? Table 3, VDC. Note the connecting vowel; cf. Table H. The root *mlk* gives the idea of reigning, being king; what would the H stem mean? (b-c) 2:4[4].

2:18 וַיַּ֨עַשׂ[1]— Work it out. Note accent: what does it suggest? When you get stuck, try 1:21[3].

מִשְׁתֶּ֣ה גָד֗וֹל[2]—(a) 1:3[5]. (b) 1:5[7]. Does the adj. agree in GNS? Then how is it used? §36.11. For the next phrase, 1:3[67].

אֵ֖ת מִשְׁתֵּ֣ה אֶסְתֵּ֑ר[4]—(a) Why is אֵת used here and not before 2:18[2]? (b-c) Note ֵה– and see Table F. Cf. 1:9[3].

וַהֲנָחָ֤ה לַמְּדִינוֹת֙ עָשָׂ֔ה[5]—(a) *hănāḥāʰ* 'holiday' (2010 1/1), root *nwḥ* 'to rest,' an H-formation noun, §24.33, obj. of verb (c)—note word order. (c) ָה–: G51 of CvC or G10 of CCY? The form could be either (but not G11 of CvC because of accent), so unless you recognize the word you may have to look up both עוּשׂ and עָשָׂה, and fit the proper word with the context. Note that the *wāw* conv. *cannot* be used unless the verb stands *first* in the clause.

וַיִּתֵּ֥ן מַשְׂאֵ֖ת כְּיַ֥ד הַמֶּֽלֶךְ׃[6]—(a) Can יִתֵּן be D10 of *ytn*? §27.117. What else could cause gemination of ? Table 7 VDC. Cf. 1:19[9]—is there a difference? (b) *maś'ēṯ* (v.4864), from *nś'*, usually means an 'uprising' or something taken by force or authority, but here (and Gen. 43:34; Jer. 40:5) it must mean something like 'gift.' (c-d) 1:7[5].

Learn the basic words in Group 23.

Analyze the following:

		וַיִּתֵּן	2:18[1]
וַיֹּאמֶר	1:13[1]	וַתִּשָּׂא	2:9[2]
וַיֹּאמְרוּ	2:2[1]	וַיִּשְׁלַח	1:22[1]
וַיִּיטַב	1:21[1]	וַיִּקְצֹף	1:12[5]
וַתִּיטַב	2:9[1]	וַיֶּאֱהַב	2:17[1]
וַיְהִי	1:1[1]	וַיַּעַשׂ	1:21[3]
וַתְּהִי	2:15[6]	וַיָּשֶׂם	2:17[5]
וַיְבַהֵל	2:9[3]	וַיְשַׁנֶּהָ	2:9[8]
וַתְּמָאֵן	1:12[1]	וַיַּמְלִיכֶהָ	2:17[6]

30

Purpose: To translate infinitives and participles
Materials: Esther 2:19-21

וּבְהִקָּבֵץ בְּתוּלוֹת שֵׁנִית וּמָרְדֳּכַי יֹשֵׁב בְּשַׁעַר־הַמֶּלֶךְ׃ 19
אֵין אֶסְתֵּר מַגֶּדֶת מוֹלַדְתָּהּ וְאֶת־עַמָּהּ כַּאֲשֶׁר צִוָּה עָלֶיהָ כ
מָרְדֳּכָי וְאֶת־מַאֲמַר מָרְדֳּכַי אֶסְתֵּר עֹשָׂה כַּאֲשֶׁר הָיְתָה
בְאָמְנָה אִתּוֹ׃ בַּיָּמִים הָהֵם וּמָרְדֳּכַי יֹשֵׁב בְּשַׁעַר־ 21
הַמֶּלֶךְ קָצַף בִּגְתָן וָתֶרֶשׁ שְׁנֵי־סָרִיסֵי הַמֶּלֶךְ מִשֹּׁמְרֵי הַסַּף
וַיְבַקְשׁוּ לִשְׁלֹחַ יָד בַּמֶּלֶךְ אֲחַשְׁוֵרֹשׁ׃

2:19 וּבְהִקָּבֵץ בְּתוּלוֹת שֵׁנִית [1]— *û* + *bᵉ* + *hiqqāḇēṣ*: Note that –ה is not H-stem. 1st rad. doubled, clue to N (VDC 2). –הִנּ is N32/65; prep. –בּ tells us it is 65, temporal, §35.421. (b) 2:2[4]. (c) 2:14[3]. The fem. form (note ת–) is used as an adverb, 'a second time.' There is no reason why this word should present a problem (see older commentaries). Under the polygamous system in vogue, the king must have ordered a collection of virgins several times during his reign. A study of the commentaries at this point, as at many others, should convince any serious student (1) that he should learn to handle the text himself, and not depend on others, and (2) that he should let the text speak for itself.

וּמָרְדֳּכַי יֹשֵׁב בְּשַׁעַר־הַמֶּלֶךְ׃ [2]— –וּ tells us what? §27.61f., 1:2[3];1:14[6]. (c) *šá'ar* 'gate' (v.8179). Does short vowel reduce in cstr.? Why not? §15.232. RSV: 'When the virgins were gathered together the second time, Mordecai was sitting at the king's gate.' *bᵉ*- + inf. cstr. 'in the being gathered to' = 'when (were) gathered.' RSV does not give right impression, however. A new phase of the story is being introduced, and what Mordecai was doing is an incidental part of it.

2:20 אֵין אֶסְתֵּר [1]–(a) 1:8[2]. אֵין usually is the neg. part. used with ptcps. 'nonexistence of, is not' (v.369). (b) Note accent; we would join this with next word. Compare this construction with 2:10, *lô'* + H11.

מַגֶּדֶת [2]—Fem. of G ptcp. (G51) is often formed by adding -*t* ת–, hence *maggîd* + *t* > **maggidt* (R. 2a) > *maggéḏeṯ* (R. 6b). –מַ (with *paṭṭāḥ*) is a strong clue for H50, §27.61, §28.31. If we remove ת—מ, what are the 3 rads.? (VDC 8). נגד 2:10[1]. 'Esther (was) not making known, telling'—i.e. she had not done so, and still was not doing so.

מוֹלַדְתָּהּ וְאֶת־עַמָּהּ [3]—(a) a:10[2]. We would expect אֵת before it, cf. 2:10[2]. (c) 2:10[2].

כַּאֲשֶׁר צִוָּה עָלֶיהָ מָרְדֳּכָי [4]—(a) 'according as.' (b) Parse first, then 2:10[3]. Does this verb take a dir. obj.? (d) Note position of subj., cf. 2:10[3]. The student with ethical sensitivity need not be offended by this statement. Unless asked, Esther would not be required to offer the information. Furthermore, in parts of Iran, even to the present, the custom of maintaining a pretense (*kitmân* or *taqiyya*) is practised for the sake of peace. Oftentimes, both parties are fully aware of the true situation, yet they observe the custom. From Ahasuerus' reaction to Esther's "revelation" in Chap. 7, we may suspect that this ancient custom was even then being observed.

וְאֶת־מַאֲמַר [5]—(a) Obj. well before the verb. (b) §24.33, 1:15[6].

עֹשָׂה [6]—Note *ô* after 1st rad., §24.23f, §27.61. 1:5[3]. Ptcp. expresses continued activity: 'the word of Mordecai she was observing.'

כַּאֲשֶׁר הָיְתָה [7]—(a) 2:20[4]. (b) תָה–, §29.71. Form here is used like our perf.: 'as she had been (doing).'

בְאָמְנָה אִתּוֹ׃ [8]—(a) Note carefully! Is it *ḇ*^{e}*'ām*^{e}*nā*^{h} or *ḇ*^{e}*'omnā*^{h}? How can you tell? §11.584. Cf. 1:1[3], 1:17[1]. 2:7[1]. אָמְנָה is fem. of G65, 'bringing up, tutelage' (545 1/1) However, it is possible that ָה is s1, for ָה > ָה in some instances, cf. *Ges.* §91*e*. (b) *'ēṯ, 'ittô* is to be distinguished from *'ēṯ, 'ôṯô* (cf. v.853 and v.854).

2:21 בַּיָּמִים הָהֵם [1]— This can be used of a reference to the past, or to the future. In the latter usage it is often an eschatological formula.

וּמָרְדֳּכַי יוֹשֵׁב בְּשַׁעַר־הַמֶּלֶךְ [2]—(b) Written full, —וֹ– should give you no trouble. Cf. 2:19[2]. The ptcp. can be used for repeated as well as continuous activity: 'M. sat there every day.'

קָצַף בִּגְתָן וָתֶרֶשׁ [3]—(a) – ַ ָ should be easy to recognize, §27.22. Cf. 1:12[5]. Verb in 3ms with compound subj. is permitted when verb precedes, §33.121. (b,c) Pr. nouns, 'Bigthan, Teresh.' Note vocalization of –וָ before accent.

שְׁנֵי־סָרִיסֵי הַמֶּלֶךְ [4]— With the help of 1:10[6], 1:5[9], and 2:14[4], you should be able to do this.

מִשֹּׁמְרֵי הַסַּף [5]— (a) Cf. 2:3[9]. What is the ending here? (b) *sap̄* (R.14) 'threshold, doorway' (v.5592).

וַיְבַקְשׁוּ לִשְׁלֹחַ יָד [6]— (a) 2:15[4]. (b) 1:22[1] *š*^{e}*lō*^{a}*ḥ yāḏ b*^{e}- is an idiom, 'to lay a hand on, stretch out a hand against, do harm to.' Finish the verse.

Learn the words in Group 24.

מַה שֶּׁשָּׂנוּא עָלֶיךָ אַל תַּעֲשֶׂה לַחֲבֵרְךָ.

What is hateful to you, don't do to your neighbor.'

(Hillel)

31

Purpose: To study the Imperfect
Materials: Esther 2:22-23

22 וַיִּוָּדַע הַדָּבָר
לְמָרְדֳּכַי וַיַּגֵּד לְאֶסְתֵּר הַמַּלְכָּה וַתֹּאמֶר אֶסְתֵּר לַמֶּלֶךְ
23 בְּשֵׁם מָרְדֳּכָי׃ וַיְבֻקַּשׁ הַדָּבָר וַיִּמָּצֵא וַיִּתָּלוּ שְׁנֵיהֶם עַל־
עֵץ וַיִּכָּתֵב בְּסֵפֶר דִּבְרֵי הַיָּמִים לִפְנֵי הַמֶּלֶךְ׃

2:22 וַיִּוָּדַע הַדָּבָר [1]—(a) Note וָּ: since it has a vowel ָ, it cannot be *šûrûq,* but must be *wāw* and strong dagesh, hence *wayyiwwāḏaʿ.* Do you see 3 radicals? What about the first? Does the pattern resemble yaC²āCēC? Why *pattāḥ* under ד? Does CCG have anything to do with it? §29.13. You should know ידע; make it passive. (b) Subj. of verb, 'the matter was known to M.'

וַיַּגֵּד לְאֶסְתֵּר [2]—(a) Do you see 3 radicals? י must be a preformative–why? §22.13. With *a*-vowel, –ַיְ suggests what stem? §28.31. Is the dagesh in גּ light or strong? R.1a. Why is it here? (R.11). H20 יַגִּיד, H40 עֲגֵּד, R.2a. VDC–7. (b) Indir. obj. 'And he told (it) to Esther.'

וַתֹּאמֶר [3]—1:13[1]. 2:2[1]; can you work it out?

בְּשֵׁם [4]—Cstr., but ֵ is not reduced, cf. 2:5[3]. Esther gave Mordecai credit when reporting the plot.

2:23 וַיְבֻקַּשׁ [1]—Note pattern: -ַּ-ֻ-ְיְ; shewa under preformative, probably D; *u*-vowel under 1st rad., passive; entire pattern, positive D-pass. VDC–1. Dpc20. בקשׁ, 2:15[4], 2:2[3]. 'And it was sought.'

וַיִּמָּצֵא [2]—Pattern -ֵ-ָּ-ִיִ should be enough for you to parse it quickly. VDC–2. 1:5[5]. 'And it was found.'

וַיִּתָּלוּ שְׁנֵיהֶם עַל־עֵץ [3]—(a) Note וּ-ָּ-ִיִ, and cf. 2:23[2]. This *could* be Nc25 of a CCY—do you think it is? §29.7, .713. תלה (v.8518) 'to hang.' (b) *šnêhem,* s5 on the word for '2.' 'The two of them were hanged.' (d) *ʿēṣ* 'tree' (v.6086). Historical monuments indicate that death by impaling on a stake was commonly used. תלה may have this meaning.

וַיִּכָּתֵב [4]—Note -ֵ-ָּ-ִיִ: what does it tell you? 2:23[2,3]. Cf. 1:19[4].

בְּסֵפֶר דִּבְרֵי הַיָּמִים לִפְנֵי הַמֶּלֶךְ׃ [5]—(a-c) The journal or day-book of royal records; cf. the title of 1-2 Chronicles, 2 Kgs. 14:28, etc. (d) 'Before,' or possibly 'in the presence of,' so that A. saw it written.

This is a good place to go over your notebook and synthesize your observations of imperf. forms, particularly the N imperfs. that you have seen.

Read through §§20.–20.5.

Read the following:

§§21., .1, .2, .3, .4, .5
§§22., .1, .2, .3, .4, .41
§§23., .1, .121, .122

Review the following:

§§24., .1, .2, .3, .4, .5, .6
§§25., .1, .2, .3, .4, .5
§§30.311, .312

Go over the following:

§§24.21, .215, .22, .221, .23, .24, .25, .26, .27, .28
§§24.3, .31, .33, .4, .5

Learn the words in Group 25.

Analyze the following verbs (using VDC if it helps you):

תָּבוֹא	יֹאמַר	וַיִּמָּצֵא	וַיְבַהֵל	יַעֲבוֹר
תָּבֹא	תֹּאמַר	וַיִּוָּדַע	וַיְבַקְשׁוּ	יֵעָשֶׂה
	תֹּאמַרְנָה	וַתִּלָּקַח	וַיְבַקֵּשׁ	וַיֶּאֱהַב
וַיָּשֶׂם	וַיֹּאמֶר	וַיִּתָּלוּ	וַתְּמָאֵן	וַיִּשְׁלַח
וַיַּעַשׂ	וַיֹּאמְרוּ	יִנָּתֵן	וַיְשַׁנֶּהָ	וַיִּיטַב
תַּגִּיד	וַתֹּאמֶר	תַּגִּיד	וַתְּהִי	וַיִּקְצֹף
		וַיִּכָּתֵב	וַיְהִי	יִמְלְאוּ

Suggested genealogy of Mordecai and Esther

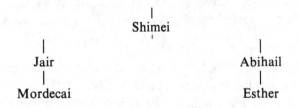

Shimei

Jair — Mordecai

Abihail — Esther

שְׁמַע עֵצָה וְקַבֵּל מוּסָר
לְמַעַן תֶּחְכַּם בְּאַחֲרִיתֶךָ׃
Listen to advice and accept instruction,
that you may gain wisdom for the future.
Proverbs 19:20

Purpose: To introduce the HtŠ-stem
Materials: Esther 3:1-3

ג CAP. III. ג

אַחַ֣ר ׀ הַדְּבָרִ֣ים הָאֵ֗לֶּה גִּדַּל֩ הַמֶּ֨לֶךְ אֲחַשְׁוֵר֜וֹשׁ אֶת־הָמָ֧ן א
בֶּן־הַמְּדָ֛תָא הָאֲגָגִ֖י וַֽיְנַשְּׂאֵ֑הוּ וַיָּ֨שֶׂם֙ אֶת־כִּסְא֔וֹ מֵעַ֕ל כָּל־
הַשָּׂרִ֖ים אֲשֶׁ֥ר אִתּֽוֹ׃ וְכָל־עַבְדֵ֨י הַמֶּ֜לֶךְ אֲשֶׁר־בְּשַׁ֣עַר הַמֶּ֗לֶךְ 2
כֹּרְעִ֤ים וּמִֽשְׁתַּחֲוִים֙ לְהָמָ֔ן כִּי־כֵ֖ן צִוָּה־ל֣וֹ הַמֶּ֑לֶךְ וּמָ֨רְדֳּכַ֔י
לֹ֥א יִכְרַ֖ע וְלֹ֥א יִֽשְׁתַּחֲוֶֽה׃ וַ֠יֹּאמְרוּ עַבְדֵ֥י הַמֶּ֛לֶךְ אֲשֶׁר־ 3
בְּשַׁ֥עַר הַמֶּ֖לֶךְ לְמָרְדֳּכָ֑י מַדּ֙וּעַ֙ אַתָּ֣ה עוֹבֵ֔ר אֵ֖ת מִצְוַ֥ת
הַמֶּֽלֶךְ׃

3:1 אַחַר ׀ הַדְּבָרִים הָאֵלֶּה [1]—Cf. 2:1. (a) R.10a. (b-c) R.1a. R.13.

גִּדַּל[2]—(a) Note CiC^2aC – ֹ– ַ– : it can only be what? Table 1 VDC, §28.21. Note that there are *two* vocalizations of this stem. גדל 'to be large, great;' D 'to make large, magnify' (v.1431). Note that the D stem often has a causative force like the H stem.

אֶת־הָמָן בֶּן־הַמְּדָתָא הָאֲגָגִי [3]—(a) Dir. obj. of verb. (b) Pr.n. 'Haman.' (c-d) Patronymic (name of father), 'son of Hammedatha.' (e) Gentilic (name of *gens* or race), note —*î* ִי—, §24.55, 'the Agagite.' This may suggest that the arch-villain was descended from Agag.

וַיְנַשְּׂאֵהוּ [4]—Note suf. ֵהוּ, see Table H. Note pattern – ּ – ַ – ְ: this should tell you the form. Note (1) shewa under preformative, (2) dagesh in middle radical, (3) *a*-vowel under 1st rad., §28.21. 'And he lifted him up.'

וַיָּשֶׂם אֶת־כִּסְאוֹ [5]—(a) Try to work it out. Then look at VDC Table 9. Then see 2:17[5]. (c) 12[7]. What suffix here? 'Ane he [the king] placed his [Haman's] chair/throne.'

מֵעַל כָּל־הַשָּׂרִים אֲשֶׁר אִתּוֹ׃ [6]—(a) *min* + *'al* 'from over' = 'higher than.' (b) *kol* with pl. = ? Note extended width of ל: certain letters (א ה ל ם ת, and in MSS also ד ר כ) are expanded to fill out the line. In printed texts these are used at line-end, but in MSS even within the line. (e) 2:20[8]. Translate.

3:2 וְכָל־עַבְדֵי הַמֶּלֶךְ [1]—(b) Cf. 1:3[7].

אֲשֶׁר־בְּשַׁעַר הַמֶּלֶךְ [2]—Cf. 2:19[2]. This is a relative clause, defining the servants (answers *which servants?*).

כֹּרְעִים [3]—Note pattern ִים– ְ– ֹ–; the long *ô* after the 1st rad. should help you, §27.611. כרע 'to bow down' (v.3766). The ptcp. often indicates continuing activity, 'were bowing down.'

וּמִשְׁתַּחֲוִים לְהָמָן[4]—(a) Note this form carefully! *mištaḥăwîm* < **miṯšaḥăwîm*; this is generally listed under שחה as HtD, but actually it is HtŠ (Hishtaph‘el) of חוה *ḥwy*, §28.13. חוה HtŠ ‘to bow down, worship’ (v.7817). (b) Indir. obj.

כִּי־כֵן צִוָּה־לוֹ הַמֶּלֶךְ[5]—(a-b) 1:8[3]. (c) 2:10[3]. Note the prep. used here.

לֹא יִכְרַע[6]—(a) Note neg. adv., generally used with finite verbs in perf. and impf. §35.221. (b) Note יִ–ְ–ַ–: your clues are (1) *i* under preformative, (2) no vowel between 1st and 2d rad. VDC Table 3. yiCCaC or *yiqtal* type impf., §27.333. For *kr‘* cf. 3:2[3].

וְלֹא יִשְׁתַּחֲוֶה׃[7]—(b) ֶה— could be 20 of CCY, in which case ו and ח are the other two rads. This leaves *yištă–* as preformative, metathesized from **yiṯšă-*. Cf. 3:2[4]. Note the difference between the ptcp. (‘the servants *were bowing down*’) and the impf. (‘but M. *would not bow down*’).

3:3 וַיֹּאמְרוּ[1]—2:2[1]. For rest of clause, 2:2[1 2].

מַדּוּעַ אַתָּה עוֹבֵר[2]—(a) Interrog. adv. ‘why?’ (v.4069), prob. from *ma*^{h} *yāḏû*$^{a‘}$ ‘what (is) known?’—but learn it as a word. (b) Independent pers. pron. 2ms (p2), §21.1 (c) Pattern tells us what? עבר has many meanings, here ‘transgressing, disobeying’ (v.5674).

אֵת מִצְוַת[3]—(a) What does this tell us? (b) *m-* (מ־) formation noun (§24.33) from צוה, *miṣwā*^{h} ‘commandment’ (v.4687). Usually in pl. when used of God’s commandments. What does ־ַת tell us? Note expanded ת, cf. 3:1[6].

Learn the words in basic vocabulary Group 26.

Note the following uses of the participle:
הוּא אֲחַשְׁוֵרוֹשׁ הַמֹּלֵךְ מֵהֹדּוּ ... ‘that (was the) Ahasuerus *who was ruling* from India ...’ (1:1)
הָעָם הַנִּמְצְאִים בְּשׁוּשַׁן ‘the people *who were found* in Susa’ (1:5)
לַחֲכָמִים יֹדְעֵי הָעִתִּים ‘to wise men *who know* the times’ (1:13)
רֹאֵי פְּנֵי הַמֶּלֶךְ ‘*who see* the king’s face’ (1:14)
הַיֹּשְׁבִים רִאשֹׁנָה בַּמַּלְכוּת ‘*who sit* first in the kingdom’ (1:14)
מְשָׁרְתָיו ‘*who serve* him’ (2:2)
Note that in every case the ptcp. is defined (definite).

Take my instruction instead of silver, And knowledge rather than choice gold.	קְחוּ־מוּסָרִי וְאַל־כָּסֶף וְדַעַת מֵחָרוּץ נִבְחָר׃

Proverbs 8:10

33

Purpose: To study "weak" verbs
Materials: Esther 3:4-6

וַיְהִי בְּאָמְרָם אֵלָיו יוֹם וָיוֹם וְלֹא שָׁמַע אֲלֵיהֶם 4
וַיַּגִּידוּ לְהָמָן לִרְאוֹת הֲיַעַמְדוּ דִּבְרֵי מָרְדֳּכַי כִּי־הִגִּיד לָהֶם
אֲשֶׁר־הוּא יְהוּדִי׃ וַיַּרְא הָמָן כִּי־אֵין מָרְדֳּכַי כֹּרֵעַ 5
וּמִשְׁתַּחֲוֶה לוֹ וַיִּמָּלֵא הָמָן חֵמָה׃ וַיִּבֶז בְּעֵינָיו לִשְׁלֹחַ יָד 6
בְּמָרְדֳּכַי לְבַדּוֹ כִּי־הִגִּידוּ לוֹ אֶת־עַם מָרְדֳּכָי וַיְבַקֵּשׁ הָמָן
לְהַשְׁמִיד אֶת־כָּל־הַיְּהוּדִים אֲשֶׁר בְּכָל־מַלְכוּת אֲחַשְׁוֵרוֹשׁ
עַם מָרְדֳּכָי׃

3:4 וַיְהִי בְּאָמְרָם אֵלָיו יוֹם וָיוֹם [1]—(a) Cf. 1:1[1]. היה is GCY, doubly weak (the medial *y* is strong). Treat it as GCC §29.11 and CCY §29.7–or better yet, learn the most common forms for immediate recognition. (b) 1:17[4]. 'CC, cf. §29.21. The Masoretic note reads *k^e'omrām*. (d-e) Idiom, 'day by day.'

וְלֹא שָׁמַע אֲלֵיהֶם [2]—(b) *šāmar*: what does the pattern tell us? – ַ – ָ. CCG §29.13. Cf. 1:18[4]. (c) אֶל + s5, cf. 1:14[2]. 'And so it was, when they spoke to him daily and he did not listen to them.'

וַיַּגִּידוּ לְהָמָן [3]—(a) Conj. –ו here is better translated 'that.' Look at *wayyaggēḏ,* 2:22[2]. In that case, the syllable was originally closed and R.2a applies. Here the ending *-û* prevented a closed syllable, so the rule does not apply. ו– – –י tells us what §27.31. – י ÷ ּ tells us what? (1) ַ under preformative, (2) dagesh in first visible rad. (could it be §13.111?), (3) long *î* before final rad. §28.31. Look at §29.42. 2:10[1]. (b) Indir. obj. 'And they told (it) to Haman.'

לִרְאוֹת [4]—*l^e* + *r^e'ôṯ*: וֹת– can be 65 of CCY, §29.71. Does this fit here? Complete the parsing. 1:14[5]. Doubly weak, C'C = CGC, §29.12, and CCY, §29.7 *l^e*- + 65 indicates purpose, 'in order to see.'

הֲיַעַמְדוּ דִּבְרֵי מָרְדֳּכַי [5]—(a) –הֲ is interrog. part., go over §22.3. The verb is GCC; note that secondary opening develops to a full vowel, study §15.2532, §15.321, §15.421, R.10c. In *yaqtul* and *yaqtil* impfs., you may be fooled by the *pattāḥ* under the preformative. עמד 'to stand' (v.5975). Direct question is used for indirect: 'to see, "would the affairs of M. stand?" ' = 'to see whether ... would stand.'

כִּי־הִגִּיד לָהֶם [6]—(a) Causal, 'for, because.' (b) –הִ-ִי looks like H10, but what is dagesh doing in גּ? Table 7 VDC. You should now know the meaning of this verb. v.5046. (c) Indir. obj., 'for he had declared to them.'

אֲשֶׁר־הוּא יְהוּדִי׃ [7]—(a) Here conj., 'that,' introduces indirect discourse, §38.82. (b-c) Noun cl., 'he (was) a Jew,' §§31.11, .21. (c) 2:5[1].

3:5 וַיַּרְא הָמָן [1]—(a) *way-yar'*, with apocopation < *yir'ê^h*, §29.72, §13.533. *Ges.* §75*q* says *pattāḥ* under *yôd* is due to influence of ר, but possibly it is an application of R.20. CC' verbs, see §29.22. (b) Subj. of verb. 'And Haman saw.'

כִּי־אֵין מָרְדֳּכַי כֹּרֵעַ [2]—(a) Conj. 'that,' introducing indir. disc. after a verb of *seeing*, or a noun cl. as obj. of 'he saw.' (b) Note the neg. part. used before ptcps. 2:20[1]. (d) R.10c. The rest of the cl. you have had in a similar form, 3:2[3 4].

וַיִּמָּלֵא הָמָן חֵמָה׃ [3]—(a) – ַ ִּ ַ : (1) dagesh in 1st rad., (2) vowel pattern. VDC Table 2. מלא 1:5[1] (b) Subj. (c) Acc. of material after verb of *filling*.

3:6 וַיִּבֶז בְּעֵינָיו [1]—(a) Note anaptyxis, *wayyíḇez*. This suggests what? §29.72. < *yiḇzê^h* יִבְזֶה, CCY, cf. 1:17[3]. (b) ָיו is s0 added to du. or pl., Table H. Cf. 1:17[3], 1:21[2]. 'And it was contemptible in his eyes.'

לִשְׁלֹחַ יָד בְּמָרְדֳּכַי לְבַדּוֹ [2]—(a-b) 2:21[7]. (d) 1:16[2]. 'To lay his hand on M. alone.'

כִּי־הִגִּידוּ לוֹ אֶת־עַם מָרְדֳּכָי [3]—(a) 'For.' (b) Cf. 3:4[6], 3:4[3]. Now figure this form out. Subj. is indefinite. (c) Indir. obj. (d-f) Dir. obj., cf. 2:10[2]; here cstr. 'For they had made known to him M.'s people.'

וַיְבַקֵּשׁ הָמָן [4]—(a) – ֵ ּ ַ ְ : (1) shewa under preform., (2) dagesh in mid. rad., (3) vowel pattern = what? §28.21. (b) Subj. of verb.

לְהַשְׁמִיד אֶת־כָּל־הַיְּהוּדִים [5]—(a) *l^e* + *hašmîḏ*. *ha – –î–* suggests what? VDC Table 3. Learn to observe such "little" differences. Complementary inf. after 'he sought.' (b-d) Dir. obj. of inf. cstr., 'to destroy all the Jews.' (d) Pl., cf. 3:4[7], 2:5[1]

אֲשֶׁר בְּכָל־מַלְכוּת [6]—(a) Rel. pron. introduces rel. cl. modifying היהודים. (b) Before *malkûṯ* what does *kol* mean? (c) Cstr. before next word. You should be able to do the rest.

Learn the words in Group 27.

---

12. In HtD forms, when the first radical is a dental or a sibilant, metathesis, assimilation, or both occur (§13.112, §13.61)

דֶּרֶךְ אֱוִיל יָשָׁר בְּעֵינָיו וְשֹׁמֵעַ לְעֵצָה חָכָם׃
The way of a fool is right in his own eyes,
but a wise man listens to advice.
Proverbs 12:15

34

Purpose: To study adjectival usages
Materials: Esther 3:7-8

7 בַּחֹדֶשׁ הָרִאשׁוֹן הוּא־חֹדֶשׁ נִיסָן בִּשְׁנַת
שְׁתֵּים עֶשְׂרֵה לַמֶּלֶךְ אֲחַשְׁוֵרוֹשׁ הִפִּיל פּוּר הוּא הַגּוֹרָל
לִפְנֵי הָמָן מִיּוֹם ׀ לְיוֹם וּמֵחֹדֶשׁ לְחֹדֶשׁ שְׁנֵים־עָשָׂר הוּא־
8 חֹדֶשׁ אֲדָר׃ וַיֹּאמֶר הָמָן לַמֶּלֶךְ אֲחַשְׁוֵרוֹשׁ יֶשְׁנוֹ
עַם־אֶחָד מְפֻזָּר וּמְפֹרָד בֵּין הָעַמִּים בְּכֹל מְדִינוֹת מַלְכוּתֶךָ
וְדָתֵיהֶם שֹׁנוֹת מִכָּל־עָם וְאֶת־דָּתֵי הַמֶּלֶךְ אֵינָם עֹשִׂים
וְלַמֶּלֶךְ אֵין שֹׁוֶה לְהַנִּיחָם׃

3:7 בַּחֹדֶשׁ הָרִאשׁוֹן הוּא־חֹדֶשׁ נִיסָן [1]—(a) 2:12[4] (b) 1:14[7], 'first' (v.7223). The adj. follows the noun it modifies and is in concord (agreement in gender, number, and definiteness). (c) Demon. pron., used as rel. pron. (§21.2), 'that (is).' (e) Nisan, the first month (late March or April), cf. 2:16[3].

בִּשְׁנַת שְׁתֵּים עֶשְׂרֵה [2]—(a) 2:16[4]. (b-c) In 2:12[4] masc. *šnêm ʿāśār,* here fem. *štêm ʿeśrēʰ,* §26.25. Note, there are no *ordinals* above 10, cf. §26.872. The numerals are generally adjs. in use, but are basically substantives, cf. §26.2. (b) Cf. 2:14[4](b). (c) Cf. 2:12[4](c). This would be 474 B.C., but see 2:16[4].

הִפִּיל פּוּר הוּא הַגּוֹרָל [3]—(a) *hippîl: hi--î-* = ? §29.4. Cf. *higgîḏ,* 3:4[6]. נפל 'to fall' (v.5307), H 'to cast, throw down.' (b) *pûr* (loanword) 'lot, chance' (6332 8/8). (c-d) Appositional cl., §36.6, a noun cl., 'that (is) the lot,' explaining the meaning of *pûr.* (d) *gôrāl* 'lot' (v.1486).

לִפְנֵי הָמָן [4]—The defined subj. of *hippîl* is Ahasuerus, but what the significance of casting a lot before Haman is, we are not told. In the light of 3:13 we may assume that it anticipates the story by telling the means of selecting the day of the genocide.

מִיּוֹם ׀ לְיוֹם וּמֵחֹדֶשׁ לְחֹדֶשׁ שְׁנֵים־עָשָׂר [5]—(a-b) Note form of מִן. Probably the lot was cast to select the specific day. We need not assume that it was cast every day for a year. (c-d) Note form of מִן. We would expect מִחֹדֶשׁ, similar to מִחוּץ (R.10a). Again we may assume that the lot was cast to select the month. (e) Cf. 2:12[4]. It is possible that a word or phrase has been dropped out, for this is not smooth.

הוּא־חֹדֶשׁ אֲדָר׃ [6]—(a) Cf. 3:7[1]. Adar was the 12th and, (except for years with intercalary Second Adar [Ve'adar]), the last month.*

---

*According to one system of calendration, the New Year began with Tishrî, the 7th month (as it does today in the Jewish calendar). But whether the year began with Nisan or Tishrî, the numbering of the months was constant; Nisan is always the 1st month, and Adar the 12th.

3:8 וַיֹּ֣אמֶר[1]—You should have no trouble with this clause.

יֶשְׁנ֣וֹ עַם־אֶחָ֗ד[2]—(a) *yēš* יֵשׁ 'existence of' (v.3426), may serve as a verb. It takes pron.sufs., here s0. 'Existence of it' = 'it exists, there is.' (c) Num. *'eḥad* 'one' (v.259), cf. §26.211, §26.81. 'One people,' more than simply 'a people,' as the following words show.

מְפֻזָּ֤ר וּמְפֹרָד֙ בֵּ֣ין הָֽעַמִּ֔ים[3]—(a) *m^e^p̄uzzār:* (1) *mêm* with shewa, (2) *u*-vowel under 1st rad., (3) doubled 2d rad. = ? Table 1 VDC. פזר 'to scatter abroad' (6340, 10/1). (b) *m^e^p̄ōrāḏ*: (1) *mêm* with shewa, (2) *u*-vowel under 1st rad. with compensatory lengthening, (3) mid. rad. rejects dagesh, = ?. Table 4 VDC. פרד N 'to be divided' (v.6504). (c) Pre. *bên* 'between' (v.996), governing the following word. We would say, 'among the peoples.'

בְּכֹ֖ל מְדִינ֣וֹת מַלְכוּתֶ֑ךָ[4]—(a) *kōl* before pl. is translated how? (b) f.p.c., §25.422. (c) s2 with connecting vowel preserved by pausal accent, Table H.

וְדָתֵיהֶ֞ם שֹׁנ֣וֹת מִכָּל־עָ֗ם[5]—(a) *dâṯ* is fem., but pl. is *dâṯîm*, and suffixial form is *dâṯê-*, here fps5. 1:8[1]. (b) *šôn-ôṯ*, f.p.a.; long vowel in *šôn-* suggests G50, cf. *šônîm* in 1:7[3]. 'And their laws (are) differing from [those of] all [other] people.'

וְאֶת־דָּתֵ֤י הַמֶּ֙לֶךְ֙ אֵינָ֣ם עֹשִׂ֔ים[6]—(a-c) Obj. of עשים. (b) f.p.c., cf. 3:8[5]. (c) Cf. *vešnô*, 3:8[2]. *'ên* + s5 'nonexistence of them' 'they are not.' (d) *'ôśî*, cf. *šônîm*, 1:7[3]. On the use of אין + ptcp., cf. *Ges.* §152*l,m*. The idea seems to be, 'they habitually do not keep the king's laws.'

וְלַמֶּ֥לֶךְ אֵין־שֹׁוֶ֖ה לְהַנִּיחָֽם׃[7]—(a) Like dat. of reference, 'as for the king.' (b) אין negates the ptcp. (c) שֹׁוֶה: note *ḥôlām* on *šîn*, not over *wāw*, which has *s^e^ḡôl*. *šôwê^h^*: ֶה could be 50 of CCY–are there other clues? שָׁוָה 'he resembled' (v.7737), but here 'it is not like (him), it is not fitting.' (d) *l^e^* + *hannîḥ* + *ām: hannî^a^ḥ* is H65 of *nû^a^ḥ*, with Aramaic doubling, §29.5115. Study this carefully. נוח 'to rest' (v.5117), H65s6 'to give them rest.'

Read over §30.251, §§30.32–30.324, §§36.–36.14.

Learn the basic words in Group 28.

---

26. When adding a consonantal sufformative (i.e. one which begins with a consonant) to a CC^2 verb which ends in a geminated consonant, the consonantal cluster which would occur is avoided by the insertion of a long vowel before the sufformative, namely וֹ (*ô*) in the perf. and ֵי (*ê^y^*) in the impf. (§15.64).

35

Purpose: To study the numerals
Materials: Esther 3:9-12a

9 אִם־עַל־הַמֶּלֶךְ טוֹב יִכָּתֵב
לְאַבְּדָם וַעֲשֶׂרֶת אֲלָפִים כִּכַּר־כֶּסֶף אֶשְׁקוֹל עַל־יְדֵי עֹשֵׂי
י הַמְּלָאכָה לְהָבִיא אֶל־גִּנְזֵי הַמֶּלֶךְ׃ וַיָּסַר הַמֶּלֶךְ אֶת־טַבַּעְתּוֹ
מֵעַל יָדוֹ וַיִּתְּנָהּ לְהָמָן בֶּן־הַמְּדָתָא הָאֲגָגִי צֹרֵר הַיְּהוּדִים׃
11 וַיֹּאמֶר הַמֶּלֶךְ לְהָמָן הַכֶּסֶף נָתוּן לָךְ וְהָעָם לַעֲשׂוֹת בּוֹ
12 כַּטּוֹב בְּעֵינֶיךָ׃ וַיִּקָּרְאוּ סֹפְרֵי הַמֶּלֶךְ בַּחֹדֶשׁ הָרִאשׁוֹן
בִּשְׁלוֹשָׁה עָשָׂר יוֹם בּוֹ

3:9 אִם־עַל־הַמֶּלֶךְ טוֹב[1]—This should give you no difficulty. 1:19[1].

יִכָּתֵב לְאַבְּדָם[2]—*yikkāṯēḇ:* יִ־ָּ־ֵ, note dagesh and vowel pattern. VDC–2. (b) l^e*'abb*^{e}*ḏām*: ־ָם is s9 (Table H); –לְ suggests what? Note dagesh in בּ: is it strong or light? R.16. CaC^{2}ēC (VDC Table 1) is what? CaC^{2}ōC is what? Which is it here? אבד D 'to kill' (v.6).

וַעֲשֶׂרֶת אֲלָפִים כִּכַּר־כֶּסֶף[3]—(a) Num., §26.24 (v.6235). (b) Num. אלף 'thousand' (v.504), in form a segolate, plur. after '10,' lit. 'ten of thousands.' (c) *kikkar* 'talent' (v.3603), sing. after a number above 10 (read §26.9), cstr. with following word. A talent was about 30 kg. (66 lbs.). (d) 1:6[9].

אֶשְׁקוֹל עַל־יְדֵי עֹשֵׂי הַמְּלָאכָה[4]—(a) Written fully (read §11.3241), but it is not a true long vowel. ---אֶ is what? §27.321. שקל 'to weigh (out)' (v.8254). (c) y^e*ḏê*^{y}: ־ֵי is what? יָד 'hand' (v.3027). (d) Written defectively for ־ֹ־ֵי–, only 2 rads., but *ô* after the first suggests G50. Ending is what? (e) m^e*lā'ḵā*^{h} 'work, business' (v.4399). 'I shall weigh into the hands of the doers of the work.'

לְהָבִיא אֶל־גִּנְזֵי הַמֶּלֶךְ׃ [5]—(a) Cf 1:11[1]. (c) g^e*nāzîm* (only pl.) 'chests, treasury' (1595, 3/2). Note form here and explain.

3:10 וַיָּסַר הַמֶּלֶךְ אֶת־טַבַּעְתּוֹ [1]—(a) Note accent shift: *way* + *yāsēr* > **wayyā́ser* VDC–9), but there is influence of ר on last vowel. סור 'to turn aside,' H 'to remove' (v.5493). (b) Subj. (c-d) Obj. *ṭabbaʿt* + *ô* could develop from *ṭabbáʿaṯ* or from *ṭabb*^{e}*ʿā*^{h}; v.2885 gives the former, 'signet-ring, seal.'

מֵעַל יָדוֹ[2]—(a) *min* + *ʿal.* If we read carefully, we shall note that Heb. is often more precise in its use of preps. than Eng. A. did not take the signet *from* his hand, but *from upon* his hand. (b) You should be able to analyze this word and translate it.

וַיִּתְּנָהּ[3]—*way* + *yitt*^{e}*n* + *āh* (note *mappîq*). Explain each morpheme. Parse the word and translate. The indirect obj. follows.

צֹרֵר הַיְּהוּדִים׃[4]—(a) —ֵֹו— (written defectively, §11.324), tells us what? צרר 'to be hostile to, harass' (v.6887c). On the analogy of עשי המלאכה we conclude that this is G52 (m.s.c.) and that (b) is in gen., rather than G50 with dir. obj. 'The harasser of the Jews.'

3:11 וַיֹּאמֶר הַמֶּלֶךְ לְהָמָן[1]—You should be able to analyze and translate this clause.

הַכֶּסֶף נָתוּן לָךְ[2]—(a) Def. because previously mentioned, 'the silver,' 1:6[9]. (b) —ָ—וּ— is what pattern? §27.13, VDC Table 5. (c) Indir. obj. Note the pausal form (Table H). 'The silver is given to you.'

וְהָעָם לַעֲשׂוֹת בּוֹ כַּטּוֹב בְּעֵינֶיךָ׃[3]—(a) Second of compound subj., §30.113. Note the pausal form with the def. art. and read §15.133. (b) ל--וֹת suggests what? §35.423. (c) s0 agrees with its antecedent, 'the people ... it'; we might say 'them.' (d-e) Cf. 1:21[1·2]. Can you figure this out? *kaṭṭôḇ* with def. art., 'according to the good' = 'according to what is good.'

3:12a וַיִּקָּרְאוּ סֹפְרֵי הַמֶּלֶךְ בַּחֹדֶשׁ הָרִאשׁוֹן[1]— (a) 2:14[8]; parse. (b) *sôpēr* 'scribe' (G50 of ספר, v.5608). (d) 2:12[4]. (e) 3:7[1].

בִּשְׁלוֹשָׁה עָשָׂר יוֹם בּוֹ[2]— (a-b) Cf. 2:12[4], 1:3[1], §26.25. (d) What is the antecedent of the pronoun?

Learn the words in Group 29.

Analyze the following:

2:2[4]	שְׁנֵי־סָרִיסֵי הַמֶּלֶךְ
2:19[3]	שֵׁנִית
2:14[3]	בֵּית הַנָּשִׁים שֵׁנִי
2:12[4]	שְׁנֵים עָשָׂר חֹדֶשׁ
1:3[1]	בִּשְׁנַת שָׁלוֹשׁ
2:12[7]	שִׁשָּׁה חֳדָשִׁים
1:6[9]	שִׁבְעַת יָמִים
1:10[6]	שִׁבְעַת הַסָּרִיסִים
2:16[4]	בִּשְׁנַת שֶׁבַע
2:9[6]	שֶׁבַע הַנְּעָרוֹת
1:10[1]	בַּיּוֹם הַשְּׁבִיעִי
1:1[9·12]	שֶׁבַע וְעֶשְׂרִים וּמֵאָה מְדִינָה
1:4[9·10]	שְׁמוֹנִים וּמְאַת יוֹם
2:16[2]	בַּחֹדֶשׁ הָעֲשִׂירִי

הֲלֹא־חָכְמָה תִקְרָא וּתְבוּנָה תִּתֵּן קוֹלָהּ׃

Does not wisdom call, does not understanding raise her voice?

Proverbs 8:1

36

Purpose: To review some of the things we have learned
Materials: Esther 3:12b-13

וַיִּכָּתֵב כְּכָל־אֲשֶׁר־צִוָּה הָמָן אֶל
אֲחַשְׁדַּרְפְּנֵי־הַמֶּלֶךְ וְאֶל־הַפַּחוֹת אֲשֶׁר ׀ עַל־מְדִינָה וּמְדִינָה
וְאֶל־שָׂרֵי עַם וָעָם מְדִינָה וּמְדִינָה כִּכְתָבָהּ וְעַם וָעָם
כִּלְשׁוֹנוֹ בְּשֵׁם הַמֶּלֶךְ אֲחַשְׁוֵרֹשׁ נִכְתָּב וְנֶחְתָּם בְּטַבַּעַת
13 הַמֶּלֶךְ׃ וְנִשְׁלוֹחַ סְפָרִים בְּיַד הָרָצִים אֶל־כָּל־מְדִינוֹת
הַמֶּלֶךְ לְהַשְׁמִיד לַהֲרֹג וּלְאַבֵּד אֶת־כָּל־הַיְּהוּדִים מִנַּעַר
וְעַד־זָקֵן טַף וְנָשִׁים בְּיוֹם אֶחָד בִּשְׁלוֹשָׁה עָשָׂר לְחֹדֶשׁ
שְׁנֵים־עָשָׂר הוּא־חֹדֶשׁ אֲדָר וּשְׁלָלָם לָבוֹז׃

3:12 וַיִּכָּתֵב כְּכָל־אֲשֶׁר־צִוָּה הָמָן [4]–(a) Est. 1:19[4]. The subj. is indefinite. (b) k^e- 'according to.' (d) –וּ– is it *šûrûq* or *wāw* with strong dagesh? 2:10[3]. (e) Subj. of verb. Translate.

אֶל אֲחַשְׁדַּרְפְּנֵי־הַמֶּלֶךְ [5]—(b) From Gk. *σατράπης*, OPers *ẖšaθrapāvan* 'ruler, satrap' (323 4/3).

וְאֶל־הַפַּחוֹת[6]—(b) *peḥā*^{h} (v.6346), prob. < **peḥḥā*^{h}, pl. **paḥḥôṯ*. Review guttural rules, §15.4ff.

וְאֶל־שָׂרֵי עַם וָעָם[7]—(a-b) You should be able to do this. What morpheme is ֵ–י? (c-d) 1:22[4]. Note the use of cstr. before two closely-joined governed nouns.

מְדִינָה וּמְדִינָה כִּכְתָבָהּ וְעַם וָעָם ׀ כִּלְשׁוֹנוֹ[8]—Review notes in 1:22.

בְּשֵׁם הַמֶּלֶךְ אֲחַשְׁוֵרֹשׁ נִכְתָּב[9]—(a) 2:5[3], 2:22[4]. Note that –ֵ does not reduce in cstr., but it does in suffixial *š^{e}mô*. (d) Masoretic note calls attention to *qāmāṣ* (pausal, §15.131) with *zāqēp̄ qāṭôn;* N10, not N50, 'it was written.'

וְנֶחְתָּם בְּטַבַּעַת הַמֶּלֶךְ׃[10]—(a) Note influence of guttural, niccāc > negcāc. Note vowels and see VDC Table 3. חתם 'to seal' (v.2856). Is it N10 or N50? (b) 3:10[1].

3:13 וְנִשְׁלוֹחַ סְפָרִים בְּיַד הָרָצִים[1]—(a) niccôc VDC Table 3, §28.42. שׁלח 1:22[1], 2:22[7]. (b) 1:22[1]. (c) *b^{e}yaḏ*, idiom = 'by.' (d) רוץ (v.7323) 'to run'; §§29.631, .6318. This form is used as a noun, 'runners, courriers.' 'And documents to be sent....'

אֶל־כָּל־מְדִינוֹת הַמֶּלֶךְ [2]—See 1:22[2].

לְהַשְׁמִיד לַהֲרֹג וּלְאַבֵּד[3]—(a) –הַ–ְ–ִי, note the vowel with ה. Explain the following: –ה, –הַ. Now note vowel after 2d rad: if –ַ, what is it? if –ִי, what? VDC T.3. §28.31. *šmd* H 'to annihilate, exterminate' (v.8045). (b) Note –ֲ–ֹ, cf. §27.65f. *hrg* 'to kill, slay' (v.2026). (c) Cf. 3:9². – ֵ ֹ ל־, §28.61. Use this opportunity to compare the inf. cstr. forms.

אֶת־כָּל־הַיְּהוּדִים [4]—Dir. obj. of the 3 preceding infs.

מִנַּעַר וְעַד־זָקֵן טַף וְנָשִׁים [5]—(a) *náʿar* 'youth' (v.5288). What morpheme is prefixed? §22., §22.42. (b) 1:5⁷. (c) *zāqēn* 'old person' (v.2205), §24.22. (d) *ṭap̄* (coll.) 'little children' (v.2945). (e) 1:9³. What morpheme is ־ִים? What gender is this word? §25.1.

בְּיוֹם אֶחָד [6]—Is this the same as יוֹם רִאשׁוֹן? Is אֶחָד cardinal or ordinal? §§26.2, .3. Do you translate it 'in one day' or 'on the first day'?

בִּשְׁלוֹשָׁה עָשָׂר לְחֹדֶשׁ שְׁנֵים־עָשָׂר [7]—(a-b) Cf. 3:12³. (c-e) Cf. 3:7⁵. Which month is this?

הוּא־חֹדֶשׁ אֲדָר [8]—See 3:7⁶.

וּשְׁלָלָם לָבוֹז׃ [9]—(a) *šᵉlālām* could be G10s0 of *šālal* or the noun *šālāl* with s0; context prefers the noun. *šālāl* 'booty, spoil' (v.7998). (b) cōc is G65 of CC²; cûc is G65 of CWC (VDC T.10). *bzz* 'to plunder, spoil' (v.962).

Study the following:

G10 cācac, + suf. > cᵉcācām, *qᵉṭālām*
G65 cucuc > cᵉcāc, + suf. > coccām, *qoṭlām, 'omrām*
CāCāC-type noun + suf. > cᵉcācām, *dᵉb̲ārām*

Memorize the words in vocabulary Group 30.

Note the following uses of the perfect:
עָשָׂה הַמֶּלֶךְ ... מִשְׁתֶּה 'the king *made* a banquet' (1:5)
כִּי־כֵן יִסַּד הַמֶּלֶךְ ... לַעֲשׂוֹת 'for thus the king *decreed* to do' (1:8)
גַּם וַשְׁתִּי ... עָשְׂתָה מִשְׁתֵּה נָשִׁים 'Vashti also *made* a women's banquet' (1:9)
לֹא־עָשְׂתָה אֶת־מַאֲמַר הַמֶּלֶךְ 'She *did not do* the king's command' (1:15)
וְלֹא־בָאָה 'and she *did not come*' (1:17)
אֲשֶׁר שָׁמְעוּ אֶת־דְּבַר הַמַּלְכָּה 'who *heard* the king's word' (1:18)
Note the consistent translation in *past* tense. Read §32.51.

He who heeds instruction is on the path to life, but he who rejects reproof goes astray.	אֹרַח לְחַיִּים שׁוֹמֵר מוּסָר וְעֹזֵב תּוֹכַחַת מַתְעֶה׃

Proverbs 10:17

Purpose: To review some of the things we have seen
Materials: Esther 3:14-15

14 פַּתְשֶׁגֶן הַכְּתָב
לְהִנָּתֵן דָּת בְּכָל־מְדִינָה וּמְדִינָה גָּלוּי לְכָל־הָעַמִּים לִהְיוֹת
טו עֲתִידִים לַיּוֹם הַזֶּה׃ הָרָצִים יָצְאוּ דְחוּפִים בִּדְבַר הַמֶּלֶךְ
וְהַדָּת נִתְּנָה בְּשׁוּשַׁן הַבִּירָה וְהַמֶּלֶךְ וְהָמָן יָשְׁבוּ לִשְׁתּוֹת
וְהָעִיר שׁוּשַׁן נָבוֹכָה׃

3:14 פַּתְשֶׁגֶן הַכְּתָב [1]—(a) *patšeḡen* 'copy' (6572 3ε). (b) k^e*ṯāḇ* 'writing' (v.3792, 9x in Est.). Explain the vowels in each word.

לְהִנָּתֵן דָּת [2]—(a) Note accent and read §17.35. Normal form *hinnāṯēn,* clues: *hin-*, dagesh in 1st rad. (VDC T.2). Does –ל tell you whether it is 32 or 65?. (b) You should know this. This sounds like documentary form, 'a copy of the writing to be given (as) law.' The following words you should know–but be sure to go over them!

גָּלוּי לְכָל־הָעַמִּים [3]—(a) For *–ûy* וי– see §29.71. גלה, cf. 2:6[1], here means 'revealed, laid bare.' (b-c) Why pl.? How would you translate it?.

לִהְיוֹת עֲתִידִים לַיּוֹם הַזֶּה׃ [4]—(a) 1:22[5]. (b) *'āṯîḏ* 'prepared, ready' (6264 6/2). The pattern CāCîC is an 'Aram.-type' pass. ptcp., see §24.255. (c-d) Cf. 1:18[1]. What is different here?

3:15 הָרָצִים יָצְאוּ [1]—(a) 3:13[1]. Note form of def. art. and review Table G. (b) *y---û*. Careful! Is *y–* a preformative (§20.212) or a radical? Look at the vowels, וּ–ְ–ָ is the pattern of what form? §27.21. Learn this *now.*

דְחוּפִים בִּדְבַר [2]—(a) CāCûC is what pattern? (VDC T.5) §27.63. *dḥp* 'to hasten' (1765 4/3). Why plural? What does it modify? (b) Note prep. b^e-, denoting agency or means. Explain vowels. Note accent ֥.

וְהַדָּת נִתְּנָה [3]—(a) You know this word. (b) Be careful! $CiC^{2e}C\bar{a}^h$ could be D11 of *ntn.* But suppose the –תּ– is the result of assimilation, and –נִ is a stem indicator–what would it be? §28.42. D10 is *nittēn*, N10 is *nittan*, but in the 11 forms, the vowel of the penult reduces and the forms lose distinction. Which makes sense in context? For the next words, cf. 1:2[10.11].

יָשְׁבוּ לִשְׁתּוֹת [4]—(a) Cf. 1:15[1] יָצְאוּ. Note vowels here. Can you figure out the form? *yšb* 'to sit, dwell,' 1:2[3]. (b) וֹת–ִ– should now "ring a bell." שתה (cf. 1:8[1]) 'to drink' (v.8354).

וְהָעִיר שׁוּשַׁן נָבוֹכָה׃ [5]—(a) Cf. v.5892, fem. gender. (b) In apposition with the preceding word (§30.251). (c) *nāḇôḵāʰ* or perhaps *nâḇôḵāʰ*, VDC–9. בּוּךְ 'to perplex, confound' (943 3/1). Accent on N11 should be *nā-ḇô-ḵāʰ*, and N51 should be *nᵉ-ḇô-ḵáʰ*. Accents here are perplexing.

Study the following carefully:

G25 CCY yiCCû: *yiglû* יִגְלוּ, *yiṣ'û* יִצְאוּ.
G25 NCC yiC²ᵉCû: *yittᵉnû* יִתְּנוּ, *yiṣṣᵉ'û* יִצְּעוּ.
G25 YCC yîCᵉCû: *yîʸtᵉḇû* יִיטְבוּ, *yîʸṣᵉ'û יִיצְאוּ.
G25 WCC yēCᵉCû: *yêṣᵉ'û* יֵצְאוּ.
G25 CWC yāCûCû: *yāqûmû* יָקוּמוּ, *yāṣû'û יָצוּאוּ.

Take some of the verbs we have had, and make similar comparative studies. Get so you know what to look for as identifying clues.

Learn the basic vocabularly in Group 31.

Read the following sections *carefully*:

§§27.–27.1112
§§27.114–27.1141
§§27.115, .1153
§§27.2, .21, .221, .232, .233
§§27.3, .31, .321, .333, .334

Read the following:

§28.1
§28.2, .21
§§28.3, .31
§§28.4, .42
§§28.5, .51
§§29., 29.02
§§32.51, .52, .53, .54
§§32.8, .81, .82, .83, .84

לֹא־יַחְפֹּץ כְּסִיל בִּתְבוּנָה כִּי אִם־בְּהִתְגַּלּוֹת לִבּוֹ׃
A fool takes no pleasure in understanding, but only in expressing his opinion.
Proverbs 18:2

38

Purpose: To review what we have been studying
Materials: Esther 4:1-3

CAP. IV. ד

ד

א וּמָרְדֳּכַי יָדַע אֶת־כָּל־אֲשֶׁר נַעֲשָׂה וַיִּקְרַע מָרְדֳּכַי אֶת־
בְּגָדָיו וַיִּלְבַּשׁ שַׂק וָאֵפֶר וַיֵּצֵא בְּתוֹךְ הָעִיר וַיִּזְעַק זְעָקָה
2 גְדוֹלָה וּמָרָה׃ וַיָּבוֹא עַד לִפְנֵי שַׁעַר־הַמֶּלֶךְ כִּי אֵין לָבוֹא
3 אֶל־שַׁעַר הַמֶּלֶךְ בִּלְבוּשׁ שָׂק׃ וּבְכָל־מְדִינָה וּמְדִינָה מְקוֹם
אֲשֶׁר דְּבַר־הַמֶּלֶךְ וְדָתוֹ מַגִּיעַ אֵבֶל גָּדוֹל לַיְּהוּדִים וְצוֹם
וּבְכִי וּמִסְפֵּד שַׂק וָאֵפֶר יֻצַּע לָרַבִּים׃

4:1 וּמָרְדֳּכַי יָדַע אֶת־כָּל־אֲשֶׁר נַעֲשָׂה [1]—(b) Remember that –י can be a radical! Note the pattern, –ַ–ָ–. (f) Examine each of the following suggestions, both for morphology and for context: G29 of CCY, N10 of CCY, G11 of NCC, D11 of CGC. Review Rule 10c,d, §28.42, §29.121, §29.42, §29.71. (c-f) Rel. cl., obj. of *yāḏaʿ*. (d-e) Subj. of *naʿăśā^{h}*, 'all that was (had been) done.'

וַיִּקְרַע מָרְדֳּכַי אֶת־בְּגָדָיו [2]—(a) Is *yiqraʿ* yiqtal or yaqtul?. Don't confuse *qrʿ* קרע with *qr'* קרא or with *krʿ* כרע. *qrʿ* 'to tear' (v.7167). (b) *béged* 'garment' (v.899); what suffix? on sing. or plur.? (Table H). §24.215.

וַיִּלְבַּשׁ שַׂק וָאֵפֶר[3]—(a) לבש 'to put on (clothing), clothe (self)' (v.3847). (b) *śaq* 'sackcloth' (v.8242). (c) *'ēp̄er* (coll.) 'ashes' (v.665).

וַיֵּצֵא בְּתוֹךְ הָעִיר [4]—(a) Review 1:17[1]. Is this form yiqtal, yaqtul, or yaqtil? (b) *b^{e}*- + *tāweḵ*, cstr. *tôḵ* (Table F), 'midst' (v.8432). (c) 3:15[5].

וַיִּזְעַק זְעָקָה גְדוֹלָה וּמָרָה׃ [5]—(a) *zʿq* 'to cry, cry out' (v.2199). (b) *z^{e}ʿāqā^{h}* 'cry' (v.2201). Cognate accusative (§30.22) (the verb is intrans.), 'to cry a cry.' (c) Adj., modifying (b), 1:5[7]. (d) Adj., also modifying (b), §30.21. *mar(r),* f. *mārā^{h}* 'bitter' (v.4751). Cf. Exod. 15:23; Ruth 1:20.

4:2 וַיָּבוֹא עַד לִפְנֵי שַׁעַר־הַמֶּלֶךְ [1]—(a) Cf. 1:19[7]. What is the difference? (b-c) 1:1[3], 1:19[3]; contrast *millip̄ānā^{y}w* '(from) before him' and *ʿaḏ lip̄nê^{y}* 'until before' = 'as far as in front of.' (d) 2:19[2].

כִּי אֵין לָבוֹא [2]—(a) Causal. (b) אין + inf. cstr. 'there is not to enter' = 'one does not enter.' Cf. Ewald, *Syntax,* §321c.

בִּלְבוּשׁ שָׂק׃[3]—(a) *b^{e}*- + *l^{e}ḇûš* 'clothing' (v.3830). Is the word in cstr.? (b) 4:1[3].

4:3 מְקוֹם אֲשֶׁר דְּבַר־הַמֶּלֶךְ וְדָתוֹ מַגִּיעַ [1]— (a) *māqôm* 'place' (v.4725), *m*– formation noun, §24.33, from קום, cstr. before rel. pron. (b) Here, 'where.' In earlier Heb.,

מְקוֹם would not be needed, cf. 2 Sam. 7:7, *bᵉkōl 'ăšer-hiṯhallákṯî* 'in every place I walked.' (f) מַגִּיעַ, cf. הִגִּיעַ in 2:12[1]. Preformative *m–* suggests what form? '(Any) place where the word of the king and his decree (were) reaching.'

אֵבֶל גָּדוֹל לַיְּהוּדִים [2]—(a) *'ēḇel* 'mourning' (v.60). (b) How is this word related to the clause? (a-c) Noun clause. 'Great mourning (was) to the Jews.' Translate smoothly.

וְצוֹם וּבְכִי וּמִסְפֵּד [3]—(a) *ṣôm* 'fasting' (v.6685). (b) *bᵉḵî* 'weeping' (v.1065). (c) *mispēḏ* 'wailing' (v.4553). How do these words fit the preceding clause?

יֻצַּע לָרַבִּים׃[4]—If you have forgotten the words preceding the verb, cf. 4:1[3]. (a) *yuṣṣaʿ*, note the *u*-vowel. CuC²aC is Dp10, hence this could be Dp10 of *yṣʿ*. yuC²aC could also be Hp20 of *nṣʿ*. Read carefully §29.34, and see §29.3411. *yṣʿ* H 'to lay, spread' (3331 4/1). 'Sackcloth and ashes were (lit. was) spread for the multitude.'

Learn the words in Group 32.

Note the following *passive participles*:
אָחוּז בְּחַבְלֵי־בוּץ '*held* with linen cords' (1:6)
הַכֶּסֶף נָתוּן לָךְ 'the money *is given* to you' (3:11)
גָּלוּי לְכָל־הָעַמִּים '*revealed* to all the peoples' (3:14)
דְּחוּפִים בִּדְבַר הַמֶּלֶךְ '*hastened* by the king's word' (3:15)
עַם־אֶחָד מְפֻזָּר וּמְפֹרָד בֵּין הָעַמִּים 'a certain people *scattered* and *dispersed* among the peoples' (3:8)
Read §32.3712.

Note the following uses of the *jussive*:
וּמַלְכוּתָהּ יִתֵּן הַמֶּלֶךְ לִרְעוּתָהּ 'and *let* the king *give* her royalty to her fellow woman' (1:19)
יְבַקְשׁוּ לַמֶּלֶךְ נְעָרוֹת '*let* them *seek* maidens for the king' (2:2)
וְיַפְקֵד הַמֶּלֶךְ פְּקִידִים 'and *let* the king *appoint* appointees' (2:3)
Note how the juss. is translated. Read §32.35f.

בַּחֵיק יוּטַל אֶת־הַגּוֹרָל וּמֵיְהוָה כָּל־מִשְׁפָּטוֹ׃
The lot is cast in the lap, but from YHWH is His every judgment.
Proverbs 16:33

39

Purpose: To review some things we have seen
Materials: Esther 4:4-6

וַתָּבוֹאינָה נַעֲרוֹת 4
אֶסְתֵּר וְסָרִיסֶיהָ וַיַּגִּידוּ לָהּ וַתִּתְחַלְחַל הַמַּלְכָּה מְאֹד
וַתִּשְׁלַח בְּגָדִים לְהַלְבִּישׁ אֶת־מָרְדֳּכַי וּלְהָסִיר שַׂקּוֹ מֵעָלָיו
וְלֹא קִבֵּל׃ וַתִּקְרָא אֶסְתֵּר לַהֲתָךְ מִסָּרִיסֵי הַמֶּלֶךְ אֲשֶׁר ה
הֶעֱמִיד לְפָנֶיהָ וַתְּצַוֵּהוּ עַל־מָרְדֳּכָי לָדַעַת מַה־זֶּה וְעַל־
מַה־זֶּה׃ וַיֵּצֵא הֲתָךְ אֶל־מָרְדֳּכָי אֶל־רְחוֹב הָעִיר אֲשֶׁר 6
לִפְנֵי שַׁעַר־הַמֶּלֶךְ׃

4:4 וַתָּבוֹאינָה נַעֲרוֹת אֶסְתֵּר וְסָרִיסֶיהָ[1]—(a) Masoretic note points out the excessive *yôḏ*; *qᵉrê wattāḇônāʰ*. נָה—תּ = ? §27.31. Cf. 1:18[2]. Subj. of verb is compound, §30.113. The nearer subj. is fem., hence the verb form. (b-d) In Bib. Heb. it is impossible to say, 'the maids and eunuchs of Esther.' Regularly the construction would be 'the maids of E. and her eunuchs.' (d) ֶיהָ– is s1 on pl., cf. Table H.

וַיַּגִּידוּ לָהּ[2]—(a) Here the verb is 3mp. Cf. 3:4[3]. (b) What suffix? Table H.

וַתִּתְחַלְחַל הַמַּלְכָּה מְאֹד[3]—(a) *wat-tiṯḥalḥal* is HtRc21, with reduplication of 1st and 2d rads., usually called Hithpalpēl and treated as HtD, §28.74. This stem is found mainly with CC^2 and CWC verbs, and often has the idea of turning or twisting. *ḥûl* 'to turn, twist, writhe' (v.2342). (c) *mᵉʾôḏ* 'exceedingly' (v.3966).

וַתִּשְׁלַח בְּגָדִים[4]—(a) Cf. 1:22[1]; what is different about this form? Parse; translate. (b) Cf. 4:1[2], בְּגָדָיו. What is the difference?

לְהַלְבִּישׁ אֶת־מָרְדֳּכַי[5]—(a) Cf. 4:1[3]. *ha—î–* tells us what?. If G means 'to put on clothing,' what does H mean? (b-c) *lbš* is intransitive in G, trans. in H, §28.3.

וּלְהָסִיר שַׂקּוֹ מֵעָלָיו[6]—(a) Cf. 3:10[1]. *lᵉha–î–*, VDC T.9. If G means 'to turn aside' (intrans.), what might H mean?. (b) Note strong dagesh. Does this explain vowel in שַׂק? (c) Note compound prep., *mēʿal–* 'from upon.'

וְלֹא קִבֵּל׃[7]—(a) Neg. part., the form usually used with finite verbs in perf./impf. (b) *qibbēl,* cic^{2}ēc: do you recognize it? Note vowel under 1st rad., VDC–1. קבל 'to receive' (6901 13/3).

4:5 וַתִּקְרָא אֶסְתֵּר לַהֲתָךְ[1]—(a) We have had the verb קרא, 3:12[1]. Can you parse it? R.15, §29.22. (b) Subj. (c) Indir. obj.

מִסָּרִיסֵי הַמֶּלֶךְ אֲשֶׁר הֶעֱמִיד לְפָנֶיהָ[2]—(a) מִן partitive, 'from among, one of.' (d) *heʿĕmîḏ,* note vowels, R.10f, §29.11, R.10c. hiCCîC > *hiqṭîl,* but with GCC >

heʿĕmîḏ. Learn this *now*. עמד 'to stand' (v.5975), in H 'whom he stood (stationed) before her.'

וַתְּצַוֵּהוּ עַל־מָרְדֳּכָי [3]—(a) Note וּ and וֵּ–which is vowel and which is consonant?. ־ֵהוּ is s0 acc. suf. on impf. (Table H). ־תְּצַוּ suggests what stem? What are the clues? Parse. 'And she commanded him concerning M.'

לָדַעַת מַה־זֶּה וְעַל־מַה־זֶּה׃ [4]–(a) 2:11[4], §29.32. (b-c) Note strong dagesh after מַה, *ma*^{h}*-zzê*^{h}, 'what (is) this?' (d-f) *ʿal-ma*^{h} 'on account of what?' = 'why?' 'And why (is) this?'

4:6 וַיֵּצֵא הֲתָךְ אֶל־מָרְדֳּכָי [1]— (a) 1:17[1]. Note the difference and explain it. (b) 4:5[1].

אֶל־רְחוֹב הָעִיר [2]— (b) *r*^{e}*ḥôḇ* 'broad place, plaza, street' (v.7339). (c) 3:15[5].

אֲשֶׁר לִפְנֵי שַׁעַר־הַמֶּלֶךְ׃ [3]— You should be able to do this without help.

Study Rules 24, 25.

Learn the words in Group 33.

Note the following ways of expressing the interrogative:

מִי בֶחָצֵר '*Who* (is) in the court?'
מַה־נַּעֲשָׂה '*What* was done?'
לְמִי יַחְפֹּץ הלמך לַעֲשׂוֹת יְקָר '*To whom* would the king delight to do honor?'
הֲיַעַמְדוּ דִּבְרֵי מרדכי 'Would Mordecai's words stand up?' (הֲ)
מַדּוּעַ אַתָּה עוֹבֵר אֵת מִצְוַת המלך '*Why* are you transgressing the king's command?'
אֵיכָכָה אוּכַל '*How* shall I be able ...?'

Note carefully every interrogative clause that you encounter. Learning comes only from meaningful encounters.

הַאֲמִינוּ בַּיהוה אֱלֹהֵיכֶם וְתֵאָמֵנוּ הַאֲמִינוּ בִנְבִיאָיו וְהַצְלִיחוּ׃
Believe in the LORD your God, and you will be established;
believe his prophets, and you will succeed.
2 Chronicles 20:20

Purpose: To examine the student's progress
Materials: Esther 2:11–3:15

The Mid-Year (Mid-Course) Examination is to be given at this point. It should be a thorough review of just about everything. At this point the student has encountered almost everything that he will see in narrative Hebrew. The exam should point out what he *needs to learn.* In the coming lessons, there will be constant review, and if the student is aware of *what to study*, he will make much better progress.

Since the verb is the biggest obstacle to most students, this will be stressed.

Note the following uses of the *imperfect*:
כִּי־יֵצֵא דְבַר־הַמַּלְכָּה 'for the queen's word *shall go forth*' (1:17)
תֹּאמַרְנָה שָׂרוֹת פָּרַס־וּמָדַי 'The princesses of Persia and Media *shall say*' (1:18)
וְלֹא יַעֲבוֹר 'and it *shall not pass away*' (1:19)
לֹא־תָבוֹא וַשְׁתִּי לִפְנֵי הַמֶּלֶךְ 'Vashti *shall not come in* before the king' (1:19)
אֲשֶׁר יַעֲשֶׂה בְּכָל־מַלְכוּתוֹ 'which he *shall cause to be done* in all his kingdom' (1:20)
Note that the impf. is consistently translated in the *future* tense. Read §32.52f.

Note the following uses of the *converted imperfect*:
וַיִּיטַב הַדָּבָר ... וַיַּעַשׂ הַמֶּלֶךְ ... וַיִּשְׁלַח סְפָרִים ... 'and the matter *was good* ... and the king *did* ... and *he sent* documents ...' (1:21-22)
Note that the conv. impf. is consistently translated in *past* tense. Read §32.533.

Go over the following verbs.

שָׁמַע	3:4^{2}	וַיֹּאמֶר	3:8^{1}	וַיַּרְא	3:5^{1}
יָצְאוּ	35^{1}	וַיֹּאמְרוּ	3:3^{1}	וַיִּבֶז	3:6^{1}
יָשְׁבוּ	3:15^{4}	וַיִּתְּנָהּ	3:10^{3}	וַיְהִי	3:4^{1}
יִכְרַע	3:2^{3}	הֲיַעַמְדוּ	3:4^{5}	עוֹבֵר	3:3^{2}
אֶשְׁקוֹל	3:9^{4}	וַיָּשֶׂם	3:1^{5}	נָתוּן	3:11^{2}
כֹּרֵעַ	3:5^{2}	וַיָּסַר	3:10^{1}	לִשְׁלוֹחַ	3:6^{2}
כֹּרְעִים	3:2^{3}	לִרְאוֹת	3:4^{4}	לַהֲרֹג	3:13^{3}
גִּדַּל	3:1^{2}	וַיְבַקֵּו	3:6^{4}	מְפֻזָּר	3:8^{3}
בַּקָּשָׁה	2:15^{4}	וַיְבַקְוּ	2:21^{6}	מְפֹרָד	3:8^{3}
צִוָּה	3:2^{5}	וַיְבֻקַּשׁ	2:23^{1}	לְאַבֵּד	3:13^{3}
				לְאַבְּדָם	3:9^{2}
הִגִּיד	3:4^{6}	וַיָּשֶׂם	3:1^{5}	לְהַשְׁמִיד	3:6^{5}
הִגִּידוּ	3:6^{3}	וַיָּסַר	3:10^{1}	לְהָבִיא	3:9^{5}
הִפִּיל	3:7^{3}	וַיַּגִּידוּ	3:4^{3}	מַגֶּדֶת	2:20^{2}
וַיַּגֵּד	2:22^{3}	וַיַּמְלִיכֶהָ	2:17^{6}	וּבְהַגִּיעַ	2:12^{1}

וְנֶחְתַּם	3:12[10]	יִכָּתֵב	3:9[2]	לְהַנִּיחָם	3:8[7]
נִכְתָּב	3:12[9]	יֵעָשֶׂה	2:11[5]	לְהִנָּתֶן־	3:14[2]
נִתְּנָה	3:15[3]	יִנָּתֶן־	2:13[3]	וּבְהִקָּבֵץ	2:19[1]
וְנִקְרְאָה	2:14[8]	וַתִּלָּקַח	2:16[1]	וְנִשְׁלוֹחַ	3:13[1]
וַיִּקָּרְאוּ	3:12[1]	וַיִּוָּדַע	2:22[1]	נָבוֹכָה	3:15[5]
וַיִּתָּלוּ	2:23[3]	וַיִּמָּצֵא	2:23[2]	וַיִּמָּלֵא	3:5[3]
מִתְהַלֵּךְ	2:11[2]	וַתִּתְחַלְחַל	4:4[3]	מִשְׁתַּחֲוֶה	3:5[2]

צֹרֵר	3:10[4]	נָתוּן	3:11[2]	בָּאָה	2:13[1]
עוֹבֵר	3:3[1]	גָּלוּי	3:14[3]	שָׁבָה	2:14[2]
שֹׁוֶה	3:8[7]	נְשֻׂאת	2:15[6]	עָשָׂה	2:20[6]
עֹשִׂים	3:8[6]	רֹאֶיהָ	2:16[1]	עֹשֵׂי	3:9[4]
שֹׁנוֹת	3:8[5]	דְּחוּפִים	3:15[2]	רָצִים	3:13[1]

לִשְׁלֹחַ	3:6[2]	בְּאָמְרָם	3:4[1]	לְהַשְׁמִיד	3:6[5]
לִשְׁתּוֹת	3:15[4]	לְאַבְּדָם	3:9[2]	לְהָבִיא	3:9[5]
הֱיוֹת	2:12[3]	וּלְאַבֵּד	3:13[3]	וּבְהַגִּיעַ	2:12[1]
לִהְיוֹת	3:14[4]	וּבְהִקָּבֵץ	2:19[1]	לְהִנָּתֵן	3:14[2]
לָדַעַת	2:11[4]	בְּאָמְנָה	2:20[3]	לַהֲרֹג	3:13[3]
לִרְאוֹת	3:4[4]	לְהַנִּיחָם	3:8[7]	לַעֲשׂוֹת	3:11[3]

Know all the words in basic vocabulary groups 1–33.

עֹבֵד אַדְמָתוֹ יִשְׂבַּע־לָחֶם וּמְרַדֵּף רֵיקִים חֲסַר־לֵב׃

He who tills his land will have plenty of bread,
but he who follows worthless pursuits has no sense.

Proverbs 12:11

41

Purpose: To review the Infinitive Construct
Materials: Esther 4:7-10

7 וַיַּגֶּד־לוֹ מָרְדֳּכַי אֵת כָּל־אֲשֶׁר קָרָהוּ
וְאֵת ׀ פָּרָשַׁת הַכֶּסֶף אֲשֶׁר אָמַר הָמָן לִשְׁקוֹל עַל־גִּנְזֵי
8 הַמֶּלֶךְ בַּיְּהוּדִיִּים לְאַבְּדָם׃ וְאֶת־פַּתְשֶׁגֶן כְּתָב־הַדָּת אֲשֶׁר־
נִתַּן בְּשׁוּשָׁן לְהַשְׁמִידָם נָתַן לוֹ לְהַרְאוֹת אֶת־אֶסְתֵּר וּלְהַגִּיד
לָהּ וּלְצַוּוֹת עָלֶיהָ לָבוֹא אֶל־הַמֶּלֶךְ לְהִתְחַנֶּן־לוֹ וּלְבַקֵּשׁ
9 מִלְּפָנָיו עַל־עַמָּהּ׃ וַיָּבוֹא הֲתָךְ וַיַּגֵּד לְאֶסְתֵּר אֵת דִּבְרֵי
מָרְדֳּכָי׃ וַתֹּאמֶר אֶסְתֵּר לַהֲתָךְ וַתְּצַוֵּהוּ אֶל־מָרְדֳּכָי׃

4:7 וַיַּגֶּד־לוֹ [1]—Note *mappîq,* normal form וַיַּגֵּד. Cf. וַיַּגִּידוּ 4:4[2]. R.2a. §15.22. The conv. impf. is *not* built on the impf., but on an originally-closed form like the juss. Subj. follows.

אֶת כָּל־אֲשֶׁר קָרָהוּ [2]—(a-d) Obj. (= ind. disc.) of 4:7[1], the first of a compound obj. (d) *qārāhû* G10s0 of קרה 'he met, it befell' (v.7136); do not confuse it with קרא (they sound alike). 'All that befell him, happened to him.' Note that the ה in this form is not the radical, but the suffix. §15.432. §29.713.

וְאֵת ׀ פָּרָשַׁת הַכֶּסֶף [3]—(a-c) Second of compound obj. Note *pāsêq.* (b) *pārāšaṯ* is obviously in cstr., hence the *qāmāṣ*s must be either long vowels or compensation vowels. *pārāšā^h* 'total, sum, declared amount' (6575 2/2).

אֲשֶׁר אָמַר הָמָן[4]—Rel. cl. defining הכסף. (c) Subj. of (b).

לִשְׁקוֹל[5]—Note ל־, R.19. Fasle plene, §11.324). *šuqul* cucuc = G65 (§27.65). 'He said to weigh,' = 'he said that he would weigh,' indirect discourse. For the following words, 3:9[5].

בַּיְּהוּדִיִּים לְאַבְּדָם׃ [6]—(a) ב־ of price, *Ges.* §119*p*, 'to pay for.' The Kt (§11.61) is the basic form of the pl. of a gentilic, *y^{e}hûḏî* + *îm*; the Qr is the developed form, *y^{e}hûḏî^{y}m*; note the violation of R.1b. (b) Cf. 3:13[3]. The form here has what suf.? R.16.

4:8 וְאֶת־פַּתְשֶׁגֶן [1]—3:14[1].

אֲשֶׁר־ נִתַּן בְּשׁוּשָׁן לְהַשְׁמִידָם [2]—(a) What kind of clause?. (b) CiC^{2}aC would be D10–but is it? What would N10 of NCC look like? G29 of NCC? N29 of CC^2? (c) ב־, place where, 'in.' (d) 3:6[5]. What is ־ָם? ל־ + 65 indicates purpose.

נָתַן לוֹ [4]—(a) Who is the subj.? (b) ל־ before substantive, indirect object.

לְהַרְאוֹת אֶת־אֶסְתֵּר [5]—(a) *l^e* + 65, purpose. לְהַ|רְא|וֹת, If *-ôṯ* tells us that the form is 65 of CCY (§29.71), why can't ה be a radical? 1:11[4]. Note that there is no syncopation (§13.5221). (b-c) The H-stem of transitive verbs takes two objects, one of which (the nearer) may take אֵת. 'To show (it) to Esther,' = 'to cause E. to see (it).'

וּלְהַגִּיד לָהּ⁶—(a) *lᵉ* + *haggîḏ* < **hangîḏ* (r.11), VDC–7. (b) Ind. obj.

וּלְצַוּוֹת עָלֶיהָ לָבוֹא⁷—(a) Note carefully! ו can be *û* or *ww*; here it is followed by a vowel וֹ, so it must be a consonant, *lᵉṣawwôṯ*, cf. 3:2⁵. (b) צוה does not take a dir. obj., but requires a prep., 2:20⁴. (c) Ind. disc.

4:8 לְהִתְחַנֶּן־לוֹ¹—(a) *lᵉ* + *hiṯḥannen*, with *nāsôḡ 'āḥôr* (§17.35), obviously HtD, and after לְ– obviously 65. חנן 'to be gracious,' HtD 'to beseech, make supplication to, seek mercy' (v.2603). (b) Is this 'from him,' 'on his behalf,' or 'to him'?

וּלְבַקֵּשׁ מִלְּפָנָיו עַל־עַמָּהּ׃⁹—(a) CaC²ēC could be what forms? VDC–2. Can you tell which it is here? 2:2³. (b) *min* + *lᵉ* + *pᵉnê* + s0. BDB 816-819. (c) *'al* 'on account of' (5921), see BDB 752-759. (d) CaC² + s1.

4:9 You should be able to do 4: 9 without help.

4:10 וַתֹּאמֶר¹—Note the incomplete way אמר is often used. When we use the Eng. verb *to say,* we expect something to follow, even if only *it.* Here it is better to translate the verb 'and she told' (even though that should be וַתַּגֵּד). התך is pr.n., 4:5¹.

וַתְּצַוֵּהוּ²—(a) For -*éhû* Table H. For צוה 4:8⁷, 3:2⁵. For ת—, §27.31. Who gave the command? To whom was it given? Note that while צוה requires a prep. before a noun-object, it can take a pron. suf. for object. 'And E. said (= told it) to H., and she commanded him (to go tell it) to M.'

Use this lesson to review the inf. cstr., its morphology and its syntax. You have not had *everything* about the inf.cstr. at this point, but you have had *most* of the common uses.

Learn the words in Group 34.

Note the following uses of the infinitive construct:
וַיִּבֶז בְּעֵינָיו לִשְׁלֹחַ יָד בְּמָרְדֳּכַי לְבַדּוֹ – *What* was contemptible?
וְלַמֶּלֶךְ אֵין שֹׁוֶה לְהַנִּיחָם – *What* is not suitable or fitting? To whom?

―――――――――

מַשְׂכִּיל עַל־דָּבָר יִמְצָא־טוֹב
וּבוֹטֵחַ בַּיהוָה אַשְׁרָיו׃
He who gives heed to the word will prosper, and happy is he who trusts in YHWH.
Proverbs 16:20

Purpose: To review verb stems
Materials: Esther 4:11-13

11 כָּל־
עַבְדֵי הַמֶּלֶךְ וְעַם מְדִינוֹת הַמֶּלֶךְ יוֹדְעִים אֲשֶׁר כָּל־אִישׁ
וְאִשָּׁה אֲשֶׁר־יָבוֹא אֶל־הַמֶּלֶךְ אֶל־הֶחָצֵר הַפְּנִימִית אֲשֶׁר
לֹא־יִקָּרֵא אַחַת דָּתוֹ לְהָמִית לְבַד מֵאֲשֶׁר יוֹשִׁיט־לוֹ הַמֶּלֶךְ
אֶת־שַׁרְבִיט הַזָּהָב וְחָיָה וַאֲנִי לֹא נִקְרֵאתִי לָבוֹא אֶל־
12 הַמֶּלֶךְ זֶה שְׁלוֹשִׁים יוֹם׃ וַיַּגִּידוּ לְמָרְדֳּכָי אֵת דִּבְרֵי אֶסְתֵּר׃
13 וַיֹּאמֶר מָרְדֳּכַי לְהָשִׁיב אֶל־אֶסְתֵּר אַל־תְּדַמִּי בְנַפְשֵׁךְ
לְהִמָּלֵט בֵּית־הַמֶּלֶךְ מִכָּל־הַיְּהוּדִים׃

4:11 כָּל־עַבְדֵי הַמֶּלֶךְ וְעַם מְדִינוֹת הַמֶּלֶךְ יוֹדְעִים [1]—Note this long clause. (a) כל is in cstr. with modifiers (1) עבדי המ׳ and (2) עם מרינות המ׳. (b) *'abdê*[y] mpc of *'ébed*, 1:3[7], §22.24, §24.241. (d-f) Chain of cstrs., last word is def., therefore all are def., 'the people of the provinces of the king.' (g) *yôd*[e]*'îm: –ô––* is what pattern? Pl. because it agrees with (b-c) and (d-f). §27.6.

אֲשֶׁר כָּל־אִישׁ וְאִשָּׁה [2]—(a) Pron. introduces ind. disc., 'knows *that* ....' (b) Modifies (c) and (d), (c-d) serving as a single expression, 'every (any) man and (or) woman.' (c) *'îš* 'man' (v.376), root **'š* (CvC), 1:8[6]. (d) *'iššā*[h] 'woman' (v.802), root **'nθ* (Arab. *'unθay, θ > š* §12.65, *nš > šš* §13.111). The cstr. *'éšet* 'wife of' probably is fem of *'îš > 'išt* (R.2a).

אֲשֶׁר־יָבוֹא [3]—(a) Introduces rel. cl. (b) *yāCôC,* CvC verb (§29.63). With yaCCuC or yaCCiC impf. of this type of verb, the *a* of the preformative remains (the syllable is not closed, hence R.18 does not apply). Don't confuse it with the clue to the H-stem.

אֶל־הֶחָצֵר הַפְּנִימִית [4]—(b) The gender of the noun must be determined by the adj. חצר appears to be masc., but the ת– on (c) proves that it is fem. 1:5[10], 2:11[3]. Table G. (c) *p*[e]*nîmî* 'inner' (v.6442), CvCîCî pattern, often used for ordinals, §26.3. Note concord (§24.59).

אֲשֶׁר לֹא־יִקָּרֵא [5]—(a) How is this particle used here? (c) Dagesh in 1st rad., vowel pattern, VDC–3. If this is not a *yqtl* perf. (cf. Akk. *iprus*), it has to be taken as = fut. perf., 'who shall enter, who shall not have been called.'

אַחַת דָּתוֹ לְהָמִית [6]——(a) §31., 'one (is) his law.' §26.21, §13.1, §13.113, §15.1411, §16.3431. (c) *hā–î–* looks like H-stem of a verb with 2 rads., prob. CvC. Does it fit? מות (v.4191) 'to die,' H 'to put to death.'

לְבַד מֵאֲשֶׁר יוֹשִׁיט־לוֹ [7]—(a) *lbd* 1:16[2], BDB 94. followed by מִן 'in separation from, apart from, besides,' *Ges.* §119*c*. (b) Analyze it. (c) יָשַׁט 'he held out, stretched forth' (3447 3/3); WCC, hence in H *yaw* > *yô*, §29.311.

אֶת־שַׁרְבִיט הַזָּהָב וְחָיָה [8]—(b) Without def. art. *šarḇîṭ* would appear to be a pr. n., but see 5:2[5]; 'scepter' (8275 4/4). There is no explanation of spirantized *ḇ* after dagesh; possibly it is a loan-word with original [v]. Scepters were often named. (c) 1:7[2]; in concord, therefore *šarḇîṭ* must be def. (see also את). (d) *ḥāyā*^{h} 'to live' (v.2421). Do not confuse חיה with היה. Gc10, 'and he shall live,' §32.54.

וַאֲנִי לֹא נִקְרֵאתִי לָבוֹא [9]—(a) Note *r*^{e}*ḇî*^{a}*ʿ* 'and as for me' (§21.1). (c) *ni–́–tî;* ––נ could be 29, but what about תִי–? If it is 14, then what is *ni–*? Could it be a stem morpheme? Note תִי–––נ, cf. נִקְטַלְתִּי, and compare the vowels under 2d rad. The CCʾ root leaves the syllable open. N14, 'I have not been called.' §29.22. (d) Purpose, or possibly ind. disc.

זֶה שְׁלוֹשִׁים יוֹם׃ [10]—(a) Demon. pron., §21.2, in sing. to agree with *yôm.* (b) The pl. of '3' is '30' (v.7970), §26.26. With numbers above 10, the noun is sing., §26.84, hence 'these 30 days.'

4:12 You should be able to do 4:12. If you need help on the verb, cf. 4:4[2].

4:13 לְהָשִׁיב[1]—(a) Cf. 3:9[5], 1:11[1]. This has to be H65 of CŷC—explain why. שׁוּב 'to return, turn; (H) to return, bring back' (v.7725). 2:14[2].

אַל־תְּדַמִּי בְנַפְשֵׁךְ [2]—(a) *ʾal* negates juss., a milder form of command. §35.223. (b) Look at this form carefully. Afformatives י–––ת, §27.31. Look at the clues: shewa, dagesh, *a*-vowel—what stem? What rad. is missing? What type of verb? דמה 'to be like; (D) to imagine' (v.1819). D43. (c) ב|נפש|ך, *népeš* 'soul, self, life' (v.5315), with s3; 'with/in your soul.'

לְהִמָּלֵט בֵּית־הַמֶּלֶךְ [3]—(a) hiC^{2}āCēC should now be familiar (VDC–2). מלט N 'to escape' (v.4422). (c) = בבית, 1:9[4]. 'Don't imagine in your soul to escape' = '. . . that you will escape,' inf. of ind. disc.

מִכָּל־הַיְּהוּדִים׃[4]—(a) *min* of comparison, 'more than (other) Jews' = 'Don't think that you will be safer.'

Be sure you know the principal characterstics of verb-stem morphology. Students struggle with the Heb. verb for years, just because they fail to learn *what to look for* in each form. The basic patterns are your best friends in this problem.

Memorize the words in Group 35.

43

Purpose: To review verb "tenses"
Materials: Esther 4:14-16

כִּי אִם־הַחֲרֵשׁ 14
תַּחֲרִישִׁי בָּעֵת הַזֹּאת רֶוַח וְהַצָּלָה יַעֲמוֹד לַיְּהוּדִים מִמָּקוֹם
אַחֵר וְאַתְּ וּבֵית־אָבִיךְ תֹּאבֵדוּ וּמִי יוֹדֵעַ אִם־לְעֵת כָּזֹאת
הִגַּעַתְּ לַמַּלְכוּת׃ וַתֹּאמֶר אֶסְתֵּר לְהָשִׁיב אֶל־מָרְדֳּכָי׃ טו
לֵךְ כְּנוֹס אֶת־כָּל־הַיְּהוּדִים הַנִּמְצְאִים בְּשׁוּשָׁן וְצוּמוּ עָלַי 16
וְאַל־תֹּאכְלוּ וְאַל־תִּשְׁתּוּ שְׁלֹשֶׁת יָמִים לַיְלָה וָיוֹם גַּם־אֲנִי
וְנַעֲרֹתַי אָצוּם כֵּן וּבְכֵן אָבוֹא אֶל־הַמֶּלֶךְ אֲשֶׁר לֹא־כַדָּת
וְכַאֲשֶׁר אָבַדְתִּי אָבָדְתִּי׃ 17

4:14 כִּי אִם־הַחֲרֵשׁ תַּחֲרִישִׁי[1]—(a-b) *kî 'im* often means 'except,' especially after a neg. Here, however, the words are not joined; they mean 'for if.' אִם 'if,' etc. (v.518), BDB 49f. (c) *haḥărēš* < **haḥrēš* (R.10c) haCCēC, VDC–3, inf. abs. (H60, §28.31). חרש 'to be silent, dumb' (v.2790). (d) *taḥărîšî* ת——ִי = 23, תַּ-ִ-ִי = H23. For the use of H60 + H23 see §35.6. 'Surely if you keep silent.'

בָּעֵת הַזֹּאת[2]—(a) b^e + *hā*, §13.521, + *'ēṯ* 'time' (v.6256). (b) Demon. pron (§21.2), note concord, including def. art. 'In this time.'

רֶוַח וְהַצָּלָה יַעֲמוֹד לַיְּהוּדִים מִמָּקוֹם אַחֵר[3]—(a) *réwaḥ* 'deliverance, relief' (7305 2/1), cf. §24.21. (b) *haṣṣālā*[h] 'deliverance' (2020 1/1), root *nṣl*, cf. §24.31. (c) *yaqtul* of GCC yaGăCōC, with false plēnē (§11.3241). For *'md*, 3:4[5]. (e) *min* + *māqôm* 'place' (v.4725), §24.33, from קום. (f) *'aḥēr* 'other, another' (v.312).

וְאַתְּ וּבֵית־אָבִיךְ תֹּאבֵדוּ[4]—(a) §21.1, < **'anti*, note strong dagesh, *'att*[e], §16.341, §16.363. (c) *'āḇ* always has *yôḏ* when adding suffix. 2:7[4·7]. *Ges.* p.282. (d) Note athnaḥ. Read §29.212, §15.623. ת——ו is 22, §27.31. R.17 only applies in nonpausal forms. For אבד, 3:13[3].

וּמִי יוֹדֵעַ אִם־לְעֵת כָּזֹאת הִגַּעַתְּ לַמַּלְכוּת׃[5]—(a) Interrog. pron, §21.4, R.10e. מִי 'who?' (v.4310). (c) 'If, whether.' (d) 4:14[2]. (e) 4:14[2]. Is there a def.art.? §22.41. (f) *higgá'aṯ* < **hinga't*, R.11, R.10c, exception to R.5. ה——ת must be H13, NCC, §27.21, §28.31. נגע 2:12[2]. Read §32.5122.

4:15 You should be able to do this verse. Cf. 4:13. For להשיב, cf. 4:13[1].

4:16 לֵךְ כְּנוֹס[1]—(a) *lēḵ* < **h*[e]*lēḵ*, §13.512, §27.4. הלך 2:11[2].(b) *k*[e]*nôs*, G32 < *CiCuC*, §24.22. כנס 'to gather, assemble' (3664 11/1). Note asyndeton, §30.364. Dir. obj. follows.

הַנִּמְצְאִים בְּשׁוּשָׁן [2]—See 1:5[5].

וְצוּמוּ עָלַי [3]—(a) —*û* could be 15/16/37, §27.41. The *û* between the two radicals tells us it is 37, see VDC–10. צום 'to fast' (v.6684). (b) עַל always has *yôḏ* with suffix, *'alay* + *î* > *'alay,* §15.72. 'On my behalf, for me.'

וְאַל־תֹּאכְלוּ וְאַל־תִּשְׁתּוּ [4]—(a) 4:13[2]. (b) ת——ו is 27/47 (§27.31). Review §29.212. For אַל and juss., §32.353. 'Don't eat.' (d) Note morphemes. Two rads., 1st syll. closed (G or H), and ִ tells us it is G. §29.713. שתה 3:15[4]. Note change of subj. from sing. (you, Mordecai) to plur. (you, all Jews).

שְׁלֹשֶׁת יָמִים לַיְלָה וָיוֹם [5]—(a) Num., §26.23; cstr., §36.14. (b) *yôm*, pl. *yāmîm*, §24.212. Note pl. after nums. 3-9. (c) *láy-lā*^{h} 'night' (v.3915), cf. §§23.2, .23. (BDB 538 rejects this explanation, but fails to account for [1] penultimate accent and [2] the frequent use of this word adverbially.)

גַּם־אֲנִי וְנַעֲרֹתַי אָצוּם כֵּן [6]—(a) 'Also' (v.1571). (b-c) Note order. (c) Form is fps4, written defectively. (d) —א is 24, cf. 4:16[3]. The pattern could be Gp50, so beware! (e) 'Thus' (v.3651).

וּבְכֵן אָבוֹא אֶל־הַמֶּלֶךְ [7]—(a) ו|ב|כן 'and in this manner. (b) This verb is irregular; we would expect *'āCûC* like *'āṣûm*, §29.63f.

אֲשֶׁר לֹא־כַדָּת [8]—(b-c) Rel. cl., verbless, 'which (is) not according to law.'

וְכַאֲשֶׁר אָבַדְתִּי אָבָדְתִּי׃ [9]—(a) When,' §36.41. (b) ־תִּי– – – is 14, vowel pattern is G. (c) Note pausal form, cf. R.15. This could be fut.perf., 'and when I have perished, I have perished' (§32.5133), or contrary-to-fact condition, 'and if I perish I perish' (§32.5141).

Learn the words in Group 36.

Note the following pronominal suffixes:

b^e*nô* *his* son
bānā^y*w* *his* sons
b^e*nî* *my* son
bānê^y*ḵā* *your* sons
binḵā *your* son
b^e*nôṯā*^{y}*w* *his* daughters

הַחֵקֶר אֱלוֹהַּ תִּמְצָא
אִם עַד־תַּכְלִית שַׁדַּי תִּמְצָא׃
Can you find out the deep things of God?
Can you find out the limit of the Almighty?
Job 11:7

44

Purpose: To work on the verb
Materials: Esther 4:17–5:2

וַיַּעֲבֹר מָרְדֳּכָי וַיַּעַשׂ כְּכֹל אֲשֶׁר־
צִוְּתָה עָלָיו אֶסְתֵּר׃

CAP. V. ה

ה
א וַיְהִי ׀ בַּיּוֹם הַשְּׁלִישִׁי וַתִּלְבַּשׁ אֶסְתֵּר מַלְכוּת וַתַּעֲמֹד בַּחֲצַר
בֵּית־הַמֶּלֶךְ הַפְּנִימִית נֹכַח בֵּית הַמֶּלֶךְ וְהַמֶּלֶךְ יוֹשֵׁב עַל־
2 כִּסֵּא מַלְכוּתוֹ בְּבֵית הַמַּלְכוּת נֹכַח פֶּתַח הַבָּיִת׃ וַיְהִי
כִרְאוֹת הַמֶּלֶךְ אֶת־אֶסְתֵּר הַמַּלְכָּה עֹמֶדֶת בֶּחָצֵר נָשְׂאָה
חֵן בְּעֵינָיו וַיּוֹשֶׁט הַמֶּלֶךְ לְאֶסְתֵּר אֶת־שַׁרְבִיט הַזָּהָב אֲשֶׁר
3 בְּיָדוֹ וַתִּקְרַב אֶסְתֵּר וַתִּגַּע בְּרֹאשׁ הַשַּׁרְבִיט׃

4:17 וַיַּעֲבֹר מָרְדֳּכָי [1]—(a) Young's Concordance lists 73 different ways עבר is translated in KJV. This word needs careful study. Here it could mean: 'M. *transgressed* (the king's command)'; '*crossed over* (the street)'; '*proceeded with* (E.'s command),' etc. *Meanings are derived from contexts, not from lexicons.* Good lexicons supply references to the contexts for our study.

וַיַּעַשׂ כְּכֹל [2]—(a) You should know this form. §29.72. §32.53. (b) k^e + k̲ōl; –כְּ 'according to.'

אֲשֶׁר־צִוְּתָה עָלָיו אֶסְתֵּר׃ [3]—(a) Rel. pron., used how? (b) –תָה– is what morpheme? §29.7131. Is –וְ– vocalic or consonantal *wāw*?

5:1 וַיְהִי ׀ בַּיּוֹם הַשְּׁלִישִׁי [1]—(a) You should know this word thoroughly. If you don't, learn it *now.* 3:4[1]. (b-c) Note use of ordinal as adj., §36.14. For morphology, §26.32.

וַתִּלְבַּשׁ אֶסְתֵּר מַלְכוּת [2]—(a) *yiqtal* type Gc20 of לבש (v.3847). §32.533. (b) How related to verb? How do you know?. (c) 1:2[8]. How does 'royalty, queenship' fit here? In Eng. we would use either an adv. or a prep., but learn to observe how it is done in Heb.

וַתַּעֲמֹד בַּחֲצַר בֵּית־הַמֶּלֶךְ הַפְּנִימִית [3]—(a) 4:14[3]. Parse form, translate. (b) 4:11[4]. Explain the different pointing. (c-d) 'Palace.' (e) Does this modify בית or חצר ? How do you know? Cf. 4:11[4].

נֹכַח [4]—(a) Noun used as prep, see BDB 647, 'in front of' (v.5227). CuCG-type noun, §24.211. This word in in cstr. with and governing the following word, which is also in cstr.

וְהַמֶּ֫לֶךְ יוֹשֵׁב עַל־כִּסֵּא מַלְכוּתוֹ בְּבֵית הַמַּלְכוּת [5]—(b-e) Cf. 1:2[3,6,7,8]. (f-g) Is this 'in the royal house,' 'in the house of royalty,' or 'in the house of the kingship' ? Note בבית, not בית, and cf. 1:9[4], 4:13[3].

נֹכַח פֶּתַח הַבָּיִת׃ [6]—(a) 5:1[4]. (b) 'Door, doorway' (v.6607), CvCG-type noun; cf. *pattāḥ*, name of the open vowel /a/.

5:2 וַיְהִי כִרְאוֹת [1]—(a) 5:1[1]. ?אם לא עכשו, אימתי (see p.35). (b) Cf. 3:4[4], 3:4[1], 2:20[8]. The 65 + כְּ– often means 'when,' but more strictly 'as, while'; the 65 + בְּ– means 'when.' You should be able to work out the rest of the clause.

עֹמֶ֫דֶת בֶּחָצֵר [2]—(a) The fem. of CôCēC is usually CôCeCt when a ptcp. (G51), which > CôCéCet, *'ômédet*. (b) Is there a def. art. on this word?. Table G.

נָשְׂאָה חֵן בְּעֵינָיו [3]—(a) ה–ָ–ְ–ָ is what form? (b) 2:15[2]. (c) Do you know the full significance of יו–ָ ?

וַיּוֹשֶׁט הַמֶּלֶךְ לְאֶסְתֵּר אֶת־שַׁרְבִיט הַזָּהָב [4]—(a) Note *wayyôšeṭ* (R.27), cf. *yôšîṭ* in 4:11[7]. Long *ô* in such forms suggests H of WCC, §29.321. Note sub., indir. obj., dir. obj., of verb. Be sure you can identify each and tell how you know. Cf. 4:11[8].

וַתִּקְרַב אֶסְתֵּר [5]—(a) ת– – – can be what morpheme? §27.31. תִּ–ְ–ַ– is what type of impf.? §27.333. קרב 'to draw near' (7126), cf. קָרוֹב 1:14[1]. (b) How is this word related to verb? §33.1.

וַתִּגַּע בְּרֹאשׁ הַשַּׁרְבִיט׃ [6]—(a) Cf. 2:12[1]. G 'to touch,' parse, translate. (b) 2:17[5]. Note use of prep. after נגע. (c) 4:11[8].

Learn the words in Group 37.

Study the following forms:

וַתָּ֫שֶׂם
וַתּ֫וֹסֶף
וַתְּדַבֵּר
וַתִּפֹּל
וַתֵּ֫בְךְּ
וַתִּתְחַנֶּן
וַתָּ֫קָם
וַתַּעֲמֹד
וַתֹּאמֶר

Study the following forms:

לְהַקְהֵל
לְהַשְׁמִיד
לַהֲרֹג
לִהְיוֹת
לְהִנָּקֵם
לְהִנָּתֵן
לְהָשִׁיב
לְהַעֲבִיר

שְׁמַע יִשְׂרָאֵל יְהוָה אֱלֹהֵינוּ יְהוָה | אֶחָד׃
Hear, O Israel, the Lord our God, the Lord is one.
Deuteronomy 6:4

45

Purpose., To introduce exegesis
Materials: Genesis 1:1-5, BDB lexicon

For the exegesis lessons we recommend that you work from your own Hebrew Bible, to get used to it. Masoretic accents will have to be supplied from your Bible.

Exegesis is the art and skill of *bringing out* (ἐξ + ἄγω) the meaning of a passage, specifically the meaning which the author intended to convey. It is both an art and a skill—an art that requires ability to perceive subtle shades of expression, structure, balance, contrast, etc., and a skill that needs to be learned, practiced, and developed. It cannot be learned by simply reading commentaries, any more than swimming or cooking can be learned by simply reading books or watching someone else. We can learn much from observation, but to succeed, we must get in and do it personally.

The first step in *grammatico-historical exegesis* is with the text itself, the words in their context, both as to form and syntax.

Gen. 1:1 בְּרֵאשִׁית בָּרָא אֱלֹהִים[1]—(a) *rēʾšît*- 'beginning' (v.7225). No def. art., hence it could be cstr. (with a finite verb—distinctly a possibility in Sem. languages). BDB 912. (b) 'He created' (v.1254), always of divine activity, but not exclusively *ex nihilo* (out of nothing), BDB 135. (c) 'God,' pl. form of אֱלֹהַּ (v.430, 433), BDB 43f., used of rulers, angels, gods (with pl. adjs. and vb. forms) and of God (with sg. adjs. and vb. forms). The pl. is explained as (1) a vestige of polytheism, (2) royal pl., (3) community of persons, either (*a*) God and his court, or (*β*) in the godhead. Use of sg. concord seems to rule out (1) and (3*a*).

אֵת הַשָּׁמַיִם וְאֵת הָאָרֶץ׃[2]—(a,c) Sign of def. dir. obj., §34.113, hence compound obj., §34.115. (b) 'Heavens' (v.8064), BDB 1029. (d) 'Earth' (v.776), BDB 75f.(b + d) Possibly a merism for 'everything, the universe, the earth beneath and the sky overhead.'

1:2 וְהָאָרֶץ הָיְתָה תֹהוּ וָבֹהוּ[1]—(a) The center of interest is earth, not the heavens. All that follows is phenomenologically (but not necessarily physically) geocentric, i.e. as it appears to us on earth.(b) G11 in concord with (a). היה is not a mere copula (§31.3), but rather emphasizes the former state, '*was*,' in the beginning of creation.(c) V.8414, BDB 1062. (d) BDB 96. Note accents. Note form of ו־ before ב when near-open, not conforming to R.8.

וְחֹשֶׁךְ עַל־פְּנֵי תְהוֹם[2]—(a) 'Darkness' (v.2822). The cl. is verbless, §31. (d) 'Abyss' (v.8415), possibly cognate with Akk. *Tiʾâmat*, the underground waters, cf. BDB 1062f. But the place of Tiʾâmat in the Bab. creation story is far different from that of *t*ᵉ*hôm*.

וְרוּחַ אֱלֹהִים מְרַחֶפֶת עַל־פְּנֵי הַמָּיִם׃[3]— (a) 'Wind, breath, spirit' (v.7307), BDB 924ff, esp. 925.9, 926.9e.(a-b) Cstr. could be 'the wind from God,' 'the breath which is God's,' 'the divine Spirit,' etc.(c) D51 of רחף 'to hover' (2x, BDB 934). Force of ptcp., '(was) hovering.'

1:3 וַיֹּאמֶר אֱלֹהִים יְהִי אוֹר[1]—(a-b) Note concord in meaning but not in morphology—regular when *'ĕlôhîm* means '(the true) God.' If 1:1[1] is taken as cstr., hence dependent cl., this is the first main cl., 'then God said.'(c) G40 of היה, §27.511, §29.72, §32.35., 'let there be.' In Lat., this is translated *fiat*, hence the term "fiat creation."(d) 'Light' (v.216), not necessarily the light of the sun, moon, and stars, BDB 21.(c-d) Direct discourse or quotation, §38.81. Be sure you understand the jussive. It is significant in Gen. 1.

וַיְהִי־אוֹר׃[2]—(a) Cf. Est. 1:1[1]. Here, however, it is the converse of the היתה of Gen. 1:2 and its darkness, hence, 'Light came into being.'

1:4 וַיַּרְא אֱלֹהִים אֶת־הָאוֹר כִּי־טוֹב[1]—(a) Is this from ירא (v.3372, BDB 431) or from ראה (v.7200, BDB 906ff)? (c-d) What is the relation of this word-group to (a-b)? §34.113. (e) Introduces a noun-clause (§31.13) after verbs of *seeing, hearing, saying,* etc. (v.3588), BDB 471.1a, *Ges.* §157*b*. (f) Pred. adj., §31.23. Supply 'it was' (§31.71).

וַיַּבְדֵּל אֱלֹהִים בֵּין הָאוֹר וּבֵין הַחֹשֶׁךְ׃[2]— (a) בדל 'to be divided, separate' (v.914), but what stem? §28.31. BDB 95. (b) How is this related to (a)? (c,e) Note that בֵּין is repeated, BDB 107.1a,d.

1:5 וַיִּקְרָא אֱלֹהִים | לָאוֹר יוֹם[1]—(a) Parse the verb. (b) Relate to the verb (subj., obj., ind. obj.?). The *pâsēq* | has no significance here (cf. J. Kennedy, *The Note-line in the Hebrew Scriptures* [1903]). (c) Note use of -לְ after קרא meaning 'to name,' BDB 896.6e. 'God cried/called "day" to the light.'

וְלַחֹשֶׁךְ קָרָא לָיְלָה[2]—(a) Gen. 1:2[2], 1:5[1](c). (b) In 3d pers. the subj. of verb must be defined unless it is clear from context. §30.3363, §33.212. Identify the subj. (c) Est. 4:16[5], here pausal.

וַיְהִי־עֶרֶב וַיְהִי־בֹקֶר יוֹם אֶחָד׃[3]—(a) Here, more like 'and/so there was.'(b) Est. 2:14[1]. (d) Est. 2:14[2]. (e-f) Cf. Est. 3:8, 13. Either 'one day' or possibly 'day one.' 'The first day' would be הַיּוֹם הָרִאשׁוֹן or יוֹם רִאשׁוֹן.

This exercise loses its point if you fail to study the words in their contexts, their meanings, the syntax, etc. Do *not* start exegesis with a commentary. Commentaries are thought-stoppers. Get all *you* can from the text, start your own thinking, and *then* turn to the commentaries.

Learn the words in Group 38.

46

Purpose: To review afformatives
Materials: Esther 5:3-6

וַיֹּאמֶר לָהּ
הַמֶּלֶךְ מַה־לָּךְ אֶסְתֵּר הַמַּלְכָּה וּמַה־בַּקָּשָׁתֵךְ עַד־חֲצִי
4 הַמַּלְכוּת וְיִנָּתֵן לָךְ׃ וַתֹּאמֶר אֶסְתֵּר אִם־עַל־הַמֶּלֶךְ טוֹב
יָבוֹא הַמֶּלֶךְ וְהָמָן הַיּוֹם אֶל־הַמִּשְׁתֶּה אֲשֶׁר־עָשִׂיתִי לוֹ׃
ה וַיֹּאמֶר הַמֶּלֶךְ מַהֲרוּ אֶת־הָמָן לַעֲשׂוֹת אֶת־דְּבַר אֶסְתֵּר
וַיָּבֹא הַמֶּלֶךְ וְהָמָן אֶל־הַמִּשְׁתֶּה אֲשֶׁר־עָשְׂתָה אֶסְתֵּר׃
6 וַיֹּאמֶר הַמֶּלֶךְ לְאֶסְתֵּר בְּמִשְׁתֵּה הַיַּיִן מַה־שְּׁאֵלָתֵךְ וְיִנָּתֵן
לָךְ וּמַה־בַּקָּשָׁתֵךְ עַד־חֲצִי הַמַּלְכוּת וְתֵעָשׂ׃

5:3 מַה־לָּךְ אֶסְתֵּר הַמַּלְכָּה ¹—(a) *māʰ* can be interrog. or indef. (§30.124, §21.5); here interrog. Note dagesh in ל, §13.36. (a-b) Idiom, 'What ails you?' 'What's with you?.' etc. (d) Def. art. used as vocative (§36.66).

וּמַה־בַּקָּשָׁתֵךְ עַד־חֲצִי הַמַּלְכוּת ²—(a) Here מַה is indef., not interrog., according to Masoretic accents, for the entire clause is joined. (b) *baqqāšāʰ* 'request, a seeking' (1246 8/7). Note preservation of fem. ת– before suf.; ֵךְ– is s3 (§23.1). Cf. 2:2³, 2:23¹, 2:15⁴, 3:6⁴. (c) *ʿad* 'until, unto, up to' (v.5704, BDB 723ff). (d) *ḥăṣî* 'half, middle' (v.2677). (e) Cf. 5:1⁵. 'And whatever (is) your request up to half of the kingdom.'

וְיִנָּתֵן לָךְ׃ ³—(a) *wᵉ* + *yinnāṯēn*, but note effect of next accent (*nāsôg 'āḥôr,* §17.35). Pattern yiC²āCēC, VDC–2. Learn to identify this pattern *now*. Is *wāw* conversive? (§32.53) (b) §23.121.

5:4 אִם־עַל־הַמֶּלֶךְ טוֹב ¹—Cf. 1:19¹.

יָבוֹא הַמֶּלֶךְ וְהָמָן הַיּוֹם ²—(a) *yāḇô'*: Cf. note on *'āḇô',* 4:16⁷. This could be G20 or G40, probably the latter: 'Let the king and H. come.' Note verb in sg. with compound subj., §33.113. (d) *hayyôm* 'today'; Eng. *today* < *the day*).

אֶל־הַמִּשְׁתֶּה אֲשֶׁר־עָשִׂיתִי לוֹ׃ ³—(b) 1:5⁸, maCCaY-type (§24.33, R.18). (d) In CCY verbs, 3d rad. *yôḏ* is preserved in certain forms (§29.712)., learn this *now*. It can't be H (no –ה). It can't be D or N (why not?). 1:5³, 1:9². (e) Note לָהֶם–E. wouldn't make a משתה for Haman, at least she would not say that to the king, hence this must be address in 3d pers. to the king, following יבוא.

5:5 מַהֲרוּ אֶת־הָמָן ¹—(a) *mahărû* < **mahhărû* (R.10a). ּו– ָ ָ would be G37; ּו– ֵ ַ would be D37. Learn to note such details. מהר D 'to hasten' (v.4116); cf. the name of Isaiah's son (Isa. 8:3). 3cp indef., probably to servants, 'Hurry up Haman.'

לַעֲשׂוֹת אֶת־דְּבַר אֶסְתֵּר[2]—(a) Why not cstr. here? §38.54. (b) Why is את used? Is the phrase def.? Why?

וַיָּבֹא הַמֶּלֶךְ וְהָמָן אֶל־הַמִּשְׁתֶּה[3]—(a) Cf. 5:4[2], here written defectively. Note again the use of sg. verb with compound subj., §33.113.

אֲשֶׁר־עָשְׂתָה אֶסְתֵּר׃[4]—(b) Cf. 1:9[2]. Note word order.

5:6 בְּמִשְׁתֵּה הַיַּיִן[1]—(a) 1:9[3]. Although משתה is generally translated 'feast,' the root שתה means 'to drink,' and the feast is described as משתה היין. For הֵ–, Table F.

מַה־שְּׁאֵלָתֵךְ וְיִנָּתֵן לָךְ[2]—(a) See notes on 5:3[1]. (b) *šᵉʼēlāʰ* (7596 14/6) 'request, petition,' root שאל (7592). Review §13.36. (c) Cf. 5:3[3].

וּמַה־בַּקָּשָׁתֵךְ עַד־חֲצִי הַמַּלְכוּת[3]—See 5:3[2].

וְתֵעָשׂ׃[4]—*wᵉtēʻāś* (in pause): —ת can be 21/22/41/42. The subj. is שאלתך, hence vb. is 21/41. Why? תֵּעָשֶׂה < **tiʻʻāśêʰ*, GCY with compensatory lengthening, §15.141, R.10a. But form here is apocopated (§13.533), which is found only in conv. impf. and juss., hence form must be N41, 'let it be done.'

Learn the words in Basic Vocabulary Group 39.

Study the following pronominal suffixes:

בַּעֲלֵיהֶן	שְׁנֵיהֶם	עַמָּהּ	עַמּוֹ	מַלְכוּתֵךְ	עָלַי
בְּעֵינֵיהֶן	לָהֶם	לָהּ	לוֹ	לָךְ	לִי
תַּמְרֻקֵיהֶן	דָּתֵיהֶם	תַּמְרוּקֶיהָ	מַלְכוּתוֹ	בְּעֵינֶיךָ	מוֹלַדְתִּי
	בְּאָמְרָם	יָפְיָהּ	לְמָלְכוֹ	אָבִיךָ	נַעֲרֹתַי
	אוֹתָם	מִמֶּנָּה	מִמֶּנּוּ		מִמֶּנִּי
	עֲלֵיהֶם	מָנוֹתֶיהָ	גְּדוּלָּתוֹ	בַּקָּשָׁתֵךְ	בַּקָּשָׁתִי
	אֵינָם	מוֹלַדְתָּהּ	חֲמָתוֹ	שְׁאֵלָתֵךְ	שְׁאֵלָתִי

הֲיִגְאֶה־גֹּמֶא בְּלֹא בִצָּה
יִשְׂגֶּה־אָחוּ בְלִי־מָיִם׃

Can papyrus grow where there is no marsh?
Can reeds flourish where there is no water?

Job 8:11

* וַתַּ֣עַן
8 אֶסְתֵּ֖ר וַתֹּאמַ֑ר שְׁאֵלָתִ֖י וּבַקָּשָׁתִֽי׃ אִם־מָצָ֨אתִי חֵ֜ן בְּעֵינֵ֣י
הַמֶּ֗לֶךְ וְאִם־עַל־הַמֶּ֙לֶךְ֙ ט֔וֹב לָתֵת֙ אֶת־שְׁאֵ֣לָתִ֔י וְלַעֲשׂ֖וֹת
אֶת־בַּקָּשָׁתִ֑י יָב֧וֹא הַמֶּ֣לֶךְ וְהָמָ֗ן אֶל־הַמִּשְׁתֶּה֙ אֲשֶׁ֣ר אֶֽעֱשֶׂ֣ה
9 לָהֶ֔ם וּמָחָ֥ר אֶֽעֱשֶׂ֖ה כִּדְבַ֥ר הַמֶּֽלֶךְ׃ וַיֵּצֵ֤א הָמָן֙ בַּיּ֣וֹם הַה֔וּא
שָׂמֵ֖חַ וְט֣וֹב לֵ֑ב וְכִרְאוֹת֩ הָמָ֨ן אֶֽת־מָרְדֳּכַ֜י בְּשַׁ֣עַר הַמֶּ֗לֶךְ
וְלֹא־קָם֙ וְלֹא־זָ֣ע מִמֶּ֔נּוּ וַיִּמָּלֵ֥א הָמָ֛ן עַל־מָרְדֳּכַ֖י חֵמָֽה׃
י וַיִּתְאַפַּ֣ק הָמָ֔ן וַיָּב֖וֹא אֶל־בֵּית֑וֹ וַיִּשְׁלַ֛ח וַיָּבֵ֥א אֶת־אֹהֲבָ֖יו
וְאֶת־זֶ֥רֶשׁ אִשְׁתּֽוֹ׃

5:7 וַתַּ֣עַן אֶסְתֵּ֖ר וַתֹּאמַ֑ר *[1]—Masoretic * before verse notes that this is the middle verse in Esther. The same fact is noted in the final Masorah at end of Esther. Cf. Fig. 5. (a) *wat* + *tá'an* < *ta'ănê^h^*, ענה 'to answer' (v.6030). (c) Pausal form; cf. first word in 5:4.

שְׁאֵלָתִ֖י וּבַקָּשָׁתִֽי׃[2]—(a) Cf. 5:5[2]; what suf. here? (b) Cf. 5:3[2]; what suf. here?. For smooth translation, sc. 'is this.'

5:8 אִם־מָצָ֨אתִי חֵ֜ן [1]—(a) 4:14[1]. (b) ־תִי--- is what morpheme? §27.21. ־ָ־ָ־ְתִי is what stem pattern? §27.22. For מצא 1:5[5], 2:23[2], v.4672. (c) 2:15[5]. You should be able to do the next two clauses.

לָתֵת֙ אֶת־שְׁאֵ֣לָתִ֔י וְלַעֲשׂ֖וֹת אֶת־בַּקָּשָׁתִ֑י [2]—(a) Cf. 2:9[5] and note difference in accents. We should note (but not construct a theory on it) that נתן is used with שאלה and עשה with בקשה. Masoretic pointing would seem to make it impossible to take the inf. cls. as subj. of noun cl., with טוב as pred.—but how else to translate it?

יָב֧וֹא הַמֶּ֣לֶךְ[3]—Cf. 5:5[3].

אֶֽעֱשֶׂ֣ה לָהֶ֔ם[4]—(a) ---א is what morpheme? §27.31. ֶה in CCY verb is what morpheme? §29.71. R.10g. (b) Here, להם, cf. 4:4[3] and notes. It is customary to speak to the king in the 3d pers.

וּמָחָ֥ר אֶֽעֱשֶׂ֖ה כִּדְבַ֥ר הַמֶּֽלֶךְ׃[5]—(a) *māḥār* 'tomorrow' (v.4279). §24.22. (b) 5:8[4]. (c) *k^e^*- 'according to,' BDB 453ff.

5:9 וַיֵּצֵ֤א הָמָן֙ בַּיּ֣וֹם הַה֔וּא [1]—(a) Cf. 1:17[1]. What is the difference here? (c-d) Cf. 1:18[1]. 1:2[1] How would you translate the phrase? §30.32.

שָׂמֵ֖חַ וְט֣וֹב לֵ֑ב[2]—(a) *śāmē^a^ḥ* is G50 of stative vb., §27.612; note *pattāḥ g^e^nûḇā^h^* (§15.4321). Many stative verbs are used in a way that makes it impossible to distinguish between G10 and G50. (bc) 'Good of heart' = 'happy.' *lēḇ* < *libb-*, §24.224.

וְכִרְאוֹת הָמָן אֶת־מָרְדֳּכַי [3]—(a) ־ו here must be translated 'but.'–כ 'when, as.' All of a sudden, Haman's joy is turned to anger.

וְלֹא־קָם וְלֹא־זָע מִמֶּנּוּ [4]—(a) *qām* could be G50 or G10; after **לא** it is more likely perf., §35.221. 'He didn't get up.' (d) *zāʻ* G50 or G10 of **זוע** 'move, tremble' (2111 3/1). (c) מִן 'because of' (cf. our idiom 'I was shaking *from* fright'). For *min* + *min* + suf., cf. 1:19[11], §23.1231.

וַיִּמָּלֵא הָמָן עַל־מָרְדֳּכַי חֵמָה׃ [5]—(a) 3:5[3]. (c) 'Against, on account of.' (e) 3:5[3].

5:10 וַיִּתְאַפַּק הָמָן וַיָּבוֹא אֶל־בֵּיתוֹ [1]—(a) *way* + *yiṯʼāppēq*: this can only be one form (VDC–1). **אפק** 'restrain self' (662 7/1). (c) Note form here and see 5:5[3]. Be sure you don't get hung up on one to the exclusion of the other!

וַיִּשְׁלַח וַיָּבֵא [2]—(a) Cf. 1:22[1], 4:4[4]. (b) Cf. 5:10[1]. What is the difference between *wayyāḇôʼ* and *wayyāḇēʼ*? between *yaqtul* and *yaqtēl*? §27.321, §28.31, cf. 1:17[6].

אֶת־אֹהֲבָיו [3]—(b) *ʼōhēḇ* would be what form? §24.233. *ʼōhăḇêʸ*? So what is this? Table H. **אהב** 'to love' (v.157), but this form is often a noun, 'friend.'

וְאֶת־זֶרֶשׁ אִשְׁתּוֹ׃ [4]—(b) Pr. n. 'Zeresh.' (c) *ʼišt* is probably fem. of *ʼîš*, §15.222, cf. 4:11[2].

Learn the words in Group 40.

Study the following uses of the negative particles:

lôʼ hēḇîʼāʰ (5:12[1])
lôʼ qibbēl (4:4[7])
lôʼ niqrēʼṯî (4:11[9])
lôʼ qām (5:9[4])
ʼăšer lôʼ yiqqārēʼ (4:11[5])
ʼăšer lôʼ ḵaddâṯ (4:16[8])
ʼêʸn lāḇôʼ (4:2[2])
ʼêʸnénnû šôwêʰ lî (5:13[1])
ʼal tᵉḏammî ḇᵉnap̄šēḵ (4:13[2])
ʼal tōʼḵᵉlû (4:16[4])
ʼal tištû (4:16[4])
ʼal tappēl dāḇār (6:10[5])

Happy is the man who finds wisdom, and the man who gets understanding.	אַשְׁרֵי אָדָם מָצָא חָכְמָה וְאָדָם יָפִיק תְּבוּנָה׃

Proverbs 3:13

Purpose: To review morphemes
Materials: Esther 5:11-13

וַיְסַפֵּר לָהֶם הָמָן אֶת־כְּבוֹד עָשְׁרוֹ
וְרֹב בָּנָיו וְאֵת כָּל־אֲשֶׁר גִּדְּלוֹ הַמֶּלֶךְ וְאֵת אֲשֶׁר נִשְּׂאוֹ
12 עַל־הַשָּׂרִים וְעַבְדֵי הַמֶּלֶךְ׃ וַיֹּאמֶר הָמָן אַף לֹא־הֵבִיאָה
אֶסְתֵּר הַמַּלְכָּה עִם־הַמֶּלֶךְ אֶל־הַמִּשְׁתֶּה אֲשֶׁר־עָשָׂתָה
כִּי אִם־אוֹתִי וְגַם־לְמָחָר אֲנִי קְרוּא־לָהּ עִם־הַמֶּלֶךְ׃ וְכָל־ 13
זֶה אֵינֶנּוּ שֹׁוֶה לִי בְּכָל־עֵת אֲשֶׁר אֲנִי רֹאֶה אֶת־מָרְדֳּכַי
הַיְּהוּדִי יוֹשֵׁב בְּשַׁעַר הַמֶּלֶךְ׃

5:11 וַיְסַפֵּר לָהֶם הָמָן [1]—(a) V.5608, D 'to recount, tell.' Note the pattern –ַ–ֵּ–ְ־ִ. You should be able to parse it. Cf. 3:12[1]. (b) Table H. Note word order. Where is the subj. of the verb?

אֶת־כְּבוֹד עָשְׁרוֹ וְרֹב בָּנָיו [2]—(b) 1:4[3]. (c) *ʿošrô*; 1:4[2], CuCC > *CŏCeC*,§24.21. (d) *rōḇ* < **rubb*, 'multitude' (v.7230). (e) Note: sg. *bēn* (CiC), pl. *bānîm* (CaC); likewise the fem., sg. *baṯ* < *bint*, §15.33, (cf. Arab. *bint*), pl. *bānôṯ*.

וְאֵת כָּל־אֲשֶׁר גִּדְּלוֹ הַמֶּלֶךְ [3]—Note use of n. cl. for dir. obj., §33.6. (d) Cf. 3:1[2], here + s0 (3ms suf.), Table H. 'And all (with) which the king had magnified him.'

וְאֵת אֲשֶׁר נִשְּׂאוֹ [4]—(c) *niśś^{e}ʾô*: –ִ–ְּ–ָ is a strong clue that form is D perf. נִשֵּׂא would be D15, but what is נִשְּׂאוֹ? Table H. For root, 2:9[2], 3:1[4]. 'And how (אשר) he had lifted him up.' You should be able to finish the verse.

5:12 אַף לֹא־הֵבִיאָה אֶסְתֵּר הַמַּלְכָּה עִם־הַמֶּלֶךְ [1]—(a) *ʾap̄* 'also' (v.637). (b) Note the neg. part., §35.221. (c) הֵ־ִי־ָה, note clues. –הֵ H perf.; –ָה perf. 3fs (11); 2 radicals, 3d not weak (note –ִי–), and no sign of weak 1st rad. (but it could be YCC defectively written) – so we try ב–א. Does it fit? (d) How is this related to the verb? *ʿim* 'with' (accompaniment, v.5973). You should be able to do the rest of the cl.

אֲשֶׁר־עָשָׂתָה [2]—(b) Cf. 1:9[2]. Form here is pausal, with a disjunctive accent that is usually relatively weak.

כִּי אִם־אוֹתִי [3]—(a-b) After a neg., *ki ʾim* often means 'but, except.' (c) Note *ʾēṯ*, *ʾôṯ-*, sign of def. dir. obj., §23.1233.

וְגַם־לְמָחָר אֲנִי קְרוּא־לָהּ עִם־הַמֶּלֶךְ׃ [4]—(a) 1:9[1]. (b) 5:8[5]. Here, something like, 'on (the) morrow.' (c) §21.1. (d) –וּ–ָ is what pattern? §27.63. (f-g) 5:12[1]. 'And also on the morrow *I* (have been) called by her with the king.'

5:13 וְכָל־זֶ֕ה אֵינֶ֥נּוּ שֹׁוֶ֖ה לִ֑י [1]— (a-b) ‘Yet all this’ (RSV). (c) אין + suf., Table H, with *nûn* energ. (§23.1221): ‘it is not’ (§31.331). (d) Note שׁ, ֹ, *šôwê*^{h} written defectively. שָׁוָה (v.7737), 3:8[7], ‘fitting, satisfactory.’ §§36.3, .31. (e) Dat. of advantage, ‘for me.’ Table H.

בְּכָל־עֵ֗ת אֲשֶׁ֨ר אֲנִ֤י רֹאֶה֙ [2]—(a) ‘In every (any) time.’ §36.123. (b) *’ēṯ* ‘time’ (v.6256), 1:13[2], 4:14[2]; < *‘*int*. (c) *’ăšer*, here, almost ‘when’. §38.51. (d-e) Like a pres. tense, ‘I see.’ (e) Learn to recognize long vowels written defectively; *rô’ê*^{y} and *rô’ē*^{h} are cstr., but is this? The rest is a ptcp. cl. modifying both the noun *mord*^{e}*ḵay* and the verb *rô’ê*^{h}. §38.43.

Learn the words in Group 41.

Study the following noun modifiers:
בַּחֹ֫דֶשׁ הָעֲשִׂירִי ‘in the tenth month’
בִּשְׁנַת שֶׁ֫בַע ‘in the seventh year’
כֶּ֫תֶר־מַלְכוּת ‘a royal crown’
יֵין מַלְכוּת רָב ‘much royal wine’
כִּסֵּא מַלְכוּתוֹ ‘his royal throne’
בֵּית הַמַּלְכוּת ‘the royal house’
שִׁשָּׁה חֳדָשִׁים ‘six months’
וְאֵת שֶׁ֫בַע הַנְּעָרוֹת הָרְאֻיוֹת ‘and the seven seemly maids’
נְעָרוֹת בְּתוּלוֹת טוֹבוֹת מַרְאֶה ‘good-looking virgin maids’
עֵינֵי מֶ֫לֶךְ ‘the king’s eyes’
בֵּיתוֹ ‘his house’
הַיּוֹם הַזֶּה ‘this day’
הַיָּמִים הָאֵ֫לֶּה ‘these days’

If YHWH does not build a house,
in vain the builders labor on it;
if YHWH does not guard a city,
in vain the watchman stays awake.

אִם־יהוה לֹא־יִבְנֶה בַיִת
שָׁוְא עָמְלוּ בוֹנָיו בּוֹ
אִם־יהוה לֹא־יִשְׁמָר־עִיר
שָׁוְא שָׁקַד שׁוֹמֵר׃

Psalm 127:1

49

Purpose: To review morphemes
Materials: Esther 5:14–6:2

14 וַתֹּאמֶר לוֹ זֶרֶשׁ אִשְׁתּוֹ וְכָל־
אֹהֲבָיו יַעֲשׂוּ־עֵץ גָּבֹהַּ חֲמִשִּׁים אַמָּה וּבַבֹּקֶר ׀ אֱמֹר לַמֶּלֶךְ
וְיִתְלוּ אֶת־מָרְדֳּכַי עָלָיו וּבֹא עִם־הַמֶּלֶךְ אֶל־הַמִּשְׁתֶּה שָׂמֵחַ
וַיִּיטַב הַדָּבָר לִפְנֵי הָמָן וַיַּעַשׂ הָעֵץ׃

ו CAP. VI. ו

א בַּלַּיְלָה הַהוּא נָדְדָה שְׁנַת הַמֶּלֶךְ וַיֹּאמֶר לְהָבִיא אֶת־
סֵפֶר הַזִּכְרֹנוֹת דִּבְרֵי הַיָּמִים וַיִּהְיוּ נִקְרָאִים לִפְנֵי הַמֶּלֶךְ׃
2 וַיִּמָּצֵא כָתוּב אֲשֶׁר הִגִּיד מָרְדֳּכַי עַל־בִּגְתָנָא וָתֶרֶשׁ שְׁנֵי
סָרִיסֵי הַמֶּלֶךְ מִשֹּׁמְרֵי הַסַּף אֲשֶׁר בִּקְשׁוּ לִשְׁלֹחַ יָד בַּמֶּלֶךְ
אֲחַשְׁוֵרוֹשׁ׃

5:14 וַתֹּאמֶר לוֹ זֶרֶשׁ אִשְׁתּוֹ וְכָל־אֹהֲבָיו[1]— Cf. 5:10[3,4]. Again, note *ḥôlām* in d.o. in אֹהֲבָיו: it must be a long *ô*. Note R.16. (a) Verb; (b) indir. obj., §35.11; (c) subj., §33.1; (d) appositive, §36.6; (e-f) second of compound subj, §33.12. The verb agrees with the nearer subj., §33.111.

יַעֲשׂוּ־עֵץ גָּבֹהַּ חֲמִשִּׁים אַמָּה[2]— (a) In sing. we can distinguish G20 from G40 (cf. §§32.34, .35) of this verb (יַעֲשֶׂה, יַעַשׂ), but in pl. the forms fall together. Here, probably G45, 'Let them make.' Indef. 3mp often = passive, 'Let a tree be made.' (b) *'ēṣ* 'tree' (v.6086), often translated 'gallows,' because of the following clause. Primitive noun (CiC); there is no reason to suppose a root עצה* as BDB 781. (c) *gāḇô*^{a}*h* 'high' (v.1364); note *mappîq* = consonantal *hê*. Note accents: not 'a high tree,' but 'a tree, a high one.' (d) '50' (v.2572), §26.2, §24.261. (e) *'ammā*^{h} 'cubit' (approx. 1.5 ft. or 0.46 m.) (v.520). 'High, 50 cubits.' Note sing. noun, §36.142.

וּבַבֹּקֶר ׀ אֱמֹר לַמֶּלֶךְ[3]— (a) 2:14[2]. CuCC > *CōCēC*, §24.21. For adv. use of prep. phrase, §35.3. (b) Note vowels! – – ָ < CuCuC (R.13a, 16, 10b), the pattern of G32/65. Here, GCC. G32 fits context, 'Say to the king.'

וְיִתְלוּ אֶת־מָרְדֳּכַי עָלָיו[4]— (a) *w*^{e}*yiṯ*^{e}*lû*: don't let *yiṯ* fool you! You need 3 rads. *yi—û* could be CCY; there is no sign of loss of 1st rad., no sign of medial *wāw* or *yôḏ*. תלה 'to hang' (v.8518). Probably G45, 'Let them hang,' or (indef. 3pl.) = pass., 'Let M. be hanged on it.' Note the form of indirect discourse. (d) Table H. In ancient Persian art, the use of sharpened stakes and impaling is attested. But whether by hanging or by impaling, a 75-ft. (23-m.) tree is hardly necessary. Perhaps it was to be set up on a high place to be seen by all.

וּבֹא עִם־הַמֶּלֶךְ אֶל־הַמִּשְׁתֶּה שָׂמֵחַ[5]— (a) *bô'* can be G32/65 of בוא (it's irregular, remember). In context, impv. is preferred: 'Say ... and go....' (f) 5:9[2], §27.612. The ptcp. modifies the verb: *how* he was to go, §35.61. I hope you're not missing the delightful way this story is being developed!

וַיִּיטַב הַדָּבָר לִפְנֵי הָמָן וַיַּעַשׂ הָעֵץ׃ [6]— (a) Cf. 1:21[1]. Note differences in the following expressions. (c-d) Prep. phr. used adverbially, §35.31. (e) 1:21[3]. (f) 5:14[2], there indef., no special tree; here, def., the tree previously mentioned. §32.221.

6:1 בַּלַּיְלָה הַהוּא נָדְדָה שְׁנַת הַמֶּלֶךְ [1]— (a) 4:16[5]. (a-b) Cf. 5:9[1], §35.31. (c) ה ָ- - - = perf. 3fs (11). The –נ can't be N-stem, for a word cannot begin with 1st and 2d rads. the same. נדד 'to flee' (v.5074). (d) This looks like 3:7[2] (1:3[1]). *šānā*^{h} 'year' and *šēnā*^{h} 'sleep' (v.8142) take the same form in cstr. (d-e) Construct phrase (noun phrase) used as subj. (§33.13).

וַיֹּאמֶר לְהָבִיא אֶת־סֵפֶר הַזִּכְרֹנוֹת דִּבְרֵי הַיָּמִים [2]— (b) You should know this. 1:11[1]. §38.82 (d-g) This is probably a title. (e) *hazzikrônôt*, sg. *zikkārôn* 'remembrance' (v.2146). Joüon (§18*d,g*) calls the dagesh "spontaneous doubling," i.e. due neither to extrinsic cause (e.g. assimilation) nor to intrinsic (e.g. denoting intensity). Syntax and accents call for cstr. here, 'The book of the memorials of the affairs of the days,' but there is a def. art. on *zikrônôt*. In advanced Heb. grammar, the student will learn that there are exceptions to rules. The use of the def. art. with a cstr. is not unknown either to Heb. or to Arab. (cf. Wright, *Arabic Grammar*, II, 222A). The book was the king's chronicles.

וַיִּהְיוּ נִקְרָאִים [3]— (a-b) Note conv. impf. + ptcp.: 'they were being read.' (b) With *niqrā'îm*, cf. *nims*^{e}*'îm* 1:1[5].

6:2 וַיִּמָּצֵא כָתוּב [1]— (a) *yimmāṣē'* – do you recognize the pattern? 2:23[2]. (b) *–ā–û–* : do you recognize the pattern? §24.244. 'And it was found written.'

אֲשֶׁר הִגִּיד מָרְדֳּכַי [2]— (a) 'Where' or 'that.' (b) 3:4[6] The account concerns (עַל) Bigthan and Teresh, cf. 2:21[3.4.5]. The Masoretic mark calls attention to a *pattāḥ* in pause (with *'atnāḥ*).

אֲשֶׁר בִּקְשׁוּ לִשְׁלֹחַ יָד [3]— Cf. 2:21[6.7]. With בִּקְשׁוּ, cf. בִּקְשָׁה, 2:15[4].

Learn the words in Group 42.

Study the following expressions:

d^e*bar hammélek w*^{e}*dâtô* (4:3[1]) 'the king's word and law'
na'ărôt 'estēr w^e*sârîsê*^{y}*hā* (4:4[1]) 'Esther's maids and eunuchs'

50

Purpose: To continue study of exegesis
Materials: Amos 7:10-15; Bible dictionary, atlas

The second element in grammatico-historical exegesis is the understanding of all historical, geographical, and similar elements in a passage. The Bible is unique among religious scriptures in the place it gives to historical and geographical details. The God of the Bible reveals himself in word and action in space and time, hence these details have significance. Some exegetes stress the necessity of identifying the life situation (*Sitz im Leben*) in order to understand the message. This is particularly true in the Prophets.

Amos 7:10 וַיִּשְׁלַח אֲמַצְיָה כֹּהֵן בֵּית־אֵל[1]— (a) Parse, translate. Cf. Est. 1:22[1]. (b) Amaziah the priest, not the king. Cf. *NBD* 29 or any good Bible dictionary. (c) *kôhēn* (> Cohen) 'priest' (v.3548). Is it 'a priest' or 'the priest'? Is it cstr.? §27.6112. (d-e) Bethel ('house of El'), *NBD* 143, *IDB* 1: 191ff. Look at a good Bible Atlas (Grollenberg, *Atlas of the Bible, The Westminster Historical Atlas,* or *The Macmillan Bible Atlas*). Bethel in the south and Dan in the north were cult centers established by Jeroboam ben Nebat, first king of the Northern Kingdom (cf. 1 Kgs. 12:26-30).

אֶל־יָרָבְעָם מֶלֶךְ־יִשְׂרָאֵל לֵאמֹר[2]— (b) *y^{e}rob̲'ām* (note *qāmāṣ-ḥăṭûp̄*) 'Jeroboam' – but was it Jeroboam I or II? *NBD* 613f. Note dates of each. (c-d) In apposition (§30.251) with (b). 'Israel' can mean (1) Jacob, (2) the entire people Israel, (3) the entire nation (Judah and Israel, the 12 tribes), or (4) the Northern Kingdom. Which is meant here?. (e) Note form. This may be translated 'quote.'

קָשַׁר עָלֶיךָ עָמוֹס בְּקֶרֶב בֵּית יִשְׂרָאֵל[3]— (a) V.7130, BDB 905, 'to conspire.' (b) Indir. obj. (§35.31). (c) *'āmôs* Amos, from Tekoa (Am. 1:1), cf. *IDB*). Was he the father of Isaiah (see Isa. 1:1)? Where was Tekoa? Was Amos a northerner? (d) V.7130, BDB 899.1f. *b^{e}qéreb̲* often = *b^e*-. (e-f) BDB 110.5dδ. What does "house of Israel" mean in this context?

לֹא־תוּכַל הָאָרֶץ לְהָכִין אֶת־כָּל־דְּבָרָיו׃[4]— (a-b) Cf. Est. 6:13. Is it 21 (3fs) or 22 (2ms)? (c) How is this word related to (a-b)? What does *hā'ā́reṣ* refer to here? the earth? the land under foot? the nation? (b) BDB 466. Here something like 'to sustain, endure, bear.' GNB reads, 'His speeches will destroy the country' – is this a literal translation? (e-f-g) How is this related to (d)? What is the relationship of (d-g) to (a-c)?

7:11 כִּי־כֹה אָמַר עָמוֹס[1]— (a) BDB 471-475. Is this 'that' after a verb of *saying* (ὅτι recitative) or 'because' (ὅτι causal)? (b) V.3541. The formula *kō^h 'āmar* ... is often found in the Prophets, frequently with יהוה as subj.

בַּחֶרֶב יָמוּת יָרָבְעָם[2]— (a) *ḥéreb̲* 'sword' (v.2719), ־בּ of instrument 'with,' BDB 89.III.2. Is it 'with a sword' or 'with the sword'? See Table G. (b) VDC–9; מוּת 'to die' (v.4191). (c) How is this related to (b)? Is it 'he caused J. to die with a sword'?

וְיִשְׂרָאֵל גָּלֹה יִגְלֶה מֵעַל אַדְמָתוֹ׃[3]— (a) How used here? Cf. 7:10[2] above. (b) VDC–6, §29.71, Est. 2:6[1]. (c) Parse. (b+c) §35.6. (a-c) Word order for emphasis. (d) *min* + *'al*. (e) *'ăḏāmā^h* 'ground, land' (v.127); cstr. *'aḏmaṯ* (< *'ăḏ^{e}maṯ*, cf. R.19, R.10d).

Amos

7:12 וַיֹּאמֶר אֲמַצְיָה אֶל־עָמוֹס[1]— (b) Cf. 7:10 above. Who said to whom? Make the Heb. give you the translation. Where was Amos – near Jeroboam or near Amaziah?

חֹזֶה לֵךְ בְּרַח־לְךָ אֶרֶץ יְהוּדָה[2]— (a) 'Seer' (v.2374), used of prophets, here in derision. (b) G32 of הלך. (c) ברח 'to flee' (v.1272), VDC–5. For asyndeton, §30.364. (d) Impv. is often followed by *l^{e}ḵā*, "ethical" dative, BDB 515.5.i(b). (g) *y^{e}hûḏā^h* 'Judah.' See art. in *NBD* or *IDB*; find Judah on a map of Israel and Judah in a Bible atlas. Locate Tekoa.

וֶאֱכָל־שָׁם לֶחֶם וְשָׁם תִּנָּבֵא׃[3]— (a) *w^e'ĕḵol* (*qāmāṣ-ḥāṭûp̄*), VDC–5; parse, translate. Est. 4:16[4]. (c) *léḥem* 'bread, food' (v.3899), perhaps sarcastically suggesting that Amos expected to earn his living by his prophetic activity. (e) *tinnāḇē'*, VDC–2. נבא N 'to prophesy' (v.5012). (b,d) Repetition of *šām* adds pointed emphasis: *there* eat bread and *there* prophesy.' Is (e) impv.?

7:13 וּבֵית־אֵל לֹא־תוֹסִיף עוֹד לְהִנָּבֵא[1]— (a) For *ûḇ^{e}ḇê^{y}ṯ-'ēl*, 'but in Bethel.' Cf. 7:10[1]. (b) *lô'* with impf., §32.5215. (c) *tôsîp̄* < **tawsîp*, VDC–9. יסף 'to add' (v.3254), followed by inf., 'to do again, more,' BDB 728f. After יסף (e) would appear to be pleonastic – but it often occurs. (f) *l^{e}hinnāḇē'*, VDC–2, §28.42.

כִּי מִקְדַּשׁ־מֶלֶךְ הוּא[2]— (a) Cf. 7:11[1]. How is *kî* used here? (b) *miqdāš* 'sanctuary' (v.4720), note vowels: abs. or cstr.? §24.33. (d) §21.2. This is a verbless clause, §31. 'For *that* is the king's sanctuary.'

וּבֵית מַמְלָכָה הוּא׃[3]— (b) 'Kingdom' (v.4467); *bêṯ mamlāḵā* is 'palace' or 'capital.' This also is a verbless clause.

7:14 וַיַּעַן עָמוֹס וַיֹּאמֶר אֶל־אֲמַצְיָה[1]— (a) Cf. Est. 5:7[1]. ענה 'to answer' (v.6030). What is the subj.? (c-e) Cf. Am. 7:12[1].

לֹא נָבִיא אָנֹכִי וְלֹא בֶן־נָבִיא אָנֹכִי[2]— (a) *lô'* may be used to negate a noun in a predicate, BDB 519.1b. (b) *nāḇî'* 'prophet' (v.5030). (a-c) Verbless clause. (c) §21.1, v.595. 'I (am) not a prophet.' (e-f) *ben-nāḇî'* 'son of a prophet,' probably meaning a member of a prophetic guild or school.

כִּי־בוֹקֵר אָנֹכִי וּבוֹלֵס שִׁקְמִים׃[3]— (a) After a neg., 'but,' BDB 474.3e. (b) Don't confuse with *bṓqer* (v.1242); *bôqēr* is denominal (§24.51), from *bāqār* 'cattle, herd' (v.1241), meaning 'herdsman' (951 1/0). (a-c) Verbless cl., 'I (am/was) a herdsman.' (d) G52 (from an unused verb, בלס) 'pincher.' The sycamore fig needs to be bruised to make it edible. (e) *šiqmā^h*, pl. *šiqmîm* 'sycamore fig' (8256 6/0). (d-e) Verbless cl., subj. omitted (§30.141), supply 'I.'

Note: This lesson is continued on page 109.

51

Purpose: To study direct and indirect discourse
Materials: Esther 6:3-6

וַיֹּאמֶר הַמֶּלֶךְ מַה־נַּעֲשָׂה יְקָר וּגְדוּלָּה 3
לְמָרְדֳּכַי עַל־זֶה וַיֹּאמְרוּ נַעֲרֵי הַמֶּלֶךְ מְשָׁרְתָיו לֹא־נַעֲשָׂה
עִמּוֹ דָּבָר׃ וַיֹּאמֶר הַמֶּלֶךְ מִי בֶחָצֵר וְהָמָן בָּא לַחֲצַר 4
בֵּית־הַמֶּלֶךְ הַחִיצוֹנָה לֵאמֹר לַמֶּלֶךְ לִתְלוֹת אֶת־מָרְדֳּכַי
עַל־הָעֵץ אֲשֶׁר־הֵכִין לוֹ׃ וַיֹּאמְרוּ נַעֲרֵי הַמֶּלֶךְ אֵלָיו הִנֵּה ה
הָמָן עֹמֵד בֶּחָצֵר וַיֹּאמֶר הַמֶּלֶךְ יָבוֹא׃ וַיָּבוֹא הָמָן וַיֹּאמֶר 6
לוֹ הַמֶּלֶךְ מַה־לַּעֲשׂוֹת בָּאִישׁ אֲשֶׁר הַמֶּלֶךְ חָפֵץ בִּיקָרוֹ
וַיֹּאמֶר הָמָן בְּלִבּוֹ לְמִי יַחְפֹּץ הַמֶּלֶךְ לַעֲשׂוֹת יְקָר יוֹתֵר
מִמֶּנִּי׃

6:3 מַה־נַּעֲשָׂה יְקָר וּגְדוּלָּה[1]— (a) Interrogative, §33.23. (b) ָה could be 10 of CCY; if so, what is –נ ? Try N10 of עשה in context. Why is there a dagesh in נ ? §13.36. (c) 1:4[5], 'value, price, honor' (v.3366). (d) *g*^{e}*ḏûlā*^{h} 'greatness' (1420 12/3), 1:4[7]. 'What honor was done and greatness to/for M. on account of this?'

וַיֹּאמְרוּ נַעֲרֵי הַמֶּלֶךְ מְשָׁרְתָיו[2]— (b-c) 2:2[1]. (d) 1:10[7].

לֹא־נַעֲשָׂה עִמּוֹ דָּבָר׃[3]— (b) 6:3[1]. (c) *'im* 'with' < *'imm*; the suf. preserves the gemination. R.5, R.6a. (d) 'a thing.' דבר ... לא 'not a thing, nothing.'

6:4 מִי בֶחָצֵר[1]— (a) Interrog., מִי personal, מַה impers., §21.4. (b) 4:11[4]. Verbless cl., 'Who (is) in the court?' §33.23.

וְהָמָן בָּא לַחֲצַר בֵּית־הַמֶּלֶךְ הַחִיצוֹנָה[2]— (b) *bā'* could be G10 or G50, 'had entered, was entering.' (e) *ḥîṣôn, -ā*^{h} 'outer(most)' (v.2435). וֹן– *-ôn* often adds the superlative idea to a noun or adj., §24.431. What word does it modify? Cf. 4:11[4].

לֵאמֹר לַמֶּלֶךְ[3]— (a) Inf. of purpose, §38.54. *l*^{e} + *'ĕmōr* (cf. 5:14[3]) > *lē'mōr*, §15.54.

לִתְלוֹת אֶת־מָרְדֳּכַי עַל־הָעֵץ[4]—(a) Inf. cstr. in indir. disc., §38.82. Direct discourse would be, "... to say, 'Hang Haman' "; indir. disc., "... to say to hang Haman." (e) Why definite? Note following clause.

אֲשֶׁר־הֵכִין לוֹ׃[5]— (b) *hēḵîn*; study the forms in §29.632. כון H 'to set up, erect' (v.3559). (c) Dat. of advantage, 'for him.'

6:5 וַיֹּאמְרוּ נַעֲרֵי הַמֶּלֶךְ אֵלָיו[1]— You should be able to do this. Cf. 6:3[2]. (d) אֶל, like עַל, always brings back an original י– when adding a suffix, cf. Table H.

הִנֵּה הָמָן עֹמֵד בֶּחָצֵר [2]— (a) *hinnêʰ* 'behold!' (v.2009). (c) – ֵ –; would you recognize it if it were – ֵ ו–? After הנה we often find the ptcp.

וַיֹּאמֶר הַמֶּלֶךְ יָבוֹא׃ [3]— (c) G20 or G40, here the latter: 'Let him enter.'

6:6 מַה־לַּעֲשׂוֹת בָּאִישׁ [1]— You should be able to do the first 2 clauses. (a-b) 1:15[2]. Why *pattāḥ* under ל ? (c) 'with the man.'

אֲשֶׁר הַמֶּלֶךְ חָפֵץ בִּיקָרוֹ [2]— A rel. cl. defining האיש. (c) *ḥāpēṣ* 'to delight, take pleasure in' (v.2654), note vowels and see §§27.23, .232. It could be G10 or G50 (§27.612). 2:14[7]. (d) 1:4[5], plus what morphemes? b^e + y^e > $bî^y$, §15.652.

בְּלִבּוֹ [3]— Cf. 5:9[2]. Explain form here. אמר בלבו is an idiom meaning 'to think.'

לְמִי יַחְפֹּץ הַמֶּלֶךְ לַעֲשׂוֹת יְקָר [4]— (a) *mî* cannot be inflected (as can, e.g., the Greek pron.), hence *l^emî* for 'to whom.' (b) *ḥāpēṣ*, impf. *yaḥpōṣ*. We generally find yiCCaC as impf. of stative verbs (R.24, §27.331). 6:6[2]. 'To whom shall (would) the king delight to do honor?'

יוֹתֵר מִמֶּנִּי׃ [5]— (a) Formally G50 of יתר 'to remain, be left over' (v.3498), but it has become a noun in late Bib. Heb. 'more' (3148 8/1, 7x in Eccl.). (b) Cf. מִמֶּנָּה, ממנו 1:19[4], 5:9[4]. מִן of comparison (§38.74); translate 'more than me.'

Learn the words in Basic Group 44.

The following is the conclusion of Lesson 50, continued from page 107.

mos

7:15 וַיִּקָּחֵנִי יְהוָה מֵאַחֲרֵי הַצֹּאן [1]— (a) *way| yiq| qāḥ| ḗnî*: analyze it. It must be conv. impf.; 1st rad. geminate (VDC–2), hence it could be from *nqḥ*, but don't forget *lqḥ* (§29.45). *-ḗnî* is s4 with connecting vowel, §23.122, §23.1231, R.23. What is left is **yilqaḥ* > *yiqqaḥ*, and the form is Gc20s4 of לקח, cf. Est. 2:7[8]. (b) The sacred name (tetragrammaton) YHWH, read *'ăḏōnāy* '(my) lord' (§11.63), originally pronounced something like [i̯a-hə-u̯ɛ]. (c) *'aḥărê^y*, cf. Est. 2:1[1], + *min*, 'from after, from behind,' BDB 30.4a. (d) *ṣô'n* 'small cattle, flock, sheep and goats.'

וַיֹּאמֶר לִי יְהוָה לֵךְ הִנָּבֵא אֶל־עַמִּי יִשְׂרָאֵל׃ [2]— (a) Who said? (b) *'ēl* + s4, indir. obj. (d) Am. 7:12[2]. (e) Cf. Am. 7:12[3], 7:13[1]; what is the form here? (g) Est. 1:5[4], here + s4. (h) Am. 7:10[2], here in apposition with *'ammî.*

Learn the basic words in Group 43.

52

Purpose: To study the use of prepositions
Materials: Esther 6:7-10

7 וַיֹּאמֶר הָמָן אֶל־הַמֶּלֶךְ אִישׁ אֲשֶׁר הַמֶּלֶךְ חָפֵץ
8 בִּיקָרוֹ׃ יָבִיאוּ לְבוּשׁ מַלְכוּת אֲשֶׁר לָבַשׁ־בּוֹ הַמֶּלֶךְ
וְסוּס אֲשֶׁר רָכַב עָלָיו הַמֶּלֶךְ וַאֲשֶׁר נִתַּן כֶּתֶר מַלְכוּת
9 בְּרֹאשׁוֹ׃ וְנָתוֹן הַלְּבוּשׁ וְהַסּוּס עַל־יַד־אִישׁ מִשָּׂרֵי הַמֶּלֶךְ
הַפַּרְתְּמִים וְהִלְבִּשׁוּ אֶת־הָאִישׁ אֲשֶׁר הַמֶּלֶךְ חָפֵץ בִּיקָרוֹ
וְהִרְכִּיבֻהוּ עַל־הַסּוּס בִּרְחוֹב הָעִיר וְקָרְאוּ לְפָנָיו כָּכָה
י יֵעָשֶׂה לָאִישׁ אֲשֶׁר הַמֶּלֶךְ חָפֵץ בִּיקָרוֹ׃ וַיֹּאמֶר הַמֶּלֶךְ
לְהָמָן מַהֵר קַח אֶת־הַלְּבוּשׁ וְאֶת־הַסּוּס כַּאֲשֶׁר דִּבַּרְתָּ
וַעֲשֵׂה־כֵן לְמָרְדֳּכַי הַיְּהוּדִי הַיּוֹשֵׁב בְּשַׁעַר הַמֶּלֶךְ אַל־
תַּפֵּל דָּבָר מִכֹּל אֲשֶׁר דִּבַּרְתָּ׃

6:7 You should be able to do this entire verse. Cf. 6:6[2].

6:8 יָבִיאוּ לְבוּשׁ מַלְכוּת[1]— (a) *yāḇîʾû*: long *î* tells us what? VDC–9. G20/40, here probably juss., 'Let them bring.' (b) *l^{e}ḇûš* 'clothing,' 4:2[3]. (b-c) How would you translate this idiom? Cf. 1:7[4].

אֲשֶׁר לָבַשׁ־בּוֹ הַמֶּלֶךְ[2]— (a) *ʾăšer* cannot be inflected, hence a resumptive prep. phr. is needed (c): *ʾăšer ... bô* = 'in which' (§36.43). (b) *lāḇaš* – do you have any trouble parsing this form? Cf. 4:1[3]. Since the impf. is *yilbaš*, we would expect perf. *lāḇēš* or *lāḇōš* (R.24, §27.331), and the form *lāḇēš* does occur.

וְסוּס אֲשֶׁר רָכַב עָלָיו הַמֶּלֶךְ[3]— (a) *sûs* 'horse' (v.5483). (b) *ʾăšer ... ʿāla^{y}w*, cf. note on 6:8[2](a) and §36.43. Translate 'on which.' (c) *rāḵaḇ* 'he mounted and rode' (v.7392); we would say simply, 'on which the king rode.'

וַאֲשֶׁר נִתַּן כֶּתֶר מַלְכוּת בְּרֹאשׁוֹ׃[4]— (a,e) Again, translate 'on whose head,' §36.43. (b) 4:8[2]. (c-d) 2:17[5].

6:9 וְנָתוֹן הַלְּבוּשׁ וְהַסּוּס[1]— (a) –וֹ–ָ is G60 (§27.64); 'and to give' = 'let them give.' (b) 6:8[1]. (c) 6:8[3].

עַל־יַד־אִישׁ מִשָּׂרֵי הַמֶּלֶךְ הַפַּרְתְּמִים[2]— (a-b) 'upon the hand of' = 'by.' RSV 'And let the robes and the horse be handed over to one of the king's most noble princes.' (d) מִן partitive, 'from the princes.' (f) 1:3[11]. The word is in apposition with שרי המלך, to define the princes more closely.

וְהִלְבִּשׁוּ אֶת־הָאִישׁ[3]— (a) ה–ִ–י–וּ must be H15 – do you know why? H of לבשׁ means 'to clothe someone.' This is Hc15, continuing a juss., hence to be translated, 'and let them (the princes) clothe the man ....' (§32.544). You should be able to do the rest of the cl. 6:6[1,2].

וְהִרְכִּיבֻהוּ עַל־הַסּוּס בִּרְחוֹב הָעִיר[4]—(a) Take it apart: וְ|הִרְכִּיבֻ|הוּ. *hirkîḇû* is obviously H15, with final vowel written defectively. Ancient scribes seem to have avoided plēnē writing of one vowel if two were in the form. הוּ– is s0 (Table H). –וְ is conv., hence Hc15s0, continuing a juss., 'and let them mount him on the horse.' (d) *r^{e}ḥôḇ* 4:6[2]. (e) 3:15[5].

וְקָרְאוּ לְפָנָיו[5]— (a) Gc15, see previous notes. A conv. perf. may be used to continue the tense and mood of a previous verb, §§32.542-.546.

כָּכָה יֵעָשֶׂה[6]— (a) *kā́ḵā^{h}* 'thus' (v.3602), adds a bit of emphasis. (b) This cannot be juss. for it is not apocopated (§29.72). 2:11[5]. You can finish the verse.

6:10 מַהֵר קַח אֶת־הַלְּבוּשׁ[1]— (a) Cf. 5:5[1]. *māhēr* < **mahhēr*, D32, 'Hurry!' (b) *qaḥ* < *l^{e}qaḥ* (§29.45). Cf. 2:7[8]. Form here is G32. **l^{e}qaḥ* could also be G65, but the inf. cstr. adds ballast-*t* after apheresis > *qáḥaṯ*, not found in Est. You should be able to complete the clause.

כַּאֲשֶׁר דִּבַּרְתָּ[2]— (a) 2:20[4]. (b) תָּ– – – is what? (§27.21). תָּ–ַ–ִ– is what stem? (§28.21). Note *i* > *a* (§15.33). For דבר, 1:22[7]. 'According as you have spoken.'

וַעֲשֵׂה־כֵן לְמָרְדֳּכַי[3]— (a) Be careful! וַ|עֲשֵׂה: *GăCē^{h}* < C^{e}CaC GCY, pattern is impv. (§27.423). The –וַ is *not* conversive! (Conv. *wāw* is only found on impf. and perf.) 'And do thus.' Complete the clause.

הַיּוֹשֵׁב בְּשַׁעַר הַמֶּלֶךְ[4]— (a) Ptcp. with def. art. often used as a relative clause (§38.414), 'who (was) sitting.' Complete the clause

אַל־תַּפֵּל דָּבָר מִכֹּל אֲשֶׁר דִּבַּרְתָּ׃[5]— (a) אַל is the neg. used with juss. (§35.223). (b) *tappēl* < **tanpēl*, vowels are our clues: H42 (§28.31). There is no neg. of impv.; to give a negative command in Heb., the following are used: לֹא + impv. (very strong), or אַל + juss. (less strong). For נפל, 3:7[3]. (c) 'Thing.' 'Don't let a thing fall from all you have spoken.' (f) 6:10[2].

Learn the meanings of the words in Group 45.

Study the following uses of the participle:

hammélek yôšēḇ 'al kissē' malkûtô (5:1[5]) 'the king was sitting on his throne'
'estēr hammalkā^{h} 'ômédeṯ (5:2[2]) 'Queen Esther was standing'
wayyēṣē' hāmā ... śāmē^{a}ḥ (5:9[2]) 'and Haman went out rejoicing'
b^{e}ḵol-'ēṯ 'ăšer 'ănî rô'ē^{h} 'eṯ-mord^{e}ḵay yôšēḇ b^{e}šá'ar hammélek (5:13[2]) 'every time I see M. sitting in the king's gate'
hayy^{e}hûḏîm hannimṣ^{e}'îm b^{e}šûšān (4:16[2]) 'the Jews who are found in Susa'
hayy^{e}hûḏî hayyôšēḇ b^{e}šá'ar hammélek (6:10[4]) 'the Jew who sits in the king's gate'
na'ărê hammélek m^{e}šār^{e}ṯā^{y}w (6:3[2]) 'the king's servants who minister to him'

53

Purpose: To review the student's progress
Materials: Esther 4:1–6:10

In the following groups of words, a Rule is illustrated by one of the words. Identify the word that illustrates the Rule.

Rule 2a וְיִפְקֵד, (b) יִכְתֹּב, (c) יַעֲבוֹר, (d) קֹדֶשׁ, (e) עַם
Rule 8. (a) וְכָתוּב, (b) וּתְדַבֵּר, (c) אָצוּם, (d) כְּטוֹב, (e) וּמָרְדֳּכַי
Rule 10c. (a) יֶאֱהַב, (b) יֹאמַר, (c) יַעֲבֹר, (d) נַעֲרָה, (e) עַיִן
Rule 11. (a) מִדְבָּר, (b) וַיִּשָּׂא, (c) מֵאָה, (d) מִכָּל־, (e) בְּהִקָּבֵץ
Rule 14. (a) טַף, (b) הַמֶּלֶךְ, (c) כְּיַד, (d) אֵם, (e) עֵת, (f) חֹק
Rule 16. (a) יוֹדְעֵי, (b) שְׁמוֹ, (c) וַיִּשְׁלַח, (d) הַיּוֹשְׁבִים, (e) יְקַטְּלוּ
Rule 19. (a) בִּשְׁנַת, (b) יִקְטְלוּ, (c) כִּכְתָבָהּ, (d) מִדְבָּר, (e) יִקְטֹל
Rule 21. (a) אֲחַשְׁוֵרוֹשׁ, (b) חֳדָשִׁים, (c) יַעֲבֹר, (d) לַעֲשׂוֹת, (e) וַחֲמֹרוֹ

You will be given a sight passage, similar to the one printed below, and asked a number of questions about it. These questions are such as you should ask yourself when working on a new passage. Observe them carefully.

וַיָּמָת כִּדְבַר־יְהוָה ׀ אֲשֶׁר־דִּבֶּר אֵלִיָּהוּ וַיִּמְלֹךְ יְהוֹרָם תַּחְתָּיו בִּשְׁנַת שְׁתַּיִם לִיהוֹרָם בֶּן־יְהוֹשָׁפָט מֶלֶךְ יְהוּדָה כִּי לֹא־הָיָה לוֹ בֵּן׃ וְיֶתֶר דִּבְרֵי אֲחַזְיָהוּ אֲשֶׁר עָשָׂה הֲלוֹא־הֵמָּה כְתוּבִים עַל־סֵפֶר דִּבְרֵי הַיָּמִים לְמַלְכֵי יִשְׂרָאֵל׃

Parse these verbal forms: וַיָּמָת (1); דִּבֶּר (1); וַיִּמְלֹךְ (1); כְּתוּבִים (4).

Parse these nonverbal forms: כִּדְבַר (1); בִּשְׁנַת (2); דִּבְרֵי (3); הֲלוֹא (4).

Explain the use of these prepositions: כִּדְבַר (1); בִּשְׁנַת (2); תַּחְתָּיו (2), לִיהוֹרָם (2); לוֹ (3); עַל (4); לְמַלְכֵי (4).

Describe or explain the dageshes in: וַיָּמָת (1); כִּדְבַר (1); דִּבֶּר (1); שְׁתַּיִם (2); בֵּן (3); הֵמָּה (4); הַיָּמִים (4).

What is the difference between: יְהוֹרָם (2) and יְהוּדָה (3)? between לֹא (3) and לוֹא (4)?

Which words have a pronominal suffix: אֵלִיָּהוּ (1); תַּחְתָּיו (2); לִיהוֹרָם (2); יְהוּדָה (3); לוֹ (3); דִּבְרֵי (3)?

What is meant by the terms: "perpetual Q^{e}re" – יְהוָה (1); "full (plene) writing" – הֲלוֹא (4); "patronymic" – בֶּן־יְהוֹשָׁפָט (2).

Work out the following proper nouns by transliteration and normalization: אֵלִיָּהוּ (1); יְהוֹשָׁפָט (2); אֲחַזְיָהוּ (3); יִשְׂרָאֵל (5).

What kind of clause is introduced by: אֲשֶׁר (1); כִּי (3); הֲלוֹא (4)?

Parse these verbal forms: וַיָּמָת (1); דִּבֶּר (1); וַיִּמְלֹךְ (1); כְּתוּבִים (4).

Parse these nonverbal forms: כִּדְבַר (1); בִּשְׁנַת (2); דִּבְרֵי (3); הֲלוֹא (4).

Explain the use of these prepositions: כִּדְבַר (1); בִּשְׁנַת (2); תַּחְתָּיו (2), לִיהוֹרָם (2); לוֹ (3); עַל (4); לְמַלְכֵי (4).

Describe or explain the dageshes in: וַיָּמָת (1); כִּדְבַר (1); דִּבֶּר (1); שְׁתַּיִם (2); בֵּן (3); הֵמָּה (4); הַיָּמִים (4).

What is the difference between: יְהוֹרָם (2) and יְהוּדָה (3)? between לֹא (3) and לוֹא (4)?

Which words have a pronominal suffix: אֵלִיָּהוּ (1); תַּחְתָּיו (2); לִיהוֹרָם (2); יְהוּדָה (3); לוֹ (3); דִּבְרֵי (3)?

What is meant by the terms: "perpetual Qᵉre" – יְהוָה (1); "full (plene) writing" – aWlḥ (4); "patronymic" – בֶּן־יְהוֹשָׁפָט (2).

Work out the following proper nouns by transliteration and normalization: אֵלִיָּהוּ (1); יְהוֹשָׁפָט (2); אֲחַזְיָהוּ (3); יִשְׂרָאֵל (5).

What kind of clause is introduced by: אֲשֶׁר (1); כִּי (3); הֲלוֹא (4)?

Which are the more nearly correct translations:
בִּשְׁנַת שְׁתַּיִם (2) 'in the second year' or 'in two years'?
אֲשֶׁר דִּבֶּר אֵלִיָּהוּ (1) 'who spoke unto him,' 'which Elijah spoke' or 'which was the word of Eliyahu'?
וַיִּמְלֹךְ יְהוֹרָם תַּחְתָּיו (1-2) 'and he reigned over Judah in his place,' 'and Jehoram succeeded him as king' or 'and he placed their law under him'?
כִּי לֹא הָיָה לוֹ בֵּן (3) 'when his son was not with him,' 'for he was not with us' or 'since he had no son'?
סֵפֶר דִּבְרֵי הַיָּמִים לְמַלְכֵי יִשְׂרָאֵל (4-5) 'he told those words to the kings of Israel, 'the book of the chronicles of the kings of Israel' or 'to guard those words for the kings of Israel' ?
Who died? (a) Jehoram, (b) Jehoshaphat, (c) Ahaziah, (d) Elijah.
Who had no son? (a) Jehoram, (b) Jehoshaphat, (c) Ahaziah, (d) Judah.
Who reigned in the place of him who died? (a) Jehoram, (b) Jehoshaphat, (c) Ahaziah, (d) Israel.

שִׁפְטוּ־דַל וְיָתוֹם עָנִי וָרָשׁ הַצְדִּיקוּ׃
Give justice to the weak and the fatherless:
Maintain the right of the afflicted and the destitute.
Psalm 82:3

54

Purpose: To note types of clauses
Materials: Esther 6:11-14

וַיִּקַּח הָמָן אֶת־הַלְּבוּשׁ
וְאֶת־הַסּוּס וַיַּלְבֵּשׁ אֶת־מָרְדֳּכָי וַיַּרְכִּיבֵהוּ בִּרְחוֹב הָעִיר
וַיִּקְרָא לְפָנָיו כָּכָה יֵעָשֶׂה לָאִישׁ אֲשֶׁר הַמֶּלֶךְ חָפֵץ בִּיקָרוֹ׃
12 וַיָּשָׁב מָרְדֳּכַי אֶל־שַׁעַר הַמֶּלֶךְ וְהָמָן נִדְחַף אֶל־בֵּיתוֹ אָבֵל
13 וַחֲפוּי רֹאשׁ׃ וַיְסַפֵּר הָמָן לְזֶרֶשׁ אִשְׁתּוֹ וּלְכָל־אֹהֲבָיו
אֵת כָּל־אֲשֶׁר קָרָהוּ וַיֹּאמְרוּ לוֹ חֲכָמָיו וְזֶרֶשׁ אִשְׁתּוֹ אִם
מִזֶּרַע הַיְּהוּדִים מָרְדֳּכַי אֲשֶׁר הַחִלּוֹתָ לִנְפֹּל לְפָנָיו לֹא־
14 תוּכַל לוֹ כִּי־נָפוֹל תִּפּוֹל לְפָנָיו׃ עוֹדָם מְדַבְּרִים עִמּוֹ
וְסָרִיסֵי הַמֶּלֶךְ הִגִּיעוּ וַיַּבְהִלוּ לְהָבִיא אֶת־הָמָן אֶל־הַמִּשְׁתֶּה
אֲשֶׁר־עָשְׂתָה אֶסְתֵּר׃

6:11 וַיִּקַּח הָמָן[1]—(a) *yiqqaḥ* < +*yilqaḥ*, cf. 6:10[1]. לקח behaves as an NCC verb (§29.45). Complete the clause, 6:8[1-3], 6:10[1].

וַיַּלְבֵּשׁ אֶת־מָרְדֳּכַי[2]—(a) Compare יִלְבַּשׁ 4:1[3] and יַלְבֵּשׁ. What is the difference? Vowel under preformative tells us what? Vowel after 2d rad. tells us what? Form here is Hc20 – translate it.

וַיַּרְכִּיבֵהוּ בִּרְחוֹב הָעִיר[3]—(a) Analyze it. Cf. 6:9[4]. Note difference in connecting vowels. –ִי–ַ–ְ tells us what? For the rest of clause, 6:9[4].

וַיִּקְרָא לְפָנָיו[4]—(a) Cf. 6:9[5]. Explain the difference here. You should be able to do the rest of the verse with the help of 6:9[6].

6:12 וַיָּשָׁב מָרְדֳּכַי [1]—(a) *wayyāšoḇ* (*qāmāṣ ḥāṭûp̄*!) < *yāšûḇ*. Impf. *yāšûḇ* < **yašûbu*, but Gc20 or G40 > *yāšōḇ* (R.2a). With conv. *wāw* accent shifts, *way* + *yāšōḇ* > *wayyā́šoḇ* (R.27). Be sure to note the differences between CWC and WCC/YCC. §32.5311.

וְהָמָן נִדְחַף [2]—(a) Note position of subj. (b) *niḏḥap̄*: the 3 rads. must be ד ח פ, since ף cannot be a sufformative or suffix. נ must therefore be either 29- or N-indicator. Which fits context? For *dḥp*, 3:15[2]. For use of N, §32.83.

אָבֵל וַחֲפוּי רֹאשׁ׃[3]—(a) *'āḇēl* 'mourning' (v.56). (b) *ḥăp̄ûy*: note vowels (cstr., reduced from –ָ–*û*–); what must it be? Note 3d rad. *yôḏ*. cf. §29.7. חפה 'to cover' (2645 12/2). Gp50 of CCY –ָ–וּי, of CCW –ָ–וּו (rare). §32.3712. (c) 2:17[5].

6:13 וַיְסַפֵּר הָמָן לְזֶרֶשׁ אִשְׁתּוֹ[1]–(a) 5:11[1]. For balance cf. 5:10[3·4].

אֵת כָּל־אֲשֶׁר קָרָהוּ [2]—(a-c) Obj. of the following verb, §34.17. (d) This could be G15 of קָרָה, but no such verb is listed. –ָהוּ could be s0 (Table H); if so, verb must be CCY. 4:7[2]. §32.5114.

וַיֹּאמְרוּ לוֹ חֲכָמָיו[3]—(a) Review §29.212. Form is yaqtil. (b) Masoretic note calls attention to dagesh, without explanation. It would appear that the words were read as one, *wayyṓ'mᵉrûllô.* §35.111. (c) 1:13[1]; explain form and vocalization. §33.13.

אִם מִזֶּרַע הַיְּהוּדִים מָרְדֳּכַי[4]—(a) Introduces conditional cl., §38.6111; read §38.6. (b) *zéraʿ* 'seed' (v.2233), review §24.211. מִן of origin. (d) Subj. of verbless cl., §31.11, §31.62.

אֲשֶׁר הַחִלּוֹתָ לִנְפֹּל לְפָנָיו[5]—(a-d) Rel. cl., §38.411. 'who ... before him' = 'before whom.' (b) *haḥillôṯā*: (1) –ה could be stem indicator, §28.3. (2) תָ– must be PGN morpheme (§27.21). (3) –וֹ– after ל with dagesh could be epenthetic (R.26). This leaves a root חלל H 'to begin' (v.2490). This verb generally requires a complement. (c) Note נ, violating R.11, *linpōl.* §§29.412, .4121, §27.6511. 3:7[3]. §34.8.

לֹא־תוּכַל לוֹ[6]—This is the main cl. (apodosis) of the condition, §38.612. (b) *tûḵal* is generally identified as Hp22 of יכל (*Ges.* §53*u*, 69*r*), but it is impf. < **tiwkal*, and has no causative significance. יכל 'to be able, prevail' (v.3201). *lô'* + impf. need not be prohibitive; it may be a simple statement, 'you will not prevail over (ל) him.' §32.5211.

כִּי־נָפוֹל תִּפּוֹל לְפָנָיו׃[7]—(a) Adversative, introducing a second apodosis. (b) Pattern tells us what? §27.64. For the use of inf. abs. to strengthen a finite verb, see §35.6. It is difficult to translate, here perhaps 'surely.' (c) VDC–7. Cf. 6:10[5]. Is the form yiqtal or yaqtul?.

6:14 עוֹדָם מְדַבְּרִים עִמּוֹ[1]—(a) עוֹד 'yet, still' (v.5750), can take a pron. suf. and serve in a verbless clause, translated by a form of the verb *to be* (cf. אַיִן, יֵשׁ). Here + s5, they (were) still speaking.' (b) מְ–ַ–ִים there are enough clues for you to parse the form. 6:10[2], 1:22[7]. (c) 6:3[3].

וְסָרִיסֵי הַמֶּלֶךְ הִגִּיעוּ[2]—(a) *wᵉ*- is best translated 'when' in this context. If you have forgotten this word, cf. 1:10[6], 6:2[2]. (c) Cf. 4:14[5], 4:3[1]. וּ– is what morpheme? Is it any different than הִ–ִי–וּ? Be sure you recognize the basic morphemes, regardless of where they occur.

וַיַּבְהִלוּ לְהָבִיא אֶת־הָמָן[3]–(a) Note the clues: וּ–ִ–ַ–וַיְ. (1) *way-* tells us what? §32.53. (2) ַ under preformative, ִ after 2d rad. (written fully or defectively?) tell us what? VDC–3. (3) וּ–––י tells us what? §27.31. For בהל 2:9[3]. (b) §34.8. You should recognize the form. 3:9[5].

אֶל־הַמִּשְׁתֶּה[4]—This clause should be fairly easy. Cf. 5:12[1,2].

Learn the words in BVG–46.

55

Purpose: To introduce exegesis of poetry
Materials: Micah 6:6-8

This lesson serves not only to study a great prophetic passage, but also to introduce Hebrew poetry. Fundamental to Heb. poetry is *parallelism*, generally found in a *distich* composed of two *stichs* (*stichoi*), or a *tristich* composed of three stichs. The parallelism may be expressed by stichs that are synonymous, or antithetical, or in expanding idea, or sometimes in other forms. See the article on "Poetry" in *IDB* 3:829-838

6:6 בַּמָּה אֲקַדֵּם יְהוָה || אִכַּף לֵאלֹהֵי מָרוֹם[1]—The siglum || indicates parallel stichs. (a) *b*^{e}- + *ma*^{h}, BDB 553.4a. (b) *qdm* 'to go before' (v.6923), VDC–1. (d) *kpp* 'to bend, bow down' (3721 5x), N24. (f) *mārôm* 'height' (v.4791) = heaven, BDB 496. Isa. 33:5; 57:15. The first stich consists of p (prep.), v (verb), o (obj.); the 2d stich of v′ O′. The prep. phrase is omitted, and a noun-phrase is used. The 2d verb (v′) is synonymous with the 1st (v), and O′ is synonymous with o. This is parallelism.

הַאֲקַדְּמֶנּוּ בְעוֹלוֹת || בַּעֲגָלִים בְּנֵי שָׁנָה׃[2]—(a) *h*-interrog. *'ăqadd*^{e}*ménnû* has *nûn energ*. + s0 (§23.1221), cf. (b) in preceding distich. Who is the antecedent of *-énnû*? Verb and obj. are combined into one word. (b) *b*^{e}- 'with, by means of.' *'ôlā*^{h} 'holocaust' (v.5930), G51 of עלה. (c) *'ēgel* 'calf' (v.5695). (d-e) *bēn* + a number (of years) = age, here 'a year old.' Note that 'with year-old calves' is the entire 2d stich, paralleling 'with burnt offerings.' We might represent the distich as v-o p || P′.

6:7 הֲיִרְצֶה יְהוָה בְּאַלְפֵי אֵילִים || בְּרִבְבוֹת נַחֲלֵי־שָׁמֶן[1]—(a) Interrog. רצה 'to be pleased with, accept' (BVG-9). (c) *'élep̄* BVG-29. (d) *'áyil* 'ram' (v.352). This stich consists of v, s(ubj.), p. (e) *rib*^{e}*bôt* 'myriad' (v.7233). (f) *náḥal* 'river' (v.5158) (g) *šémen* 'oil' (BVG-21). This stich consists of only a prep. phrase P′, which is synonymous with 'thousands of rams' (i.e. as an offering). We may therefore diagram the distich as: v s p || P′.

הַאֶתֵּן בְּכוֹרִי פִּשְׁעִי || פְּרִי בִטְנִי חַטַּאת נַפְשִׁי׃[2]—(a) *h*- interrog. Have you forgotten נתן? (b) *b*^{e}*k̲ôr* 'first-born' (v.1060) + s4. (c) *péšaʿ* 'transgression, rebellion' (v.6587) + s4. 'Shall I give my first-born (for) my transgression?' (d) *p*^{e}*rî* 'fruit' (v.6529), cstr. (e) *béṭen* 'belly, womb, body' (v.990) + s4. (f) *ḥaṭṭa't̲* 'sin, sin-offering' (v.2403), cstr. But since the parallel word is *péšaʿ*, which cannot mean 'tresspass-offering,' we must translate *ḥaṭṭa't̲* here as 'sin.' (g) BVG-35. Note that the verb is omitted in the 2d stich, 'fruit of my body' צצ 'my first-born' and 'sin of my soul' || 'my transgression.' v o_1 o_2 || O_1' O_2'.

6:8 ||הִגִּיד לְךָ אָדָם מַה־טּוֹב[1]—(a) Est. 2:10[1]. Indef. subj. = passive (*Ges.* §144*d*, LXX *ἀνηγγέλη*); it is also possible to consider YHWH as the subj. (c) *'āḏām* 'man (generic, male and female)' (v.120), vocative. (d-e) Verbless cl., obj. of *higgîḏ*. I take this as a stich, parallel with the next.

וּמָה יְהוָה דּוֹרֵשׁ מִמְּךָ[2]—(a) Indef. pron. (§21.5), obj. of *dôrēš*. (b) Subj. of following ptcp. (c) *drš* 'to seek' (v.1875). (d) §23.1231. 'One made clear to you, O man, what is good || and what YHWH is seeking from you.' There are other ways of analyzing this portion.

|| כִּי אִם־עֲשׂוֹת מִשְׁפָּט[3]—(a-b) 'But, except.' This may indicate that the preceding *māʰ*-clause is interrog. (c) G65 in elliptical cl., 'He [is seeking from you] to do ....' (d) *mišpāṭ* 'judgment (the act, the sentence, the execution)' (v.4941, BDB 1048f, cf. Leon Morris, *The Biblical Doctrine of Judgment* [1960] 7-25).

|| וְאַהֲבַת חֶסֶד[4]—I understand this as the second stich in a tristich. (a) *'ăhāḇāʰ* 'love' (v.160), cstr. (b) *ḥéseḏ* is a very important and rich word, which we shall study further in Lesson 60. 'Mercy' is too restricted a meaning; 'covenant loyalty, fidelity to the covenantal obligations' is closer. Cf. N. Glueck, Hesed *in the Bible* (1967).

וְהַצְנֵעַ לֶכֶת עִם־אֱלֹהֶיךָ׃[5]—(a) *ṣnʿ* 'to be modest, humble' (6800 1x), H60 used as adv. (b) We might expect לָלֶכֶת. (c) *'im* 'with' of accompaniment. 'Your God' could mean any god, but this is highly unlikely in a strong prophet of YHWH.

If I have analyzed this correctly, the tristich, as often, serves to bring the passage to a climax. The last word has not yet been written on Hebrew poetry. The discovery of Ugaritic poetry has made obsolete a number of former theories. The student should study the poetical passages in the Bible, rather than read about them in other books. Facts should always control theories.

For further study of poetry, cf. Stanley Gevirtz, *Patterns in the Early Poetry of Israel* (1963); Theodore H. Robinson, *The Poetry of the Old Testament* (1947); and G. Buchanan Gray, *The Forms of Hebrew Poetry* (1915). My study, "An Approach to Hebrew Poetry through the Masoretic Accents," is scheduled for publication in an early issue of *Jewish Quarterly Review*.

Learn the Words in Vocabulary Group 47.

שַׁאֲלוּ שְׁלוֹם יְרוּשָׁלָםִ יִשְׁלָיוּ אֹהֲבָיִךְ׃

Pray for Jerusalem's peace; those that love thee shall have tranquillity.

Psalm 122:6

56

Purpose: To study conditional clauses
Materials: Esther 7:1-4

CAP. VII. ז   ז

וַיָּבֹא הַמֶּלֶךְ וְהָמָן לִשְׁתּוֹת עִם־אֶסְתֵּר הַמַּלְכָּה׃ וַיֹּאמֶר א 2
הַמֶּלֶךְ לְאֶסְתֵּר גַּם בַּיּוֹם הַשֵּׁנִי בְּמִשְׁתֵּה הַיַּיִן מַה־שְּׁאֵלָתֵךְ
אֶסְתֵּר הַמַּלְכָּה וְתִנָּתֵן לָךְ וּמַה־בַּקָּשָׁתֵךְ עַד־חֲצִי הַמַּלְכוּת
וְתֵעָשׂ׃ וַתַּעַן אֶסְתֵּר הַמַּלְכָּה וַתֹּאמַר אִם־מָצָאתִי חֵן 3
בְּעֵינֶיךָ הַמֶּלֶךְ וְאִם־עַל־הַמֶּלֶךְ טוֹב תִּנָּתֶן לִי נַפְשִׁי
בִּשְׁאֵלָתִי וְעַמִּי בְּבַקָּשָׁתִי׃ כִּי נִמְכַּרְנוּ אֲנִי וְעַמִּי לְהַשְׁמִיד 4
לַהֲרוֹג וּלְאַבֵּד וְאִלּוּ לַעֲבָדִים וְלִשְׁפָחוֹת נִמְכַּרְנוּ הֶחֱרַשְׁתִּי
כִּי אֵין הַצָּר שֹׁוֶה בְּנֵזֶק הַמֶּלֶךְ׃ ה

7:1 לִשְׁתּוֹת[1]—Note *wayyāḇô'* with compound subj., and see §33.124. (a) Inf. of purpose, §35.423. VDC–6. 3:15[4].

עִם־אֶסְתֵּר[2]—(a) Note difference between b^e- 'with' (instrument) and *'im* 'with' (accompaniment). See BDB 767f.

7:2 גַּם בַּיּוֹם הַשֵּׁנִי [1]—(a) 1:9[1] (v.1571). (b-c) 2:14[3], 1:10[1]. For balance, cf. 5:6.

7:3 תִּנָּתֶן לִי נַפְשִׁי בִּשְׁאֵלָתִי[1]—For several parts of this verse, cf. 5:6-8. (a) 2:13[3]. What is the difference? (c) 4:13[2]. (d) Note suffix, cf. 5:7[2]. Various explanations of –בְּ: price, essence, instrument, etc. When we have a lot of repetition from a previous passage, it's a good time for careful review.

וְעַמִּי בְּבַקָּשָׁתִי׃ [2]—(a) Second subj. of *tinnāṯen lî*; verb agrees with nearer, §33.123. (b) 7:3[1]. 5:7[2].

7:4 כִּי נִמְכַּרְנוּ אֲנִי וְעַמִּי[1]—(a) Causal, §38.53, BDB 473.3. (b) נִ——וּ: if *-nû* is sufformative, *ni-* must be stem-indicator. Why? *mkr* 'to sell' (v.4376). Parse first, then translate. (c-d) Compound subj., §33.1111 not applying. 7:1[1].

לְהַשְׁמִיד לַהֲרוֹג וּלְאַבֵּד [2]—Cf. 3:13[3]. Here we might expect passives, but the Heb. inf. cstr. is a verbal adj. and can be translated 'for destruction, etc.' §30.381

וְאִלּוּ לַעֲבָדִים וְלִשְׁפָחוֹת נִמְכַּרְנוּ[3]—(a) *'illû* (< *'in lû*) 'if indeed' (432 2/1), followed by perf. it represents a contrary-to-fact condition, §38.6112. (b) 'for, as.' 1:3[7]. (c) $\check{s}i\underline{p}\d{h}\bar{a}^h$ 'female slave' (v.8198). (d) §38.6112. 7:4[1].

הֶחֱרַשְׁתִּי [4]—R.10c. *ḥrš* 'to be silent, dumb' (v.2790a). Strong lists it under *ḥrš* 'to plow,' but one is from PS *$\d{h}r\theta$, the other from PS **ḥrš*. Study conditional clauses. This is contrary-to-fact, 'If we had been sold ...' (we weren't; we were condemned to death), 'I would have kept silent' (I didn't; I'm speaking out.' §32.514.

כִּי אֵין הַצָּר שֹׁוֶה[5]—(a) §38.53. (b) אֵין negates ptcp. (c) *ṣār* is usually translated 'enemy' (v.6862), but this is from *ṣrr*, and should be *ṣar* (R.14). *ṣār* could be from צור*, cf. Arab. *ḍâr* 'to injure, harm,' and if so, we could read it, 'the harm would not be equal to ....' RSV translates 'our affliction,' cf. v.6862b. (d) *šôwêʰ*, cf. 3:8[7]; 'worth' fits here and in 3:8 and 5:13

בְּנֵזֶק הַמֶּלֶךְ׃[6]—(a) *nḗzeq* 'damage, injury' (5143 1/1). 'Damage of the king' = that suffered by the king, objective genitive. Cf. RSV.

Memorize the meanings of the words in **BVG–48**.

Study the following pronominal suffixes:

בַּעֲלֵיהֶן	שְׁנֵיהֶם	עַמָּהּ	עַמּוֹ	מַלְכוּתֵךְ	עָלַי
בְּעֵינֵיהֶן	לָהֶם	לָהּ	לוֹ	לָךְ	לִי
תַּמְרֻקֵיהֶן	דָּתֵיהֶם	תַּמְרוּקֶיהָ	מַלְכוּתוֹ	בְּעֵינַיִךְ	מוֹלַדְתִּי
	בְּאָמְרָם	יָפְיָהּ	לְמָלְכוֹ	אָבִיךְ	נַעֲרֹתַי
	אוֹתָם	מִמֶּנָּה	מִמֶּנּוּ		מִמֶּנִּי
	עֲלֵיהֶם	מָנוֹתֶיהָ	גְּדוּלָּתוֹ	בַּקָּשָׁתֵךְ	בַּקָּשָׁתִי
	אֵינָם	מוֹלַדְתָּהּ	חֲמָתוֹ	שְׁאֵלָתֵךְ	שְׁאֵלָתִי

Note the following pronominal suffixes:

'ôṯî *me*
'ēlî to *me*
'ālay on *my* behalf
'āḥî my brother
'aḥay *my* brothers
šᵉlāḥánî he sent *me*
wayyišlāḥḗnî and he sent *me*
šᵉ'ēlāṯî *my* petition
na'ărôṯay *my* maids

מִצִּיּוֹן מִכְלַל־יֹפִי אֱלֹהִים הוֹפִיעַ׃
Out of Zion, the perfection of beauty, God shines forth.
Psalm 50:2

57

Purpose: To study the use of the converted imperfect
Materials: Esther 7:5-8

וַיֹּאמֶר הַמֶּלֶךְ
אֲחַשְׁוֵרוֹשׁ וַיֹּאמֶר לְאֶסְתֵּר הַמַּלְכָּה מִי הוּא זֶה וְאֵי־זֶה
6 הוּא אֲשֶׁר־מְלָאוֹ לִבּוֹ לַעֲשׂוֹת כֵּן׃ וַתֹּאמֶר אֶסְתֵּר אִישׁ
צַר וְאוֹיֵב הָמָן הָרָע הַזֶּה וְהָמָן נִבְעַת מִלִּפְנֵי הַמֶּלֶךְ
7 וְהַמַּלְכָּה׃ וְהַמֶּלֶךְ קָם בַּחֲמָתוֹ מִמִּשְׁתֵּה הַיַּיִן אֶל־גִּנַּת
הַבִּיתָן וְהָמָן עָמַד לְבַקֵּשׁ עַל־נַפְשׁוֹ מֵאֶסְתֵּר הַמַּלְכָּה כִּי
8 רָאָה כִּי־כָלְתָה אֵלָיו הָרָעָה מֵאֵת הַמֶּלֶךְ׃ וְהַמֶּלֶךְ שָׁב
מִגִּנַּת הַבִּיתָן אֶל־בֵּית ׀ מִשְׁתֵּה הַיַּיִן וְהָמָן נֹפֵל עַל־הַמִּטָּה
אֲשֶׁר אֶסְתֵּר עָלֶיהָ וַיֹּאמֶר הַמֶּלֶךְ הֲגַם לִכְבּוֹשׁ אֶת־
הַמַּלְכָּה עִמִּי בַּבָּיִת הַדָּבָר יָצָא מִפִּי הַמֶּלֶךְ וּפְנֵי הָמָן חָפוּ׃

7:5 מִי הוּא זֶה וְאֵי־זֶה הוּא [1]—(a-c) Verbless, §31.224, §31.31. (d) 'Where?')v.335). In Mod. Heb. אֵיזֶהוּ means 'who/which is it?' but here, probably 'where is he?'

אֲשֶׁר־מְלָאוֹ לִבּוֹ לַעֲשׂוֹת כֵּן׃ [2]—(b) מלא is usually stative (§32.21), but here is fientive (§32.22), taking an obj. *Ges.* (§74*g*) suggests this is the reason for the *qāmāṣ* (normally *ṣêrê*). Note suffix. (c) §36.6.

7:6 אִישׁ צַר וְאוֹיֵב הָמָן הָרָע הַזֶּה [1]—This is direct discourse (§38.81). We can almost hear Esther biting off each word. (b) *ṣar* 'enemy' (v.6862). (c) G50 of איב, but a very common noun 'enemy' (v.340), and should be listed as such. (e) *ra'* 'evil, wicked' (v.7451).

וְהָמָן נִבְעַת [2]—(b) ַ-ת could be fsc, but this does not fit context (§33.11). -נִ could be what? - ַ - ִנ is what pattern? §28.42. בעת (N) 'to be terrified' (v.1204). §32.51, .5111.

וְהַמֶּלֶךְ קָם בַּחֲמָתוֹ [1]—(b) G10 or G50? §29.631. Which does context require? (c) 1:12[6]. Adv. phrase, §35.31, describing circumstances of the action.

אֶל־גִּנַּת הַבִּיתָן [2]—We would insert לבוא, but this could be looked upon as a "pregnant" construction. 'The king stood up into the garden.' *Ges.* §119*ee*. §36.54. (b) 1:5[10].

וְהָמָן עָמַד [3]—(b) 3:4[5]. Note how the conv. impf. is avoided in this story. §32.533f.

לְבַקֵּשׁ עַל־נַפְשׁוֹ מֵאֶסְתֵּר [4]—(a) 2:15[4], 4:8[9]. (b) 'on behalf of.' (c) 7:3[1]. (d) What is the force of מִן? Purpose clause, §38.542, tells the purpose of the action of the main verb.

כִּי רָאָה כִּי־כָלְתָה אֵלָיו הָרָעָה מֵאֵת הַמֶּלֶךְ׃ [5]—(a) §38.53. (b) §29.71. (c) Introduces indirect discourse, §38.82. (d) §29.7131, VDC–6. כלה ‘to finish,’ but with רעה ‘was determined’ (v.3615). (f) f. of *ra‘*, for **ra‘^{a}ā^h*, 7:6[1]. (g) *min* + *’ēṯ*, ‘from, by’ (of author or composer).

7:8 וְהַמֶּלֶךְ שָׁב מִגִּנַּת הַבִּיתָן [1]—(b) 2:14[2], 6:12[1]. G10 or G50? (c-d) Cf. 7:7[2].

אֶל־בֵּית [2]—Cf. 7:7[1].

וְהָמָן נֹפֵל עַל־הַמִּטָּה אֲשֶׁר אֶסְתֵּר עָלֶיהָ [3]—(b) 6:13[5-7], 3:7[3]. Did Haman ‘fall’ *after* the king returned, or *before*? Read §32.5114. (d) 1:6[9]. (e-g) 6:8[2-3].

הֲגַם לִכְבּוֹשׁ אֶת־הַמַּלְכָּה עִמִּי בַּבָּיִת [4]—(a) Interrog. –הֲ, §35.23. (b) *kbš* ‘to conquer, subdue’ (v.3533), here ‘to ravish.’ (e-f) ‘with me in the house,’ §35.31. Note the ellipsis, ‘Is (he) even (going) to rape the queen ...?’

הַדָּבָר יָצָא מִפִּי הַמֶּלֶךְ [5]—(a) Here, ‘statement, words.’ (b) YCC and CC’, §29.8. (c) פֶּה ‘mouth’ (v.6310), with מִן of source. *pî* may be an old genitive ending, §25.3ff.

וּפְנֵי הָמָן חָפוּ׃ [6]—(a) 1:14[5]. (c) Two radicals – which is lacking? VDC–6 or VDC–10? If this is G15 of חפה ‘to cover’ (2645 12/2), 6:12[3], we would expect אֵת before the obj. (a-b). Some emend to read ‘Haman’s face grew red (*ḥammû*).’In vv. 6-7 there are seven main clauses with the noun preceding the verb. Don’t let anyone tell you that the verb normally stands first in Hebrew. The conv. impf. is used in this part of the story only for the formula ‘and ... said.’ *Use your eyes!*

Learn the words in BVG–49.

Note the following pronominal suffixes:
b^{e}nap̄šēḵ in *your* (f.s.) soul
lāḵ to *you* (f.s.)
’āḇîḵ *your* (f.s.) father
š^e’ēlāṯēḵ *your* (f.s.) petition
l^{e}ḵā to *you* (m.s.)
b^e‘ê^{y}né^{y}ḵā in *your* (m.s.) eyes
b^e‘ê^{y}né^{y}ḵem in *your* (m.p.) eyes
lāḵem to *you* (m.p.)

עַד־אָנָה מֵאַנְתֶּם לִשְׁמֹר מִצְוֹתַי וְתוֹרֹתָי
How long do you refuse to keep my commandments and my laws?
Exodus 16:28

58

Purpose: To learn something about relative clauses
Materials: Esther 7:9–8:2

וַיֹּאמֶר חַרְבוֹנָה אֶחָד מִן־הַסָּרִיסִים לִפְנֵי הַמֶּלֶךְ גַּם הִנֵּה־ 9
הָעֵץ אֲשֶׁר־עָשָׂה הָמָן לְמָרְדֳּכַי אֲשֶׁר דִּבֶּר־טוֹב עַל־הַמֶּלֶךְ
עֹמֵד בְּבֵית הָמָן גָּבֹהַּ חֲמִשִּׁים אַמָּה וַיֹּאמֶר הַמֶּלֶךְ תְּלֻהוּ
עָלָיו׃ וַיִּתְלוּ אֶת־הָמָן עַל־הָעֵץ אֲשֶׁר־הֵכִין לְמָרְדֳּכָי וַחֲמַת י
הַמֶּלֶךְ שָׁכָכָה׃

ח CAP. VIII. ח

בַּיּוֹם הַהוּא נָתַן הַמֶּלֶךְ אֲחַשְׁוֵרוֹשׁ לְאֶסְתֵּר הַמַּלְכָּה אֶת־ א
בֵּית הָמָן צֹרֵר הַיְּהוּדִיִּים וּמָרְדֳּכַי בָּא לִפְנֵי הַמֶּלֶךְ כִּי־
הִגִּידָה אֶסְתֵּר מַה הוּא־לָהּ׃ וַיָּסַר הַמֶּלֶךְ אֶת־טַבַּעְתּוֹ 2
אֲשֶׁר הֶעֱבִיר מֵהָמָן וַיִּתְּנָהּ לְמָרְדֳּכָי וַתָּשֶׂם אֶסְתֵּר אֶת־
מָרְדֳּכַי עַל־בֵּית הָמָן׃

7:9 אֶחָד מִן־הַסָּרִיסִים[1]—(b) *min* partitive, 'one from, one of (a larger group).'

גַּם הִנֵּה־הָעֵץ[2]—(a) This seems unusual to me (cf. BDB 169), possibly introducing a climax, 'Yea.' (b) *hinnê^h* 'behold! here is!' (v.2009). (c) 2:23[3]. The sentence is broken with two relative clauses. After הנה we may expect a ptcp., which we find after the rel. cls.

אֲשֶׁר־עָשָׂה הָמָן[3]—Rel. cl., defining *hā'ēṣ*, §38.4

אֲשֶׁר דִּבֶּר־טוֹב[4]—(a) Introduces second rel. cl., this one describing Mordecai, §38.4. (b) Note accent and pointing. The D10 of this word often is closely joined to the next word. (c) This word can be an adj. 'good,' or an adv. 'well.'

עֹמֵד בְּבֵית הָמָן[5]—(a) The ptcp. resumes the main cl., after *hinnê^h hā'ēṣ*. The cl. is verbless, cf. §31.24, although in Eng. we would consider 'the tree' as obj. of 'behold,' and 'standing' as describing 'the tree.' Learn to think in Heb. style. Does the following prep. phrase describe Haman, the house, or the tree?

תְּלֻהוּ עָלָיו׃[6]—(a) 5:14[4]. Defective writing, G37s0, note accent.

7:10 וַיִּתְלוּ אֶת־הָמָן[1]—Take care! If -יתְ is HtD and -וּ is ending, what is the root? Will it fit VDC–11? What is ו—י are afformatives? Parse and *then* translate. Who or what is/are subj. of verb? §32.114.

אֲשֶׁר־הֵכִין לְמָרְדֳּכָי[2]—(a) What is the antecedent? (b) 6:4[5]. Who or what is the subj. of this verb? Think out each phrase and clause.

וַחֲמַת הַמֶּלֶךְ שָׁכָכָה׃ [3]—(a) 2:1[2]. (c) 2:1[2] (7918 5/2), G11 with pausal accent.

8:1 צֹרֵר הַיְּהוּדִיִּים [1]—The first part of the verse consists of: prep. phr. (temporal), verb, subj., appositive, indir. obj., appositive, dir. obj with modifier. (a) 3:10[4].

כִּי־הִגִּידָה [2]—(a) Tells *why* Mordecai came, §38.53. (b) 2:10[1]. What did Esther make known?.

8:2 וַיָּסַר הַמֶּלֶךְ אֶת־טַבַּעְתּוֹ [1]—(a-d) 3:10[1] In contrast with 7:7-8, we now find eleven clauses starting with conv. impfs. in vv. 2-4. Read §§32.53, .5312, .533.

אֲשֶׁר הֶעֱבִיר מֵהָמָן [2]—Rel. cl. (a) What is the antecedent? (b) This word is translated in many ways. How does it fit best in this context? (c) If *to* indicates indir. obj. after verbs of *giving*, does *min* do the same after verbs of *taking*? In both cases, it is better to think of the prep. phrase as an adverbial modifier of the verb, cf. §35.11.

יִּתְּנָהּ לְמָרְדֳּכָי [3]—(a) What is the antecedent of ־ָהּ? Note *mēhāmān ... lᵉmordᵉḵay* – do the preps. help us to translate *heʿᵉḇîr*? Perhaps something like 'to cause to pass, to transfer.' Meanings are established by contexts.

וַתָּשֶׂם [4]—(a) 2:17[5]. What is subj. of this verb? What is obj.? How is the prep. phrase used?

Learn the words in Vocabulary Group 50.

Study the use of the accusative אֵת:

וַיִּקַּח הָמָן   אֶת־הַלְּבוּשׁ
וְאֶת־הַסּוּס (6:11)

וַיְסַפֵּר לָהֶם הָמָן   אֶת־כְּבוֹד עָשְׁרוֹ וְרֹב בָּנָיו
וְאֵת כָּל־אֲשֶׁר גִּדְּלוֹ הַמֶּלֶךְ
וְאֵת אֲשֶׁר נִשְּׂאוֹ עַל־הַשָּׂרִים וְעַבְדֵי הַמֶּלֶךְ (5:11)

וְאֶת־פַּתְשֶׁגֶן כְּתָב־הַדָּת ... נָתַן לוֹ

מַצְרֵף לַכֶּסֶף וְכוּר לַזָּהָב
וּבֹחֵן לִבּוֹת יהוה׃

A crucible is for silver and a furnace for gold, but YHWH tries hearts.

Proverbs 17:3

59

Purpose: To observe phrases and clauses
Materials: Esther 8:3-6

וַתּ֣וֹסֶף אֶסְתֵּ֗ר וַתְּדַבֵּר֙ לִפְנֵ֣י 3
הַמֶּ֔לֶךְ וַתִּפֹּ֖ל לִפְנֵ֣י רַגְלָ֑יו וַתֵּ֣בְךְּ וַתִּתְחַנֶּן־ל֗וֹ לְהַעֲבִיר֙ אֶת־
רָעַת֙ הָמָ֣ן הָאֲגָגִ֔י וְאֵת֙ מַחֲשַׁבְתּ֔וֹ אֲשֶׁ֥ר חָשַׁ֖ב עַל־הַיְּהוּדִֽים׃
וַיּ֤וֹשֶׁט הַמֶּ֙לֶךְ֙ לְאֶסְתֵּ֔ר אֵ֖ת שַׁרְבִ֣ט הַזָּהָ֑ב וַתָּ֣קָם אֶסְתֵּ֔ר 4
וַֽתַּעֲמֹ֖ד לִפְנֵ֥י הַמֶּֽלֶךְ׃ וַתֹּאמֶר֩ אִם־עַל־הַמֶּ֨לֶךְ ט֜וֹב וְאִם־ 5
מָצָ֧אתִי חֵ֣ן לְפָנָ֗יו וְכָשֵׁ֤ר הַדָּבָר֙ לִפְנֵ֣י הַמֶּ֔לֶךְ וְטוֹבָ֥ה אֲנִ֖י
בְּעֵינָ֑יו יִכָּתֵ֞ב לְהָשִׁ֣יב אֶת־הַסְּפָרִ֗ים מַחֲשֶׁ֜בֶת הָמָ֤ן בֶּן־
הַמְּדָ֙תָא֙ הָאֲגָגִ֔י אֲשֶׁ֣ר כָּתַ֗ב לְאַבֵּד֙ אֶת־הַיְּהוּדִ֔ים אֲשֶׁ֖ר
בְּכָל־מְדִינ֥וֹת הַמֶּֽלֶךְ׃ כִּ֠י אֵיכָכָ֤ה אוּכַל֙ וְֽרָאִ֔יתִי בָּרָעָ֖ה 6
אֲשֶׁר־יִמְצָ֣א אֶת־עַמִּ֑י וְאֵֽיכָכָ֤ה אוּכַל֙ וְֽרָאִ֔יתִי בְּאָבְדַ֖ן
מוֹלַדְתִּֽי׃

8:3 וַתּ֣וֹסֶף אֶסְתֵּ֗ר וַתְּדַבֵּר֙[1]—(a) יסף 'to add' (v.3254), followed by another verb, 'to do ... again.' **tawsip*, §29.311. (c) 1:22[7].

וַתִּפֹּ֖ל לִפְנֵ֣י רַגְלָ֑יו[2]—(a) 3:7[3]. (c) *rég̲el* 'foot' (v.7272), dual §25.423. (b-c) Prep. phrase, adverbial, modifying verb, telling *where* she fell.

וַתֵּ֣בְךְּ וַתִּתְחַנֶּן־ל֗וֹ[3]—(a) Note form, read §29.72 carefully, then read §29.721. בכה 'to weep' (v.1058). (b) 4:8[9]. VDC–1. (a-b) Note sequence of conv. impfs. Note §32.5333. Some of the statements in §§32.533ff. I have drawn from the standard grammars against my better judgment. There is still *very much to be done* in study of the conv. impf. and conv. perf.

לְהַעֲבִיר֙ אֶת־רָעַת֙ הָמָ֣ן[4]—(a) Cf. 8:2[2]. (c) Est. 7:6[1]. Here רָעָה 'evil' (v.7451), < **raʿʿat*. In this context, how translate העביר? §38.54.

מַחֲשַׁבְתּ֔וֹ אֲשֶׁ֥ר חָשַׁ֖ב[5]—(a) *maḥăšéb̲et̲* 'device, plan' (v.4284), 2d of compound obj. of verb. (b) Introduces rel. cl.; what does it modify? (c) *ḥāšab̲* 'he thought, devised' (v.2803). The verb is modified by the adverbial prep. phrase that follows.

8:4 וַיּ֤וֹשֶׁט[1]—(a) 4:11[7]. For following words, 4:11.

וַתָּ֣קָם[2]—(a) 5:9[4]. VDC–9. Note *qāmāṣ*'s. Note position of verb and subj.

וַֽתַּעֲמֹ֖ד[3]—(a) 3:4[5]. R.9c. The adverbial phrase that follows tells *where* she stood.

8:5 וְכָשֵׁ֤ר[1]—You should be able to read this verse to the r^{e}ḇî^{a}ʿ. (a) *kāšēr* 'right, proper' (3787 3/1). In Ashkenazic pronunciation, this word > "kosher."

וְטוֹבָה אֲנִי[2]—(a-b) Verbless cl., §31. Pred. adj., §31.23. Word order, §31.43. Actually there are *four* "if" clauses (protases, §38.611), but *'im* is omitted before the last two, §30.14. §31.233.

יִכָּתֵב לְהָשִׁיב אֶת־הַסְּפָרִים[3]—(a) 1:19[4]. G20 or G40? §32.3511. (b) 4:13[1]. (d) 1:22[1]. (b-d) Indir. disc., §38.82. For use of inf. cstr., §32.3823. This is the main cl. (apodosis, §38.612) of the condition. The condition is "general" (it does not assume either alternative), hence the apodosis takes any kind of verb, here jussive. 'If I have found favor ... let it be written ... (and if not, then obviously it won't be written).'

מַחֲשֶׁבֶת הָמָן[4]—(a) 8:3[5]. Appositional cl. (§38.33), explaining the "letters." This is further explained (defined) by the clauses which follow.

אֲשֶׁר כָּתַב לְאַבֵּד[5]—(a) What is the antecedent? (c) 3:9[2]. Indir. disc., cf. §32.3823, §38.82. It can also be taken as a purpose cl. Either 'which he wrote (saying) to destroy ...,' or 'which he wrote in order to destroy ....' To what does the following rel. cl. relate?

8:6 כִּי אֵיכָכָה אוּכַל[1]—(a) Causal, tells *why* Esther is so acting. (b) *'ê*^{y}*k̲āk̲â* and *'ê*^{y}*k̲āk̲â* (Eccl.), 'How?' (349 4/2). (c) 6:13[6]. §28.322.

וְרָאִיתִי בָּרָעָה[2]—(a) ָֽ is *ga'yâ* or grave metheg. According to *David Ḳimḥi's Hebrew Grammar* [Ḳimḥi 1160-1235 C. E.) §4d, it has a full vowel sound (ָ). It is not found in 8:6[4]. Since the penult is open, we cannot tell if *wāw* is conversive (§17.342), but after impf. it probably is (§32.5422). רָאָה בְּ– 'to gaze upon,' BDB 908.8a(3). (b) 8:3[4].

אֲשֶׁר־יִמְצָא [3]—Adj. cl., §38.4, defining which word? How should we translate (b) – 'which my people shall find' or 'which shall find my people'?

וְרָאִיתִי בְּאָבְדַן[4]—(a) Cf. 8:6[2]. (b) *'ob̲d̲ān* 'destruction' (13 1/1), cstr., but *-ân* should not reduce. In effect, this is conditional, 'How can I endure if I shall have gazed upon ... ?'

Memorize the basic vocabulary in Group 51.

קְדֹשִׁים תִּהְיוּ כִּי קָדוֹשׁ אֲנִי יְהוָה אֱלֹהֵיכֶם׃

Holy shall you be, for holy am I YHWH your God.

Leviticus 19:2

Purpose: To study exegesis of poetry
Materials: Psalm 136:10-22

כִּי לְעוֹלָם חַסְדּוֹ׃	לְמַכֵּה מִצְרַיִם בִּבְכוֹרֵיהֶם	10
כִּי לְעוֹלָם חַסְדּוֹ׃	וַיּוֹצֵא יִשְׂרָאֵל מִתּוֹכָם	11
כִּי לְעוֹלָם חַסְדּוֹ׃	בְּיָד חֲזָקָה וּבִזְרוֹעַ נְטוּיָה	12
כִּי לְעוֹלָם חַסְדּוֹ׃	לְגֹזֵר יַם־סוּף לִגְזָרִים	13
כִּי לְעוֹלָם חַסְדּוֹ׃	וְהֶעֱבִיר יִשְׂרָאֵל בְּתוֹכוֹ	14
כִּי לְעוֹלָם חַסְדּוֹ׃	וְנִעֵר פַּרְעֹה וְחֵילוֹ בְיַם־סָרוּף	15
כִּי לְעוֹלָם חַסְדּוֹ׃	לְמוֹלִיךְ עַמּוֹ בַּמִּדְבָּר	16
כִּי לְעוֹלָם חַסְדּוֹ׃	לְמַכֵּה מְלָכִים גְּדֹלִים	17
כִּי לְעוֹלָם חַסְדּוֹ׃	וַיַּהֲרֹג מְלָכִים אַדִּירִים	18
כִּי לְעוֹלָם חַסְדּוֹ׃	לְסִיחוֹן מֶלֶךְ הָאֱמֹרִי	19
כִּי לְעוֹלָם חַסְדּוֹ׃	לְעוֹג מֶלֶךְ הַבָּשָׁן	20
כִּי לְעוֹלָם חַסְדּוֹ׃	וְנָתַן אַרְצָם לְנַחֲלָה	21
כִּי לְעוֹלָם חַסְדּוֹ׃	נַחֲלָה לְיִשְׂרָאֵל עַבְדּוֹ	22

Psalm 136 This is an introduction to the rubric of the Israelite cult, namely an antiphonal psalm. The reader (or Group A) recited the words at the beginning of each verse, and the congregation (or Group B) recited the response, in this example, *kî lᵉʿôlām ḥasdô*. I have set a portion of this Psalm in columns for visual help. Note that the right-hand column is a "recital of the great deeds of Yahweh." Much of Israel's worship was centered about the Lord's revelatory and redemptive activity, many portions of which are brought into liturgical passages of the Bible repeatedly. Look for this as you work in the Scriptures.

:10¹ (a) *lᵉmakkêʰ* < *nky* H 'to smite' (v.5221), 'to the smiter of.' (b) *miṣráyim* pr.n. 'Egypt.' (c) *bib̲ᵉk̲ôrêhem*: *bᵉk̲ôr* 'first-born' (v.1060, BVG-47. *bᵉ*- is perhaps the *beth essentiae*, specifying the part of Egypt that was smitten.

:10² (a) *kî* causal. The psalm opens with the words, *hôd̲û la'd̲ônāy kî ṭôb̲* 'Give thanks to YHWH for he is good.' The antiphonal gives the reason in a refrain repeated 26 times. (b) *lᵉʿôlām*: *ʿôlām* 'long duration (past or future)' (v.5769). The idea of 'eternity' is more Greek than Hebrew. (c) *ḥésed̲* 'covenant obligation/loyalty' (v.2619). This psalm affords an outstanding definition of *ḥésed̲*. While the mercy of YHWH is shown to Israel, the people of his covenant, there is no mercy to those who oppose him or his people.

:11 (a) *wayyôṣēʾ*: note long-*ô*, §29.311. 'He caused to come out, brought out.' (c) *mittôk̲ām: min* + *tôk* (v.8432) + s5.

:12 (b) *ḥăzāqāʰ* 'strong, firm' (v.2389). *zᵉrôᵃʿ* 'arm, shoulder' (v.2220,BVG-46). (d) *nṭʰ*, V.5186, Gp51 'outstretched.' The words *bᵉyād̲ ḥăzāqāʰ ûb̲izrôᵃʿ nᵉṭûyāʰ* are part of the Passover Seder. Cf. Exod. 6:1. 6; Deut. 4:34.

:13 (a) *l*^{e}*gôzēr*: *gzr* ‘to cut, divide’ (1504 13x), G52. (b-c) *yam-sûp̄* ‘sea of reeds‘ (5488, BDB 693), a name given only to arms of the Red Sea; later the Greeks applied the name *θάλασσα ἐρυθρά* ‘Red Sea’ to the arms as well. Read a good article in *NBD, IDB, ISBE,* or another Bible encyclopedia. (d) *liḡzārîm*: *gézer* ‘portion’ (1506 2x).

:14 (a) *w*^{e}*heʿeḇîr*: what stem? You certainly know עבר by now! (c) *b*^{e}*ṯôḵô*, cf. Ps. 136:11(c).

:15 (a) *w*^{e}*niʿēr*: *nʿr* ‘to shake, shake out/off’ (5287 12x). What stem? (b) *parʿō*^{h} ‘Pharaoh.’ (c) *ḥáyil* ‘might, army’ (v.2428). (d-e) Cf. 136:13(b-c).

:16 (a) *l*^{e}*môlîḵ*: הלך acts like WCC, BDB 236, ‘the one who caused to walk.’ (b) You should know *ʿam*. (c) *bammiḏbār*: *miḏbār* ‘steppe, wilderness’ (v.4057), with def. art. often = the wilderness of the wanderings (in the Sinai peninsula).

:17 (a) *l*^{e}*makkê*^{h}, 136:10. (b) *m*^{e}*lāḵîm*. pl. of *méleḵ*. *Is it definite? (c) g*^{e}*ḏôlîm,* v. 1419. Why pl.? Why not def.?

:18 (a) *wayyahărōḡ,* Est. 3:13³. Is it H or G?. (b) See 136:17. (c) *ʾaddîrîm*: *ʾaddîr* ‘majestic’ (v.117).

:19 (a) *l*^{e}*sîḥôn* pr.n. ‘Sihon.’ (e) *hāʾĕmôrî*, gentilic, ‘the Amorite,’ collective.

:20 (a) *ûl*^{e}*ʿôḡ*: *ʿôḡ* pr.n. ‘Og.’ (c) *habbāšān*: pr.n. ‘Bashan,’ usually with def. art.

:21 (a) What various meanings does נתן have? (b) *ʾarṣām*: Do you recognize the word if you take off the s5?. ‘Their land.’ (c) *l*^{e}*naḥălā*^{h}: *naḥălā*^{h} ‘possession, property, inheritance’ (v.5159).

:22 With the help of the previous word, you should be able to do this portion.

Review what you have learned about poetry in Lesson 55. Then read the right-hand column of this psalm as printed at the top of this lesson. Now analyze the stichs as I have suggested them. Whether you agree with what I have done is beside the point – do you understand what I have tried to do? Start now to analyze every poetic passage that you see in the Hebrew Bible.

Know the basic vocabulary in Group 52.

A strophic analysis of Psalm 136

1 ‖ 2 ‖ 3	10 ‖ 11 ‖ 12	23 ‖ 24 ‖ 25
4	13 ‖ 14 ‖ 15	26
5 ‖ 6	16	
7 ‖ 8 ‖ 9	17 ‖ 18	
	19 ‖ 20	
	21 ‖ 22	

61

Purpose: More on phrases and clauses
Materials: Esther 8:7-9

וַיֹּאמֶר הַמֶּלֶךְ אֲחַשְׁוֵרֹשׁ לְאֶסְתֵּר הַמַּלְכָּה 7
וּלְמָרְדֳּכַי הַיְּהוּדִי הִנֵּה בֵית־הָמָן נָתַתִּי לְאֶסְתֵּר וְאֹתוֹ
תָּלוּ עַל־הָעֵץ עַל אֲשֶׁר־שָׁלַח יָדוֹ בַּיְּהוּדִיִּים׃ וְאַתֶּם 8
כִּתְבוּ עַל־הַיְּהוּדִים כַּטּוֹב בְּעֵינֵיכֶם בְּשֵׁם הַמֶּלֶךְ וְחִתְמוּ
בְּטַבַּעַת הַמֶּלֶךְ כִּי־כְתָב אֲשֶׁר־נִכְתָּב בְּשֵׁם־הַמֶּלֶךְ וְנַחְתּוֹם
בְּטַבַּעַת הַמֶּלֶךְ אֵין לְהָשִׁיב׃ וַיִּקָּרְאוּ סֹפְרֵי־הַמֶּלֶךְ בָּעֵת־ 9
הַהִיא בַּחֹדֶשׁ הַשְּׁלִישִׁי הוּא־חֹדֶשׁ סִיוָן בִּשְׁלוֹשָׁה
וְעֶשְׂרִים בּוֹ וַיִּכָּתֵב כְּכָל־אֲשֶׁר־צִוָּה מָרְדֳּכַי אֶל־
הַיְּהוּדִים וְאֶל הָאֲחַשְׁדַּרְפְּנִים וְהַפַּחוֹת וְשָׂרֵי הַמְּדִינוֹת
אֲשֶׁר ׀ מֵהֹדּוּ וְעַד־כּוּשׁ שֶׁבַע וְעֶשְׂרִים וּמֵאָה מְדִינָה
מְדִינָה וּמְדִינָה כִּכְתָבָהּ וְעַם וָעָם כִּלְשֹׁנוֹ וְאֶל־הַיְּהוּדִים
כִּכְתָבָם וְכִלְשׁוֹנָם׃ י

8:7 הִנֵּה בֵית־הָמָן נָתַתִּי[1]—(a) 'Behold!' (v.2009). Masoretic accents appear to make this an independent cl.; 'Behold Haman's house!' The absence of אֵת confirms this. (d) §13.1111.

וְאֹתוֹ תָּלוּ[2]—(a) §34.113. Note word order: emphasis. (b) VDC–10. The prep. phrase is adverbial; explain why.

עַל אֲשֶׁר־שָׁלַח יָדוֹ[3]—(a-b) 'on account of (the fact) that' = *because*. BDB 758.IIIa. §38.53. (c) 2:21[7].

8:8 וְאַתֶּם כִּתְבוּ[1]—(a) §21.1. To whom does this refer? (Note the number.) (b) §27.422. §32.32, §32.1121. 'Now *you* write ....'

כַּטּוֹב[2]—(a) Is there a def. art.? You should be able to do the rest of the clause.

וְחִתְמוּ[3]—(a) 3:12[10] §37.422. Does §32.324 apply here? Watch the context! You should be able to do the rest of the clause.

כִּי־כְתָב אֲשֶׁר־נִכְתָּב[4]—(a) *kî* causal, BDB 473. (b) 1:22[3], 3:14[1] (c) Introduces rel. cl., subj. of *niḵtāḇ*. (d) N10 or N50? VDC–3. §32.831. If ptcp., then we have a verbless cl., with *'ăšer* as subj., and *niḵtāḇ* as pred., §31.123, §31.24.

וְנַחְתּוֹם בְּטַבַּעַת הַמֶּלֶךְ[5]—Also a rel. cl., with *'ăšer* omitted. (a) VDC- 3. §28.42. §32.391. (b) 3:10[1]. In both clauses, there are prep. phrases used adverbially. Identify them.

אֵין לְהָשִׁיב׃[6]—(a-b) §32.3812. ‘There is no recalling’ = ‘it cannot be recalled.’

8:9 וַיִּקָּרְאוּ[1]—(a) Vowel-pattern tells us what? 3:12[1]. For the following words, 3:12[1], 1:13[2]. §26.32. Does §33.13 apply?

בַּחֹדֶשׁ הַשְּׁלִישִׁי[2]—The main verb is modified by 3 adv. phrases, the 2d of which is modified by an appositional phr. Identify them. Cf. 3:12[2]. 3:12[3], 5:1[1], 1:1[10]. *Sîwân*, 3d month, is approximately May-June. §26.262. The word *yôm* is usually omitted in date-formulas.

וַיִּכָּתֵב[3]—Cf. 3:12[4]. Indefinite, ‘let it be written,’ §32.114. *kᵉ*- does not properly introduce a comparative clause (§38.7), but rather the noun (here *kōl*), the rest being a rel. cl., cf. *Ges.* §155*g*.

הָאֲחַשְׁדַּרְפְּנִים[4]—3:12[5]. For the rest of the verse, 3:12 and 1:1.

Learn the words in Vocabulary Group 53.

Note the following uses of אֲשֶׁר:

עִם־הַגֹּלָה אֲשֶׁר הָגְלְתָה עִם יְכָנְיָה ‘with the captivity *which* was taken captive ...’
מִסָּרִיסֵי הַמֶּלֶךְ אֲשֶׁר הֶעֱמִיד לְפָנֶיהָ ‘from the eunuchs *whom* he stationed before her’
הַשָּׂרִים אֲשֶׁר אִתּוֹ ‘the princes *who* (were) with him’
הִגִּיד לָהֶם אֲשֶׁר־הוּא יְהוּדִי ‘he told them *that* he (was) a Jew’
לְבוּשׁ אֲשֶׁר לָבַשׁ־בּוֹ המלך ‘clothing *in which* the king dressed’
וְסוּס אֲשֶׁר רָכַב עָלָיו המלך ‘and a horse *on which* the king rode’
עַל־הַמִּטָּה אֲשֶׁר אסתר עָלֶיהָ ‘on the couch *on which* Esther (was)’
בְּכָל־עֵת אֲשֶׁר אֲנִי רֹאֶה ‘every time *when* I see’
וְכַאֲשֶׁר אָבַדְתִּי אָבָדְתִּי ‘and *when* I have perished, I have perished’
וּבְכֵן אָבוֹא אל־המלך אֲשֶׁר לֹא־כַדָּת ‘and thus I shall go in to the king, *which* (deed) is not according to custom’
כַּאֲשֶׁר דִּבַּרְתָּ ‘according *as* you have spoken’

Be sure you understand the various different usages that are illustrated here.

It is better to hear the rebuke of a wise man
than the song of fools.

טוֹב לִשְׁמֹעַ גַּעֲרַת חָכָם
מֵאִישׁ שֹׁמֵעַ שִׁיר כְּסִילִים׃

Ecclesiastes 7:5

Purpose: To observe the infinitives
Materials: Esther 8:10-13

וַיִּכְתֹּב בְּשֵׁם הַמֶּלֶךְ אֲחַשְׁוֵרֹשׁ וַיַּחְתֹּם
בְּטַבַּעַת הַמֶּלֶךְ וַיִּשְׁלַח סְפָרִים בְּיַד הָרָצִים בַּסּוּסִים
11 רֹכְבֵי הָרֶכֶשׁ הָאֲחַשְׁתְּרָנִים בְּנֵי הָרַמָּכִים׃ אֲשֶׁר נָתַן
הַמֶּלֶךְ לַיְּהוּדִים ׀ אֲשֶׁר בְּכָל־עִיר־וָעִיר לְהִקָּהֵל וְלַעֲמֹד
עַל־נַפְשָׁם לְהַשְׁמִיד לַהֲרֹג וּלְאַבֵּד אֶת־כָּל־חֵיל עַם
12 וּמְדִינָה הַצָּרִים אֹתָם טַף וְנָשִׁים וּשְׁלָלָם לָבוֹז׃ בְּיוֹם
אֶחָד בְּכָל־מְדִינוֹת הַמֶּלֶךְ אֲחַשְׁוֵרוֹשׁ בִּשְׁלוֹשָׁה עָשָׂר
13 לְחֹדֶשׁ שְׁנֵים־עָשָׂר הוּא־חֹדֶשׁ אֲדָר׃ פַּתְשֶׁגֶן הַכְּתָב
לְהִנָּתֵן דָּת בְּכָל־מְדִינָה וּמְדִינָה גָּלוּי לְכָל־הָעַמִּים וְלִהְיוֹת
11 הַיְּהוּדִיים עֲתוּדִים לַיּוֹם הַזֶּה לְהִנָּקֵם מֵאֹיְבֵיהֶם׃

8:10 וַיִּכְתֹּב[1]—Cf. 3:12[9,10], 3:13[1]. Note the different G20 forms. For בַּסּוּסִים, 6:8[3].

רֹכְבֵי הָרֶכֶשׁ הָאֲחַשְׁתְּרָנִים בְּנֵי הָרַמָּכִים׃[2]—(a) *rkb* 'to ride' (v.7392. What form? §27.611. (b) *réḵeš* 'courser, swift steed' (7409 4/2). (c) *'ăḥaštᵉrānîm* 'royal (steeds?),' from Pers. adj. *ḫšatra* 'royal' (BDB 31), taken to modify (b). However, the pl. seems to indicate that it modifies (a). (d) *ben* can mean 'member of a class or guild.' (e) *rammāḵ*, usually 'mare' or 'dromedary' (7424 1/1), but CaC^{2}āC suggests occupation or habit (§24.26), hence possibly 'breeder' or the like. Meanings are derived from contexts.

8:11 לְהִקָּהֵל וְלַעֲמֹד עַל־נַפְשָׁם[1]—The verse begins with *'ăšer*, and appears to be indir. disc., giving the content of the documents, 'that the king has given to the Jews ....' The second *'ăšer* introduces an adj. cl. Then follow 5 infs. cstr. (purpose) spelling out the king's decree. (a) *qhl* 'to assemble, gather' (v.6950). §§28.42, .421, possibly reflexive (§32.83) 'to gather themselves together. (b) 3:4[5]. (b-d) Idiom, 'to stand for their lives,' cf. 7:3[1]. What suffix? For the following words, 3:13[3].

אֶת־כָּל־חֵיל עַם וּמְדִינָה[2]—Possibly the dir. obj. of all three preceding infs. cstr. (b) *kol* before sg. 'each, any.' (c) 1:3[8]. Here, probably 'force, (armed) power.' 'Any army of people or state.'

הַצָּרִים אֹתָם[3]—(a) Usually taken to be from *ṣrr*, but the form must be G55, and G55 of *ṣrr* should be *haṣṣôrᵉrîm* (§29.522). G55 of *ṣûr* would be either *haṣṣārîm* or *haṣṣôrîm* (§29.631). צוּר 'to besiege, assault' (v.6696). For ptcp. with def. art., §38.414.

טַף וְנָשִׁים וּשְׁלָלָם לָבוֹז׃[4]—(a,b) 3:13[5]. (c,d) 3:13[9].

8:12 You should be able to do this verse. On what day of what month? §26.25.

8:13 לְהִנָּקֵם מֵאֹיְבֵיהֶם׃[1]—See 3:14 for first part of verse. *paṯšeḡen hakkᵉṯāḇ* is n. phr., subj. of the inf. cstr. (a) נקם 'to avenge' (v.5358). §28.42. (b) *'ôyēḇ* 7:6[1]. What morphemes can you identify? This verse sounds as if it might be the language of the document.

Learn the meanings of the words in BVG–54.

Study the following uses of the infinitive:

אָמַר ... לְהָבִיא אתושתי ... לְהַרְאוֹת הָעַמִּים ... אֶת־יָפְיָהּ He said, *Bring* Vashti ... *to show* the people her beauty.
וַתְּמָאֵן ... ושתי לָבוֹא and Vashti refused *to enter*.
מַה־לַּעֲשׂוֹת בַּמַּלְכָּה What *is to be done* with the queen?
כְּשֹׁךְ חמת המלך *When* the king's anger *was assuaged*.
לָדַעַת את־שלום אסרת *in order to know* Esther's welfare.
וּבְהַגִּיעַ תר נערה ונערה לָבוֹא אל־המלך and *when* each girl's turn *came to go in* to the king.
ויבקשו לִשְׁלֹחַ יד במלך and they sought *to stretch forth* their hand against the king.
יִכָּתֵב לְאַבְּדָם Let it be written, *Destroy them.*
כִּי אֵין לָבוֹא אל־שער המלך For it is not permitted *to enter* the king's gate.
ותשלח בגדים לְהַלְבִּישׁ את־מרדכי And she sent garments *to clothe* Mordecai.
אחת דתו לְהָמִית His law is clear: *Put (him) to death.*
אל־תדמי בנפשך לְהִמָּלֵט Don't suppose *that you will be delivered.*

I sought the Lord and He answered me,
and from all my terrors He delivered me.

דָּרַשְׁתִּי אֶת־יהוה וְעָנָנִי
וּמִכָּל־מְגוּרוֹתַי הִצִּילָנִי׃

Psalm 34:4 (MT 5)

63

Purpose: To observe participles
Materials: Esther 8:14-17

הָֽרָצִים
רֹכְבֵי הָרֶכֶשׁ הָֽאֲחַשְׁתְּרָנִים יָֽצְאוּ מְבֹהָלִים וּדְחוּפִים בִּדְבַר
טו הַמֶּלֶךְ וְהַדָּת נִתְּנָה בְּשׁוּשַׁן הַבִּירָה׃ וּמָרְדֳּכַי יָצָא ׀
מִלִּפְנֵי הַמֶּלֶךְ בִּלְבוּשׁ מַלְכוּת תְּכֵלֶת וָחוּר וַעֲטֶרֶת זָהָב
גְּדוֹלָה וְתַכְרִיךְ בּוּץ וְאַרְגָּמָן וְהָעִיר שׁוּשָׁן צָהֲלָה וְשָׂמֵחָה׃
16 17 לַיְּהוּדִים הָֽיְתָה אוֹרָה וְשִׂמְחָה וְשָׂשֹׂן וִיקָר׃ וּבְכָל־
מְדִינָה וּמְדִינָה וּבְכָל־עִיר וָעִיר מְקוֹם אֲשֶׁר דְּבַר־הַמֶּלֶךְ
וְדָתוֹ מַגִּיעַ שִׂמְחָה וְשָׂשׂוֹן לַיְּהוּדִים מִשְׁתֶּה וְיוֹם טוֹב
וְרַבִּים מֵעַמֵּי הָאָרֶץ מִֽתְיַהֲדִים כִּֽי־נָפַל פַּֽחַד־הַיְּהוּדִים
עֲלֵיהֶם׃

8:14 מְבֹהָלִים וּדְחוּפִים—For the first part, cf. 8:10[2]. (a) *m*ᵉ*ḇōhālîm* 2:9[3], *u*-type vowel tells us what? §28.22, §32.81, .815. (b) 3:15[2]. §32.3712.

8:15 יָצָא ׀[1]—Can you recognize 1st rad. י and preformative י in יָצָא and יֵצֵא? If not, learn it *now*.

בִּלְבוּשׁ מַלְכוּת תְּכֵלֶת וָחוּר[2]—(a) 4:2[3], cf. 1:11[3]. (c) 1:6[3] (v.8504). (d) 1:6[1] (2353 2/2). This verse is in contrast with 4:1[2].

וַעֲטֶרֶת זָהָב גְּדוֹלָה[3]—(a) *ʿăṭārā*ʰ 'crown' (v.5850). (b) 1:6[9]. Does this modify (a)? §36.31. (c) 1:5[7]. What word does this modify? §36.11.

וְתַכְרִיךְ בּוּץ וְאַרְגָּמָן[4]—(a) *takrîḵ* 'garment' (8509 1/1). Since Sem. roots with the same 1st and 3d rads. are very rare, this appears to be a loan-word (*pace* BDB 501). (b) 1:5[5]. (c) 1:5[6].

וְהָעִיר שׁוּשָׁן צָהֲלָה וְשָׂמֵחָה׃[5]—This cl. is in contrast with 3:15[5]. (c) צהל 'to rejoice' (6670 9/1), G11, possibly inchoative, §32.5125. (d) Pausal G11 of stative verb; adj. would be *ś*ᵉ*mēḥā*ʰ, nonpausal G11 *śām*ᵉ*ḥā*ʰ. *śmḥ* 'to rejoice' (v.8056). Cf. §32.5125. Read §32.51.

8:16 לַיְּהוּדִים הָֽיְתָה אוֹרָה וְשִׂמְחָה וְשָׂשֹׂן וִיקָר׃—(a-b) There is no verb *to have* in Heb. One way to express possession is by the idiom הָיָה לְ– (which in certain other contexts means 'to become'); 'to the Jews was ....' (a) *'ôrā*ʰ 'light' (219 4/1). (e) *śāśōn* 'joy' (v.8342). (f) 1:4[5]. Note the concord: verb in fs with 4 subjs. §33.12, .122.

8:17 Cf. 4:3. Again, this is a planned contrast, a stylistic device of the author.

וְרַבִּים מֵעַמֵּי הָאָרֶץ מִתְיַהֲדִים[1]—(a) 1:4[8], here subsantival. (b) *min* partitive, 'many from' = 'many of.' (c) Gen. 1:1[2] (Lesson 45). The word can mean: the planet Earth, land, country, nation, or a small piece of land. (d) Denom. verb used in HtD 'to become Jews' (3054 1/1), §32.842.

פַּחַד־הַיְּהוּדִים[2]—(a) *páḥad* 'fear' (v.6343). Subj. of verb is a noun-phrase (§33.13).

Memorize the words in Group 55.

Note the following uses of the participle:
והמלך יוֹשֵׁב עַל־כִּסֵּא מַלְכוּתוֹ 'and the king (was) *sitting* on his royal throne'
וַיֵּצֵא הָמָן שָׂמֵחַ 'and Haman went out *rejoicing*'
וַיִּהְיוּ נִקְרָאִים לפני המלך 'and they were *being read* before the king'
עוֹדָם מְדַבְּרִים עִמּוֹ 'while they (were) still *speaking* with him'
לְכָל־אֹהֲבָיו 'to all his *friends*'
בְּשֹׂנְאֵיהֶם 'on *those who hate* them'
גָּלוּי לְכָל־הָעַמִּים '*revealed* to all the peoples'
מִסְפַּר הַהֲרוּגִים 'the number of *those who were killed*'
וְהַיָּמִים הָאֵלֶּה נִזְכָּרִים וְנַעֲשִׂים 'and those days (are) *being remembered* and *being observed*'
עַם־אֶחָד מְפֻזָּר וּמְפֹרָד 'one people *scattered* and *divided*'
הַיְּהוּדִים הַנִּמְצְאִים בְּשׁוּשָׁן 'the Jews *who were found* in Susa'
הָרָצִים 'the *couriers*'
רֹכְבֵי הָרֶכֶשׁ 'the *riders* of the swift horses'

Every time you come across a participle, note exactly how it used – as a verb, a noun, an adjective, a relative clause, or whatever.

Prove me, O Lord, and try me,	בְּחָנֵנִי יהוה וְנַסֵּנִי
Refine my emotions and my intellect.	צָרְופָה כִלְיוֹתַי וְלִבִּי׃
For Thy covenant love is before my eyes,	כִּי־חַסְדְּךָ לְנֶגֶד עֵינָי
And I go about in Thy faithfulness.	וְהִתְהַלַּכְתִּי בַּאֲמִתֶּךָ׃

Psalm 26:2-3

Purpose: To study phrases and clauses
Materials: Esther 9:1-4

ט CAP. IX. ט

א וּבִשְׁנֵים עָשָׂר חֹדֶשׁ הוּא־חֹדֶשׁ אֲדָר בִּשְׁלוֹשָׁה עָשָׂר יוֹם
בּוֹ אֲשֶׁר הִגִּיעַ דְּבַר־הַמֶּלֶךְ וְדָתוֹ לְהֵעָשׂוֹת בַּיּוֹם אֲשֶׁר
שִׂבְּרוּ אֹיְבֵי הַיְּהוּדִים לִשְׁלוֹט בָּהֶם וְנַהֲפוֹךְ הוּא אֲשֶׁר
2 יִשְׁלְטוּ הַיְּהוּדִים הֵמָּה בְּשֹׂנְאֵיהֶם׃ נִקְהֲלוּ הַיְּהוּדִים
בְּעָרֵיהֶם בְּכָל־מְדִינוֹת הַמֶּלֶךְ אֲחַשְׁוֵרוֹשׁ לִשְׁלֹחַ יָד
בִּמְבַקְשֵׁי רָעָתָם וְאִישׁ לֹא־עָמַד בִּפְנֵיהֶם כִּי־נָפַל פַּחְדָּם
3 עַל־כָּל־הָעַמִּים׃ וְכָל־שָׂרֵי הַמְּדִינוֹת וְהָאֲחַשְׁדַּרְפְּנִים
וְהַפַּחוֹת וְעֹשֵׂי הַמְּלָאכָה אֲשֶׁר לַמֶּלֶךְ מְנַשְּׂאִים אֶת־
4 הַיְּהוּדִים כִּי־נָפַל פַּחַד־מָרְדֳּכַי עֲלֵיהֶם׃ כִּי־גָדוֹל מָרְדֳּכַי
בְּבֵית הַמֶּלֶךְ וְשָׁמְעוֹ הוֹלֵךְ בְּכָל־הַמְּדִינוֹת כִּי־הָאִישׁ
מָרְדֳּכַי הוֹלֵךְ וְגָדוֹל׃

9:1 אֲשֶׁר הִגִּיעַ דְּבַר־הַמֶּלֶךְ וְדָתוֹ לְהֵעָשׂוֹת[1]—For the first part, cf. 8:12 (b) 2:12[1]. (f) If you have not learned how to recognize the N65, do it *now*. Two temporal cls. introduced with ־בְּ, and an appositional cl. (verbless). *'ăšer* introduces another temporal clause, 'when.'

בַּיּוֹם אֲשֶׁר שִׂבְּרוּ אֹיְבֵי הַיְּהוּדִים לִשְׁלוֹט בָּהֶם[2]—(a-b) on the day that' = 'when.' §38.51. (c) *śbr* D 'to hope' (7663 8/1). Subj. follows (noun-phrase). (f) *šlṭ* 'to rule, domineer' (7980 9/2). 'Sultan' comes from this root, through Arabic. Inf. cstr. after verb of *thinking, hoping,* etc., §38.82.

וְנַהֲפוֹךְ הוּא[3]—(a) *hpk* 'to turn, overturn' (v.2015). §28.42. Verbless cl., 'and that (the hope expressed) [was] overturned.' §32.3925.

יִשְׁלְטוּ הַיְּהוּדִים הֵמָּה בְּשֹׂנְאֵיהֶם׃ [4]—(a) 9:1[2]. Subj. follows. Cf. §32.524. (d) *śônē'* from *śn'* 'to hate' (v.8130). The sentence is hardly in classical style: "When the king's word and decree came to be done, when the enemies of the Jews hoped to domineer over them, and that was overturned, when the Jews themselves domineered over those who hated them."

9:2 נִקְהֲלוּ הַיְּהוּדִים בְּעָרֵיהֶם[1]—(a) 8:11[1]. (c) f.s. עִיר (3:15[5]), f.p. עָרִים, §25.6.

לִשְׁלֹחַ יָד בִּמְבַקְשֵׁי רָעָתָם[2]—(a-b) 2:21[7]. (c) Shewa under preform. *mêm* tells us what? Why no dagesh in ק? §13.41, .412. Why ־בִּ? §15.651. Translate 'on those who were seeking.' (d) ־ָם is what? §23.121. Cf. 8:3[4] and 8:6[2]. Would *-ām* represent subjective or objective genitive? §36.323f.

וְאִישׁ לֹא־עָמַד בִּפְנֵיהֶם[3]—(a-b) = 'no man.' (d) בִּפְנֵי 'in the face of' BDB 816.II.3, here 'against them' reads better.

כִּי־נָפַל פַּחְדָּם[4]—(a) Causal, §38.53. (c) 8:17[2]. Explain form here.

9:3 וְכָל־שָׂרֵי הַמְּדִינוֹת וְהָאֲחַשְׁדַּרְפְּנִים וְהַפַּחוֹת וְעֹשֵׂי הַמְּלָאכָה[1]—(a) *'ăḥašdarpᵉnîm* 'protectors of the realm,' Pers. *ẖšatřapâvan*. 3:12[5], 8:9[4]. This is the longest word (incl. bound morphemes) that I have found in the Heb. Bible. (b) 3:12[6]. (c-d) 3:9[4].

מְנַשְּׂאִים[2]—(a) 3:1[4]. It is difficult to determine whether such a cl. is verbal or verbless. We could take the subj. as a compound n. cl., from the beginning of the verse, and the pred. as this ptcp. and its complement.

9:4 וְשָׁמְעוֹ הוֹלֵךְ[1]—(a) Caution! Not שָׁמְעוּ but *šom'ô* from *šṓma'* 'report' (8089 4/1). G65s0 of the verb would take the same form, cf. 29:18. (b) '[was] going, spreading.'

הוֹלֵךְ וְגָדוֹל׃[2]—(a-b) Idiom, G50 of *hlk* + adj., 'becoming continually greater,' cf. BDB 233 I.4d.

Learn the words in Vocabulary Group 56.

Note the following pronominal suffixes:

ba'ălêʸhen *their* husbands
mᵉrûqēʸhen *their* cleansers
bᵉ'ārēʸhem in *their* (m.p.) cities
bāhem in *them*
'ôṯām *them* (dir. obj.)
paḥdām the fear of *them*
yāḏām *their* hand
dâṯēʸhem *their* customs
šnêʸhem the two of *them*
lᵉhannîḥām to indulge *them*

Those who trust in YHWH:
Like Mount Zion he shall not be shaken,
For ever he shall dwell securely.

הַבֹּטְחִים בַּיהוָה
כְּהַר־צִיּוֹן לֹא־יִמּוֹט
לְעוֹלָם יֵשֵׁב׃

Psalm 125:1

65

Purpose: To continue the study of exegesis
Materials: Genesis 12:1-3; 15:4-7

Gen. ויאמר יְהוָה אֶל־אַבְרָם[1]—(b) יהוה is the covenant-name of the God of Israel
12:1 (6,518x as יְהוָה Q *'ăḏônāy* and 305x as יֱהוִה Q *'ĕlôhîm*). The use of the name as a criterion for distinguishing J from E cannot be carried out satisfactorily. (d) Pr.n. 'Abram,' later changed to *'aḇrāhām* 'Abraham,' Gen. 17:5.

לֶךְ־לְךָ מֵאַרְצְךָ וּמִמּוֹלַדְתְּךָ וּמִבֵּית אָבִיךָ[2]—(a) G32 – do you recognize it? (b) "Ethical dative," like "get yourself out of ...." Translate (a-b) simply 'Go.' (c) ־אַרְצְ־ > ? (d) Est. 2:10[2]. (e) If you haven't learned to spot מִן as a bound morpheme (§22), do it *now*.

אֶל־הָאָרֶץ אשר אַרְאֶךָּ׃[3]—(b) Definite because defined by the following rel. cl. (d) *'ar'ekkā* < **'ar'enkā,* §23.1221. The root is ראה; what stem (vowel under preformative)? Cf. Est. 1:11[4].

12:2 וְאֶעֶשְׂךָ לְגוֹי גָּדוֹל[1]—(a) וְ|אֶ|עֶשְׂ|ךָ – what root? what stem? perf. or impf.? what PGN? (b) *l*^{e}- here something like 'into.' *gôy* 'nation, gentile' (v.1471). Indefinite, 'a great nation.'

וַאֲבָרֶכְךָ וַאֲגַדְּלָה שְׁמֶךָ[2]—(a) Break it into its parts. *brk* (D) 'to bless' (v.1288). Shewa under preformative, compensatory lengthening under 1st rad. = ? (b) Follow the same steps as for (a). Est. 3:1[2]. §27.531. §32.342. (c) Est. 2:5[3]. Obj. of (b).

וֶהְיֵה בְּרָכָה׃[3]—(a) G32 of *hy*^{h}. §32.325. RSV "so that you will be a blessing," is based on this principle, but the intent is stronger: 'so be a blessing!'

12:3 וַאֲבָרֲכָה מְבָרְכֶיךָ[1]—(a) Cf. 12:2[2](b) and (c) – which is this? (b) Preformative ־מְ tells what? ־ֵי before s2 tells what? Is it 'the one who blesses' or 'those who bless'?

וּמְקַלֶּלְךָ אָאֹר[2]—(a) *qll* 'to be small, trifling; (D) to belittle, make contemptible' (v.7043). Stem? Sg. or pl.? (b) *'ā'ōr* for **'a'rōr*; *'rr* 'to curse' (v.779), G24 of CC^2, §§29.511, .5114.

וְנִבְרְכוּ בְךָ כֹּל מִשְׁפְּחֹת הָאֲדָמָה׃[3]—(a) Can ו—נ be 29? N15? N37? What is the subj. of this verb? (b) Agent. (d) *miśpāḥā*^{h} 'clan, family' (v.4940). (e) *'ăḏāmā*^{h} 'ground, land, earth' (v.127). Possibly this word is used here rather than *'éreṣ* so there will be no tendency to limit the effect to the land promised to Abram. The obvious relationship of *'ăḏāmā*^{h} to *'āḏām* suggests that all mankind is in view.

15:4 וְהִנֵּה דְבַר־יְהוָה אֵלָיו לֵאמֹר[1]–You should be able to do this portion. דבר־יהוה is a much used expression in the Bible. The antecedent of *'ēlā*^{y}*w* is Abram, 15:3. לאמר = 'quote.'

לֹא יִירָשְׁךָ זֶה[2]—(c) 'This one' = Eliezer, 15:3, subj. of the negated verb. (b) *yrš* 'to take possession, inherit' (v.3423). Read §29.3211. Note use of suffix, 'he shall not inherit you' = 'he shall not be your heir.'

כִּי־אִם אֲשֶׁר יֵצֵא מִמֵּעֶיךָ הוּא יִירָשֶׁךָ׃[3]—(a-b) After neg. a strong adversative, 'but rather,' BDB 475.2b. (c) *'ăšer* 'the one who,' subj. of verbless cl. (e) **mē'ā*^{h}, only pl. cstr. and suf., 'internal parts, bowels, the source of procreation' (v.4578). (f) 'He' or 'that one.' (g) Cf. 15:4[2]; form here is pausal.

Gen. וַיּוֹצֵא אֹתוֹ הַחוּצָה[1]—(a) G, N, or H? (c) *ḥûṣ* '(the) outside' (v.2399), + *-ā*^{h} loc. In
15:5 Eng. 'outside' can be adverbial but in Heb. it must have ָה or a prep. to make it such.

ויאמר הַבֶּט־נָא הַשָּׁמַיְמָה[2]—(b) *nbṭ* (H) 'to look at, regard' (v.5027), H32 + *nâ'*, §32.327. Who is the subj. of (b)? of (a)? (c) Gen. 1:1[2]. Note unaccented ָה.

וּסְפֹר הַכּוֹכָבִים אִם־תּוּכַל לִסְפֹּר אֹתָם[3]—(a) Cf. Est. 3:12[1]. *spr* 'to count,' here G32. (b) *kôkāḇ* 'star' (v.3556); definite because well known. (c-f) Cond. cl., hence protasis, and (a-b) apodosis: 'If you're able, count the stars.' (d) Cf. Est. 6:13[6]. 'To be able' requires a complementary inf., (e). (e) Compare this with (a). What difference do you see? Don't overlook a dagesh!

ויאמר לו כֹּה יִהְיֶה זַרְעֶךָ׃[5]—(a-b) Who said to whom? (c) Amos 7:11[1] (Lesson 50). (d) You should know it. (e) Est. 6:13[4]. Form here, + s2 pausal.

15:6 וְהֶאֱמִן בַּיהוָה[1]—(a) Cf. Est. 2:7[1] In H this word means 'to trust, believe,' and followed by ־בּ 'to believe in, commit yourself to.'

וַיַּחְשְׁבֶהָ לּוֹ צְדָקָה׃[2]—(a) *ḥšb*, cf. Est. 8:3[5]. The word also means 'to reckon, account,' BDB 363.II.3. The s1 refers back to Abram's act of faith. (b) I.e. to Abram. (c) *ṣ*^{e}*dāqā*^{h} 'righteousness' (v.6666, cf. BDB 842).

15:7 ויאמר אליו אני יהוה אשר הוֹצֵאתִיךָ מֵאוּר כַּשְׂדִּים[1]—(a-e) You should be able to read this. (f) הוֹ—תִי suggests what stem, what type of verb, what person? VDC–9. Do you know יצא? Note that the verb agrees in PGN with the antecedent of אשר, viz. אני. (g) *'ûr* pr.n. 'Ur.' Look it up on a map of ancient Mesopotamia. (h) *kaśdîm* pr.n. 'Chaldees.' Look it up in a good Bible dictionary. Akk. *kašdu* later > *kaldu*; the Heb. reflects an earlier or dialectal form.

לָתֶת לְךָ אֶת־הָאָרֶץ הַזֹּאת לְרִשְׁתָּהּ׃[2]—(d-e) What land? (f) G65 of *yrš* is *rešeṯ*, §29.322. Can you work from *rešeṯ* to *l*^{e}*riśtāh*? To whom or what does ָה refer? For *yrš*, Gen. 15:4[2].

These passages are foundational for the biblical concept of election. It has a purpose that extends far beyond the person or persons chosen. For an elementary discussion, cf. W. S. LaSor, *Israel, A Biblical View* (1976), 32-36. For fuller study, cf. H. H. Rowley, *The Biblical Doctrine of Election* (1950).

Learn the words in Vocabulary Group 57.

66

Purpose: To read with understanding
Materials: Esther 9:5-11

וַיַּכּוּ הַיְּהוּדִים בְּכָל־אֹיְבֵיהֶם מַכַּת־ ה
חֶרֶב וְהֶרֶג וְאַבְדָן וַיַּעֲשׂוּ בְשֹׂנְאֵיהֶם כִּרְצוֹנָם׃ וּבְשׁוּשַׁן 6
הַבִּירָה הָרְגוּ הַיְּהוּדִים וְאַבֵּד חֲמֵשׁ מֵאוֹת אִישׁ׃

וְאֵת ׀ 7
פַּרְשַׁנְדָּתָא וְאֵת ׀
דַּלְפוֹן וְאֵת ׀
אַסְפָּתָא׃ וְאֵת ׀ 8
פּוֹרָתָא וְאֵת ׀
אֲדַלְיָא וְאֵת ׀
אֲרִידָתָא׃ וְאֵת ׀ 9
פַּרְמַשְׁתָּא וְאֵת ׀
אֲרִיסַי וְאֵת ׀
אֲרִידַי וְאֵת ׀
וַיְזָתָא׃ עֲשֶׂרֶת י
בְּנֵי הָמָן בֶּן־הַמְּדָתָא צֹרֵר הַיְּהוּדִים הָרָגוּ וּבַבִּזָּה לֹא
11 שָׁלְחוּ אֶת־יָדָם׃ בַּיּוֹם הַהוּא בָּא מִסְפַּר הַהֲרוּגִים בְּשׁוּשַׁן
12 הַבִּירָה לִפְנֵי הַמֶּלֶךְ׃

9:5 וַיַּכּוּ[1]—VDC–11. When there is *only one* radical, it has to be NCY, hence נכה H 'to smite' (v.5221). Note preform. with *pattāḥ*. The verb is followed by –בּ, cf. 'to beat up on.'

מַכַּת חֶרֶב וְהֶרֶג וְאַבְדָן[2]—(a) From root נכה, so try to guess the meaning. *makkā*^{h} 'plague, stroke, wound' (v.4347). It is defined by 3 nouns, unusual for cstr. to have more than one governed noun. (b) *héreḇ* 'sword' (v.2719). (c) *héreḡ* 'slaughter' (2027 5/1). (d) Cf. 8:6[4]. Strong lists the words separately (12 1/1), but BDB 2 lists both as one entry – in my opinion, correctly.

כִּרְצוֹנָם׃[3]–Cf. 1:8[6].

9:6 הָרְגוּ הַיְּהוּדִים וְאַבֵּד חֲמֵשׁ מֵאוֹת אִישׁ׃[1]—(a) 3:13[3]. (c) 3:13[3] Note sequence: *hār*^{e}*gû* G15, *w*^{e}*'abbēḏ* D60, §32.391, *Ges.* §113*z*. (d-e) §26.273. §36.14.

9:7-9 The 10 sons of Haman are "hanged" in the text layout. Reasons for the large and small letters, noted in marginal masorah, are not known to me. It is traditional to read these names as rapidly as possible.

9:10 עֲשֶׂרֶת בְּנֵי הָמָן[1]—(a) §26.24. (c) Definite, hence 'the 10 sons of Haman.'

וּבַבִּזָּה לֹא שָׁלְחוּ אֶת־יָדָם׃[2]—(a) *bizzā^{h}* 'spoil, booty' (961 10/3), cf. 3:13[9], 8:11[4]. In this cl. the conj. *wāw* is better read 'but.'

9:11 You should be able to translate this entire verse.

Memorize the words in BVG–58.

Review the various vowel-patterns of the verb in G-impf.:

G20	yaqtul		yiqtal		yaqtil	
CCC	יִסְגֹּר	*yisgōr*	יִשְׁכַּב	*yiškaḇ*		
GCC	תַּעֲבֹד	*ta'ăḇōḏ*	יֶחֱזַק	*yeḥĕzaq*	יַעֲלֶה	*ya'ălê^{h}* (?)
CGC	יִטְרֹף	*yiṭrōp̄*	יִשְׁחַט	*yišḥaṭ*		
CCG			יִשְׁלַח	*yišlaḥ*	יֹאמַר	*yō'mar*
'CC	יֶאֱסֹף	*ye'ĕsōp̄*	יֶאֱנַף	*ye'ĕnap̄*	יֹאבֵד	*yō'ḇēḏ*
	יֶאְסֹר	*ye'sōr*				
CC'			יִמְצָא	*yimṣā'*		
WCC			יִירַד	*yî^{y}raḏ*	יֵצֵא	*yêṣē'*
YCC			יִיטַב	*yî^{y}ṭaḇ*		
YṢC	יִצֹּק	*yiṣṣōq*	תִּצַּת	*tiṣṣaṯ*		
NCC	יִפֹּל	*yippōl*	יִגַּשׁ	*yiggaš*	יִתֵּן	*yittēn*
CC[2]	יָסֹב	*yāsōḇ*	תֵּקַל	*tēqal*		
	יִדֹּם	*yiddōm*				
CWC	יָמוּת	*yāmûṯ* (?)	יֵבוֹשׁ	*yēḇôš* (?)	יֵשֵׁב	*yêšēḇ*
CYC					יָדִין	*yāḏîn* (?)
CCY			יִהְיֶה	*yihyê^{h}*	יֹאבֶה	*yō'ḇê^{h}* (?)
hlk					יֵלֵךְ	*yêlēḵ*
lqḥ			יִקַּח	*yiqqaḥ*		

Wait eagerly for YHWH;
Be strong and be bold (in) your heart,
And wait eagerly for YHWH.

קַוֵּה אֶל־יהוה
חֲזַק וְיַאֲמֵץ לִבֶּךָ
וְקַוֵּה אֶל־יהוה׃

Psalm 27:14

67

Purpose: To examine the student's progress
Materials: Esther 6:1–9:4

With your Hebrew Bible open to Exodus 13:1-10 work over the following questions.

Which word(s) illustrate(s) the following:

Strong dagesh ("doubler")	קַדֶּשׁ־לִי	1
Weak dagesh ("hardener")	וּבַבְּהֵמָה	2
"Zero" shewa	בִּבְנֵי	3
Maqqeph	חָמֵץ׃	4
"Vocal" shewa	אֶתְכֶם	5
Silluq	וְהַחִוִּי	6
Geminate (doubled) *wāw*	מִמִּצְרַיִם	7
Nasog 'aḥor	הוּא	8
Shuruq	יְהוָה	9
Perpetual q^erê	וְהָיָה	10

Which word(s) illustrate(s) the following:

qāmāṣ ḥăṭûp̄	הוּא	1
Quiescent *ʾālep̄*	יֵאָכֵל	2
"Heavy" ending	הָעָם	3
Penultimate accent	לַאֲבֹתֶיךָ	4
Compensatory lengthening	כָּל־רֶחֶם	5
Pausal form	גְּבֻלֶךָ	6
Rule 19	הוֹצִאֲךָ	7
Rule 21	יְצָאתֶם	8
Connecting vowel with accent	אֵת	9
Defective writing of long vowel	בִּבְנֵי	10

Parse the following, giving stem, person, gender, number, any affixes, root, and meaning.

קַדֶּשׁ־לִי	v. 2	זָבַת	v. 5
זָכוֹר	v. 5	וְעָבַדְתָּ	v. 5
יְצָאתֶם	v. 3	תֹּאכַל	v. 6
הוֹצִיא	v. 3	יֵרָאֶה	v. 7
יֵאָכֵל	v. 4	וְהִגַּדְתָּ	v. 8
יֹצְאִים	v. 5	בְּצֵאתִי	v. 8
יְבִיאֲךָ	v. 5	הוֹצִאֲךָ	v. 9
נִשְׁבַּע	v. 5	וְשָׁמַרְתָּ	v.10

Parse, giving gender, number, state, any affixes, lexical form, and meaning.

v. 2	בָּאָדָם	v. 6	מַצֹּת
v. 2	וּבַבְּהֵמָה	v. 7	גְּבֻלֶךָ
v. 3	הַזֶּה	v. 8	לִבְנְךָ
v. 3	מִבֵּית	v. 9	לְאוֹת
v. 3	עֲבָדִים	v. 9	עֵינֶיךָ
v. 3	מִזֶּה	v. 9	תּוֹרַת
v. 5	הָעֲבֹדָה	v.10	לְמוֹעֲדָהּ
v. 6	שִׁבְעַת	v.10	יָמִימָה

Parse the following verbs. Give stem, person, gender, number, any affixes, root, and meaning.

4:1	וַיִּקְרַע	4:16	אָצוּם
4:1	וַיֵּצֵא	5:2	וַיּוֹשֶׁט
4:3	יֻצַּע	5:2	וַתִּגַּע
4:4	וַתָּבוֹאנָה	5:4	עָשִׂיתִי
4:4	וַיַּגִּידוּ	5:5	מַהֲרוּ
4:4	וַתִּתְחַלְחַל	5:10	וַיִּתְעַפֵּק
4:5	וַתְּצַוֵּהוּ	5:14	וַעֲשׂוּ
4:7	קָרָהוּ	6:1	נָדְדָה
4:7	לְאַבְּדָם	6:3	נַעֲשָׂה
4:13	לְהִמָּלֵט	6:8	יָבִיאוּ
4:16	לֵךְ	6:9	נָתוֹן
4:16	וְצוּמוּ	6:10	קַח

Parse the following substantives, giving gender, number, state, any affixes (including the def. art.), lexical form, and meaning.

4:1	גְּדוֹלָה	4:11	עַבְדֵי
4:3	וְדָתוֹ	4:11	יוֹדְעִים
4:4	לָרַבִּים	4:11	הֶחָצֵר
4:4	נַעֲרוֹת	4:11	אַחַת
4:4	וְסָרִיסֶיהָ	4:13	בְּנַפְשֵׁךְ
4:6	הֲתָךְ	4:14	אֲבִיךְ
4:8	עִמָּה	4:16	שְׁלֹשֶׁת
4:16	וְנַעֲרֹתַי	5:9	שָׂמֵחַ
5:1	בַּחֲצַר	5:9	מִמֶּנּוּ
5:1	פֶּתַח	5:10	אֹהֲבָיו
5:2	בְּרֹאשׁ	5:10	אִשְׁתּוֹ
5:3	בַּקָּשָׁתֵךְ	5:11	עָשְׁרוֹ
5:3	חֲצִי	6:2	מִשֹּׁמְרֵי
5:6	בְּמִשְׁתֵּה	6:3	מְשָׁרְתָיו
5:7	שְׁאֵלָתִי	6:6	בְּלִבּוֹ
5:8	לָהֶם	6:14	עוֹדָם

Know the words in vocabulary groups 46-58 and 12-33.

Purpose: To read with understanding
Materials: Esther 9:12-15

וַיֹּאמֶר הַמֶּלֶךְ לְאֶסְתֵּר הַמַּלְכָּה
בְּשׁוּשַׁן הַבִּירָה הָרְגוּ הַיְּהוּדִים וְאַבֵּד חֲמֵשׁ מֵאוֹת אִישׁ
וְאֵת עֲשֶׂרֶת בְּנֵי־הָמָן בִּשְׁאָר מְדִינוֹת הַמֶּלֶךְ מֶה עָשׂוּ
13 וּמַה־שְּׁאֵלָתֵךְ וְיִנָּתֵן לָךְ וּמַה־בַּקָּשָׁתֵךְ עוֹד וְתֵעָשׂ׃ וַתֹּאמֶר
אֶסְתֵּר אִם־עַל־הַמֶּלֶךְ טוֹב יִנָּתֵן גַּם־מָחָר לַיְּהוּדִים אֲשֶׁר
בְּשׁוּשָׁן לַעֲשׂוֹת כְּדָת הַיּוֹם וְאֵת עֲשֶׂרֶת בְּנֵי־הָמָן יִתְלוּ
14 עַל־הָעֵץ׃ וַיֹּאמֶר הַמֶּלֶךְ לְהֵעָשׂוֹת כֵּן וַתִּנָּתֵן דָּת בְּשׁוּשָׁן
טו וְאֵת עֲשֶׂרֶת בְּנֵי־הָמָן תָּלוּ׃ וַיִּקָּהֲלוּ הַיְּהוּדִיים אֲשֶׁר־
בְּשׁוּשָׁן גַּם בְּיוֹם אַרְבָּעָה עָשָׂר לְחֹדֶשׁ אֲדָר וַיַּהַרְגוּ
בְשׁוּשָׁן שְׁלֹשׁ מֵאוֹת אִישׁ וּבַבִּזָּה לֹא שָׁלְחוּ אֶת־יָדָם׃

9:12 בִּשְׁאָר מְדִינוֹת הַמֶּלֶךְ מֶה עָשׂוּ[1]—You should be able to read the first part. (a) *ś^e'ār* 'rest, remainder' (v.7605). (a-c) Cstr. chain. (d) Note vowel, cf. Table G. The balance of the verse you should be able to do. Cf. 5:6, 7:2.

9:13 וַתֹּאמֶר אֶסְתֵּר[1]—(a) Can you explain this form? Learn it *now*. §32.5311, .5312, §32.533.

אִם־עַל־הַמֶּלֶךְ טוֹב[2]—Does this give you any trouble? Is it verbal or verbless? §31. Is it a protasis or an apodosis? §38.611, .612.

יִנָּתֵן גַּם־מָחָר[3]—(a) Note pattern yiC^2āCēC – do you recognize it? You should! §28.42. Master these basic patterns. (c) 5:8[5]. The story seems to deteriorate at this point.*

לַעֲשׂוֹת כְּדָת הַיּוֹם[4]—(a) Comp. inf., §34.8, after נתן 'to permit to ____.' (b-c) 'according to today's decree.' §38.71.

וְאֵת עֲשֶׂרֶת בְּנֵי־הָמָן יִתְלוּ[5]—(b) 9:10[1]. (e) Prob. G45. §32.352. There are two apodoseis in this sentence, §38.612, cf. §32.356. The sons of Haman were already killed, 9:7-10; does Esther want their dead bodies publicly hanged? Why?

9:14 This verse should be easy to translate. Note לְהֵעָשׂוֹת, and remember R.10a.

9:15 You should be able to do this. Cf. 9:2, 6.

---

*Those of us who believe in the doctrine of Inspiration need not be concerned by such a statement. Inspiration does not guarantee literary excellence, only doctrinal authority.

Memorize the words in Group 59.

Note the following uses of ל־:

וְיִנָּתֵן לָךְ 'and let it be given *to* you'
וְהָמָן בָּא לַחֲצַר בית־המלך 'and Haman was coming in *to* the court ...'
שְׁלוֹשָׁה עָשָׂר לְחֹדֶשׁ שְׁנֵים עָשָׂר 'on the 13th *of* the 12th month'
ויאמר לָהּ המלך 'and the king said *to* her'
אֲנִי קָרוּא לָהּ 'I (was) called *by* her'
אַל־תְּדַמִּי בְנַפְשֵׁךְ לְהִמָּלֵט 'Don't imagine that you will be spared' (lit., *to* be delivered)
וַתִּשְׁלַח בְּגָדִים לְהַלְבִּישׁ מרדכי 'and she sent clothing *in order to* clothe Mordecai'
וַיְבַקֵּשׁ הָמָן לְהַשְׁמִיד אֶת־כָּל־הַיְּהוּדִים 'and Haman sought *to* destroy all the Jews'
אֵין לָבוֹא אֶל־שַׁעַר־המלך בִּלְבוּשׁ שָׂק 'It is forbidden to enter (lit. there is not *to* enter) the king's gate in sackcloth'
לאמר למלך לִתְלוֹת את־מרדכי '*to* say *to* the king *to* hang Mordecai'

זֹבֵחַ תּוֹדָה יְכַבְּדָנְנִי
וְשָׂם דֶּרֶךְ אַרְאֶנּוּ בְּיֵשַׁע אֱלֹהִים׃

The one who brings a sacrifice of thanksgiving
I will honor him,
And the one who establishes his manner of life
I will show him the salvation of God.

Psalm 50:23

Because of the repetitious and sometimes aimless nature of the next portion, students often become restless and fail to use their time well. I have therefore marked the material as three *supplementary* readings, to be omitted, read hastily, or used otherwise, as the teacher thinks best. Lesson 69 resumes the required material, and from there to the end there should be continuous effort to learn something new each day.

SR-1

Purpose: To complete the material in Esther
Materials: Esther 9:16-19

16 וּשְׁאָר הַיְּהוּדִים אֲשֶׁר בִּמְדִינוֹת הַמֶּלֶךְ נִקְהֲלוּ ׀ וְעָמֹד
עַל־נַפְשָׁם וְנוֹחַ מֵאֹיְבֵיהֶם וְהָרוֹג בְּשֹׂנְאֵיהֶם חֲמִשָּׁה
17 וְשִׁבְעִים אָלֶף וּבַבִּזָּה לֹא שָׁלְחוּ אֶת־יָדָם׃ בְּיוֹם־שְׁלוֹשָׁה
עָשָׂר לְחֹדֶשׁ אֲדָר וְנוֹחַ בְּאַרְבָּעָה עָשָׂר בּוֹ וְעָשֹׂה אֹתוֹ
18 יוֹם מִשְׁתֶּה וְשִׂמְחָה׃ וְהַיְּהוּדִיים אֲשֶׁר־בְּשׁוּשָׁן נִקְהֲלוּ
בִּשְׁלוֹשָׁה עָשָׂר בּוֹ וּבְאַרְבָּעָה עָשָׂר בּוֹ וְנוֹחַ בַּחֲמִשָּׁה
19 עָשָׂר בּוֹ וְעָשֹׂה אֹתוֹ יוֹם מִשְׁתֶּה וְשִׂמְחָה׃ עַל־כֵּן הַיְּהוּדִים
הַפְּרָוזִים הַיֹּשְׁבִים בְּעָרֵי הַפְּרָזוֹת עֹשִׂים אֵת יוֹם אַרְבָּעָה
עָשָׂר לְחֹדֶשׁ אֲדָר שִׂמְחָה וּמִשְׁתֶּה וְיוֹם טוֹב וּמִשְׁלֹחַ
כ מָנוֹת אִישׁ לְרֵעֵהוּ׃

9:16 וּשְׁאָר הַיְּהוּדִים אֲשֶׁר בִּמְדִינוֹת הַמֶּלֶךְ[1]—(a) 9:12[1], i.e. those *not* in Susa, cf. 3:8[2,3].

נִקְהֲלוּ ׀ וְעָמֹד עַל־נַפְשָׁם[2]—(a) 9:2[1]. (b) Defective writing, §11.3241; would you recognize עָמוֹד? Cf. 9:12. Read §32.391 again. (b-d) Cf. 8:11[1].

וְנוֹחַ מֵאֹיְבֵיהֶם וְהָרוֹג בְּשֹׂנְאֵיהֶם[3]—(a) נוח 'to rest' (v.5117), G60, §32.391. (c) Also G60. In this sentence we have N15 followed by 3 infs. abs.

חֲמִשָּׁה וְשִׁבְעִים אָלֶף[4]—(c) 3:9[3]. Note how this number is expressed, cf. §26.262, §26.284. For balance of verse, cf. 9:10[2].

9:17 בְּיוֹם־שְׁלוֹשָׁה עָשָׂר לְחֹדֶשׁ אֲדָר[1]—The text seems to be corrupt. We should expect an account of the death and destruction on the 13th day and the rest on the 14th.

וְעָשֹׂה אֹתוֹ יוֹם מִשְׁתֶּה וְשִׂמְחָה׃[2]—(a) §29.71. §32.3911. (c) Cstr. 'And to make it a day of drinking (or banquet) and joy.'

9:18 This verse summarizes the days for the Jews in Susa. Compare it with the previous verses.

9:19 עַל־כֵּן הַיְּהוּדִים הַפְּרָוזִים[1]—(a-b) 'Wherefore, on account of this.' (d) *p^{e}rāzîm* (Q), pl. of *p^{e}rāzî* 'dweller in a hamlet, rural population' (6521 3/1). Kt (§11.61) appears to be Gp55 of an unused verb *prz* 'to remove, separate,' BDB 826.

הַיֹּשְׁבִים בְּעָרֵי הַפְּרָזוֹת[2]—(a) 1:14[6], here 'dwellers, those who were dwelling.' (b) 3:15[5], 9:2[1]. (c) *p^{e}rāzā^h* 'open region, hamlet' (6519 3/1). This cl. modifies *hayy^{e}hûḏîm happ^{e}rāzîm*.

עֹשִׂים אֵת יוֹם אַרְבָּעָה עָשָׂר לְחֹדֶשׁ אֲדָר שִׂמְחָה וּמִשְׁתֶּה וְיוֹם טוֹב [3]—This cl. should not be difficult for you.

וּמִשְׁלֹחַ מָנוֹת אִישׁ לְרֵעֵהוּ׃[4]—(a) *mišlō^{a}ḥ* 'outstretching, sending' (4916 3/2). *mānā^{h}* 2:9[4]. (c-d) Idiom, 'to one another.' (d) *rē^{a}ʿ* 'neighbor' (v.7453).

SR-2

Purpose: To complete the material in Esther
Materials: Esther 9:20-25

וַיִּכְתֹּב מָרְדֳּכַי אֶת־הַדְּבָרִים הָאֵלֶּה
וַיִּשְׁלַח סְפָרִים אֶל־כָּל־הַיְּהוּדִים אֲשֶׁר בְּכָל־מְדִינוֹת
21 הַמֶּלֶךְ אֲחַשְׁוֵרוֹשׁ הַקְּרוֹבִים וְהָרְחוֹקִים׃ לְקַיֵּם עֲלֵיהֶם
לִהְיוֹת עֹשִׂים אֵת יוֹם אַרְבָּעָה עָשָׂר לְחֹדֶשׁ אֲדָר וְאֵת
22 יוֹם־חֲמִשָּׁה עָשָׂר בּוֹ בְּכָל־שָׁנָה וְשָׁנָה׃ כַּיָּמִים אֲשֶׁר־נָחוּ
בָהֶם הַיְּהוּדִים מֵאֹיְבֵיהֶם וְהַחֹדֶשׁ אֲשֶׁר נֶהְפַּךְ לָהֶם מִיָּגוֹן
לְשִׂמְחָה וּמֵאֵבֶל לְיוֹם טוֹב לַעֲשׂוֹת אוֹתָם יְמֵי מִשְׁתֶּה
וְשִׂמְחָה וּמִשְׁלֹחַ מָנוֹת אִישׁ לְרֵעֵהוּ וּמַתָּנוֹת לָאֶבְיֹנִים׃
וְקִבֵּל הַיְּהוּדִים אֵת אֲשֶׁר־הֵחֵלּוּ לַעֲשׂוֹת וְאֵת אֲשֶׁר־כָּתַב 23
מָרְדֳּכַי אֲלֵיהֶם׃ כִּי הָמָן בֶּן־הַמְּדָתָא הָאֲגָגִי צֹרֵר כָּל־ 24
הַיְּהוּדִים חָשַׁב עַל־הַיְּהוּדִים לְאַבְּדָם וְהִפִּל פּוּר הוּא
הַגּוֹרָל לְהֻמָּם וּלְאַבְּדָם׃ וּבְבֹאָהּ לִפְנֵי הַמֶּלֶךְ אָמַר עִם־ כה
הַסֵּפֶר יָשׁוּב מַחֲשַׁבְתּוֹ הָרָעָה אֲשֶׁר־חָשַׁב עַל־הַיְּהוּדִים
עַל־רֹאשׁוֹ וְתָלוּ אֹתוֹ וְאֶת־בָּנָיו עַל־הָעֵץ׃

9:20 הַקְּרוֹבִים וְהָרְחוֹקִים׃[1]–The first part you should be able to do. (a) *haqq^{e}rôḇîm,* 1:14[1]. Note unusual קְּ (R.1b). (b) *rāḥôq* 'far, distant' (v.7350). These two adjs. modify what word? §36.11.

9:21 לְקַיֵּם עֲלֵיהֶם[1]—(a) *qayyēm* appears to be a late and analogic formation, D65 of קום. For the normal form, §29.631. Read §29.6326. To establish, enjoin upon them.'

לִהְיוֹת עֹשִׂים[2]—'To be doing/making,' cf. §32.375.

בְּכָל־שָׁנָה וְשָׁנָה׃[3]–Cf. 3:14[2], 1:8[6]. For distributives, §33.125.

9:22 כַּיָּמִים אֲשֶׁר־נָחוּ בָהֶם[1]—(a) *kayyāmîm*, comparison, 'as the days.' (b-d) 'in which they rested' – explain the construction.

וְהַחֹדֶשׁ אֲשֶׁר נֶהְפַּךְ לָהֶם מִיָּגוֹן לְשִׂמְחָה[2]—(a) We might expect *kaḥōḏeš*. (c) niCCaC > neGcaC; is it G29 or N10? 9:1[3]. (e) *yāḡôn* 'sorrow' (3015 14/1).

וּמֵאֵבֶל לְיוֹם טוֹב[3]—(a) 4:3[2]. You should be able to do the next part.

וּמַתָּנוֹת לָאֶבְיוֹנִים׃[4]—(a) *mattānā*^{h} 'gift' (v.4979) < **mantanat* – do you recognize the root? *mattān* is collective 'gifts'; the fem. is *nomen unitatis*, a single unit of a class (e.g. m. *fleet*, f. *ship;* m. *hair* [of the head], f. *single hair*), *Ges.* §122*t*. (b) *'eḇyôn* 'poor, needy' (v.34). Why –לָ?

9:23 וְקִבֵּל הַיְּהוּדִים אֵת אֲשֶׁר־הֵחֵלּוּ לַעֲשׂוֹת[1]—(a) 4:4[7]. Note sg. followed by pl. subj., §33.1111. Two dir. objs. (§34.115) follow, in each instance a "that which" clause. (e) *ḥll* H 'to begin'; *hēḥēllû*, read §29.51 and note §29.511. (f) Complementary inf. after (e), 'to begin to do,' §34.8.

וְאֵת אֲשֶׁר־כָּתַב[2]—Second of compound obj. of לַעֲשׂוֹת, §34.115.

9:24 חָשַׁב עַל־הַיְּהוּדִים לְאַבְּדָם[1]—Causal cl. (a) *ḥāšaḇ*, 8:3[5]. (d) 3:9[2].

וְהִפִּל פּוּר הוּא הַגּוֹרָל[2]—(a) Is second *ḥîrîq* long-*î* or short-*i*? Know the Short-Vowel Chart! Cf. 3:7[3].

לְהֻמָּם[3]—(a) *hmm* 'to discomfit' (2000 13/1). G65s5, basic pattern CuC^2, §29.511, before dagesh ◌ֻ.

9:25 וּבְבֹאָהּ[1]—Antecedent of the suffix is not clear: Esther? the plot? This part is a rehash of the story, and it is much inferior in style (see footnote on 9:12[3]).

יָשׁוּב מַחֲשַׁבְתּוֹ הָרָעָה [2]—(a) Gp50 of ישב or G20 of שוב? (G40 would be יֵשֵׁב). (c) modifies (b). 'His evil plan shall return.'

עַל־רֹאשׁוֹ[1]—Adv. modifier of *yāšûḇ*, §35.31. You should be able to finish the sentence.

SR-3

Purpose: To complete the material in Esther
Materials: Esther 9:26-28

26 עַל־כֵּן קָרְאוּ
לַיָּמִים הָאֵלֶּה פוּרִים עַל־שֵׁם הַפּוּר עַל־כֵּן עַל־כָּל־דִּבְרֵי
הָאִגֶּרֶת הַזֹּאת וּמָה־רָאוּ עַל־כָּכָה וּמָה הִגִּיעַ אֲלֵיהֶם׃
27 קִיְּמוּ וְקִבְּלֻ הַיְּהוּדִים ׀ עֲלֵיהֶם ׀ וְעַל־זַרְעָם וְעַל כָּל־
הַנִּלְוִים עֲלֵיהֶם וְלֹא יַעֲבוֹר לִהְיוֹת עֹשִׂים אֶת־שְׁנֵי הַיָּמִים
28 הָאֵלֶּה כִּכְתָבָם וְכִזְמַנָּם בְּכָל־שָׁנָה וְשָׁנָה׃ וְהַיָּמִים הָאֵלֶּה
נִזְכָּרִים וְנַעֲשִׂים בְּכָל־דּוֹר וָדוֹר מִשְׁפָּחָה וּמִשְׁפָּחָה מְדִינָה
וּמְדִינָה וְעִיר וָעִיר וִימֵי הַפּוּרִים הָאֵלֶּה לֹא יַעַבְרוּ מִתּוֹךְ
הַיְּהוּדִים וְזִכְרָם לֹא־יָסוּף מִזַּרְעָם׃

9:26 This explains the name "Purim." The sentence should end with *happûr*.

עַל־כָּל־דִּבְרֵי הָאִגֶּרֶת הַזֹּאת[1]—(d) *'iggéreṯ* 'letter' (107 10/2) 'On account of all the words of this letter.' Has a portion of the letter become attached to the story? This could account for the change in style.

וּמָה־רָאוּ עַל־כָּכָה[2]—A second phrase governed by עַל, which is highly irregular. 'On account of what they had seen concerning this.'

וּמָה הִגִּיעַ אֲלֵיהֶם׃[3]—Yet a third phrase goverened by *'al*. The prep. is usually repeated before each of its objects. 'On account of what had happened to them.' For this use of perf., §32.5114. The sentence continues into 9:27.

9:27 קִיְּמוּ וְקִבְּלֻ[1]—(a) Analogic D15 of קוּם, cf. §29.6326. (b) Kt D10, Q D15. Subj. follows, 'The Jews established and received upon them(selves).'

וְעַל־זַרְעָם וְעַל כָּל־הַנִּלְוִים עֲלֵיהֶם[2]—(b) *zéra'* 6:13[4]. (e) *lāwā^h* 'he joined, attached to' (v.3867), N reflexive, §32.83, 'upon all who were attached to them.' Note the repetition of the preps., cf. 9:26.

וְלֹא יַעֲבוֹר לִהְיוֹת עֹשִׂים[3]—(a) *lô'* + impf., §32.5215. (c) Comp. inf., §34.8. (c-d) 'to be doing, observing,' obj. (noun phrase) follows, 'these two days.'

כִּכְתָבָם וְכִזְמַנָּם[4]—(a) 1:22[3]. (b) *z^eman* 'time' (2165 4/2); why do I write it with *pattāḥ*? (R.14). Note dagesh.

9:28 נִזְכָּרִים וְנַעֲשִׂים[1]—(a) 2:1[3], 'being remembered and being done (observed).'

דּוֹר וָדוֹר מִשְׁפָּחָה וּמִשְׁפָּחָה[2]—(a) *dôr* 'generation' (v.1765); Akk. *dâru* was a 50-yr. cycle. (c) *mišpāḥā^h* 'family' (v.4940).

וִימֵי הַפּוּרִים הָאֵלֶּה לֹא יַעַבְרוּ[3]—(a) **w^ey^emê* > *wî^ymê*, §15.652.

מִתּוֹךְ הַיְּהוּדִים[4]—(a) *min* + *tôḵ* 'midst,' 4:1[4]. 'From amongst the Jews.'

וְזִכְרָם לֹא־יָסוּף מִזַּרְעָם׃[5]—(a) *zēḵer* 'memorial, remembrance' (v.2143). (c) *sûp̄* 'to come to an end, perish' (5486 8/1).

I would praise the name of God with a song, and I would magnify Him with thanksgiving. This will please YHWH more than an ox or a bull with horns and hooves.	אֲהַלְלָה שֵׁם־אֱלֹהִים בְּשִׁיר וַאֲגַדְּלֶנּוּ בְתוֹדָה׃ וְתִיטַב לַיהוָה מִשּׁוֹר פָּר מַקְרִן מַפְרִיס׃

Psalm 69:30-31

69

Purpose: To read with understanding
Materials: Esther 9:29-32

29 וַתִּכְתֹּב
אֶסְתֵּר הַמַּלְכָּה בַת־אֲבִיחַיִל וּמָרְדֳּכַי הַיְּהוּדִי אֶת־כָּל־
ל תֹּקֶף לְקַיֵּם אֵת אִגֶּרֶת הַפֻּרִים הַזֹּאת הַשֵּׁנִית׃ וַיִּשְׁלַח
סְפָרִים אֶל־כָּל־הַיְּהוּדִים אֶל־שֶׁבַע וְעֶשְׂרִים וּמֵאָה מְדִינָה
31 מַלְכוּת אֲחַשְׁוֵרוֹשׁ דִּבְרֵי שָׁלוֹם וֶאֱמֶת׃ לְקַיֵּם אֶת־יְמֵי
הַפֻּרִים הָאֵלֶּה בִּזְמַנֵּיהֶם כַּאֲשֶׁר קִיַּם עֲלֵיהֶם מָרְדֳּכַי הַיְּהוּדִי
וְאֶסְתֵּר הַמַּלְכָּה וְכַאֲשֶׁר קִיְּמוּ עַל־נַפְשָׁם וְעַל־זַרְעָם דִּבְרֵי
32 הַצּוֹמוֹת וְזַעֲקָתָם׃ וּמַאֲמַר אֶסְתֵּר קִיַּם דִּבְרֵי הַפֻּרִים
הָאֵלֶּה וְנִכְתָּב בַּסֵּפֶר׃

9:29 You should be able to read this verse with little help. תֹּקֶף 'authority' (8633 3/2). What do הַזֹּאת and הַשֵּׁנִית modify? For אִגֶּרֶת cf. 9:26[1]. I know of no explanation for the large ת.

9:30 You should be able to do this verse. שָׁלוֹם 2:11[4]. אֱמֶת 'truth' (v.571) < *'*imint*, root אמן.

9:31 Most of this verse is repetition of what we have covered several times. הַצּוֹמוֹת 4:3[3]. זַעֲקָתָם 4:1[5].

9:32 This verse, too, is familiar material. מאמר 1:15[6] (3882 3/3).

Learn the vocabulary in Group 60.

Note the following pronominal suffixes:

yāḏēnû *our* hand
bᵉśārēnû *our* flesh
'āḥînû *our* brother

בְּךָ־יְהוָה חָסִיתִי אַל־אֵבוֹשָׁה לְעוֹלָם׃
In Thee, O Lord, I have put my trust;
I would never be put to shame!
Psalm 71:1

THE ALEPPO CODEX (two-thirds of full size)

The page contains 1 Chr. 2:26–3:4. The Aleppo Codex is the oldest MS of the complete Hebrew Bible and is considered to be the most exact of all such codices.

70

Purpose: To note the Final Masorah
Materials: Esther 10:1-3 and Final Masorah

י Cap. X. י

א 2 וַיָּשֶׂם הַמֶּלֶךְ אֲחַשְׁרֹשׁ ׀ מַס עַל־הָאָרֶץ וְאִיֵּי הַיָּם׃ וְכָל־
מַעֲשֵׂה תָקְפּוֹ וּגְבוּרָתוֹ וּפָרָשַׁת גְּדֻלַּת מָרְדֳּכַי אֲשֶׁר גִּדְּלוֹ
הַמֶּלֶךְ הֲלוֹא־הֵם כְּתוּבִים עַל־סֵפֶר דִּבְרֵי הַיָּמִים לְמַלְכֵי
3 מָדַי וּפָרָס׃ כִּי ׀ מָרְדֳּכַי הַיְּהוּדִי מִשְׁנֶה לַמֶּלֶךְ אֲחַשְׁוֵרוֹשׁ
וְגָדוֹל לַיְּהוּדִים וְרָצוּי לְרֹב אֶחָיו דֹּרֵשׁ טוֹב לְעַמּוֹ וְדֹבֵר
שָׁלוֹם לְכָל־זַרְעוֹ׃

סכום פסוקי דמגלת אסתר מאה וששים ושבעה. וסימנו כבדני
נא נגד זקני עמי. וחציו ותען אסתר ותאמר. וסדריו חמשה.
וסימנו וזה גב המזבח׃

10:1 וַיָּשֶׂם הַמֶּלֶךְ אֲחַשְׁרֹשׁ ׀ מַס עַל־הָאָרֶץ וְאִיֵּי הַיָּם׃[1]—(a) 2:17[5]. (c) Note that Q adds a vowel where consonantal *wāw* is missing. (d) *mas* 'tribute' (v.4522). (g) *ʾî* 'isle, coastland' (v.336). (h) *yām* 'sea.'

10:2 וְכָל־מַעֲשֵׂה תָקְפּוֹ וּגְבוּרָתוֹ[1]—(b) *maʿăśê*^{h} 'act, work, deed' (v.4639). Is הֵ– abs. or cstr. Table F. (c) 9:29, note *qāmāṣ ḥāṭûp̄*. (d) *g*^{e}*ḇûrā*^{h} 'might, strength' (v.1369).

וּפָרָשַׁת גְּדֻלַּת מָרְדֳּכַי[2]—(a) 4:7[3] (6575 2/2). Here, something like 'the account of.' (b) Written defectively, cf. 1:4[7], (1420 12/3).

הֲלוֹא־הֵם כְּתוּבִים[3]—(a) הֲ interrog., לוא neg. (c) Note pattern. Gp55, pres. state as result of past activity.

עַל־סֵפֶר דִּבְרֵי הַיָּמִים לְמַלְכֵי מָדַי וּפָרָס׃[4]—(a) 'Upon.' The title of the book follows, cf. the title of 1-2 Chronicles. (c-d) 'Affairs of the days' = journal, diary, the official record of events. (e) 'Of/for the kings of Media and Persia.'

10:3 מִשְׁנֶה[1]—Causal. *mišnê*^{h} 'second, next' (v.4932).

וְרָצוּי לְרֹב אֶחָיו[2]—(a) The ending וּי– is Gp50 of CCY, §29.71. רצה 'to like, please,' Gp 'to be liked by, acceptable to' (v.7521). (b) 5:11[2]. (e) *ʾāḥ* 'brother' (v.251); note *ʾeḥā*^{y}*w* as if from **ʾaḥḥ-* or **ʾiḥḥ-*.

דֹּרֵשׁ טוֹב לְעַמּוֹ וְדֹבֵר שָׁלוֹם לְכָל־זַרְעוֹ׃[3]—(a) *drš* 'to seek' (v.1875). (d) Unusual stem, for דבר is usually in D. It occurs in G mostly as ptcp.

סכום פסוקי דמגלת אסתר מאה וששים ושבעה. —(a) $s^e\underline{k}\hat{u}m$ 'total of.' (b) $p^e s\hat{u}q\hat{e}$ 'verses.' (c) d^e- Aram. 'of,' the the rest is in Heb.

וסימנו כבדני נא נגד זקני עמי. [2]—(a) *sîmânô* 'its sign,' followed by quotation of part of 1 Sam. 15:30, to get the word זְקֵנַי. ז = 7, ק = 100, נ = 50, י = 10, total 167, the number of verses in Esther. The use of a portion of a verse precludes any chance of error in the figure.

וחציו ותען אסתר ותאמר. [3]—(a) $w^e\d{h}e\d{s}y\hat{o}$ 'and its middle,' followed by a quotation from Est. 5:7, the middle verse of Esther, an additional check on the number of verses.

וסדריו חמשה. [4]—(a) $\hat{u}s^e\underline{d}\bar{a}r\bar{a}^y w$ 'and its $s^e\underline{d}\bar{a}r\hat{i}m$, sections, paragraphs,' (b) '5.' These are not marked in our text.

וסימנו וזה גַּב המזבח: [5]—(a) $w^e s\hat{i}m\hat{a}n\hat{o}$ 'and its sign,' followed by a quotation from Ezek. 43:13, to set out the word גַּב, ג = 3, ב = 2, total 5. All this was to ensure the accuracy of the count to protect the text from additions or losses.

Learn the words in BVG–61.

Analyze the following verbs (using VDC if it helps you):

תָּבוֹא	יֹאמַר	וַיִּמָּצֵא	וַיְבַהֵל	יֵעוֹר
תָּבֹא	תֹּאמַר	וַיִּוָּדַע	וַיְבַקְשׁוּ	יֵעָשֶׂה
	תֹּאמַרְנָה	וַתִּלָּקַח	וַיְבַקֵּשׁ	וַיֶּאֱהַב
וַיָּשֶׂם	וַיֹּאמֶר	וַיִּתָּלוּ	וַתְּמָאֵן	וַיִּשְׁלַח
וַיַּעַשׂ	וַיֹּאמְרוּ	יִנָּתֵן	וַיְשַׁנֶּהָ	וַיִּיטַב
תַּגִּיד	וַתֹּאמֶר	תַּגִּיד	וַתְּהִי	וַיִּקְצֹף
		וְיִכָּתֵב	וַיְהִי	יִמְלְאוּ

Blessed be the Lord day by day,
He bears us up, the God of our salvation.
Selah.

בָּרוּךְ אֲדֹנָי יוֹם יוֹם
יַעֲמָס־לָנוּ הָאֵל יְשׁוּעָתֵנוּ סֶלָה׃

Psalm 68:19

71

Purpose: To continue the study of exegesis
Materials: Hosea 1:2-5

Hosea 1:2 תְּחִלַּת דִּבֶּר־יְהוָה בְּהוֹשֵׁעַ[1]—(a) *t*^{e}*ḥillā*^{h} 'beginning' (v.8642), cstr. before a finite verb (§35.7) = dependent cl. There are enough examples of cstr. before a finite verb, both in the Heb. Bible and in comparative Sem. studies, that emendation should no longer be suggested. (b) D10. (c) Subj. (d) *b*^{e}- of agent. *hôšē*$^{a\text{ʿ}}$ pr.n. 'Hosea,' from *yšʿ* 'to save.'

לֵךְ קַח־לְךָ אֵשֶׁת זְנוּנִים וְיַלְדֵי זְנוּנִים[2]—(a) VDC–10. (b) VDC–10. (c) Cf. Gen. 12:1[2] (Lesson 65). (d) *ʾēšeṯ* 'wife' (v.802b) < **ʾišt*, perhaps fem. of *ʾîš* but not cognate with *ʾiššā*^{h} (< **ʾnθ*). (e) *z*^{e}*nûnîm* 'harlotries' (2183 11x). (f) m.p.c. of *yéleḏ* 'child.'

כִּי־זָנֹה תִזְנֶה הָאָרֶץ מֵאַחֲרֵי יהוה׃[3]—(a) Causal. (b) CāCôC = ?. (b-d) §35.6. Translate something like, 'for the land has indeed gone into harlotry.' (d) To what does this refer? (e-f) To us, elliptical, but a common idiom in Heb., 'to commit adultery from (after)' = to be unfaithful to, cf. BDB 275.3.

1:3 וַיֵּלֶךְ וַיִּקַּח אֶת־גֹּמֶר בַּת־דִּבְלָיִם[1]—(a) Subj. is what? Remember the irregularities of הלך and לקח! (d) Pr.n. 'Gomer,' also a man's name (Gen. 10:2, etc.). (e-f) Patronymic, 'daughter of Diblaim.'

וַתַּהַר וַתֵּלֶד לוֹ בֵּן׃[2]—(a) הרה 'to conceive' (v.2029), CCY, §29.72. (b) *yld* 'to bear' (v.3205), WCC, §17.341, R.27. (c) "Dat. of advantage" – of course, there is no dative in Bib. Heb. (d) Indef., 'a son.'

1:4 ויאמר יהוה אליו[1]—You should have no trouble with this.

קְרָא שְׁמוֹ יִזְרְעֶאל[2]—(a) VDC–5. (b) Est. 2:5[3]. (c) Pr.n. 'Jezreel,' from *yizraʿ ʾēl* 'El will sow (sows).'

כִּי־עוֹד מְעַט וּפָקַדְתִּי אֶת־דְּמֵי יִזְרְעֶאל עַל־בֵּית יֵהוּא[3]—(a) Causal. (b-c) 'Yet a little, in a little while.' *m*^{e}*ʿaṭ* 'a little, a few' (v.4592). (d) BVG-16, v.6485, note accent, §17.342: conv. perf., §32.54. (f) *dām* in pl. = blood shed in quantity or by violence, BDB 196.2f. (g) Jezreel, a place-name; look it up in an atlas. (j) Pr.n. 'Jehu.' 'The house of Jehu' can mean the building he lives in, his family, or his dynasty. Which here? Look up "Jehu" in a Bible dictionary.

וְהִשְׁבַּתִּי מַמְלְכוּת בֵּית יִשְׂרָאֵל׃[4]—(a) הִ—תִּי should immediately suggest stem, aspect, person, gender, number. *šbt* 'to cease, rest; (H) to cause to cease, destroy' (v.7673). Note accent, §17.342. (b) *maml^{e}ḵûṯ* 'kingdom' (4468 9x, cf. מַלְכוּת and מַמְלָכָה). (c-d) See note on Amos 7:10[2,3], Lesson 50.

1:5 וְהָיָה בַּיּוֹם הַהוּא וְשָׁבַרְתִּי אֶת־קֶשֶׁת יִשְׂרָאֵל בְּעֵמֶק יִזְרְעֶאל׃[1]—(a) Hc10 'and it shall be.' (b-c) 'In that day' often refers to a future time of judgment or blessing. (d) *šbr* 'to break' (v.7665). (f) *qéšeṯ* 'bow (weapon or rainbow)' (v.7198), cstr., since after את and no def. art. (k) *'ēmeq* 'valley,' often a plain alongside a mountain (or half-valley) (v.6010). Look up the Valley of Jezreel in an atlas.

This is not an exercise in exegesis unless you attempt to ascertain the complete meaning. Simply identifying forms and meanings of words and translating is but the first step to exegesis.

Learn the words in Basic Vocabulary Group 62.

גַּם כִּי־אֵלֵךְ בְּגֵיא צַלְמָוֶת לֹא־אִירָא רָע
כִּי־אַתָּה עִמָּדִי
שִׁבְטְךָ וּמִשְׁעַנְתֶּךָ הֵמָּה יְנַחֲמֻנִי׃

Even if I should walk in a valley of deep darkness, I would not fear evil, for Thou art with me; Thy rod and Thy staff, they comfort me.

Psalm 23:4

Purpose: To continue the study of exegesis
Materials: Hosea 1:6-9

Hosea וַתַּהַר עוֹד וַתֵּלֶד בַּת[1]—(a,c) Cf. 1:3[1]. (d) Why no def. art.?

1:6 ויאמר לו קְרָא שְׁמָהּ לֹא רֻחָמָה[2]—(a-b) Who said to whom? (c-d) Cf. 1:4[2]. What is the difference? (e-f) Pr.n. 'Lo-ruhamah'; *rḥm* 'to have compassion' (v.7355). **ruḥḥāmā^h^* would be Dp11 paus., 'she has not received (or will not, §§32.513, .5132) compassion.'

כִּי לֹא אוֹסִיף עוֹד אֲרַחֵם אֶת־בֵּית יִשְׂרָאֵל[3]—(a) Causal. (c) Est. 8:3[1], here what PGN? (e) Note: shewa (compound) under preformative, ח in 2d rad. therefore no gemination and no compensatory lengthening, §15.1411. For *rḥm* see preceding note. Observe the idiom, 'I will not add again I will not have compassion on ....' Put it in proper English.

כִּי־נָשֹׂא אֶשָּׂא לָהֶם׃[4]—(b) Vowel pattern! (a-b) §35.6.1 (b) < *'*enśā*' < *'*inśa*' yiqtal, NC', §29.8. *nś'* has several meanings; which fits best here? Is RSV a good translation? Before you answer, look at BDB 670.1b(3), 671.3e. Use your large lexicon constantly.

1:7 וְאֶת־בֵּית יְהוּדָה אֲרַחֵם וְהוֹשַׁעְתִּים בַּיהוָה אֱלֹהֵיהֶם[1]—(a) *w^e^*- 'but.' (d) See Hos. 1:6[3], above. (e) ו|הושעתי|ם – does הו—תי suggest anything? *yš'* (H) 'to deliver, save' (v.3467); which suffix? §23.122. (f) *b^e^* of agent, 'by means of YHWH their God.'

וְלֹא אוֹשִׁיעֵם בְּקֶשֶׁת וּבְחֶרֶב וּבְמִלְחָמָה בְּסוּסִים וּבְפָרָשִׁים׃[2]—(a) *w^e^*- 'but.' (b) Analyze it; אוֹ-ִי- should tell you stem, WCC, and PGN of impf. Which suffix? For ישע see previous note. (c) Hos. 1:5[1]. *b^e^*- 'by.' (d) Amos 7:11[2]. *û*- 'or.' (e) *milḥāmā^h^* 'war, battle' (v.4421). (f) Est. 6:8[3]. (g) *pārāš* 'horseman' (v.6571). What does this statement mean?

1:8 וַתִּגְמֹל אֶת־לֹא רֻחָמָה וַתַּהַר וַתֵּלֶד בֵּן׃[1]—(a) *gml* 'to deal fully, bountifully; to wean' (v.1580, BDB 168.2). 'And she weaned Lo-ruhamah.' You should be able to finish the verse, cf. 1:3,6.

1:9 ויאמר קרא שמו לֹא־עַמִּי[1]—You should be able to read (a-c) even without the points, cf. 1:4,6. (d-e) Pr.n. 'Lo-ammi,' 'not my people.' Some commentators suggest that this son (and possibly the previous daughter) were not Hosea's children, but children of Gomer's harlotry.

כִּי אַתֶּם לֹא עַמִּי וְאָנֹכִי לֹא־אֶהְיֶה לָכֶם׃[2]—(a) Causal. (b) §21.1. To whom does this refer? Who is speaking? (c-d) Does this refer to the child or to whom? (e) Amos 7:14[2]. To whom does this refer? Does it add emphasis? (g) Do you associate this with יִהְיֶה? (g-h) 'To be to' = to belong to, hence 'I will not be yours,' i.e. 'your God.'

At this point, consult the commentaries – *after* you have gone carefully through the passage. There is much debate over the interpretation. For an excellent survey of the views, cf. H. H. Rowley, "The Marriage of Hosea," *Bulletin of the John Rylands Library*, 39,1 (Sept. 1956): 200-233, reprinted in *id., Men of God* (1963) 66-97. *Never read a commentary before you have worked over the text thoroughly!* To do so is to submit to brainwashing or the like. Don't let someone else tell you what to think. Let the text tell you. This should be the first rule of exegesis.

Note that Hos. 1:10-11 in the Eng. Bible is 2:1-2 in the Heb. Bible. Watch for such details, for references in your reading may be to one or the other system.

Learn the words in vocabulary Group 63.

Review the following sections on verb morphology:
- §§27.11-.1172
- §§27.13, .14
- §§27.2, .21, .221,. 232, .233
- §§27.31, .321, .333, .334
- §§27.422, .423, .424
- §27.6122
- §§27.64, .651

Review the following sections on verb syntax:
- §§30.12, .122, .22, .23, .33-.3395
- §§30.381-.3821
- §§32.-32.13
- §§32.5-.524

אַךְ טוֹב וָחֶסֶד יִרְדְּפוּנִי כָּל־יְמֵי חַיָּי
וְשַׁבְתִּי בְּבֵית יהוה לְאֹרֶךְ יָמִים׃

Surely good and covenant loyalty shall pursue me all the days of my life,
And I shall return into the house of YHWH at length of days.

Psalm 23:6

73

Purpose: To read with understanding
Materials: Genesis 37:5-9

In this and the remaining lessons, you are reading for pleasure (I hope), with a minimum of help. Work from your biblical text and use the notes only as necessary.

37:5 וַיַּחֲלֹם יוֹסֵף חֲלוֹם וַיַּגֵּד לְאֶחָיו[1]—(a) *ḥlm* 'to dream' (v.2492). (b) Pr.n. 'Joseph,' *yôsēp̄* is G50 of *ysp* 'to add,' cf. Gen. 30:24. (c) Noun; cf. (a) and guess meaning (v.2472). Cognate acc., §34.2f. (d) Est. 2:22[2]. (e) *'āḥ* (v.251), pl. *'aḥîm*, note vowel changes.

וַיּוֹסִפוּ עוֹד שְׂנֹא אֹתוֹ׃[2]—(a) Est. 8:3[1]. (b) V.5750. (c) – –̇ –ָ tells us what? V.8130.

37:6 שִׁמְעוּ־נָא הַחֲלוֹם הַזֶּה אֲשֶׁר חָלָמְתִּי׃[1]—(a) V.8085. *ḥîrîq* under 1st rad. tells us what? VDC–1 or –5? (b) *nâ'* 'I pray' (v.4994). (c-d) §36.54. (c,f) Cf. 37:5[1] (a,c).

37:7 הִנֵּה אֲנַחְנוּ מְאַלְּמִים אֲלֻמִּים בְּתוֹךְ הַשָּׂדֶה[1]— (a) V.2009, often (but not always) followed by ptcp. (b) §21.1. (c) *'lm* D 'to bind (sheaves)' (v.481). (d) *'ălummîm* 'sheaves' (485 5x). §34.2. (e) V.8432. Est. 4:1[4]. (f) *śāḏê*^{h} '(open) field' (v.3704).

וְהִנֵּה קָמָה אֲלֻמָּתִי וְגַם־נִצָּבָה[2]—(b) Note accent, §29.6318 – is this G11 'stood' or G51 'were standing'? (c) F.s.s4, cf. 37:7[1]. (d) V.1571. (e) *nṣb* 'to stand upright/erect' (v.5324). Note vowels: is it D11 or N11?.

וְהִנֵּה תְסֻבֶּינָה אֲלֻמֹּתֵיכֶם וַתִּשְׁתַּחֲוֶיןָ לַאֲלֻמָּתִי׃[3]—(b) §§29.511, .5113. *sbb* 'to surround' (v.5437). (c) F.p.s7. (d) ןָ– – –ת or נָה– – –ת tell us what? §27.31. For this verb, §28.13, §28.9.

37:8 הֲמָלֹךְ תִּמְלֹךְ עָלֵינוּ[1]—(a) CāCôC, §27.64. What is –הֲ? §22.3. (a-b) §35.6. Translate something like, 'will you indeed reign over us?' (c) *'al* + s9, §23.121.

אִם־מָשׁוֹל תִּמְשֹׁל בָּנוּ[2]—(a) *'im* sometimes introduces a question (v.518, BDB 49f.). (b) *mšl* 'to rule, have dominion over' (v.4910). Note the prep. that follows.

עַל־חֲלֹמֹתָיו וְעַל־דְּבָרָיו׃[3]—(a) *'al* 'on account of.' (b) F.p.s0: (d) M.p.s0.

37:9 וַיַּחֲלֹם עוֹד חֲלוֹם אַחֵר וַיְסַפֵּר אֹתוֹ לְאֶחָיו[1]—(a-c) You should be able to do this, cf. 37:5. (d) *'āḥēr* 'another, different' (v.312). (e-g) You should be able to do this. (e) *spr* v.5608. (g) 37:5[1].

וְהִנֵּה הַשֶּׁמֶשׁ וְהַיָּרֵחַ וְאַחַד עָשָׂר כּוֹכָבִים[2]—(b) *šémeš* 'sun' (v.3121). (c) *yārēaḥ* 'moon' (v.3394). (d-e) §26.25. (f) *kôkāb* 'star' (v.3556).

Go over the story several times, until you can read it with comparative ease. Any language is enjoyable when you can read it without having to look up every word or parse every form.

Memorize the vocabulary in Group 64.

Review the use of *wāw* with the verb:
§§32.53-.549
§§32.8-.849

Review the following sections with regard to the D-stem:
§§28.1, .2-.222
§§29.523, .6326, .711
§§32.222, .24
§§32.81-815

Review the following sections with regard to the H-stem:
§§28.3-.33
§§29.311, .313, .332, .511
§§29.632, .6322-.6325, .6412, .6413
§29.711
§§32.82-.824

God has ascended with a shout,	עָלָה אֱלֹהִים בִּתְרוּעָה
YHWH, with the sound of a ram's horn.	יהוה בְּקוֹל שׁוֹפָר׃
Sing praises to God, sing praises!	זַמְּרוּ אֱלֹהִים זַמֵּרוּ
Sing praises to our king, sing praises!	זַמְּרוּ לְמַלְכֵּנוּ זַמֵּרוּ׃

Psalm 47:6-7

74

Purpose: To read with understanding
Materials: Genesis 37:10-14

37:10 וַיְסַפֵּר אֶל־אָבִיו וְאֶל־אֶחָיו וַיִּגְעַר־בּוֹ אָבִיו[1]—(c) *'āḇîw,* note that *'āḇ* always retains its final *-î* when adding a suffix, cf. §24.6. Pronounce it [ɑˈvi·v]. (f) *g'r* 'to rebuke' (1605 13x). Note that it does not take a dir. obj. (h) Subj. of (f).

מָה הַחֲלוֹם הַזֶּה אֲשֶׁר חָלָמְתָּ[2]—Verbless cl., §31.224. (e) *ḥālā́mtā,* pausal. How do you translate *-tā*? *-tî*?

הֲבוֹא נָבוֹא אֲנִי וְאִמְּךָ וְאַחֶיךָ לְהִשְׁתַּחֲוֹת לְךָ אָרְצָה׃[3]—(a) Note that –הֲ! G60 + G29 of בוא – how would you translate it? §35.6. (c-e) Compound subj. (3 subjs.) with pl. verb. §33.12. (f) Note that –וֹ– after a vowel is *-wô-*. –וֹת– –לְ tells us what? (h) *-āʰ* is directive (note accent), read §23.2, 'earthward, to(ward) the earth.'

37:11 וַיְקַנְאוּ־בוֹ אֶחָיו[1]—(a) R.1b! *qn'* (D) 'to be jealous, zealous, envious' (v.7065). Note use of prep., position of subj.

וְאָבִיו שָׁמַר אֶת־הַדָּבָר׃[2]—(b) *šmr* 'to keep, guard, watch over, protect' (v.8104). (d) *dāḇār* has many meanings besides 'word,' cf. BDB 182ff.

37:12 וַיֵּלְכוּ אֶחָיו לִרְעוֹת אֶת־צֹאן אֲבִיהֶם בִּשְׁכֶם׃[1]—(a) *hlk* is often formed like WCC, §29.321. Subj. follows. (c) *r'y* to tend, pasture, graze' (v.7462); –וֹת– tells us what? VDC–6. (e) *ṣô'n* (< *ṣa'n*, CaCC, with *a'* acting as quasi long-*â* > *ô*) 'sheep, goats, flock, small cattle' (v.6629). Is it definite? (f) s5. Pay attention to the pron. suffixes! (g) *šᵉḵem* pr.n. 'Shechem' – locate it in your Bible atlas. Use exegetical tools from now on.

37:13 ויאמר ישראל אל־יוסף[1]— Learn to read without vowel-points; it's faster. (b) Joseph's father was Jacob, also known as 'Israel,' cf. Gen. 32:29.

הֲלוֹא אַחֶיךָ רֹעִים בִּשְׁכֶם[2]—Verbless, ptcp. for predicate, §31.24. (c) 37:12[1](c). (d) 37:12[1](g).

לְכָה וְאֶשְׁלָחֲךָ אֲלֵיהֶם ויאמר לו הִנֵּנִי׃[3]—(a) G32 + *āʰ*, §27.43f., 'come, now,' or just 'come.' (b) *'ešlāḥăḵā*, G24/44s2, *šlḥ* 'to send' (v.7971). Translate possibly 'I would like to send you,' cf. §32.5213. (f) *hinnēʰ* + s4, 'Here am I,' but in the context, more like 'OK, I'll go.'

37:14 לֶךְ־נָא רְאֵה אֶת־שְׁלוֹם אַחֶיךָ וְאֶת־שְׁלוֹם הַצֹּאן[1]—(a-b) G32 of *hlk* + *nâ'*, 'come/go, I pray.' (c) G32 of *r'y* 'to see,' here more like 'look into, find out about.' (e) *šālôm* 'peace, welfare,' cstr. 'the welfare of' = 'how they are.'

וַהֲשִׁבֵנִי דָּבָר[2]—(a) *wahăšîḇēnî*, H32s4; note that the pron. suf., in our way of speaking, is indir. obj., 'bring back word *to me*.' We can also say, 'Bring me word,' but *me* in such a sentence is not dir. obj.

וַיִּשְׁלָחֵהוּ מֵעֵמֶק חֶבְרוֹן וַיָּבֹא שְׁכֶמָה׃[3](a) *wayyišlāḥēhû.* In this and the preceding verb, note connecting vowel, §23.1321. What suf. here? §23.122. (b) *min* + *'ēmeq* 'valley' (v.6010). (c) *ḥeḇrôn*, pr.n. 'Hebron.' Find it on a map. (e) *šᵉkémāʰ*, §23.2. Learn to spot the *hê*-directive/locative; note the accent. About how far was it from Hebron to Shechem?.

Learn the words in BVG 65.

Review the imperative (impv.) in the following:
§§27.42-.441, .74
§§28.21, .31, .41, .51
§§29.322, 7122, .93
§§32.32-.327
§32.543

Review the jussive (juss.) and cohortative (cohort.):
§§27.5-531
§§28.21, .31
§§29.7122, .7422
§§32.34-.345
§§32.35-35.7
§§32.544-.545

Review noun morphology; see pp. 23, 25.

A righteous man knows the rights of the poor;
a wicked man does not understand such knowledge.

יֹדֵעַ צַדִּיק דִּין דַּלִּים
רָשָׁע לֹא־יָבִין דָּעַת׃

Proverbs 29:7

75

Purpose: To read with understanding
Materials: Genesis 37:15-19

37:15 וַיִּמְצָאֵהוּ אִישׁ וְהִנֵּה תֹעֶה בַּשָּׂדֶה[1]—(a) *way|yimṣā'|ēhû*: do you understand each segment? *mṣ'* v.4672. (b) Indef., 'a man.' (d) תעה 'to err, wander about' (v.8582), parse. (e) 37:7[1]. (c-e) Verbless cl., ptcp. and modifier for pred., subj. omitted ('he').

וַיִּשְׁאָלֵהוּ הָאִישׁ לֵאמֹר מַה־תְּבַקֵּשׁ׃[2]—(a) *way|yiš'āl|ēhû*: *š'l* 'to ask' (v.7592). Who asked whom? (b) Definite, the aforementioned man. (c) = 'quote.' (d-e) 'What are you looking for?' §34.1.

37:16 אֶת־אַחַי אָנֹכִי מְבַקֵּשׁ[1]—(a-b) Dir. obj. Note s4 added to pl. אָחִי 'my brother,' אַחַי 'my brothers.' (c) *'ânôḵî* 'I' (v.595). אני is used more often than אנכי in the later books of OT, but both *'ănî* and *'ânôḵî* are found in the earliest and latest levels of Heb. (d) Almost a pres. tense, 'I am looking for.'

הַגִּידָה־נָּא לִי אֵיפֹה הֵם רֹעִים׃[2]—(a-b) *haggîḏā^h-nâ'*, note vowel under הַ: H11 would have הִ; H32/60/65 have הַ, VDC–7. With *-ā^h* and *nâ'* it must be impv., cf. §§32.326, .327. (d) *'ê^ypō^h* 'where?' (375 10x). (e-f) Verbless, 'they [are] shepherding,' with ptcp. for pred., modified by adv. of place.

37:17 נָסְעוּ מִזֶּה כִּי שָׁמַעְתִּי אֹמְרִים נֵלְכָה דֹּתָיְנָה[1]— (a) *nās^e'û*: נסע 'to pull up stakes, set out, move on' (v.5265). (b) *min* + *zê^h* 'from this [place].' (c) Causal or explicative, BDB 473. 3c. (d) *šm'* v.8085. (e) Ptcp., subj. not defined, 'I heard (them) saying.' (f) *nêl^eḵā^h*, lengthened impf./juss., cf. §§32.34, .341, < *hlk,* 'Let us go.' (g) *dôṯā́ynā^h*, pr.n. 'Dothan,' + loc. ה ָ. Cf. 37:17[2](f).

וַיֵּלֶךְ יוסף אַחַר אחיו וַיִּמְצָאֵם בְּדֹתָן׃[2]—(a-b) Verb, subj. (c-d) Modifier, tells where he went. (e) *way|yimṣā'|ēm*: what suf.? §23.122. (f) Adv. phr. telling where he found them. *dôṯān* is the more common form, cf. 37:17[1](g).

37:18 ויראו אתו מרחוק[1]—(a) From ראה. Can you point it?. (b) *'ittô* or *'ôṯô*? (c) *min* + *rāḥôq* 'far, distance' (v.7350). Who saw whom? Where?

וּבְטֶרֶם יִקְרַב אֲלֵיהֶם וַיִּתְנַכְּלוּ אתו לַהֲמִיתוֹ׃[2]—(a) *b^e* + *ṭérem* 'when not yet, before' (v.2962), generally with impf., BDB 382. (d) *yiṯ– – –û,* VDC–1. *nkl* 'to be crafty, deceitful,' HtD 'to deal deceitfully with' (5230 4x). (f) *l^e*- + inf. cstr., purpose, 'fo cause him to die.'

37:19 ויאמרו איש אל אחיו[1]—(b-d) §33.125. Can you point (or pronounce) the unpointed words? Keep trying! When you can read the consonants without looking at the vowels, you'll read much more rapidly.

הנה בַּעַל הַחֲלֹמוֹת הַלָּזֶה בָּא׃[2]—Direct quotation. (b) *bá'al* 'lord, owner, husband,' cstr., 'the lord of dreams.' (d) BDB 229, *hallāz* (1975 7x), *hallāzê*[h] (1976 2x), *hallāzû* (1977 1x) 'this.' (g) G10 'has come,' or G50 'is coming'? After הנה which is more likely?

Learn the words in Basic Vocabulary Group 66.

Review the participle (ptcp.):
§§27.61-.632
§§28.21, .22, .31, .32, .42, .51, .61
§29.6318
§31.24
§§32.37-.376, .5363, .545

Review the infinitive absolute (inf.abs.):
§§27.64-6411
§§28.21, .22, .31, .32, .42, .51
§29.6319
§§32.39-.393

Review the verb forms on pp. 35, 51, 53, 55.

Be still and know that I am God;	הַרְפּוּ וּדְעוּ כִּי־אָנֹכִי אֱלֹהִים
I will be exalted among the nations,	אָרוּם בַּגּוֹיִם
I will be exalted in the earth.	אָרוּם בָּאָרֶץ׃

Psalm 46:10 (MT 11)

76

Purpose: To read with understanding
Materials: Genesis 37:20-24

37:20 וְעַתָּה לְכוּ וְנַהַרְגֵהוּ[1]—(a) *'attā^{h}* 'now' (v.6258). (b) *hlk* G37. (c) *w^{e}|naharg|ēhû*: G29/49s0 *hrg* 'to kill,' read §32.355.

וְנַשְׁלִכֵהוּ בְּאַחַד הַבֹּרוֹת וְאָמַרְנוּ חַיָּה רָעָה אֲכָלָתְהוּ[2]—(a) *šlk* (H) 'to throw, cast' (v.7993). You should now know ־ֵהוּ. Can you parse *našlîḵ*? Note vowels. VDC–3. (b) Cstr. (c) *bō'r* 'cistern, dug well, pit' (v.877). (d) Gc15. (e) *ḥayyā^{h}* 'beast, wild animal' (v.2416). (f) V.7453. (g) *'akālāṯ|hû*: note §27.221, §27.72, and the ת– on G11s0.

וְנִרְאֶה מַה־יִּהְיוּ חֲלֹמֹתָיו׃[3]—(a) ־ֶה, VDC–6; if CCY, then –נ must be 29 (N10 would be ־ָה), 'we shall see.' (b-d) N. cl., dir. obj. of verb, = indir. disc. (c) 'Be, come to be, become.' 'We shall see what his dreams will become' or 'what will become of his dreams.'

37:21 וַיִּשְׁמַע רְאוּבֵן וַיַּצִּלֵהוּ מִיָּדָם[1]—(b) Pr.n., 'Reuben,' < *r^{e}'û bēn* 'see, a son!' cf. Gen. 29:32. (c) *nṣl* 'to snatch, rescue, deliver' (v.5337), Hc20s0. (d) *min* + *yāḏ* + s5.

וַיֹּאמֶר לֹא נַכֶּנּוּ נָפֶשׁ׃[2]—(c) *nakkénnû* < **nankê^{h}* + *n* + *hû*, §27.714, prob. H49, for the energic would not apocopate; *nky* H 'to smite' (v.5221). (d) *Ges.* §117*ll* takes this as a 2d acc. to define the obj., 'Let us not smite him (in) the life.' It could also be taken as an appositive, 'a soul, a living being,' hence not be treated as an animal.

37:22 ויאמר אלהם | ראובן אַל־תִּשְׁפְּכוּ־דָם[1]—(b) Usually אליהם. Verb, obj., subj. (d-e) *'al* usually with juss. for neg. command, §32.353. (e) *špk* 'to pour out' (v.8210). (f) V.1818.

הַשְׁלִיכוּ אֹתוֹ אֶל־הַבּוֹר הַזֶּה אֲשֶׁר בַּמִּדְבָּר[2]—(a) *šlk* (H) 'to throw, fling' (v.7993), ־ִי־ ־וּ–הַ must be H37 (VDC–3). (b) *bôr* 'pit, cistern, dug well' (v.953), cf. בֹּאר. (g) *midbār* 'steppe, wilderness' (v.4057). Since *midbār* is often used of pasture-land, it is not to be considered as 'desert,' and even 'wilderness' often conveys the wrong idea. Study words *in contexts*!

וְיָד אַל־תִּשְׁלְחוּ בוֹ[3]—Note word order. (a) 'A hand.' (b-c) §32.353. For *šlḥ yāḏ*, cf. Est. 2:21[6].

לְמַעַן הַצִּיל אֹתוֹ מִיָּדָם לַהֲשִׁיבוֹ אֶל־אָבִיו׃[4]—(a) *l^{e}má'an* 'for the sake of, in order that' (v.4616, see BDB 775). (b) *haṣṣîl*: note that *pattāḥ*! H65 of נצל after למען, 'in order to deliver him.' (d) *min* + *yāḏ* + s5. (e) *lahăšîḇô*: *l^{e}*- + H65s0 of *šûḇ*. Is this a second purpose cl., or a result cl.?

37:23 וַיְהִי כַּאֲשֶׁר־בָּא יוֹסֵף אֶל־אֶחָיו[1]—(a) Est. 1:1, και εγενετο. (b) Temporal cl. (c) G10 or G50? Try to read the clause without the pointing. Then check your results against the pointed text.

וַיַּפְשִׁיטוּ אֶת־יוֹסֵף אֶת־כֻּתָּנְתּוֹ[2]—(a) *pšṭ* 'to strip off, (H) to strip' (v.6584). (b,d) Unusual to have both objs. of H-stem indicated by את. (e) *kuttont* > *kuttṓneṯ* 'tunic' (v.3801).

אֶת־כְּתֹנֶת הַפַּסִּים אֲשֶׁר עָלָיו׃[3]—This cl. is appositional, describing the tunic (§36.65). (b) *k*ᵉ*ṯṓneṯ*, a variant form of v.3801; the forms are used interchangeably. Cstr. (d) *pas* 'palm of hand, sole of foot' (6446 5x, always of a garment). We know this as 'a coat of many colors,' but *k*ᵉ*ṯṓneṯ happassîm* seems to mean a tunic with long sleeves (to the wrist) and skirt (to the feet), in contrast to the sleeveless, knee-length tunic.

37:24 וַיִּקָּחֻהוּ וַיַּשְׁלִכוּ אֹתוֹ הַבֹּרָה[1]—(a) *way|yiqqāḥū́|hû*: remember that לקח often behaves as if NCC. Note obj. expressed here by s0, in next cl. by *'ōṯô*. (b) *wayyašlīḵû*: note the vowels, cf. with preceding word. Cf. 37:22[2]. (d) *habbṓrāʰ*: note accent; when loc. ־ָה is used, the def. art. may also be used, 'to the pit.'

וְהַבּוֹר רֵק אֵין בּוֹ מָיִם׃[2]—(a) *rêq*, also *rêʸq*, 'empty' (7386 14x). If you didn't know the meaning, could you figure it out from (c-e)? (e) *máyim* 'water' (v.4325).

Learn the words in Vocabulary Group 67.

Review the N-stem in the following sections:
§§28.4-.421
§§29.311, .3122, .6322
§§32.83-.833

Review the HtD-stem in the following:
§§28.5-.53
529.523
§§32.84-.844

וִיהִי נֹעַם אֲדֹנָי אֱלֹהֵינוּ עָלֵינוּ
וּמַעֲשֵׂה יָדֵינוּ כּוֹנְנָה עָלֵינוּ
וּמַעֲשֵׂה יָדֵינוּ כּוֹנְנֵהוּ׃

Let the favor of the Lord our God be upon us,
And the work of our hands establish Thou upon us,
Yea, the work of our hands, establish Thou it.

(Psalm 90:12)

77

Purpose: To read with understanding
Materials: Genesis 37:25-30

Gen. 37:25 וַיֵּשְׁבוּ לֶאֱכָל־לֶחֶם וַיִּשְׂאוּ עֵינֵיהֶם[1]—(a) Is this from ישב or שוב? Note *ṣêrê*. (b) Is it *qāmāṣ* or *qāmāṣ-ḥăṭûp̄*? What difference does it make? (c) BVG-34. (d) If there were a dagesh in שׁ would it help? (e) עין can mean 'eye' or 'spring' – which is it here?

וַיִּרְאוּ וְהִנֵּה אֹרְחַת יִשְׁמְעֵאלִים בָּאָה מִגִּלְעָד[2]—(c) *'ôr^{e}ḥā^{h}* 'caravan' (736 2x, G53 of *'rḥ* #731). (d) Pr.n. 'Ishmaelites.' (e) G11 or G51? Note accent! (f) Pr.n. 'Gilead.' Look it up on a map.

וּגְמַלֵּיהֶם נֹשְׂאִים נְכֹאת וּצְרִי וָלֹט[3]—(a) BVG–63. Note geminate ל. (b) Note vowel pattern. Note various meanings of *nś'*. (c) *n^{e}ḵô't̲* 'spices' (5219 2x; Arab. *naka'at*). (d) *ṣ^{e}rî* or *ṣŏrî* 'balsam' (6875 6x). (e) *lōṭ* 'myrrh' (3910 2x, BDB 538).

הוֹלְכִים לְהוֹרִיד מִצְרָיְמָה׃[4]—(a) Note vowel pattern: is it H of **wlk* or G of *hlk*? (b) *yrd* 'to go down, descend' (v.3881). (a-b) Note the expression, 'going to go down,' i.e., traveling for the purpose of going down to Egypt. It is not a compound verb like Eng. *going to do* – in Heb. that would be *'md l^{e}-*. (c) Pr.n. *miṣráyim* 'Egypt.' What is the unaccented *-ā^{h}*?.

37:26 ויאמר יְהוּדָה אל־אחיו[1]—(b) *y^{e}hûḏā^{h}* 'Judah,' Gen. 29:35. Did you read אחיו *'eḥā^{y}w* or *'āḥi^{y}w*?

מַה־בֶּצַע כִּי נַהֲרֹג אֶת־אָחִינוּ וְכִסִּינוּ אֶת־דָּמוֹ׃[2]—(b) *béṣa'* 'unjust gain, profit' (v.1215). (c) Introduces a condition, BDB 473.2b, *Ges.* §159*aa, bb*. (d) N-stem or G29? BVG-30. (e) Sing. + s9. (f) *w^{e}kissînû*: note vowels; Dc19 of כסה 'to cover, conceal' (v.3680). Note ellipsis in apodosis: 'If we kill ... and conceal ..., what profit [is there for us]?'

37:27 לְכוּ וְנִמְכְּרֶנּוּ לישמעאלים וְיָדֵנוּ אַל־תְּהִי־בוֹ[1]—(a) G37 of *hlk*. Learn it! (b) Est. 7:4[1]. What is the difference between the forms? §32.342. (c) Gen. 37:25[2]. (d) s9. Subj. of following verb. The form could be f.d.s9 written defectively. 'Our hand(s), let it not be on him.'

כִּי־אָחִינוּ בְשָׂרֵנוּ הוּא[2]—(a) Causal. Verbless cl. with a pred. and an appositive. (c) *bāśār* 'flesh' (v.1320). s9 on a noun can be *-nû* or *-ēnû*, §23.121.

וַיִּשְׁמְעוּ אחיו׃[3]—(a) Would you translate this 'they heard' or 'they agreed'? Why?

37:28 וַיַּעַבְרוּ אֲנָשִׁים מִדְיָנִים סֹחֲרִים[1]—(a) עבר is not easy to translate. Had the men 'passed by' or were they 'passing by' or 'about to pass by'? (c) Appositional. *miḏyānîm* 'Midianites.' Because both Reuben and Judah seek to rescue Joseph, and because both Ishmaelites and Midianites are mentioned, some scholars believe that two stories have been conflated. (d) Another appositive. *sḥr* 'to travel (as a merchant)' (v.5503), G55 'merchants.'

וַיִּמְשְׁכוּ וַיַּעֲלוּ את־יוסף מִן־הַבּוֹר[2]—(a) *mšk* 'to drag, draw, draw out' (v.4900). (b) This form could be Gc25 or Hc25 – which is it? (e-f) Cf. 37:20[2].

וימכרו את־יוסף לישמעאלים בְּעֶשְׂרִים כָּסֶף[3]—(a) 37:27[1]. Here see §32.533. (e) *b*[e]- of measure, price, BDB 90.III.3b. *'eśrîm* v.6242. (f) *késep̄* 'silver,' but since coinage was unknown at this date, we should probably understand '20 [shekels of] silver,' BDB 494.8b. You should be able to finish the verse. For *miṣráymā*[h], cf. 37:25[4].

37:29 וַיָּשָׁב ראובן אל־הַבּוֹר והנה אין־יוסף בַּבּוֹר[1]—(a) Is this from *šûḇ* or *yšb*? You should be able to do the rest of the clause.

ויקרע את־בגדיו׃[2]—Cf. Est. 4:1[2].

37:30 וישב אל־אחיו ויאמר[1]—You should be able to read this – even without pointing!

הַיֶּלֶד אֵינֶנּוּ וַאֲנִי אָנָה אֲנִי־בָא׃[2]—(a) BVG-20. Joseph was 17, but as next-to-youngest he was a *yéleḏ*. (b) §23.1221. (c,e) §21.1. (d) *'ā́nā*[h] < *'ān* 'where?' (v.575) + ה-directive, BDB 33. (f) G10 and G50 of CWC can be confused – but what of G14 and G50?

Learn the words in Basic Vocabulary Group 68.

אַחַת דִּבֶּר אֱלֹהִים שְׁתַּיִם־זוּ שָׁמָעְתִּי
כִּי־עֹז לֵאלֹהִים׃
וּלְךָ־אֲדֹנָי חָסֶד
כִּי־אַתָּה תְשַׁלֵּם לְאִישׁ כְּמַעֲשֵׂהוּ׃

Once God has spoken, twice have I heard this,
That power belongs to God,
Even to You, my Lord, covenant loyalty,
For You will reward a man according to his work.

Psalm 62:11-12 (MT 12-13)

Purpose: To read with understanding
Materials: Genesis 37:31-36

37:31 וַיִּקְחוּ אֶת־כְּתֹנֶת יוֹסֵף וַיִּשְׁחֲטוּ שְׂעִיר עִזִּים[1]—(a) If you haven't learned to recognize forms of לקח yet, do it *now*. (c) 37:23. (e) *šḥṭ* 'to slaughter' (v.7819). (f) *śā'îr* 'he-goat, buck' (v.8163); abs. or cstr.? (g) *'ēz* 'she-goat' (v.5795).

וַיִּטְבְּלוּ אֶת־הַכֻּתֹּנֶת בַּדָּם׃[2]—(a) *ṭbl* 'to dip' (v.2881). (c) 37:23. (d) Is it 'in blood' or 'in the blood'?

37:32 וַיְשַׁלְּחוּ אֶת־כְּתֹנֶת הַפַּסִּים וַיָּבִיאוּ אֶל־אֲבִיהֶם[1]—(a) BVG-14. Is it G, D, or N? (c,d) 37:23. (e) What stem-indicators do you see at once? (g) 37:10. Note the rather strange juxtaposition of 'and they sent ... and they brought ....'

ויאמרו זאת מָצָאנוּ[2]—(b) §21.2. (c) נוּ– is what morpheme? §27.21.

הַכֶּר־נָא הַכְּתֹנֶת בִּנְךָ הִוא אִם־לֹא׃[3]—(a) D32 of *hkr* or H32 of *nkr*? *nkr* 'to observe, regard' (v.5234). (c) Since this word is in cstr., we must read הַ– as interrog. In a few instances, *hê*-interrog. takes *pattāḥ* and the strong dagesh, *Ges.* 101*l*. (d) *bēn* + s2; we should expect **benkā* (Short Vowel Chart). (e) In Pentateuch (only!), *hî'* is always written הִוא – a fact which the theory of a Hexateuch does not satisfactorily explain. (f-g) 'Or not.' (c-g) Verbless correlative cls., '[Is] that the tunic of your son or [is it] not?'

37:33 וַיַּכִּירָהּ ויאמר כְּתֹנֶת בְּנִי[1]—(a) Hc20s1: if you don't understand that analysis, review your verb-forms. *nkr,* 37:32[3]. (d) *bēn* + s4. (c-d) Verbless, '[It is] my son's tunic.'

חַיָּה רָעָה אֲכָלָתְהוּ טָרֹף טֹרַף יוסף׃[2]—(a) *ḥayyā^h* BVG-30. (b) *rā'ā^h* BVG-49, Est. 7:6[1]. (c) Remember that G11 preserves original ת– in suffixial forms. §27.721. This is G11s0 pausal. (d) *ṭrp* 'to tear, rend' (v.2963). CāCôC is what form? §27.64. (e) *Be careful!* The *ḥôlām* could be *ô* < *â* (R.2b), or it could be a *u*-vowel with compensatory lengthening before ר. What would **ṭurrap̄* be? VDC–1. 'Joseph has surely been torn to pieces!'

37:34 וַיִּקְרַע יַעֲקֹב שִׂמְלֹתָיו וַיָּשֶׂם שַׂק בְּמָתְנָיו[1]—(a) Est. 4:1[2]. (b) Gen. 37:1. (c) *śimlā^h* 'mantle, wrapper; pl. clothes' (v.8071). (d) Est. 2:17[5]. (e) Est. 4:1[3]. (f) *moṯnáyim* 'loins' (v.4975).

וַיִּתְאַבֵּל עַל־בְּנוֹ ימים רבים׃[2]—(a) Est. 6:12[3]. (b) 'On account of.' (d-e) Est. 1:4[8].

Gen. וַיָּקֻמוּ כָל־בָּנָיו וְכָל־בְּנֹתָיו לְנַחֲמוֹ[1]—(a) Would you recognize it better as וַיָּקוּמוּ? (b-
37:35 d) Two subjects, each a noun-phrase. (e) Est. 2:7[8]. Note that the pl. of *bat̲* is
bānôt̲. (f) *nḥm* (d) 'to comfort' (v.5162). Parse it.

וַיְמָאֵן לְהִתְנַחֵם ויאמר כִּי־אֵרֵד אֶל־בְּנִי אָבֵל שְׁאֹלָה[2]—(a) Cf. Est. 1:12[1]. (b) Comp. inf. Cf. 37:35[1](f). (e) *'êrēd̲* < **'ayridu*, §29.321; cf. 37:25[4]. (h) *'āb̲ēl*, Est. 6:12[3]. (i) *šᵉ'ôl* 'Sheol, the underworld, the realm of the dead' (v.7585). Note unaccented *-āʰ*. (d-i) Direct discourse, put in his own words: 'I shall go down to my son, to Sheol, weeping.'

וַיֵּבְךְּ אֹתוֹ אָבִיו׃[3]—(a) Cf. Est. 8:3[3]. (b) Note that the Heb. verb takes a dir. obj.: we translate 'his father wept *for* him.'

37:36 וְהַמְּדָנִים מָכְרוּ אֹתוֹ אֶל־מִצְרָיִם[1]—(a) *mᵉd̲ānîm* variant form of *mid̲yānîm* (37:28),
the former attributed to E, the latter to JE – but the scant evidence is mixed, cf.
BDB 193. (b) Gen. 37:27. (e) Gen. 37:25. 'They sold him into Egypt' is rather
elliptical, and the following phrase is needed.

לְפוֹטִיפַר סְרִיס פַּרְעֹה שַׂר הַטַּבָּחִים׃[2]—(a) This is the indir. obj. of מכרו. Pr. n. 'Potiphar.' (b) You haven't forgotten this word, have you? (c) *par'ōʰ* 'Pharaoh' (Egypt. *pr-'* 'great house'). (e) *ṭabbāḥ* 'butcher, cook, bodyguard' (v.2876), but (d-e) always = 'captain of bodyguard.' To whom does it refer – Pharaoh or Potiphar?

Learn the words in Vocabulary Group 69.

Review the infinitive construct (inf. cstr.):

§§27.65-.654, .75, .752
§§28.21, .22, .31, .32
§§29.2213, .322, .93
§§31.141, .142
§§32.38-.386, 5364

Of the making of many books there is no end,
And much studying is a wearying of flesh.

עֲשׂוֹת סְפָרִים הַרְבֵּה אֵין קֵץ
וְלַהַג הַרְבֵּה יְגִעַת בָּשָׂר׃

Ecclesiastes 12:12

Purpose: To read with understanding
Materials: Genesis 45:4-10

Gen. וַיֹּאמֶר יוסף אל־אחיו גְּשׁוּ־נָא אֵלַי וַיִּגָּשׁוּ[1]—(a-d) No problem. (e) *ngš* 'to draw near,
45:4 approach' (v.5066), VDC–10. (h) Compare this form with (e). §32.533.

ויאמר אני יוסף אחיכם אשר־מְכַרְתֶּם אֹתִי מִצְרָיְמָה׃[2]—(a) Note *r*^{e}*bî*$^{a e}$. (e) + s7. (b-e) You should be able to translate; verbless, subj., pred., appositive. (f) Gen. 37:27[1], Est. 7:4[1] ־תֶּם tells us what? (f-g) 'who you sold me' = 'whom you sold.' (h) Unaccented ־ָה. This is not indir. obj., 'you sold to Egypt,' but directional, 'Egyptward,' i.e. to be taken to Egypt. RSV 'sold into Egypt.'

45:5 ועתה אַל־תֵּעָצְבוּ וְאַל־יִחַר בְּעֵינֵיכֶם[1]—(a) *'attā*^{h} 'now' (BVG-11). (c) תֵּ--ָ-וּ: what stem? PGN? *'ṣb* 'to grieve; (N) to be grieved, full of grief' (v.6087). Read §32.353: what mood or aspect? §32.832. (e) חרה 'to be angry, burn with anger' (v.2734), G40, probably referring to the incident. RSV 'do not ... be angry with yourselves,' taken literally would require G47, but it gives the sense. (f) What does עין mean here? (v.5869).

כי־מכרתם אתי הֵנָּה[2]—(a) 'That you sold me,' n. cl., defining the subj. of *yiḥar*. (a-c) 45:4[2]. (d) *hḗnnā*^{h} 'hither, to this (place/time)' (v.2008, BDB 244).

כי לְמִחְיָה שְׁלָחַנִי אלהים לִפְנֵיכֶם׃[3]—(a) Causal. (b) *miḥyā*^{h} 'preservation of life' (4241 8x; cf. BDB 313). (c) ־ַנִי §17.32, §27.712. *šlḥ* BVG-14. (e) *lip̄nê* + s7.

45:6 כִּי־זֶה שְׁנָתַיִם הָרָעָב בְּקֶרֶב הָאָרֶץ[1]—(c) Dual, 'two years' (*šānā*^{h} BVG-3). 'This two years' = 'it is now the second year.' (d) *rā'āb* 'famine, hunger' (v.7458). (e) *b*^{e}*qéreb* often = *b*^{e}- (BVG-11).

וְעוֹד חָמֵשׁ שָׁנִים אשר אֵין־חָרִישׁ וְקָצִיר׃[2]—(b) §26.23. (c) Both *šānîm* and *šānôt* are found; cf. 45:6[1]. (e) applies to the next two words as a unitary idea. (f) *ḥārîš* 'plowing, plowing-time' (2758 3x), cf. v.2790. (g) *qāṣîr* 'harvest, harvesting' (v.7105). '[There will be] yet five years where no plowing-and-harvesting' – put it in smooth Eng.

45:7 וַיִּשְׁלָחֵנִי אלהים לפניכם לָשׂוּם לָכֶם שְׁאֵרִית בָּאָרֶץ[1]—(a) §27.712. Gen. 45:5[3]. (d) *śûm*, v. 7760, here 'to establish,' BDB 963.3. (f) *š*^{e}*'ērîṯ* 'remnant, remainder' (v.7611). (g) To what does this refer?

וּלְהַחֲיוֹת לָכֶם לִפְלֵיטָה גְּדֹלָה׃[2]—(a) ־לְהַ does not > ־לָ when ה is the stem-indicator. BVG-30, v.2421. (c) *p*^{e}*lîṭā*^{h} 'escape, deliverance' (v.6413). RSV 'to keep alive for you many survivors' – evaluate.

45:8 וְעַתָּה לֹא־אַתֶּם שְׁלַחְתֶּם אֹתִי הֵנָּה כי האלהִים[1]—(a) Gen. 45:5[1]. (b-c) The position of לא stresses 'it was not *you* ... but *God*.' 'You did not send me' fails to bring this out. (d) תֶּם–: you should know it! (f) 45:5[2]. (g) After neg., 'but.' (h) Def. = 'the (true) God),' i.e. YHWH.

וַיְשִׂימֵנִי לְאָב לְפַרְעֹה וּלְאָדוֹן לְכָל־בֵּיתוֹ וּמֹשֵׁל בכל־ארץ מצרים׃[2]—(b) §27.713, Gen. 45:7[1]. Who is the subj.? (c) 'For a father.' (d) Gen. 37:36[2]. (e) *'ādôn* 'lord' (BVG-13). (f-g) Whose house? What does 'house' mean here? (h) *mšl* 'to rule, have dominion over' (v.4910), G50, followed by –ב.

45:9 מַהֲרוּ וַעֲלוּ אֶל־אָבִי וַאֲמַרְתֶּם אֵלָיו[1]—(a) Est. 5:5[1]. (b) What is the difference between וְעָלוּ and וַעֲלוּ? VDC–6 and –10. (d) Is there reason for using *'āḇî* rather than *'āḇînû?* (e) §32.543.

כֹּה אָמַר בִּנְךָ יוֹסֵף[2]—(a-b) The formula כֹּה אָמַר יְהוָה is used often in the prophets; here it is 'Thus says thy son.'

שָׂמַנִי אלהים לְאָדוֹן לכל־מצרים[3]—(a) CWC, G10s0, cf. 45:7[1], 8[2]. Who/what is the subj.? (d) 45:8[2].

רְדָה אֵלַי אַל־תַּעֲמֹד׃[4]—(a) *yrd*, Gen. 37:25[4]. §27.43. §29.322. §32.326. (d) *'md* 'to stand' (BVG-7), here 'to tarry, delay,' BDB 764.3c.

45:10 וְיָשַׁבְתָּ בְאֶרֶץ־גֹּשֶׁן וְהָיִיתָ קָרוֹב אֵלַי[1]—(a) Note pointing! וְ—ָ—ְ—ָתָּ should be c12 – but is it? of what verb? (c) Pr.n. 'Goshen.' Look it up! (d) Why no accent shift? §17.341. (e) BVG-11.

אַתָּה וּבָנֶיךָ וּבְנֵי בָנֶיךָ וְצֹאנְךָ וּבְקָרְךָ וְכָל־אֲשֶׁר־לָךְ׃[2]—You should be able to read this with little difficulty. (c-d) 'Grandsons.' (e) 'Small cattle, flocks' (BVG-65). (f) 'Large cattle, herds' (BVG-43).

Learn the words in BVG–70. At this point you should know at least half of the words in the Basic Vocabulary. Aim to learn the rest, until you can translate easily any word that occurs fifteen times or more (approximately 1,500 words).

טוֹב אַחֲרִית דָּבָר מֵרֵאשִׁיתוֹ
טוֹב אֶרֶךְ־רוּחַ מִגְּבַהּ רוּחַ׃

Better is the end of a matter than the beginning,
and the patient in spirit than the proud in spirit.

Ecclesiastes 7:8

Purpose: To prepare for the final examination
Materials: The work of the entire course

Use the following passage for review, with the help of the analytical notes.

וּלְכֹהֵן מִדְיָן שֶׁבַע בָּנוֹת וַתָּבֹאנָה וַתִּדְלֶנָה וַתְּמַלֶּאנָה אֶת־הָרְהָטִים לְהַשְׁקוֹת צֹאן אֲבִיהֶן׃ וַיָּבֹאוּ הָרֹעִים וַיְגָרְשׁוּם וַיָּקָם מֹשֶׁה וַיּוֹשִׁעָן וַיַּשְׁקְ אֶת־צֹאנָם׃ וַתָּבֹאנָה אֶל־רְעוּאֵל אֲבִיהֶן וַיֹּאמֶר מַדּוּעַ מִהַרְתֶּן בֹּא הַיּוֹם׃ וַתֹּאמַרְןָ אִישׁ מִצְרִי הִצִּילָנוּ מִיַּד הָרֹעִים וְגַם־דָּלֹה דָלָה לָנוּ וַיַּשְׁקְ אֶת־הַצֹּאן׃ וַיֹּאמֶר אֶל־בְּנֹתָיו וְאַיּוֹ לָמָּה זֶּה עֲזַבְתֶּן אֶת־הָאִישׁ קִרְאֶן לוֹ וְיֹאכַל לָחֶם׃

Answer these questions (number refers to line of text):
(1) *ûlᵉḵōhēn*: Does §16.31 apply? Abs. or cstr.? *miḏyān* is pr.n. (2) *ʾeṯ-hārᵉhāṭîm*: Is *ʾeṯ* the prep. or sign of obj.? Is there a def. art.? How would you locate this word in lexicon? (2) *ʾăḇîhen*: What pron. suf.? Antecedent? (3) *wayᵉgārᵉšûm*: To whom/what does pron.suf. refer? (3) *wayyôšíʿān*: To whom/what does pron.suf. refer? (3) *wayyašq*: In context is this Gc20 or Hc20? (5) *bōʾ*: How is this inf.cstr. used? (5) *hiṣṣîlā́nû*: To whom does the pron.suf. refer? How is it related to the verb? (7) *wᵉyôʾḵal*: In context how is the *wāw* used? What kind of clause is it?

Identify the verb-forms (= parse them) from the morphological patterns:
(1) *wattaCōʾnā* §27.117 §29.6315
(2) *wattaCᵉCénā* §27.31 §29.7122
(2) *lᵉhaCCôṯ* §28.31 §29.71
(2) *wattᵉCaC^{2}éʾnā* §28.21 §29.2211
(3) *wayᵉCāGᵉCûm* §13.411 §29.122 §29.711
(3) *wayyāCōC* §29.113
(3) *wayyôCîCān* §27.712 §29.311
(3) *wayyaCC* §13.5332 §29.721
(4) *CiGaCten* §28.21 §29.12
(5) *hiC^{2}CîCā́nû* §27.712 §28.31 §29.4
(6) *CāCô^h* §27.64 §29.71
(7) *GăCaCten* §27.221 §29.11
(7) *CiCʾen* §27.42 *Ges.* §47*f*
(7) *wᵉyôʾCaC* §29.212 (§27.117?)

Review noun morphology, using the following words:
(1) *kôhēn* §15.223 §24.23
(1) *šéḇaʿ* §15.431 §17.11 §24.211

(2) *rᵉhāṭîm* §15.611 §24.216 §24.211
(2) *ṣôʾn* §15.63
(2) *ʾāḇîhen* §24.121
(3) *rôʿîm* §24.23
(5) *yôm* §15.7212 §24.212
(5) *ʾîš* §24.12
(5) *miṣrî* §24.55
(5) *yaḏ* §24.12
(7) *lā́hem* §15.112 §15.131 §24.211

וַיְהִי בִּימֵי בִּלְקִיס מַלְכַּת־שְׁבָא וּשְׁלֹמֹה יוֹשֵׁב עַל־כִּסֵּא יְרוּשָׁלַיִם תַּחַת דָּוִד אָבִיו וּבִלְקִיס יְפַת־תֹּאַר וְטוֹבַת־מַרְאֶה׃ וַתִּסַּע בִּלְקִיס הַמַּלְכָּה לָלֶכֶת יְרוּשָׁלַיְמָה בְּחַיִל כָּבֵד מְאֹד וַתָּבֹא אֶל־הָעִיר׃ וַיֵּצֵא לִקְרַאת אֹתָהּ אִישׁ הָאֱלֹהִים וּשְׁמוֹ אֲחִיָּה הוּא נָבִיא יְהוָה׃ וַיֹּאמֶר אֵלֶיהָ לָמָּה בָאתְ הֵנָּה הָאִשָּׁה׃ וַתַּעַן אֵלָיו וַתֹּאמֶר שָׁמַעְתִּי אֶת־שֵׁמַע שְׁלֹמֹה הַמֶּלֶךְ וְלִלְמֹד עַל־מְקוֹר חָכְמָתוֹ בָּאתִי הֵנָּה׃ וַיֹּאמֶר אֲחִיָּה הַנָּבִיא הִנֵּה הַיָּמִים בָּאִים וַיָּקֶם יְהוָה גָּדוֹל מִשְּׁלֹמֹה וְחָכָם מִמֶּנּוּ וּמְלָכִים יָבֹאוּ מֵאַפְסֵי־אֶרֶץ וְיִשְׁתַּחֲווּ־לוֹ אַף־מַלְכֵי שְׁבָא וּסְבָא יַקְרִיבוּ מִנְחָה אֵלָיו׃ וְכִרְאוֹת בִּלְקִיס אֵת כָּל־חָכְמַת שְׁלֹמֹה וְהַבַּיִת אֲשֶׁר בָּנָה אָמְרָה אֵלָיו אֱמֶת הָיָה הַדָּבָר אֲשֶׁר שָׁמַעְתִּי בְּאַרְצִי וְהִנֵּה לֹא־הֻגַּד־לִי הַחֵצִי׃ וַיֶּאֱהַב שְׁלֹמֹה אֶת־בִּלְקִיס וַתָּשָׁב לְאַרְצָהּ וַתֵּלֶד בֵּן וַתִּקְרָא אֶת־שְׁמוֹ מְנָלִיךְ כִּי אָמְרָה לְקַחְתִּיו מִן־הַמֶּלֶךְ שְׁלֹמֹה׃

Proper names: מְנָלִיךְ, סְבָא, אֲחִיָּה, דָּוִד , יְרוּשָׁלַיִם , שְׁלֹמֹה, שְׁבָא, בִּלְקִיס.
Difficult words: אֶפֶס BVG 64; מִנְחָה BVG 63; נָסַע BVG 66; שֵׁמַע report; מָקוֹר source.

Don't bother trying to look up this passage. It is composed of bits from various portions of the Old Testament, plus some legendary details, cast in "biblical" form by me. If you have problems, parse the verbs, work out the clauses, and do it bit by bit. You *may* get a sight-translation in the final exam.

If you plan to take Hebrew seriously, continue to read the Hebrew Bible in increasingly larger portions. Work your way through the *Handbook* again–better still, teach it to someone else. כֹּל טוֹב וּבְרָכוֹת.

יְבָרֶכְךָ יהוה וְיִשְׁמְרֶךָ׃
יָאֵר יהוה פָּנָיו אֵלֶיךָ וִיחֻנֶּךָּ׃
יִשָּׂא יהוה פָּנָיו אֵלֶיךָ וְיָשֵׂם לְךָ שָׁלוֹם׃

May YHWH bless you and protect you.
May YHWH cause his face to shine on you and may he show you grace.
May YHWH lift his face to you and appoint for you wholeness.

Numbers 6:24-25

BASIC VOCABULARY GROUPS

These groups have been selected on the following bases: (1) The word occurs at least 40x in the OT; (2) It is in the current lesson or close thereby; (3) It is cognate with such a word; (4) It is similar in sound or meaning to such a word. By grouping cognates, the student is able to learn two or more words with little more effort than it takes to learn one word.

Basic Vocabulary Group–1 Lesson 4

–בְּ *bᵉ-* in, with, by
–הַ *ha-* the
הוּא *hû'* he, that; הִיא *hî'* she, that (1931)
הָיָה *hāyāʰ* he was (1961)
–וְ *wᵉ-* –וָ *wā-* and
יוֹם *yôm* day (3117); יוֹמָם *yômām* daily (3119)
מָלַךְ *mālak̲* he ruled (4427); מַלְכוּת *malk̲ût̲* kingdom (4438)
מֶלֶךְ *mélek̲* king (4428); מַלְכָּה *malkāʰ* queen (4436)
מִן *min* from (4480)
עַד *ʿad̲* up to, until (5704)

Basic Vocabulary Group–2 Lesson 5

הֵמָּה *hémmāʰ* הֵם *hēm* they (m., 1992); הֵנָּה *hénnāʰ* הֵן *hēn* they (f., 2004)
יָשַׁב *yāšab̲* he sat (3427)
מוֹשָׁב *môšab̲* seat, dwelling-place (4186)
עַל *ʿal* upon, unto (5921);
מַעַל *máʿal* upwards (4605)
עֶלְיוֹן *ʿelyôn* highest (5945)
מַעֲלָה *maʿălāʰ ascent, stairs (4609)*
שֶׁבַע *šébaʿ* N he swore, sevened himself (7650)
שְׁבִיעִי *šᵉb̲îʿî* 7th (7637); שִׁבְעִים *šib̲ʿîm* 70 (7657)

Basic Vocabulary Group–3 Lesson 6

דִּין *dîn* דּוּן *dûn* he judged (1777); דִּין *dîn* legal case, judgment (1779)
–כְּ *kᵉ-* as, like
כִּסֵּא *kissēʾ* throne, seat of honor (3678)
מֵאָה *mēʾāʰ* 100 (3967); מָאתַיִם *māʾt̲áyim* 200
מְדִינָה *mᵉd̲înāʰ* province (4082)
עָלָה *ʿālāʰ* he climbed, it went up (5927); עֹלָה *ʿôlāʰ* whole burnt offering (5930)
עֶשֶׂר *ʿéśer* עֲשָׂרָה *ʿăśārāʰ* 10 (6235)
עָשָׂר *ʿāśār* עֶשְׂרֵה *ʿeśrēʰ* -teen (6235-b)
עֲשִׂירִי *ʿăśîrî* 10th (6224); עֶשְׂרִים *ʿeśrîm* 20 (6242)
שָׁנָה *šānāʰ* pl. שָׁנִים *šānîm* year (8141)

Basic Vocabulary Group–4 Lesson7

אֲשֶׁר *'ăšer* which, that (834)
וֹ– *-ô* הוּ– *-hû* his, him; הָ– *-āh* הָ– *-hā* her
כֹּל *kōl* all, every, each (3606); כָּלִיל *kālîl* entire, whole (3632)
לְ– *le*- to, for, in regard to
מִשְׁתֶּה *mištêh* feast, drink (4961); שָׁתָה *šāṯāh* he drank (8534)
עָשָׂה *'āśāh* he did, made (6213); מַעֲשֶׂה *ma'ăśêh* deed, work (4639)
מַעֲשֵׂר *ma'ăśēr* tithe, tenth (4643); עָשׂוֹר *'āśôr* 10, decade (6218)
עִשָּׂרוֹן *'iśśārôn* 1/10 ephah (6241)

Basic Vocabulary Group–5 Lesson 8

אֵת *'ēṯ,* אֶת־ *'eṯ,* אֹת– *'ōṯ-* sign of def. dir. obj. (857)
גָּדוֹל *gāḏôl* great (1419); גָּדַל *gāḏal* he was strong (1431); מִגְדָּל *migdāl* tower (4026)
חַיִל *ḥáyil* power, wealth, army (2428)
יָקָר *yāqār* rare, precious (3368)
מָצָא *māṣā'* he found (4672)
עַם *'am* people (5971)
לִפְנֵי *lip̄nê* before (6440)
רָאָה *rā'āh* he saw (7200; מַרְאֶה *mar'êh* sight, appearance (4758)
רַב *raḇ* many, great, chief (7227); רַבָּה *rabbāh* great; רָבָה *rāḇāh* he became great (7235)

Basic Vocabulary Group–6 Lesson 9

אֵלֶּה *'ēllêh* these (428)
חָצֵר *ḥāṣēr* court, enclosure (2691)
כָּבוֹד *kāḇôḏ* might, glory, honor (3519); כָּבֵד *kāḇēḏ* to be heavy (3513); heavy (3515)
מָלֵא *mālē'* to be full (4390), full (4392); מְלֹא *melô'* fulness (4393)
עֹשֶׁר *'ōšer* riches (6239)
קָטָן *qāṭān* small (6996); קָטֹן *qāṭōn* small (6994)
שְׁמֹנֶה *šemônêh* 8 (8083); שְׁמֹנִים *šemônîm* 80 (8084); שְׁמִינִי *šemînî* 8th (8066)
תִּפְאֶרֶת *tip̄'ereṯ* beauty, glory (8597)

Basic Vocabulary Group–7 Lesson 10

אָחַז *'āḥaz* he held, seized (270); אֲחֻזָּה *'ăḥuzzāh* possession (272)
אַרְגָּמָן *'argāmān* purple (713)
זָהָב *zāhāḇ* gold (2091)
חֶבֶל *ḥéḇel* cord, rope (2256); כֶּסֶף *késep̄* silver, money (3701)
נָטָה *nāṭāh* he stretched out (5186); מַטֶּה *maṭṭêh* staff, rod (4294)
עָמַד *'āmaḏ* he stood (5975); עַמּוּד *'ammûḏ* pillar, column (5982)
שֵׁשׁ *šēš* byssus, fine linen (8336)
כְּלִי *kelî* vessel (3627); כְּלָיוֹת *kelāyôṯ* kidneys (3629)

Basic Vocabulary Group–8 Lesson 11

אַיִן *'áyin,* אֵין *'ên* there is/was not, nonexistence of (369)
אִישׁ *'îš* man, male, husband (376); אִשָּׁה *'iššā^{h}* woman, wife (802)
בַּיִת *báyit̲* house (1004)
גַּן *gan* garden, enclosure (1588)
יָד *yād̲* hand (3027); יָדָה *yād̲ā^{h}* (H) to give thanks (3034)
יַיִן *yáyin* wine (3196)
יָסַד *yāsad̲* he established, founded (3245)
כִּי *kî* that, for, when, because (3588); כִּי אִם *kî 'im* except
כֵּן *kēn* thus, so (3651); לָכֵן *lāk̲ēn* therefore

Basic Vocabulary Group–9 Lesson 14

אָמַר *'āmar* he said (559); אֹמֶר *'ōmer* word, saying (561)
גַּם *gam* also, together with (1571)
טוֹב *ṭôb̲* he was good, pleasant (2895), good (2896); טוֹבָה *ṭôb̲ā^{h}* good (things), well-being
לֵב *lēb̲* heart, mind, will (3820); לֵבָב *lēb̲āb̲* heart, mind, will (3824)
נָשִׁים *nāšîm* women (802); אֲנָשִׁים *'ănāšîm* men (582)
סָרִיס *sārîs* eunuch (5631)
פָּנִים *pānîm* face (6440); פָּנָה *pānā^{h}* he turned, faced (6437)
רָצוֹן *rāṣôn* good will, favor (7522); רָצָה *rāṣā^{h}* he was pleased with, accepted (7521)
שָׁקָה *šāqā^{h}* (H) to water, give to drink (8248)

Basic Vocabulary Group–10 Lesson 15

בּוֹא *bô'* to enter (935); תְּבוּאָה *t^{e}b̲û'ā^{h}* income, product (8393)
דָּבָר *dāb̲ār* word, thing (1697); דָּבַר *dāb̲ar* (d) to speak (1696)
חָכָם *ḥāk̲ām* wise, skillful, clever (2450); חָכְמָה *ḥok̲mā^{h}* wisdom, experience (2451)
חֵמָה *ḥēmā^{h}* heat, rage, poison (2534)
יָפֶה *yāp̄ê^{h}* beautiful, fair (3303)
מְאֹד *m^{e}'ōd̲* very, exceedingly (3966)
מָאֵן *mā'ēn* (D) to refuse (3985)
קָצַף *qāṣap̄* he was angry, wroth (7107)
שָׁרַת *šārat̲* (D) to minister, serve (8334)

Basic Vocabulary Group–11 Lesson 16

אֶל *'el,* אֶל־ *'el* to, towards (413); אֵל *'ēl* God, god (410)
בָּעַר *bā'ar* it burned (1197)
יָדַע *yād̲a'* he knew (3045); דַּעַת *dá'at̲* knowledge (1847)
מַדּוּעַ *maddû^{a}'* why? (4069)
לֹא *lô',* לוֹא *lô'* not, no (3808)
מַה *ma^{h}* what? (4100); לָמָה *lấmā^{h}* for what reason? why?
עֵת *'ēt̲* time (6256); עַתָּה *'attā^{h}* now (6258)
קָרוֹב *qārôb̲* near (7138); קָרַב *qārab̲* he came near (7126)
קֶרֶב *qéreb̲* midst, inward part (7130); קָרְבָּן *qorbān* offering (7133)

Basic Vocabulary Group–12 Lesson 17

בָּזָה *bāzā*[h] he despised (959)
בַּעַל *báʻal* lord, owner, husband (1167)
דַּי *day* enough (1767)
זֶה *zê*[h] this (m.) (2088); זֹאת *zôʼt* this (f.) (2063)
יָצָא *yāṣāʼ* he went/came out, exited (3318)
לְבַד– *l*[e]*badd-* alone (+ pron. suf.) (905)
עָוֹן *ʻāwôn* iniquity, guilt, punishment (5771)
עַיִן *ʻáyin* eye, spring (5869)
רִאשׁוֹן *riʼšôn* former, first (7223); רֹאשׁ *rôʼš* head (7218); רֵאשִׁית *rēʼšît* beginning (7225)
שָׁמַע *šāmaʻ* he heard (8085)

Basic Vocabulary Group–13 Lesson 18

אֶבֶן *ʼében* stone, gem, weight (69)
אָדוֹן *ʼādôn* lord, master (113); אֲדֹנָי *ʼădônāy* (my) Lord אִם *ʼim* if (518)
כָּתַב *kātab* he wrote (3789)
נָתַן *nātan* he gave, put, determined (5414)
עָבַר *ʻābar* he passed over/through/by (5674); עֵבֶר *ʻéber* region across/beyond (5676)
עוֹלָם *ʻôlām* long duration, eternity (5769); בַּעֲבוּר *baʻăbûr* for, because of (5668)
רֵעַ *rē*[a]*ʻ* friend, companion (7453); רָעָה *rāʻā*[h] **he tended, pastured, grazed (7462)**
שָׂרַף *śārap̄* he/it burned (8313)

Basic Vocabulary Group–14 Lesson 19

יָטַב *yāṭab* it goes well with, (H) to do good to (3190)
יָרֵא *yārēʼ* he was afraid, feared, was in awe (3372); יִרְאָה *yirʼê*[h] reverence, fear (3374)
כְּסִיל *k*[e]*sîl* stupid, dull, fool (3684)
לָשׁוֹן *lāšôn* tongue (3956);
סָפַר *sāp̄ar* he counted, (D) to recount, tell (5608); סֵפֶר *sép̄er* writing, document (5612)
מִסְפָּר *mispār* number (4557)
פָּלַל *pālal* (HtD) to intercede, pray (6419); תְּפִלָּה *t*[e]*p̄illā*[h] prayer (8605)
קוֹל *qôl* voice, sound (6963)
שָׁלַח *šālaḥ* he sent, stretched out (hand) (7971)
שָׂבַע *śābaʻ* he was satisfied, sated (7646)

Basic Vocabulary Group- 15 Lesson 20

אָח *ʼaḥ* brother (251); אָחוֹת *ʼāḥôt* sister (269)
אֵשׁ *ʼēš* fire (784)
דֶּרֶךְ *dérek* way, road, manner (1870); דָּרַךְ *dārak* he marched, trod (1869)
הָלַךְ *hālak* he walked, came, went (1980)
הִנֵּה *hinnê*[h], הֵן *hēn* behold! (2009)
הַר *har* mountain (2022)
יַחַד *yáḥad* together in unison (3162); יַחְדָּו *yaḥdāw* together (3162)
יָסַר *yāsar* he admonished, disciplined; (D) to establish (3256)
מוּסָר *mûsār* chastening (4148)
מָאַס *māʼas* he rejected, refused (3988)

אַחַר *'aḥar,* אַחֲרֵי *'aḥărê* after (310); אָחוֹר *'āḥôr* the back part (268)
אַחֲרוֹן *'aḥărôn* last, latter, afterward (314); אַחֲרִית *'aḥărîṯ* end, latter time, posterity (319)
בִּקֵּשׁ *biqqēš* (D) he sought (1245)
בְּתוּלָה *bᵉṯûlāʰ* unmarried woman, virgin (1330)
דָּם *dām* blood; pl. shed blood (1818)
זָכַר *zāḵar* he remembered (2142)
נַעַר *náʿar* boy, youth, servant (5288); נַעֲרָה *naʿărāʰ* girl, damsel (5291)
נְעוּרִים *nᵉʿûrîm* youth, early life (5271)
פָּקַד *pāqaḏ* he visited, observed, mustered (*see* 6485)
פְּקֻדָּה *pᵉquddāʰ* oversight, visitation (6486)

Basic Vocabulary Group–17 Lesson 22

אוֹ *'ô* or, or if, except (176)
אַךְ *'āḵ* surely (389)
עֵד *ʿēḏ* witness, evidence (5707); עֵדוֹת *ʿēḏôṯ* testimonies (5713)
עֵדֻת, עֵדוּת *ʿēḏûṯ* testimony (5717)
עוּד *ʿûḏ* H to admonish, bear witness (5749)
עֵדָה *ʿēḏāʰ* congregation (5712); מוֹעֵד *môʿēḏ* place of meeting (4150)
שָׁמַר *šāmar* he kept, watched, preserved (8104)
מִשְׁמֶרֶת *mišméreṯ* guard, charge (4931)
קָבַץ *qāḇaṣ* he gathered, collected (6908)
תַּחַת *táḥaṯ* under, below, succeeding (8478)
קֶצֶף *qéṣep̄* wrath (7110)

Basic Vocabulary Group–18 Lesson 23

בֵּן *bēn* son, member of a group (1121); בַּת *baṯ* (< **bint*) daughter (1323)
בָּנָה *bānāʰ* he built (1129)
גָּלָה *gālāʰ* he uncovered, revealed, went into exile
גּוֹלָה *gôlāʰ* exile (1473)
יָמִין *yāmîn* right (hand/side), south (3225)
שְׂמֹאל *śᵉmōʾl* left (hand/side), north (8040)
עִם *ʿim* with (5973)
עֻמָּה *ʿummāʰ* close by, parallel to, agreeing with (5980)
שֵׁם *šēm* name (8034)
שָׁמֵם *šāmēm* he was desolated, appalled (8074)
שְׁמָמָה *šᵉmāmāʰ* devastation, waste (8077)

Basic Vocabulary Group–19 Lesson 24

אָב *ʾāḇ* father, ancestor (1); אֵם *ʾēm* mother (517)
אָבָה *ʾāḇāʰ* he was willing, consented (14)
אָמַן *ʾāman* he endured; H to trust, believe (539); אָמֵן *ʾāmēn* surely, Amen! (543)
אֱמוּנָה *ʾĕmûnāʰ* faithfulness (530)
אֱמֶת *ʾĕmeṯ* (< **ʾĕment*) faithfulness, truth (5710)
דּוֹד *dôḏ* beloved, uncle (f. aunt) (1730)
לָקַח *lāqaḥ* he took, received (3947)
מוּת *mûṯ* to die (4191); מָוֶת *máweṯ* death (4194)
אֹרַח *ʾōraḥ* way, path, traveler (734)
אֹרֶךְ *ʾōreḵ* length (753)
אָרַךְ *ʾāraḵ* it was long, H to lengthen (748)

Basic Vocabulary Group–20 Lesson 25

בָּהַל *bāhal* N to be disturbed, D to hasten, terrify (926)
חֶסֶד *ḥésed* kindness, covenant loyalty/love (2618)
חָסִיד *ḥāsîd* loyal/pious one (2623)
יֶלֶד *yéled* boy, (f) girl; child (3206 ; יָלַד *yālad* G11 she bore; H to beget (3205)
מוֹלֶדֶת *môlédet* kindred (4137); תּוֹלְדוֹת *tôlᵉdôt* generations, history (8435)
נֶגֶד *néged* in front of, opposite (5048);' נָגִיד *nāgîd* leader, prince (5057)
נָגַד *nāgad* H to proclaim, declare (5046)
נָשָׂא *nāśā᾽* he lifted, carried (5375); נָשִׂיא *nāśî᾽* chief, prince (5387)
מַשָּׂא *maśśā᾽* load, burden (4853)
צִוָּה *ṣiwwāʰ* D he charged, commanded; מִצְוָה *miṣwāʰ*commandment (4687)

Basic Vocabulary Group–21 Lesson 27

בֶּשֶׂם *béśem,* בֹּשֶׂם *bōśem* spice, balsam (1314)
חֹדֶשׁ *ḥōdeš* new moon, month (2320); חָדָשׁ *ḥādāš* new, rcent, fresh (2319)
מַר *mar(r)* bitter/-ness (4751)
נָגַע *nāgaᶜ* he touched, reached, struck (5060) ; נֶגַע *négaᶜ* stroke, plague, mak (5061)
קֵץ *qēṣ* end, extremity (7093); קָצֶה *qāṣêʰ* end, extremity (7097)
שָׁלוֹם *šālôm* welfare, completeness, peace (7965)
שֶׁלֶם *šélem* pl. peace-offering (8002)
שָׁלֵם *šālēm* he was complete, sound (7999)
שֶׁמֶן *šémen* fat, oil, olive oil (8081)
שֵׁשׁ *šēš,* שִׁשָּׁה *šiššāʰ* six (8337); שִׁשִּׁים *šiššîm* sixty

Basic Vocabulary Group–22 Lesson 28

בֹּקֶר *bōqer* morning (1242)
חֵן *ḥēn* favor, grace, charm (2580); חִנָּם *ḥinnām* for nothing, in vain (2600)
חָנַן *ḥānan* he was gracious (2603); תְּחִנָּה *tᵉḥinnāʰ* favor, supplication (8467)
חָפֵץ *ḥāpēṣ* he delighted in, desired (2654)
חֵפֶץ *ḥēpeṣ* delight, pleasure (2656)
עֶרֶב *ᶜéreb* evening (6153)
עֲרָבָה *ᶜărābāʰ* desert-plain, Arabah (6160)
פִּילֶגֶשׁ *pîlégeš* concubine (6370)
שְׁנַיִם *šnáyim,* שְׁתַּיִם *štáyim* two (8147)
שֵׁנִי *šēnî* second (8145)
מִשְׁנֶה *mišnêʰ* double, copy, second (4932

Basic Vocabulary Group–23 Lesson 29

אָהֵב *᾽āhēb* he loved (157)
אַהֲבָה *᾽ahăbāʰ* love (160)
יָעַץ *yāᶜaṣ* he advised, N to counsel together (3289); עֵצָה *ᶜēṣāʰ* counsel, advice (6098)
עוֹד *ᶜôd* still, yet, again (5750)
עַד *ᶜad,* וָעֶד *wāᶜed* forever (5704)
פַּעַם *páᶜam* time, occurrence (6471)
קָרָא *qārā᾽* he called, named (7121);
קָרָה *qārāʰ* he met, it befell (7136)
שׁוּב *šûb* to turn back, return (7725)
שׂוּם *śûm,* שִׂים *śîm* to put, set, place, appoint (7760)
תֵּשַׁע *tēšaᶜ,* תִּשְׁעָה *tišᶜāʰ* nine (8672)

Basic Vocabulary Group–24 Lesson 30

אֶדֶן *ʾéden* base, pedestal (134)
אֹהֶל *ʾōhel* tent, dwelling (168)
אוֹת *ʾôṯ* sign, symbol, miracle (226, cf. #853)
אֵת *ʾēṯ*, –אִתּ *ʾitt-* with (854, cf. #853)
בָּמָה *bāmāʰ* high place (1116)
חֹק *ḥōq*, –חֻק *ḥuqq-* statute, decree (2706)
חֻקָּה *ḥuqqāʰ* statute (2708)
פֹּעַל *pṓʿal* deed, work (6467); פָּעַל *pāʿal* he did, made (6466)
שַׁעַר *šáʿar* gate (8179); שֹׁעֵר *šôʿēr* porter, door-tender (7778)
תָּלָה *tālāʰ* he hanged (8518)

Baasic Vocabulary Group–25 Lesson 31

אוּלַי *ʾûlay* if, perhaps (194)
אָז *ʾāz* then (227)
אֹזֶן *ʾōzen* ear (241); אָזַן *ʾāzan* H to give ear, hear (238)
אָרוֹן *ʾārôn* ark (of covenant) (727)
הָלַל *hālal* D to praise, HtD to boast (1984)
תְּהִלָּה *tᵉhillāʰ* (song of) praise (8416)
מָגֵן *māḡēn* shield, buckler (4043)
נֶגֶב *néḡeḇ* southland, Negev (5045)
עֵץ *ʿēṣ* tree, pl. pieces/articles of wood (6086)
שֵׁן *šēn* tooth, ivory (8127)

Basic Vocabulary Group–26 Lesson 32

אַתָּה *ʾattāʰ* you (m.s.) (859); אַתֶּם *ʾattem* you (m.p.) (859)
אַתְּ *ʾatt* you (f.s.) (859)
זָבַח *zāḇaḥ* he slaughtered, sacrificed (2076)
זֶבַח *zéḇaḥ* sacrifice (2077)
מִזְבֵּחַ *mizbēᵃḥ* altar (place of sacrifice) (4196)
חָוָה *ḥāwāʰ* HtŠ to prostrate self, worship (7817)
חָנָה *ḥānāʰ* he encamped, retired (2853)
מַחֲנֶה *maḥănêʰ* camp (4264)
כָּרַע *kāraʿ* He bowed/knelt down (3766)
שָׁכַן *šāḵan* he settled down, dwelt (7931); מִשְׁכָּן *miškān* dwelling-place, tabernacle (4948)

Basic Vocabulary Group–27 Lesson 33

אָסַר *ʾāsar* he bound, imprisoned (631)
אֵצֶל *ʾēṣel* beside (681)
–הֲ *hă-* interrogative particle (cf. §22.3ff.)
יָשָׁר *yāšār* straight, right, just (3477)
צָפוֹן *ṣāp̄ôn* north (6828)
קָבַר *qāḇar* he buried (69120; קֶבֶר *qéḇer* grave (6913)
שָׁכַב *šāḵaḇ* he lay down (7901)
מִשְׁכָּב *miškāḇ* place/act of lying down, couch (4904)
שֻׁלְחָן *šulḥān* table (7979)
שָׁמַד *šāmaḏ* N to be exterminated; H to annihilate, destroy (8045)

Basic Vocabulary Group–28 Lesson 34

אֶחָד *ʾeḥāḏ* one (259)
אַחֵר *ʾāḥēr* other, another, different (312)
אֵפוֹד *ʾēp̄ôḏ* Ephod (worn by priest) (646)
בִּין *bîn* to discern, perceive (995)
בִּינָה *bînāʰ* understanding (998); תְּבוּנָה *tᵉḇûnāʰ* understanding (8394)
בֵּין *bên* between (996)
גּוֹרָל *gôrāl* lot, portion (1486)
יֵשׁ *yēš* there is/are (3426)
נָפַל *nāp̄al* he fell, lay (5307)
נָוֶה *nāwêʰ* abode of shepherd/sheep (5116)
נוּחַ *nûaḥ* to rest (5117)

Basic Vocabulary Group–29 Lesson 35

אֶלֶף *ʾélep̄* thousand (504)
אַלּוּף *ʾallûp̄* chief, chiliarch (441)
טַבַּעַת *ṭabbáʿaṯ* signet-ring, seal (2885)
כִּכָּר *kikkār* talent, round weight (3603)
מַלְאָךְ *malʾāḵ* messenger, angel (4379)
מְלָאכָה *mᵉlāʾḵāʰ* work, business (4399)
סוּר *sûr* to turn aside, H to take away (5490)
צַר *ṣar(r)* adversary, foe (6862); צָרַר *ṣārar* he was hostile toward (6887)
צָרָר *ṣārār* distress (6869)
שֶׁקֶל *šéqel* (a weight) (8255)
מִשְׁקָל *mišqāl* weight (4948)

Basic Vocabulary Group–30 Lesson 36

אָבַד *ʾāḇad* he perished, was lost (7)
בָּזַז *bāzaz* he took as plunder (962)
הָרַג *hāraḡ* he killed (2026)
זָקֵן *zāqēn* old (man), elder (2205)
חָיָה *ḥāyāʰ* he lived, was alive (2421); חַי *ḥay(y)* alive (2416)
חַיָּה *ḥayyāʰ* animal, beast (2416); חַיִּים *ḥayyîm* life (2416)
טַף *ṭap(p)* little children (coll.) (2945)
עָזַב *ʿāzaḇ* he left, forsook (5860)
רוּץ *rûṣ* to run (7323)
שָׁלָל *šālāl* plundered, plunder, booty (7998)
תָּעָה *tāʿāʰ* he erred, wandered about (8582)

Basic Vocabulary Group–31 Lesson 37

יָבֵשׁ *yāḇēš* it was dried up (3001)
יָרָה *yārāʰ* he threw; H to teach (3884)
תּוֹרָה *tôrāʰ* Torah, instruction, law (8451)
יָתַר *yāṯar* it remained, was left over (3498); יֶתֶר *yéṯer* remainder, excess (3499)
כֹּחַ *kōaḥ* strength, power (3581)
כָּנָף *kānāp̄* wing, extremity (3671)
כָּתֵף *kāṯēp̄* shoulder (-blade), side (3802)
עִיר *ʿîr* town, city (5892)
קָוָה *qāwāʰ* he waited for (6960)
תִּקְוָה *tiqwêʰ* hope (8615)

Basic Vocabulary Group–32 Lesson 38

אָבַל *ʾāḇal* he mourned, lamented (56)
בֶּגֶד *béḡeḏ* garment (899)
בָּגַד *bāḡaḏ* he acted treacherously (898)
בָּכָה *bāḵā*^{h} he wept (1058); בְּכִי *b*^{e}*ḵî* weeping (1065)
זָעַק *zāʿaq* he cried (out), called (2199)
צָעַק *ṣāʿaq* he cried (out), called (6817)
לָבֵשׁ *lāḇēš* he put on clothing (3847); לְבוּשׁ *l*^{e}*ḇûš* clothing (3830)
סָפַד *sāp̄aḏ* he wailed, lamented (5594)
קָרַע *qāraʿ* he tore, rent (7167)
שַׂק *śaq(q)* sackcloth (8242)

Basic Vocabulary Group–33 Lesson 39

אָשָׁם *ʾāšām* guilt, guilt-offering (817)
חוּל *ḥûl,* חִיל *ḥîl* he twisted, writhed, danced (2342)
חֵיק *ḥêq,* חֵק *ḥêq* bosom (2436)
צָלַח *ṣālaḥ,* צָלֵחַ *ṣālē*^{a}*ḥ* he advanced, prospered (6743)
קוּם *qûm* to arise, stand (6965)
מָקוֹם *māqôm* (standing-) place (4725); קוֹמָה *qômā*^{h} height (6667)
רֹחַב *rṓḥaḇ* breadth, width (7341)
רְחוֹב *r*^{e}*ḥôḇ* open place, plaza, street (7339)
רַק *raq* only, surely (7535)
תָּוֶךְ *táweḵ,* תּוֹךְ *tôḵ* midst (8432)

Basic Vocabulary Group–34 Lesson 41

בָּטַח *bāṭaḥ* he trusted, was secure (982); בֶּטַח *béṭaḥ* security, securely (983)
לֶחֶם *léḥem* bread, food (3899)
לָחַם *lāḥam* N to fight, do battle (3898); מִלְחָמָה *milḥāmā*^{h} fight, battle, war (4421)
רָדַף *rāḏap̄* he pursued, chased, persecuted (7291)
רִיב *rîḇ* to strive, contend, conduct a law-suit (7378)
רִיב *rîḇ* strife, dispute, law-suit (7379)
שׁוֹר *šôr* a head of cattle, ox, bullock (7794)
שֶׂה *śê*^{h} a sheep/goat (7716)
שָׂכַל *śāḵal* he was prudent; H to ponder, prosper (7919)
שָׂפָה *śāp̄āh*^{h} lip, shore, speech (8193)

Basic Vocabulary Group–35 Lesson 42

אַל *ʾal* not (408)
אַלְמָנָה *ʾalmānā*^{h} widow (490)
אֲנִי *ʾănî* I (589); אָנֹכִי *ʾânôḵî* I (595)
אֲרִי *ʾărî;* אַרְיֵה *ʾaryē*^{h} lion (738)
בַּל *bal* not, nothing (1077); בְּלִי *b*^{e}*lî* not, without (1097)
דָּמָה *dāmā*^{h} he resembled, was like; D to liken, imagine (1819)
דָּמַם *dāmam* he was still, motionless, dumb (1826)
מָלַט *mālaṭ* N to slip away, escape; D to let escape, deliver (4422)
נֶפֶשׁ *népeš* soul, person, self (5315)
פְּנִימִי *p*^{e}*nîmî* inner (6442)

Basic Vocabulary Group–36 — Lesson 43

אָכַל *ʾāḵal* he ate, fed (398); אֹכֶל *ʾōḵel* food (400)
מַאֲכָל *maʾăḵāl* food (3978)
בּוֹשׁ *bôš* to be ashamed; H to shame (954)
בִּלְתִּי *biltî* only, beside, except;
לְבִלְתִּי *l^{e}ḇiltî* so as not to, in order not to (1115)
בְּעַד *b^{e}ʿaḏ,* בַּעַד *báʿaḏ* away from, behind, about, in behalf of (1157)
חָרַשׁ *ḥāraš* H to be silent, dumb (2790 < *ḫrš, Arab. *ḫarasa*)
חָרָשׁ *ḥārāš* artisan, engraver, artificer (2796 < *ḥrθ Arab. *ḥaraṯa*)
כַּאֲשֶׁר *kaʾăšer* according as, in so far as, when
לַיְלָה *láylā^{h},* לַיִל *láyil* night, at night (3915)
מִי *mî* who? (4310)

Basic Vocabulary Group–37 — Lesson 44

גָּאַל *gāʾal* he redeemed, acted as kinsman (1350)
גְּבוּל *g^{e}ḇûl* border, boundary (1366)
גּוּר *gûr* to sojourn, dwell; גֵּר *gēr* stranger, sojourner (1616)
דָּבַק *dāḇaq* he kept close/clung to (1692)
דְּבַשׁ *d^{e}ḇaš* honey (1706)
דֶּלֶת *délet* door (1817)
חוֹמָה *ḥômā^{h}* wall (of city) (2346)
נֹכַח *nōḵaḥ* in front of (5227)
פָּתַח *pāṯaḥ* he opened (6605); פֶּתַח *péṯaḥ* opening, doorway (6607)
שָׁמַיִם *šāmáyim* heaven(s), sky (8064)

Basic Vocabulary Group–38 — Lesson 45

אוֹר *ʾôr* light, luminary (216)
אוֹר *ʾôr* to be/become light., H to give light, cause to shine (215)
אֱלוֹהַּ *ʾĕlô^{a}h* God, god (433); אֱלֹהִים *ʾĕlôhîm* God, gods, judges, angels (430)
אֶרֶץ *ʾéreṣ* earth, land, country (776)
אֶרֶז *ʾérez* cedar (730)
בָּדַל *bāḏal* H to divide, separate; N to separate, withdraw (914)
בָּרָא *bārāʾ* he created, fashioned (1254)
חֹשֶׁךְ *ḥōšeḵ* darkness (2822)
רוּחַ *rû^{a}ḥ* breath, wind, spirit (7307); רֵיחַ *rê^{a}ḥ* scent, odor (7381)
רוּעַ *rû^{a}ʿ* H to raise a shout, give a blast on horn (7321)
תְּרוּעָה *t^{e}rûʿā^{h}* shout of war/alarm/joy (8643)

Basic Vocabulary Group–39 — Lesson 46

בְּהֵמָה *b^{e}hēmā^{h}* animal, beast, cattle (999)
בָּחַר *bāḥar* he chose, tested (977); בָּחוּר *bāḥûr* young man (970)
בָּקַע *bāqaʿ* he cleft, split, broke open (1234)
זוּר *zûr* to be a stranger, G50 stranger (2114)
חֲצִי *ḥăṣî,* חֵצִי *ḥēṣî* half, middle (2677); חֵץ *ḥēṣ* arrow (2071)
יָכַח *yāḵaḥ* H to judge, convict, reprove, rebuke (3198)
לוּן *lûn,* לִין *lîn* to lodge, pass the night (3885)
מָהַר *māhar* D to hasten (4116)
שָׁאַל *šāʾal* he asked, inquired, asked for (7592)
שְׁאוֹל *š^{e}ʾôl* Sheol, underworld (7585)

Basic Vocabulary Group–40 Lesson 47

אָדָם *ʾāḏām* man, mankind (120); אֲדָמָה *ʾăḏāmāʰ* ground, land, earth (127)
בַּרְזֶל *barzel* iron (1270)
גִּבְעָה *giḇʿāʰ* hill (1398)
גֶּפֶן *gép̄en* vine (1612)
מָחָר *māḥār* tomorrow (4279); מָחֳרָת *moḥŏrāṯ* on the morrow (4283)
עָנָה *ʿānāʰ* he answered (6030)
עָנָה *ʿānāʰ* he was afflicted, bowed down (6031)
עֳנִי *ʿŏnî* affliction, poverty; עָנִי *ʿānî* poor, afflicted, weak (6041)
שָׂמַח *śāmaḥ* he rejoiced; D to gladden (8055)
שִׂמְחָה *śimḥāʰ* gladness, mirth, joy (8037)

Basic Vocabulary Group–41 Lesson 48

אַף *ʾap̄* also (637); אַף *ʾap̄* (< *ʾnp) nose, anger (639)
חָרֵב *ḥāreḇ* it was dry/dried up; H to dry up (tr.) (351)
חֵלֶב *ḥēleḇ* fat, choice (2459); חָלָב *ḥālāḇ* milk (2461)
חָלָה *ḥālāʰ* he became weak, was sick (2470)
חָלָל *ḥālāl* pierced, slain (2491)
עָמָל *ʿāmāl* labor, toil (5999)
יָחַל *yāḥal* N, D, H to wait, await (5176)
רָעָב *rāʿāḇ* famine, hunger (7858)
רָשָׁע *rāšāʿ* wicked, criminal (7563); רֶשַׁע *réšaʿ* wickedness (7562)

Basic Vocabulary Group–42 Lesson 49

אָמָה *ʾāmāʰ* handmaid (519)
אַמָּה *ʾammāʰ* forearm, cubit (length of forearm) (520)
גָּבַהּ *gāḇah* he/it was high, exalted (1361); גָּבֹהַּ *gāḇôᵃh* high, tall, proud (1364)
חָמָס *ḥāmās* violence, wrong (2555)
חָמֵשׁ *ḥāmēš*, חֲמִשָּׁה *ḥămiššāʰ* 5 (2568); חֲמִישִׁי *ḥămîšî* 5th (2549)
חֲמִשִּׁים *ḥămiššîm* 50 (2572)
לָכַד *lāḵaḏ* he captured, seized, took (3920)
קֹדֶשׁ *qōḏeš* sacredness, holiness (6944)
קָדַשׁ *qāḏaš* N to set apart, consecrate; H to sanctify (6942)
רָחַץ *rāḥaṣ* he washed, bathed (7364)

Basic Vocabulary Group–43 Lesson 50

בָּקָר *bāqār* herd, large cattle (1241)
בָּרַח *bāraḥ* he passed through, fled; H he chased (1272)
חָזָה *ḥāzāʰ* he saw, beheld (2372); חָזוֹן *ḥāzôn* vision, sight (2377)
חֶרֶב *ḥéreḇ* sword (2719)
כֹּהֵן *kôhēn* priest (3548)
כּוּן *kûn* it was established/proper/fixed; H to establish (3559)
מַמְלָכָה *mamlāḵāʰ* dominion, kingdom (4467)
נָבָא *nāḇāʾ* N to prophesy; HtD to act as a prophet (5012); נָבִיא *nāḇîʾ* prophet (5030)
שָׁם *šām* there, thither (8033)
קָדוֹשׁ *qāḏôš* sacred, holy (6918); מִקְדָּשׁ *miqdāš* sanctuary (4724)

Basic Vocabulary Group–44 — Lesson 51

חוּץ *ḥûṣ* outside, abroad (2351)
מִגְרָשׁ *migrāš* common/open land, pasture (4054)
גָּרַשׁ *gāraš* he drove out/away, cast out (1644)
מָדַד *mādad* he measured (4058); מִדָּה *middāʰ* measure (4060)
מִזְמוֹר *mizmôr* psalm, melody (4210); זָמַר *zāmar* D to sing, praise (2167)
מִקְנֶה *miqnêʰ* cattle, possession (4735)
קָנָה *qānāʰ* he got, acquired, bought (7069)
קָנֶה *qānêʰ* reed, stalk, measuring-rod (7070)
שִׁיר *šîr* to sing (7891)
שִׁיר *šîr* song (7892)

Basic Vocabulary Group–45 — Lesson 52

חָלַק *ḥālaq* he divided, apportioned (2505); חֵלֶק *ḥéleq* portion, share, territory (2507)
מַחֲלֹקֶת *maḥălṓqet* share, division (4256)
יָצַב *yāṣab* HtD to take one's stand (3320, cf. #5324)
מַצֵּבָה *maṣṣēbāʰ* pillar, sacred pillar (4676)
כֹּה *kōʰ* here, now, thus (3541)
כָּכָה *kā́kāʰ* thus (3602)
נֵר *nēr* lamp (5369); מְנוֹרָה *mᵉnôrāʰ* lampstand (4501)
סוּס *sûs* horse (5483)
רָכַב *rākab* he (mounted and) rode (7392)
רֶכֶב *rékeb* chariot(ry), rider, millstone (7393)
מֶרְכָּבָה *merkābāʰ* chariot (4818)

Basic Vocabulary Group–46 — Lesson 54

דַּל *dal(l)* poor, weak, oppressed (1800)
זֶרַע *zéraᶜ* seed, sowing, offspring (2233 < *zrᶜ)
זָרַע *zāraᶜ* he scattered seed, sowed (2232)
זְרוֹעַ *zᵉrôaᶜ* strength, arm (2220 < *δrᶜ)
חָלַל *ḥālal* N to be defiled; D to defile, profane; H to begin (2490)
יָכֹל *yākōl* he was able (3201)
יָתוֹם *yātôm* orphan, fatherless (3490)
נְאֻם *nᵉʾûm* (cstr.) utterance of (a prophet or deity) (5002)
נָגַשׁ *nāgaš* he drew near, approached (5066)
צָדֹק *ṣādōq* he was just, righteous (6663); צַדִּיק *ṣaddîq* just, righteous (6662)
קִיר *qîr* wall (7023)

Basic Vocabulary Group–47 — Lesson 55

בֶּטֶן *béṭen* belly, womb, body (990)
בְּכוֹר *bᵉkôr* first-born (1060)
דָּרַשׁ *dāraš* he sought, inquired, consulted (1875)
חָטָא *ḥāṭāʾ* he missed, went wrong, sinned; D to make a sin-offering (2398)
חַטָּאת *ḥaṭṭāʾt* sin, sin-offering (2403); חֵטְא *ḥēṭʾ* guilt, punishment, offence (2399)
פְּרִי *pᵉrî* fruit (6529)
פֶּשַׁע *péšaᶜ* transgression, rebellion (6587); פָּשַׁע *pāšaᶜ* he rebelled, transgressed (6586)
רוּם *rûm* he was exalted, lifted; L, H to raise, erect (7311)
מָרוֹם *mārôm* height, elevation, high place (4791)
תְּרוּמָה *tᵉrûmāʰ* contribution, offering (8641)

Basic Vocabulary Group–48 Lesson 56

אַיִל *ʾáyil* ram; leader, chief (352)
כֶּבֶשׂ *kébeś* lamb, young ram (3532)
מָכַר *mākar* he sold (4376)
נָהָר *nāhār* stream, river (5104)
נַחַל *náḥal* wady, torrent-bed (5158)
עֵגֶל *ʿēgel* calf (5695)
קֶדֶם *qédem* front, east, aforetime, beginning (6924); קָדִים *qādîm* east, east wind (6921)
שִׁפְחָה *šipḥāʰ* maid, maid-servant (8198)
שָׁפַט *šāpaṭ* he judged, governed (8199); שׁוֹפֵט *šôpēṭ* judge (8199)
מִשְׁפָּט *mišpāṭ* judgment (4941)

Basic Vocabulary Group–49 Lesson 57

אֵי *ʾê* where? (335); אַיֵּה *ʾayyêʰ* where? (346)
אָיַב *ʾāyab* he was hostile , אֹיֵב *ʾôyēb* enemy (340)
זָר *zār* strange, stranger (2114)
כָּלָה *kālāʰ* it was complete/finished; D to complete (3615)
כַּלָּה *kallāʰ* daughter-in-law, bride (3618)
כַּף *kap(p)* palm of hand, sole of foot (3709)
כֶּרֶם *kérem* vineyard (3754)
רַע *raʿ* evil, distress, calamity, bad(ness) (7453)
רָעַע *rāʿaʿ* he was evil, bad., H to hurt, do evil (7489)
רָעָה *rāʿāʰ* evil, misery, distress, injury (7451)
שָׁאַר *šāʾar* N to remain, be left over; H to leave over, spare (7604)
שְׁאֵרִית *šᵉʾērîṯ* rest, residue, remainder, remnant (7611)

Basic Vocabulary Group–50 Lesson 58

חָרָה *ḥārāʰ* he was/became angry (2734)
חָרוֹן *ḥārôn* burning anger (2740)
עוֹר *ʿôr* skin, hide (5785)
עוּר *ʿûr* to rouse oneself, awake (5782)
עָרַךְ *ʿārak* he arranged, set in order (6186); עֵרֶךְ *ʿérek* order, row, estimate (6187)
פֹּה, פּוֹ, פֹּא *pô(ʾ)* here, hither (6311)
פֶּה *pêʰ* mouth (6310); לְפִי *lᵉpî,* כְּפִי *kᵉpî* according to
קָטַר *qāṭar* D, H to burn sacrifices (6999); קְטֹרֶת *qᵉṭóreṯ* smoke, incense (7004)
קָצַר *qāṣar* he reaped, harvested (7114); קָצִיר *qāṣîr* harvest (-time) (7105)

Basic Vocabulary Group–51 Lesson 59

אָסַף *ʾāsap̄* he gathered, collected
יָסַף *yāsap̄* he added H to add + inf. = to do again (3254)
אֵיךְ *ʾêk* how? how! (349); אֵיכָה *ʾêkāʰ* how! (351)
חָשַׁב *ḥāšab* he thought, reckoned, regarded (2803)
מַחֲשָׁבָה *maḥăšābāʰ* thought, device (4284)
טָהֵר *ṭāhēr* he was clean, pure; D he cleansed (2891); טָהוֹר *ṭāhôr* clean, pure (2889)
כָּפַר *kāpar* D to cover, atone for sin (3722)
כְּפִיר *kᵉpîr* young lion (3715)
כָּבַס *kābas* D he washed, cleansed (3526)
כָּעַס *kāʿas* he was angry; H he provoked (3707)
רֶגֶל *régel* foot (7272)

Basic Vocabulary Group–52 Lesson 60

חָזַק *ḥāzaq* he grew strong, was firm, it was urgent; D he strengthened (2388)
חָזָק *ḥāzāq* hard, strong, firm, severe (2389)
טָמֵא *ṭāmēʾ* he was/became unclean; D he defiled (2930)
טָמֵא *ṭāmēʾ* unclean (2931); טֻמְאָה *ṭumʾā*ʰ uncleanness (2932)
מִדְבָּר *midbār* steppe, wilderness (4057)
נָחַל *nāḥal* he took possession, inherited; H to cause to inherit, give as possession (5157)
נַחֲלָה *naḥălā*ʰ possession, inheritance, property (5159)
נָכָה *nākā*ʰ H to strike, smite (5221); מַכָּה *makkā*ʰ blow, wound, plague (4347)
עָנָן *ʿānān* cloud (-mass) (6052
עוֹף *ʿôp̄* flying things, fowl (5776)

Basic Vocabulary Group–53 Lesson 61

אֲנַחְנוּ *ʾănáḥnû* we (587)
הֵיכָל *hêkāl* palace, temple (1964)
הָמָה *hāmā*ʰ he murmured, roared (1993); הָמוֹן *hāmôn* sound, roar, tumult (1995)
חַג *ḥag(g)* feast, festival (2282)
חָרַף *ḥārap̄* he reproached, taunted (2778); חֶרְפָּה *ḥerpā*ʰ reproach, contumely (2781)
יָצַק *yāṣaq* he poured, cast (3332)
יָצַר *yāṣar* he formed, shaped (3335)
לָמַד *lāmad* he studied, learned; D he taught (3925)
קֶרֶן *qéren* horn (7161)

Basic Vocabulary Group–54 Lesson 62

נָדַח *nādaḥ* H to thrust out, banish, impel; N pass. of same (5080)
נָדַר *nādar* he vowed (5087); נֶדֶר *néder* vow (5088)
נוּס *nûs* to flee, escape (5127)
נֶסֶךְ *nések* drink-offering (5262)
נָקָה *nāqā*ʰ N to be cleaned, purged, free from obligation; D to acquit (5352)
נָקִי *nāqî* clean, innocent, exempt (5355)
צוּר *ṣûr* to confine, shut in, besiege (6696); מָצוֹר *māṣôr* siege (4692)
צוּר *ṣûr* rock, cliff (6697)
קָהַל *qāhal* N to assemble (intrans.); H to assemble (trans.) (6950)
קָהָל *qāhāl* assembly, convocation (6951)

Basic Vocabulary Group–55 Lesson 63

מִזְרָח *mizrāḥ* (place of) sunrise, east (4217)
מָשַׁח *māšaḥ* he anointed (4886); מָשִׁיחַ *māšîᵃḥ* anointed (-one), (later) messiah (4899)
נְחֹשֶׁת *nᵉḥőšet* copper, bronze, fetters (5178); נָחָשׁ *nāḥāš* serpent (5175)
פַּחַד *páḥad* dread (6343)
סָגַר *sāḡar* he shut, closed (5462)
עָזַר *ʿāzar* he helped, succored (5826)
עָפָר *ʿāp̄ār* dry earth, dust (6083)
עֶצֶם *ʿéṣem* bone, substance, self (6106)
עָצוּם *ʿāṣûm* mighty, numerous (6099)
צַוָּאר *ṣawwāʾr* (back of) neck (66770

Basic Vocabulary Group–56 Lesson 64

הָפַךְ *hāpak* he overturned, turned (back) (2015)
פֵּאָה *pē'ā*^{h} corner, side (6285)
פָּדָה *pādā*^{h} he ransomed (6299)
פּוּץ *pûṣ* it was dispersed, scattered; N to be scattered (6327)
פָּלָא *pālā'* N to be extraordinary, hard to understand; H to do marvelous things (6381)
פֶּן *pen* lest (6435)
צָבָא *ṣābā'* army, host; pl. YHWH of hosts (6635)
שָׁבָה *šābā*^{h} he took captive (7617)
שְׁבִי *š*^{e}*bî* captivity, captive (7628); שְׁבִית *š*^{e}*bît* , שְׁבוּת *š*^{e}*bût* captivity (7622)
שֵׁבֶט *šēbeṭ* staff, sceptre, tribe (7626)
שֶׁקֶר *šéqer* lie, falsehood, deception, deceit (8267)

Basic Vocabulary Group–57 Lesson 65

אָרַר *'ārar* he cursed, called a curse upon (779)
בְּרִית *b*^{e}*rît* covenant, contract (1285)
בָּרַךְ *bārak* he knelt; D to bless (1288); בְּרָכָה *b*^{e}*rākā*^{h} blessing (1293)
גּוֹי *gôy* nation, people, pl. gentiles (1471)
יָרַשׁ *yāraš* he took possession, inherited (3423)
כּוֹכָב *kôkāb* star (3556)
כָּרַת *kārat* he cut off/down, made (a covenant) (3772)
צֶדֶק *ṣédeq* rightness, righteousness (6664)
צְדָקָה *ṣ*^{e}*dāqā*^{h} righteousness, justification (6666)
קָלַל *qālal* it was slight, trifling, swift (7043) קְלָלָה *q*^{e}*lālā*^{h} curse (7045)

Basic Vocabulary Group–58 Lesson 66

יָרֵךְ *yārēk* thigh, loins, side (3409)
כְּרוּב *k*^{e}*rûb* cherub (3742)
מִשְׁפָּחָה *mišpāḥā*^{h} clan, division of tribe (4940)
נָבַט *nābaṭ* H to look at, regard, show regard for (5027)
נָחַם *nāḥam* N to be sorry, repent; H to comfort (5162)
פַּר *par(r)* young bull, steer (6499)
שָׁחַת *šāḥat* N to be marred, spoiled, corrupt; H active of same (7843)
שָׁכַח *šākaḥ* he forgot (7911)
שָׁכַם *šākam* H to rise/start early (7925)
תָּמִיד *tāmîd* continuously, continuity (8548)
תָּמִים *tāmîm* complete, sound (8549); תָּמַם *tāmam* it was complete, finished (8552)

Basic Vocabulary Group–59 Lesson 68

אֶבְיוֹן *'ebyôn* poor, needy (34)
אַרְבַּע *'arba'*, אַרְבָּעָה *'arbā'ā*^{h} 4 (703)
אַרְבָּעִים *'arbā'îm* 40 (705); רְבִיעִי *r*^{e}*bî'î* 4th (7244)
דּוֹר *dôr* age, generation, life-time, dwelling-place (1755)
חֲמוֹר *ḥămôr* he-ass (2543)
רָחַק *rāḥaq* he was/became distant, it was far (7368)
רָחוֹק *rāḥôq* distant, far, distance (7350)
שָׁדַד *šādad* he dealt violently with, despoiled (7703)
שׁוֹפָר *šôpār* ram's horn, trumpet (7782)
שִׁית *šît* to put, set, appoint (7896)
תּוֹעֵבָה *tô'ēbā*^{h} abomination (8441)

Basic Vocabulary Group–60 Lesson 69

הֶבֶל *hébel* vapor, breath, vanity (1892)
חָרַם *ḥāram* H to devote to a deity, ban, completely destroy (2763)
כָּשַׁל *kāšal* he stumbled, staggered (3782)
נָטַע *nāṭaᶜ* he planted (5193)
נָצַח *nāṣaḥ* D to act as overseer, conductor (5329)
נֵצַח *nḗṣaḥ* eminence, perpetuity, everlastingness (5331)
נָצַר *nāṣar* he watched, guarded, kept (5341)
סֶלָה *sélāʰ* Selah! lift up! exalt! (5542); סֶלַע *sélaᶜ* crag, cliff, rock (5553)
סָלַח *sālaḥ* he forgave, pardoned (5545)
סֹלֶת *sṓleṯ* fine flour (5560)
עֶרְוָה *ᶜerwāʰ* nakedness, pudenda (6172)

Basic Vocabulary Group–61 Lesson 70

אִי *ʾî* (*ʾyy*) island, coastland, region (339)
גֶּבֶר *gébeṟ* man (not woman), male (1397); גִּבּוֹר *gibbôr* mighty man, hero (1368)
גְּבוּרָה *gᵉḇûrāʰ* strength, might (1369)
חָתַת *ḥāṯaṯ* it was shattered, he was dismayed (2865)
יָם *yām*, pl. *yamm-*, sea, west (3220)
נָשַׂג *nāśaḡ* H to reach, overtake (5381)
פָּרַר *pārar* H to break, frustrate (6565)
פָּרַץ *pāraṣ* he broke through/into/down/in pieces (6555)
פָּרַשׂ *pāraś* he spread, spread out (6566)
רָנַן *rānan* he cried (in joy, exultation, distress) (7442); רִנָּה *rinnāʰ* ringing cry (7440)

Basic Hebrew Vocabulary–62 Lesson 71

הָרָה *hārāʰ* G11 she conceived, became pregnant (2029)
זָנָה *zānāʰ* he committed fornication; G11 she was a harlot; G51 harlot (2181)
יָשַׁע *yāšaᶜ* H to deliver, save, give victory (3467); יֵשַׁע *yḗšaᶜ* deliverance, salvation (3468)
יְשׁוּעָה *yᵉšûᶜāʰ* salvation, deliverance, victory (3744)
תְּשׁוּעָה *tᵉšûᶜāʰ* deliverance, salvation (8668)
מְעַט *mᵉᶜaṭ* a little, a few, fewness (4592)
רָחַם *rāḥam* D to have compassion, be compassionate (7355)
רַחֲמִים *raḥămîm* compassion, love (7356)
שָׁבַת *šāḇaṯ* he ceased, rested; H to cause to cease, destroy (7673);
שַׁבָּת *šabbāṯ* Sabbath (7676)
תָּקַע *tāqaᶜ* he thrust, gave a blow/blast, struck (8268)

Basic Hebrew Vocabulary–63 Lesson 72

גָּמָל *gāmāl* camel (1581)
מִנְחָה *minḥāʰ* gift, cereal offering
עֵמֶק *ᶜémeq* valley, deep place (6010) פָּרָשׁ *pārāš* horseman (6571)
קָשַׁב *qāšaḇ* H to give attention, attend (7181)
קָשַׁר *qāšar* he bound, conspired (7194)
קֶשֶׁת *qéšeṯ* bow (weapon, rainbow) (7198)
רָגַז *rāḡaz* he was agitated, excited, he quivered, quaked (7264)
רָפָא *rāpāʰ* he healed (7495)
רָפָה *rāpāʰ* it sank down, dropped, he relaxed; H to abandon (7503)
שָׁבַר *šāḇar* he broke; D to shatter (7665)
שֵׁבֶר *šḗḇer*, שֶׁבֶר *šéḇer* breaking, fracture, breach (7667)

Basic Hebrew Vocabulary–64 Lesson 73

אָמֵץ *ʾāmēṣ* he was strong; D to strengthen, harden; H to exhibit strength; HtD to determine (553)
אֶפֶס *ʾép̄es* end, none at all, zero; *ʾép̄es kî* howbeit (657)
חֲלוֹם *ḥălôm* dream (2472)
יְאוֹר *yᵉʾôr* river (usually Nile) (2975) יַעַר *yáʿar* thicket, wood, forest (3293)
יְרִיעָה *yᵉrîʿāʰ* curtain, tent-coth (3407)
מָשַׁל *māšal* he ruled, had dominion over (4910) נָא *nāʾ* prithee, I pray (9994)
נָצַב *nāṣab̲* N to take one's stand; H to station, fix (5324)
סָבַב *sāb̲ab̲* he turned, turned around, surrounded (5437)
סָבִיב *sāb̲îb̲* round about, the surrounding region (5439)
תָּפַשׂ *tāp̄aś* he grasped, wielded (8610)

Basic Hebrew Vocabulary–65 Lesson 74

לְאֹם *lᵉʾōm* people, folk, nation (3816)
לוּחַ *lûᵃḥ* tablet, board (3871)
לִשְׁכָּה *liškāʰ* room, chamber, hall, cell (3957)
עֹל *ʿōl* (*ʿll*) yoke (5923)
צֵל *ṣēl* (*ṣll*) shadow (6738)
עָצַר *ʿāṣar* he restrained, retained (6113)
צֹאן *ṣōʾn* small cattle, flock (6629)
צָפָה *ṣāp̄āʰ* D to overlay, plate (6823)
צִפּוֹר *ṣippôr* bird (6833)
קָנָא *qānāʾ* D to be envious, excited to anger (7065); קִנְאָה *qinʾāʰ* jealousy, zeal (7068)
שָׂדֶה *śād̲êʰ* field, land (7704)

Basic Hebrew Vocabulary–66 Lesson 75

בָּלַל *bālal* he mixed, confounded, mingled (1101)
בָּלַע *bālaʿ* he swallowed, swallowed up (1104)
גִּיל *gîl,* גּוּל *gûl* he exulted rejoiced (1523)
גִּלּוּל *gillûl* pl. amulets, idols (1544)
טֶרֶם *ṭérem* not yet; בְּטֶרֶם *bᵉṭérem* before (when not yet) (2962)
מוֹל *môl,* מוּל *mûl* in front of, facing (4136)
מַצָּה *maṣṣāʰ* unleavened bread, matsah (4682)
מָתַי *māt̲ay* when? (4970)
נָסַע *nāsaʿ* he pulled up (tent-pegs). set out, journeyed (5265)
סָתַר *sāt̲ar* N to hide self, be concealed (5641)
רָצַח *rāṣaḥ* he murdered, slew (7523) שֶׁמֶשׁ *šémeš* sun (8121)

Basic Hebrew Vocabulary–67 Lesson 76

אָרַב *ʾārab̲* he lay in wait for, ambushed (693)
בְּאֵר *bᵉʾēr* dug-well, pit (875); בּוֹר *bôr,* בֹּאר *bôʾr* cistern, pit, well (953, 877)
בְּרִיחַ *bᵉrîᵃḥ* bar, bolt (1281)
גָּאוֹן *gāʾôn* exaltation, majesty, pride (1347)
חָגַר *ḥāgar* he girded himself (2296)
לְמַעַן *lᵉmáʿan* for the sake of, on account of, in order that (4616)
מַיִם *máyim* water (4325)
נָכְרִי *nok̲rî* foreign, alien (5237)
נָצַל *nāṣal* H to snatch away, rescue, deliver (5337)
פָּגַע *pāgaʿ* he reached, met, encountered (6293)
שָׁפַךְ *šāp̄ak̲* he poured, poured out (8230)

Basic Vocabulary Group–68 — Lesson 77

דֶּבֶר *débeṟ* pestilence, plague (1698)
דָּגָן *dāgān* grain, corn (1715)
הָרַס *hāras* he threw down, broke down (2040); זוּב *zûḇ* to flow, gush (2100)
זָרָה *zārāʰ* he fanned, winnowed, scattered (2219)
חָלַץ *ḥālaṣ* he drew off; D he delivered, rescued (2502)
חָמַל *ḥāmal* he spared, had compassion (2550)
חֲנִית *ḥănîṯ* spear (2595)
חָרְבָּה *ḥorbāʰ* waste, ruin, desolation (2723); מְעָרָה *meʿārāʰ* cave (4631)
נָטַשׁ *nāṭaš* he left, forsook, abandoned (5203)
נָתַץ *nāṯaṣ* he pulled down, broke down (5422)

Basic Vocabulary Group–69 — Lesson 78

בָּשָׂר *bāśār* flesh (1320); יָרַד *yāraḏ* he went down, descended (3381)
כָּסָה *kāsāʰ* D to cover, conceal, clothe (3680)
מוֹט *môṭ* to totter, slip, shake (4131); מָטָר *māṭār* rain (4306)
מֵעִים *mēʿîm* (pl.) bowels, inward parts (4578)
מָרָה *mārāʰ* he was disobedient, rebellious, stubborn; H to display (these qualities) (4784)
מָשַׁךְ *māšaḵ* he drew, led, dragged, drew out, prolonged (4900)
מָשָׁל *māšāl* proverb, parable, similitude (4912)
סָמַךְ *sāmaḵ* he leaned, supported, upheld, placed (hand) (5564)
פֶּסַח *pésaḥ* Passover (6453)
שָׁלַךְ *šālaḵ* H to throw, fling, cast (7993)

Basic Vocabulary Group–70 — Lesson 79

מָעוֹז *māʿôz* place/means of safety, protection, stronghold (4581)
מָתְנַיִם *moṯnáyim* loins (4975)
נָכַר *nāḵar* H to regard, observe, recognize, acknowledge (5234)
עֵז *ʿēz* (*ʿizz*) she-goat (5795)
פָּשַׁט *pāšaṭ* he stripped off, made a dash; D, H to strip (6584)
שָׁחַט *šāḥaṭ* he slaughtered; Gp50 hammered, beaten (7819)
שָׂחַק *śāḥaq* he laughed; D to play, jest, make sport (7832)
שִׂמְלָה *śimlāʰ* mantle, wrapper (8071)
שָׂעִיר *śāʿîr* he-goat, buck (8163); שֵׂעָר *śēʿār* hair (animal or human) (8181)
שְׂעֹרָה *śeʿōrāʰ* barley (8184)

✡

RULES

RULES

1a. A *dagesh* in a *begadkepat* at the beginning of a word or following a shewa is a light dagesh, indicating stopped pronunciation (§11.44). A dagesh in any other letter, or in a begadkepat in any other position, is a strong dagesh, indicating a geminate (doubled) consonant (§11.43). A strong dagesh in a begadkepat both doubles and hardens it (§11.442).

1b. Consonants with shewa, except begadkepat and מ, frequently lose the strong dagesh (§13.41). This particularly applies to י.

2a. *Pure-long vowels* do not reduce except in originally-closed syllables (§15.22), where they become the corresponding short vowel, subject to the short-vowel rules (§15.222)

2b. Long *â* became long *ô* in the Canaanite dialects (§14.11).

3. Words joined by maqqeph and words in construct have only one major accent (§17.12).

4. Original short vowels in final open syllables have generally vanished (§§15.51, ,52).

5. A doubly-closed syllable never occurs within a word and rarely occurs at word-end (§16.34).

6. When a doubly-closed syllable would result from the loss of a short vowel (Rule 4), one of the following occurs:
  a. If a geminate consonant would result, it loses gemination (§13.42);
  b. If a consonantal cluster would result, an anaptycitic vowel is inserted (§15.61);
  c. In a few cases, the doubly-closed syllable remains (§16.3423).

7. Syllables do not begin with consonantal clusters, except in forms of the word for 'two' (§16.35).

8. The conjunction —ו, when it occurs before labials (ב, מ, פ, called *bûmep̄*), or before consonants with shewa, develops to vocalic וּ *û*; before yod with shewa, however, long *î* is formed (§15.652).

9. At word-end, original *-cw > *-cû* and *-cy > *-cî* (§15.67).

10a. *Gutturals* reject dagesh (§11.432); before א, ע, and ר there is compensatory lengthening (§15.141*.
  b. Gutturals do not take simple vocal shewa (§15.42).
  c. Gutturals often vocalize a silent shewa (§15.421).
  d. Gutturals prefer *a*-class vowels, especially before them (§15.43).
  e. At word-end, ע, ח, or הּ (*he*^{h} with mappiq) attract pattaḥ furtive after *i*- or *u*-class vowels (§15.4321).
  f. *i* > *e* (*ḥîrîq* > *s*^{e}*ḡôl*) before nonfinal gutturals (§15.434).
  g. Initial א prefers *i*-class vowels when near the accent (§15.433).
  h. א at word-end and frequently at syllable-end is quiescent (§15.54).

11. Nun נ assimilates to a following consonant when no vowel separates (§13.111).

12. In HtD forms, when the first radical is a dental or a sibilant, metathesis, assimilation, or both occur (§13.112, §13.61)

13. Short vowels normally *lengthen* in accented or near-open syllables, and *reduce* in distant-open syllables (§15.11, §15.12, §15.23)
  b. Compensatory vowels do not reduce (§15.233).

c. The original vowel of a segolate does not reduce in sg. cstr. (§15.232). It does, however, reduce in pl. abs. forms.

d. In many forms, *ṣêrê* does not reduce (§15.223).

14. Short *a* does not lengthen in *erstwhile doubly-closed syllables* except in pause (§15.111, cf. §15.132).

15. Short *a* does not lengthen in accented-closed syllables in finite verbal forms, except in pause (§15.113).

16. In *near-open* syllables, *i-* or *u*-class short vowels *reduce* to shewa when preceded by a long *syllable* or by no syllable at all (§15.241).

17. In finite verbal forms *without sufformatives,* the accent is on the *ultima* (§17.21). In such forms *with sufformatives,* the following rules prevail:

a. If the *ultima* is *closed,* the accent is on the ultima, and the form follows the short-vowel chart (§17.221).

b. If the *ultima* is *open* and the *penult* is *long,* the accent is on the *penult,* and the form follows the short-vowel chart (§17.222).

c. If the *ultima* is open and the *penult* is *short,* in *nonpausal* forms the accent is on the *ultima,* the vowel of the *penult* reduces to shewa, and the vowel of the antepenult ha its pausal form (lengthened) and is marked by metheg (§17.223).

d. Under the same conditions (17c) but in *pausal form*, the accent is on the *penult,* and the form follows the short-vowel chart (§17.2231).

18. Short *a* frequently attenuates to short *i* in unaccented closed syllables (§15.32).

19. When two successive simple (vocal) shewas would occur, the first becomes *ḥîrîq* and the second becomes zero-shewa (§15.651).

20. In originally closed accented syllables, in certain forms original short *i* becomes short *a* (§15.33).

21. When *simple (vocal) shewa* would occur before *compound shewa,* the simple shewa is changed to the normal short vowel of the same vowel-class as the compound shewa (§15.653).

22. When *compound shewa* would occur before simple (vocal) shewa, the compound shewa develops to its corresponding normal short vowel, and the simple shewa becomes zero shewa (§15.2532).

23. The connecting vowel of a pronominal suffix, if any, takes the accent (§17.32). If a shewa precedes the suffix, it is zero shewa and the ך/כ of the suffix is spirantized.

24. In verbal forms, thematic *a* in G-perf. generally yields thematic *u* in G-impf., and thematic *i* or *u* in G-perf. yields thematic *a* in G-impf. (§27.331).

25. In G-impf., the vowell of the preformative is determined usually by the thematic vowel, as follows: thematic *a* preformative *i,* thematic *i* or *u* preformative *a* (§27.332).

26. When adding a consonantal sufformative (i.e. one which begins with a consoant) to a CC² verb which ends in a geminated consonant, the consonantal cluster which would occur is avoided by the insertion of a long vowel before the sufformative, namely וֹ (*ô*) in the perf. and ֵי (*êʸ*) in the impf. (§15.64).

27. Nonpausal converted impf. forms which have a closed ultima and an open penult are accented on the *penult* (§17.341)

28. Nonpausal converted perf. forms ending in תָּ (*-tā*) or תִּי (*-tî*) generally are accented on the *ultima* (§17.342).